Fodor's Second Editi

W9-CDF-823

Prague and Budapest

The complete guide, thoroughly up-to-date

Packed with details that will make your trip

The must-see sights, off and on the beaten path

What to see, what to skip

Mix-and-match vacation itineraries

City strolls, countryside adventures

Smart lodging and dining options

Essential local do's and taboos

Transportation tips, distances and directions

Key contacts, savvy travel tips

When to go, what to pack

Clear, accurate, easy-to-use maps

Helpful vocabulary

Excerpted from *Fodor's Eastern and Central Europe*

Fodor's Travel Publications • New York, Toronto, London, Sydney, Auckland
www.fodors.com

Fodor's Prague and Budapest

EDITORS: Bonnie Bills, Matt Lombardi, Julie Tomasz, Kirsten Weisenberger

Editorial Contributors: Mark Baker, Ky Krauthamer, Alan Levy, Betsy Maury, Paul Olchváry, Julie Tomasz, Matt Welch

Editorial Production: Ira-Neil Dittersdorf

Maps: David Lindroth, *cartographer*; Rebecca Baer and Robert Blake, *map editors*

Design: Fabrizio La Rocca, *creative director*; Guido Caroti, *art director*; Jolie Novak, *senior picture editor*

Cover Design: Pentagram

Production/Manufacturing: Angela L. McLean

Cover Photograph: Sylvain Grandadam/Tony Stone Images

Copyright

Second Edition

ISBN 0–679–00731–8

ISSN 1530-5384

Important Tip

Although all prices, opening times, and other details in this book are based on information supplied to us at press time, changes occur all the time in the travel world, and Fodor's cannot accept responsibility for facts that become outdated or for inadvertent errors or omissions. So **always confirm information when it matters,** especially if you're making a detour to visit a specific place.

Special Sales

PRINTED IN THE UNITED STATES OF AMERICA

10 9 8 7 6 5 4 3 2 1

CONTENTS

Maps and Charts

ON THE ROAD WITH FODOR'S

EVERY VACATION IS IMPORTANT. So here at Fodor's we've pulled out all stops in preparing *Fodor's Prague and Budapest.* To guide you in putting together your vacation, we've created multiday itineraries and neighborhood walks. And to direct you to the places that are truly worth your time and money, we've rallied the team of endearingly picky know-it-alls we're pleased to call our writers. Having seen all corners of the regions they cover for us, they're real experts. If you knew them, you'd poll them for tips yourself.

Minnesota-born **Ky Krauthamer,** who updated the Prague chapter, came to Prague in 1992 and settled in as a journalist and freelance writer specializing in travel and culture. He has contributed to several Fodor's guides, including the two previous editions of *Fodor's Eastern and Central Europe.*

Betsy Maury, a former senior editor with the U.S. publisher Bantam Doubleday Dell, spent four years in Slovenia before settling in Budapest, where she now lives with her husband and works as a freelance writer. She updated the Budapest dining and lodging reviews for our guide.

Upon receiving an MA in writing in 1990, **Paul Olchváry,** a western New York native, moved to the land of his ancestors, Hungary, expecting to stay a year or so.

He stayed for ten. Initially a university composition instructor, he went on to hold a fellowship at the U.S. Embassy in Budapest before becoming founding editor of an English-language digest of Hungarian news. From the mid-1990s on, he focused on his own writing, literary translation, and copyediting. In addition to updating our Budapest chapter, he has published numerous stories and essays, many in Hungarian translation, and written three novels, two of them set in present-day Hungary. He has also rendered seven books and numerous shorter works from Hungarian to English.

We would like to thank Malév Hungarian Airlines for its help with realizing the Hungary chapter.

Don't Forget to Write

Keeping a travel guide fresh and up-to-date is a big job. So we love your feedback—positive and negative—and follow up on all suggestions. Contact the Prague and Budapest editor at editors@fodors.com or c/o Fodor's, 280 Park Avenue, New York, NY 10017. And have a wonderful trip!

Karen Cure
Editorial Director

Eastern and Central Europe

Czech Republic (Česká Republika)

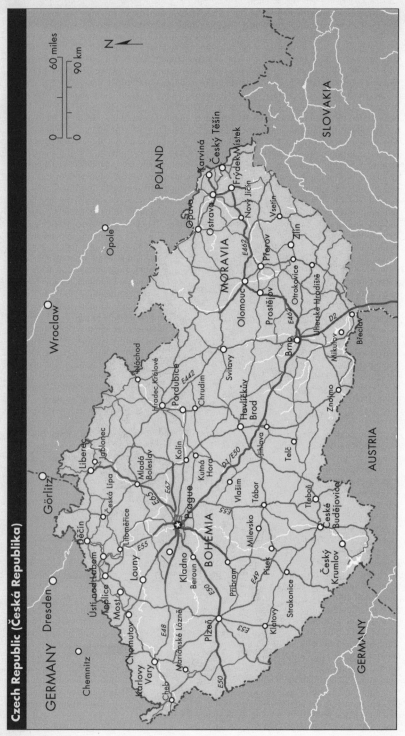

Hungary (Magyarország)

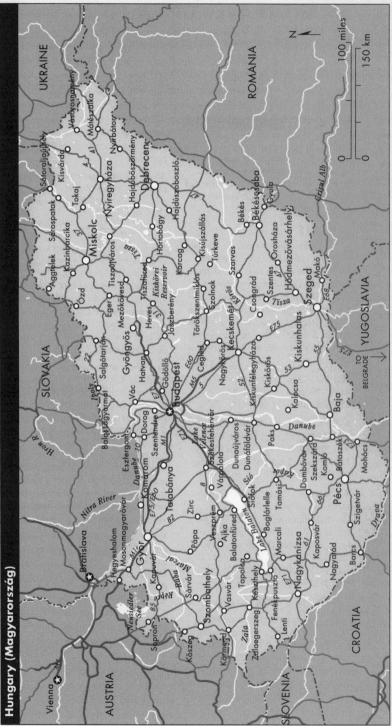

UKRAINE

ROMANIA

SLOVAKIA

YUGOSLAVIA

AUSTRIA

CROATIA

SLOVENIA

TO BELGRADE

100 miles
150 km

Vienna

Bratislava

Sopron

Kőszeg

Szombathely

Körmend

Zalaegerszeg

Lenti

Nagykanizsa

Kaposvár

Szigetvár

Pécs

Mohács

Nagyatád

Barcs

Fenékpuszta

Keszthely

Marcali

Boglárlelle

Siófok

Lake Balaton

Balatonfüred

Tapolca

Ajka

Veszprém

Pápa

Zirc

Vasvár

Sárvár

Kapuvár

Mosonmagyaróvár

Hegyeshalom

Győr

Tatabánya

Várpalota

Székesfehérvár

Lake Velence

Dunaújváros

Dunaföldvár

Paks

Szekszárd

Dombóvár

Tamási

Komló

Baranyék

Baja

Kalocsa

Kiskőrös

Kiskunfélegyháza

Kiskunhalas

Nagykőrös

Cegléd

Budapest

Gödöllő

Vác

Szentendre

Dorog

Esztergom

Komárom

Szentlőrinc

Hatvan

Gyöngyös

Salgótarján

Balassagyarmat

Vác

Jászberény

Törökszentmiklós

Szolnok

Kecskemét

Csongrád

Szentes

Szeged

Makó

Hódmezővásárhely

Orosháza

Szarvas

Túrkeve

Kisújszállás

Karcag

Hajdúszoboszló

Hortobágy

Debrecen

Hajdúböszörmény

Nyíregyháza

Nyírbátor

Mátészalka

Vásárosnamény

Sátoraljaújhely

Sárospatak

Kisvárda

Tokai

Miskolc

Kazincbarcika

Aggtelek

Ózd

Eger

Mezőkövesd

Tiszaújváros

Tiszafüred

Kiskörei Reservoir

Heves

Kiskörei

Kisköre

Heves

Kiskunmajsa

Békés

Békéscsaba

Gyula

Crişul Alb

Tisza

Danube

Drava

Hron R

Nitra River

Mur

Raab

Mura

Répce

Zala

Kapos

Sió

Marcal

Rába

Neusiedler See

E75/E60

M1

E71

M5

M3

E79

E73

E68

E75

M0

41
3
38
37
35
21
22
10
8
82
84
86
76
61
66
67
7
81
52
53
55
47
44
5

SMART TRAVEL TIPS A TO Z

Basic Information on Traveling in Prague and Budapest, Savvy Tips to Make Your Trip a Breeze, and Companies and Organizations to Contact

AIR TRAVEL

BOOKING

When you book **look for nonstop flights** and **remember that "direct" flights stop at least once.** Try to avoid connecting flights, which require a change of plane.

CARRIERS

In most cases, flights from the United States on major U.S. airlines have a European co-carrier that provides a connecting flight from a gateway in Europe. Some European national airlines offer nonstop service from the United States to their own countries as well as connecting flights; others only provide connections within Europe.

➤ MAJOR AIRLINES: **Continental** (☎ 800/231–0856). **Delta** (☎ 800/241–4141). **Northwest** (☎ 800/447–4747). **United** (☎ 800/538–2929).

➤ FROM THE U.K.: **British Airways** (✉ 156 Regent St., London W1R 5TA, ☎ 0207/434–4700; 0845/722–2111 outside London). **Czech Airlines** (☎ 0207/255–1898 in London).

➤ NATIONAL AIRLINES WITH SERVICE FROM U.S.: The Czech Republic: **Czech Airlines** (CSA; ☎ 212/765–6022, in 02/2010–4310 in Prague). Hungary: **Malév Hungarian Airlines** (☎ 212/757–6446, in Budapest, ☎ 1/235–3535; 06/40–212–121 toll free; 1/235–3804 [ticketing]).

CHECK-IN & BOARDING

Assuming that not everyone with a ticket will show up, airlines routinely overbook planes. When everyone does, airlines ask for volunteers to give up their seats. In return, these volunteers usually get a certificate for a free flight and are rebooked on the next flight out. If there are not enough volunteers, the airline must choose who will be denied boarding. The first to get bumped are passengers who checked in late and those

flying on discounted tickets, so **get to the gate and check in as early as possible,** especially during peak periods.

Always **bring a government-issued photo I.D. to the airport.** You may be asked to show it before you are allowed to check in.

CUTTING COSTS

The least expensive airfares to Central and Eastern Europe must usually be purchased in advance and are nonrefundable; the same fare may not be available the next day. Always **check different routings** and look into using different airports. Travel agents, especially low-fare specialists (☞ Discounts & Deals, *below*), are helpful.

Consolidators are another good source. They buy tickets for scheduled international flights at reduced rates from the airlines, then sell them at prices that beat the best fare available directly from the airlines, usually without restrictions. Sometimes you can even get your money back if you need to return the ticket. Carefully read the fine print detailing penalties for changes and cancellations, and **confirm your consolidator reservation with the airline.**

➤ CONSOLIDATORS: **Cheap Tickets** (☎ 800/377–1000). **Discount Airline Ticket Service** (☎ 800/576–1600). **Unitravel** (☎ 800/325–2222). **Up & Away Travel** (☎ 212/889–2345). **World Travel Network** (☎ 800/409–6753).

ENJOYING THE FLIGHT

For more legroom, **request an emergency-aisle seat.** Don't sit in the row in front of the emergency aisle or in front of a bulkhead, where seats may not recline. If you have dietary concerns, **ask for special meals when booking.** These can be vegetarian, low-cholesterol, or kosher, for example. On long flights, try to maintain a normal routine, to help fight jet lag.

At night, **get some sleep.** By day, **eat light meals, drink water** (not alcohol), and **move around the cabin** to stretch your legs.

HOW TO COMPLAIN

If your baggage goes astray or your flight goes awry, complain right away. Most carriers require that you **file a claim immediately.**

➤ AIRLINE COMPLAINTS: U.S. Department of Transportation **Aviation Consumer Protection Division** (✉ C-75, Room 4107, Washington, DC 20590, ☎ 202/366–2220, airconsumer@ost.dot.gov, www.dot.gov/airconsumer). **Federal Aviation Administration Consumer Hotline** (☎ 800/322–7873).

AIRPORTS

For more in-depth airport information, and for the best way to get between the airport and your destination, *see* Arriving and Departing in the A to Z section at the end of each city's chapter.

➤ CZECH REPUBLIC: Prague: **Ruzyně Airport** (☎ 02/2011–1111).

➤ HUNGARY: Budapest: **Ferihegy Repülőtér** (Ferihegy Airport) (☎ 1/296–9696 or for same-day flight information; 1/296–8000 for arrivals, 1/296–7000 for departures; 1/296–8108 for lost & found).

BIKE TRAVEL

The prevalence of bicycles varies greatly from country to country within Eastern and Central Europe. While, for instance, bike touring and mountain biking are gaining popularity in the Czech Republic, in Romania recreational cycling is uncommon and on some roads can be dangerous. Most major cities have some sort of bike rental available, and in less populated areas it's sometimes possible to arrange rentals through informal sources; your hotel is often a good resource for finding rentals. For more information, *see* the Pleasures and Pastimes and Outdoor Activities and Sports sections *in* individual city's chapters.

BIKES IN FLIGHT

Most airlines accommodate bikes as luggage, provided they are dismantled and boxed. For bike boxes, often free at bike shops, you'll pay about $5 from airlines (at least $100 for bike bags). International travelers can sometimes substitute a bike for a piece of checked luggage at no charge; otherwise, the cost is about $100. Domestic and Canadian airlines charge $25–$50.

BOAT & FERRY TRAVEL

Ferries offer a pleasant and cheap mode of transportation to Eastern and Central Europe, although you have to be fairly close to your destination already to hop a Europe-bound ferry or hydrofoil. Flying into the appropriate hub, however, is an option. A hydrofoil shuttles visitors from Vienna to Budapest, Hungary. For further country-specific information, *see* Arriving and Departing in the A to Z section in Budapest (Chapter 3). In Hungary, ferries operate on the Danube River and on Lake Balaton.

➤ FERRY LINES: Hungary: **MAHART Tours** (✉ V, Belgrád rakpart, Budapest, ☎ 1/484–4025; 1/484–4010 for information).

BUS TRAVEL

Bus travel is generally more costly than travel by train, although this varies by country. In some instances, especially where trains are largely local (and stop seemingly every 100 feet), buses are actually speedier than rail travel. Comfort is minimal, though; roads tend to be bumpy and seats lumpy. Buses are generally tidier; train bathrooms are notoriously rank. It's a bit of a gamble; seats on buses are a rarity during prime traveling hours, and drivers don't always stop where they should, although most leave punctually (especially when you're still waiting in line for a ticket). Comfort and fares vary drastically by nation. *See* Arriving and Departing by Bus *in* the A to Z section at the end of each city's chapter.

FROM THE U.K.

Unless you latch onto a real deal on airfare, a bus ticket from London's Victoria Terminal (☎ 0171/730–0202) is probably the cheapest transit from the United Kingdom to Eastern and Central Europe, although it may take a little research, as regularly scheduled routes to all cities except Warsaw and Prague are practically nonexistent. Check newspaper ads for eastbound passage.

BUSINESS HOURS

For country-specific opening and closing times and business hours, *see* Opening and Closing Times in the A to Z section at the end of each city's chapter.

CAMERAS & PHOTOGRAPHY

In general, people are pleased to be photographed, but ask first. Never photograph Gypsies, however colorful their attire, without explicit permission and payment clearly agreed upon. Photographing anything military, assuming you'd want to, is prohibited.

➤ PHOTO HELP: **Kodak Information Center** (☎ 800/242–2424). *Kodak Guide to Shooting Great Travel Pictures,* available in bookstores or from Fodor's Travel Publications (☎ 800/533–6478; $18 plus $5.50 shipping).

EQUIPMENT PRECAUTIONS

Always **keep your film and tape out of the sun.** Carry an extra supply of batteries, and **be prepared to turn on your camera or camcorder** to prove to security personnel that the device is real. Always **ask for hand inspection of film,** which becomes clouded after repeated exposure to airport X-ray machines, and **keep videotapes away from metal detectors.**

FILM & DEVELOPING

Major brands of film are available throughout the region, and 24-hour developing is the rule rather than the exception in large and medium-size cities. The variable is cost—prices fluctuate widely from place to place.

VIDEOS

Due to differing television systems, VHS tapes bought in Europe will run about 30% shorter than the time indicated on the box when operated with U.S. equipment. Also note that tapes may be hard to find outside of major urban areas.

CAR RENTAL

Major rental agencies are represented throughout the region, but **don't** overlook local firms; they can offer bargains, but watch for hidden insurance conditions. Rates and regulations vary widely from country to country. For more information, *see* the A to Z sections *in* individual city's chapters.

➤ MAJOR AGENCIES: **Alamo** (☎ 800/327–9633; 020/8759–6200 in the U.K.). **Avis** (☎ 800/331–1212; 800/331–1084 in Canada; 02/9353–9000 in Australia; 09/525–1982 in New Zealand; 0870/606–0100 in the U.K.). **Budget** (☎ 800/527–0700; 0144/227–6266 in the U.K.). **Dollar** (☎ 800/800–4000; 0124/622–0111 in the U.K., where it is known as Sixt; 02/9223–1444 in Australia). **Hertz** (☎ 800/654–3131; 800/263–0600 in Canada; 020/8897–2072 in the U.K.; 02/9669–2444 in Australia; 09/256–8690 in New Zealand). **National Car Rental** (☎ 800/227–7368; 0845/722–2525 in the U.K., where it is known as National Europe).

CUTTING COSTS

To get the best deal, **book through a travel agent who will shop around.** Do **look into wholesalers,** companies that do not own fleets but rent in bulk from those that do and often offer better rates than traditional car-rental operations. Payment must be made before you leave home.

➤ WHOLESALERS: **Auto Europe** (☎ 207/842–2000 or 800/223–5555, FAX 800/235–6321, www.autoeurope. com). **DER Travel Services** (✉ 9501 W. Devon Ave., Rosemont, IL 60018, ☎ 800/782–2424, FAX 800/282–7474 for information; 800/860–9944 for brochures, www.dertravel.com). **Kemwel Holiday Autos** (☎ 800/678–0678, FAX 914/825–3160, www.kemwel.com).

INSURANCE

When driving a rented car you are generally responsible for any damage to or loss of the vehicle. Before you rent see what coverage your personal auto-insurance policy and credit cards already provide.

Before you buy collision coverage, check your existing policies—you may already be covered. However, collision policies that car-rental companies sell for European rentals usually do not include stolen-vehicle coverage.

REQUIREMENTS & RESTRICTIONS

In most Eastern and Central European countries, visitors need an International Driver's Permit; U.S. and Canadian citizens can obtain one from the American or Canadian Automobile Association, respectively. In Hungary, many car rental agencies will accept an international license, but the formal permit is technically required. If you intend to drive across a border, ask about **restrictions on driving into other countries.** The minimum age required for renting is usually 21 or older, and some companies also have maximum ages; be sure to inquire when making your arrangements.

SURCHARGES

Before you pick up a car in one city and leave it in another, **ask about drop-off charges or one-way service fees,** which can be substantial. Note, too, that some rental agencies charge extra if you return the car before the time specified in your contract. To avoid a hefty refueling fee, **fill the tank just before you turn in the car,** but be aware that gas stations near the rental outlet may overcharge.

CAR TRAVEL

The plus side of driving is an itinerary free from the constraints of bus and train schedules and lots of trunk room for extra baggage. The negatives are many, however (☞ Car Rental, *above*), not the least of which are shabbily maintained secondary roads, the risk of theft and vandalism, and difficulty finding gas. Crowded roads and fast and/or careless drivers add to the danger element, particularly in Poland. However, car travel does make it much easier to get to out-of-the-way monasteries and other sights not easily accessible by public transportation. Good road maps are usually available.

A word of caution: If you have any alcohol whatsoever in your body, do not drive. Penalties are fierce, and the blood-alcohol limit is practically zero. (In Hungary, it *is* zero.)

AUTO CLUBS

➤ IN THE CZECH REPUBLICH AND HUNGARY: Czech Republic: **Autoturist** (⊠ Prague 4, Na Strži 9, ☎ 02/6110–4333). Hungary: **Hungarian Automobile Club** (⊠ Budapest II, Rómer Flóris u. 4/A, ☎ 212–0300).

➤ IN AUSTRALIA: **Australian Automobile Association** (☎ 02/6247–7311).

➤ IN CANADA: **Canadian Automobile Association** (CAA, ☎ 613/247–0117).

➤ IN NEW ZEALAND: **New Zealand Automobile Association** (☎ 09/377–4660).

➤ IN THE U.K.: **Automobile Association** (AA, ☎ 0990/500–600). **Royal Automobile Club** (RAC, ☎ 0990/722–722 for membership; 0345/121–345 for insurance).

➤ IN THE U.S.: **American Automobile Association** (☎ 800/564–6222).

EMERGENCY SERVICES

In case of a breakdown, your best friend is the telephone. Try contacting your **rental agency** or the appropriate national breakdown service.

➤ CONTACTS: Czech Republic: ABA (☎ 124, or 0124 in rural areas) or ÚAMK (☎ 123, or 0123 in rural areas). **Hungary:** Hungarian Automobile Club (☎ 188).

FROM THE U.K.

Theoretically it's possible to travel by car from the United Kingdom to the Czech Republic and Hungary, although it's really not recommended due to lack of parts and mechanical know-how. However, if you do choose to drive your own vehicle, don't leave home without the car registration, third-party insurance, driver's license, and (if you're not the car's owner) a notarized letter of permission from the owner. The vehicle must bear a country ID sticker.

The best ferry ports for Prague and Budapest are Rotterdam, Holland, or Ostende, Belgium, from which you drive to Cologne (Köln), Germany, and then through either Dresden or Frankfurt and on to Prague.

GASOLINE

Gas stations are easy to come by on major thoroughfares and near large cities. Many are open around the clock, particularly in the Czech Republic and Hungary. At least two grades of gasoline are sold in Eastern and Central European countries, usually 90–93 octane (regular) and 94–98 octane (super). Lead-free gasoline is now available in most gas stations.

For additional country-specific information relating to roads, gasoline, and insurance, *see* Getting Around by Car in the A to Z section at the end of each city's chapter.

ROAD CONDITIONS

The main roads in the Czech Republic and Hungary are built to a fairly high standard. There are now quite substantial stretches of highway on main routes, and a lot of rebuilding is being done.

ROAD MAPS

In the **Czech Republic,** the ubiquitous 24-hour gas stations often sell road maps, or try a bookstore. In Prague, the downstairs level of the **Jan Kanzelsberger bookshop** on Wenceslas Square (✉ Václavské nám. 42, ☎ 02/2421–7335) has a good selection of hiking maps and auto atlases. In **Hungary,** good maps are sold at most large gas stations. In Budapest, the **Globe Térképbolt** (Globe Map Store; ✉ VI, Bajcsy-Zsilinszky út 37, ☎ 1/312–6001) has an excellent supply of domestic and foreign maps.

RULES OF THE ROAD

Throughout the Czech Republic and Hungary, driving is on the right and the same basic rules of the road practiced in the the United States and the rest of Europe apply. For further information *see* Getting Around by Car in the A to Z section at the end of each city's chapter.

CHILDREN IN PRAGUE AND BUDAPEST

Be sure to plan ahead and **involve your youngsters** as you outline your trip. When packing, include things to keep them busy en route. On sightseeing days try to schedule activities of special interest to your children. If

you are renting a car, don't forget to **arrange for a car seat** when you reserve.

FLYING

If your children are two or older, **ask about children's airfares.** As a general rule, infants under two not occupying a seat fly at greatly reduced fares or even for free. When booking, **confirm carry-on allowances** if you're traveling with infants. In general, for babies charged 10% of the adult fare you are allowed one carry-on bag and a collapsible stroller; if the flight is full, the stroller may have to be checked or you may be limited to less.

Experts agree that it's a good idea to use safety seats aloft for children weighing less than 40 pounds. Airlines set their own policies: U.S. carriers usually require that the child be ticketed, even if he or she is young enough to ride free, since the seats must be strapped into regular seats. Do **check your airline's policy about using safety seats during takeoff and landing.** And since safety seats are not allowed just everywhere in the plane, get your seat assignments early.

When reserving, **request children's meals or a freestanding bassinet** if you need them. But note that bulkhead seats, where you must sit to use the bassinet, may lack an overhead bin or storage space on the floor.

LODGING

Most hotels in Prague and Budapest allow children under a certain age to stay in their parents' room at no extra charge, but others charge for them as extra adults; be sure to **find out the cutoff age for children's discounts.** Some spa hotels don't allow children under 12.

The **Novotel** chain, which has hotels in Budapest, allows up to two children under 12 to stay free in their parents' room. The **Budapest Hilton** has an unusual policy allowing children of any age—even middle-aged adults—to stay for free in their parents' room.

Young visitors to Prague will enjoy staying at one of the picturesque floating "botels." For further information contact the Czech Tourist Authority (☞ Visitor Information, *below*). Prague's luxurious Palace and Savoy hotels, managed by Vienna International, allow children under 12 to stay free in their parents' room.

➤ BEST CHOICES: **Novotel** (☎ 800/221–4542). **Budapest Hilton** (☎ 1/214–3000 in Budapest).

SIGHTS & ATTRACTIONS

Places that are especially appealing to children are indicated by a rubber duckie icon in the margins throughout the book.

SUGGESTED READING

The Adventures of Mickey, Taggy, Pupo, and Cica and How They Discover Budapest, by Kati Rekai (Canadian Stage Arts Publications, Toronto), is an animal fantasy story set in Budapest, written by a Hungarian-born author. *The Trumpeter of Krakow* by Eric P. Kelly is a delightful, Newbery medal–winning book set in Kraków in the early Renaissance; though first published in 1928, it was reprinted in 1992. Intricate illustrations of Prague fill Czech-American Peter Sis's *The Three Golden Keys* (Doubleday); aimed at young readers, it evokes the city of the author's childhood.

SUPPLIES & EQUIPMENT

In Prague and Budapest, disposable diapers and formula are generally available in larger grocery stores and (with less frequency in some areas) pharmacies. For crayons and craft supplies, try a stationer's.

TRANSPORTATION

In the Czech Republic, car passengers under 12 years of age, or less than 150 cm (5 ft) in height, must ride in the back seat.

COMPUTERS ON THE ROAD

Bring an adapter for your laptop plug. Adapters are inexpenseive, and some models have several plugs suitable for different systems throughout the world. Some hotels lend adapters to guests for use during their stay.

At the airport, **be prepared to turn on your laptop** to prove to security personnel that the device is real. Security X-ray machines are damaging to a laptop, but **keep computer disks away from metal detectors.**

CONSUMER PROTECTION

Whenever buying travel services for a trip to Eastern and Central Europe, **pay with a major credit card** so you can cancel payment or get reimbursed if there's a problem. This is also a good philosophy when making purchases during your trip, but be aware that credit cards are not as widely accepted in the region as they are in western Europe and the United States—many hotels and restaurants operate on a cash-only basis. If you're doing business with a travel-services company for the first time, **contact your local Better Business Bureau and the attorney general's offices** in your own state and the company's home state, as well. Have any complaints been filed? Finally, if you're buying a package or tour, always **consider travel insurance** that includes default coverage (☞ Insurance, *below*).

➤ BBBs: **Council of Better Business Bureaus** (✉ 4200 Wilson Blvd., Suite 800, Arlington, VA 22203, ☎ 703/276–0100, ℻ 703/525–8277 www.bbb.org).

CUSTOMS & DUTIES

When shopping, **keep receipts** for all purchases. Upon reentering the country, **be ready to show customs officials what you've bought.** If you feel a duty is incorrect or object to the way your clearance was handled, note the inspector's badge number and ask to see a supervisor. If the problem isn't resolved, write to the appropriate authorities, beginning with the port director at your point of entry.

IN AUSTRALIA

Australian residents who are 18 or older may bring home $A400 worth of souvenirs and gifts (including jewelry), 250 cigarettes or 250 grams of tobacco, and 1,125 ml of alcohol (including wine, beer, and spirits). Residents under 18 may bring back $A200 worth of goods. Prohibited items include meat products. Seeds, plants, and fruits need to be declared upon arrival.

➤ INFORMATION: **Australian Customs Service** (Regional Director, ✉ Box 8, Sydney, NSW 2001, Australia, ☎ 02/9213–2000, ℻ 02/9213–4000, www.customs.gov.au).

IN CANADA

Canadian residents who have been out of Canada for at least 7 days may bring home C$500 worth of goods duty-free. If you've been away less than 7 days but more than 48 hours, the duty-free allowance drops to C$200; if your trip lasts 24–48 hours, the allowance is C$50. You may not pool allowances with family members. Goods claimed under the C$500 exemption may follow you by mail; those claimed under the lesser exemptions must accompany you. Alcohol and tobacco products may be included in the 7-day and 48-hour exemptions but not in the 24-hour exemption. If you meet the age requirements of the province or territory through which you reenter Canada, you may bring in, duty-free, 1.14 liters (40 imperial ounces) of wine or liquor *or* 24 12-ounce cans or bottles of beer or ale. If you are 16 or older you may bring in, duty-free, 200 cigarettes and 50 cigars. Check ahead of time with Revenue Canada or the Department of Agriculture for policies regarding meat products, seeds, plants, and fruits.

You may send an unlimited number of gifts worth up to C$60 each duty-free to Canada. Label the package UNSOLICITED GIFT—VALUE UNDER $60. Alcohol and tobacco are excluded.

➤ INFORMATION: **Revenue Canada** (✉ 2265 St. Laurent Blvd. S, Ottawa, Ontario K1G 4K3, Canada, ☎ 613/993–0534; 800/461–9999 in Canada, FAX 613/991–4126, www.ccra-adrc.gc.ca).

IN THE CZECH REPUBLIC AND HUNGARY

You may import duty-free 250 cigarettes or the equivalent in tobacco, 1 liter of spirits, and 2 liters of wine into Hungary. In addition to the above, you are permitted to import gifts valued up to 30,500 Ft into Hungary. You may import duty-free into the Czech Republic tobacco products equivalent to 200 cigarettes, 100 cigarillos, 250 grams of tobacco, or 50 cigars; 1 liter of spirits, 2 liters of wine, and personal medicines, as well as gifts and personal items valued at up to 6,000 Kč (3,000 Kč for visitors under 15) (about $170/$85).

If you are bringing into any of these countries any valuables or foreign-made equipment from home, such as cameras, it's wise to carry the original receipts with you or register the items with U.S. Customs before you leave (Form 4457). Otherwise you could end up paying duty upon your return. Be aware that leaving the country without expensive items declared upon entering can present a huge hassle with airport police.

IN NEW ZEALAND

Homeward-bound residents 17 or older may bring back $700 worth of souvenirs and gifts. Your duty-free allowance also includes 4.5 liters of wine or beer; one 1,125-ml bottle of spirits; and either 200 cigarettes, 250 grams of tobacco, 50 cigars, or a combination of the three up to 250 grams. Prohibited items include meat products, seeds, plants, and fruits.

➤ INFORMATION: **New Zealand Customs** (Custom House, ✉ 50 Anzac Ave., Box 29, Auckland, New Zealand, ☎ 09/300–5399, FAX 09/359–6730), www.customs.govt.nz.

IN THE U.K.

From countries outside the EU, including the Czech Republic and Hungary, you may bring home, duty-free, 200 cigarettes or 50 cigars; 1 liter of spirits or 2 liters of fortified or sparkling wine or liqueurs; 2 liters of still table wine; 60 ml of perfume; 250 ml of toilet water; plus £136 worth of other goods, including gifts and souvenirs. If returning from outside the EU, prohibited items include meat products, seeds, plants, and fruits.

➤ INFORMATION: **HM Customs and Excise** (✉ Dorset House, Stamford St., Bromley, Kent BR1 1XX, U.K., ☎ 020/7202–4227, www.hmce.gov.uk).

IN THE U.S.

U.S. residents who have been out of the country for at least 48 hours (and who have not used the $400 allowance or any part of it in the past 30 days) may bring home $400 worth of foreign goods duty-free.

U.S. residents 21 and older may bring back 1 liter of alcohol duty-free. In addition, regardless of your age, you are allowed 200 cigarettes and 100 non-Cuban cigars. Antiques, which the U.S. Customs Service defines as objects more than 100 years old, enter duty-free, as do original works of art done entirely by hand, including paintings, drawings, and sculptures.

You may also mail or ship packages home duty-free: up to $200 worth of goods for personal use, with a limit of one parcel per addressee per day (except alcohol or tobacco products or perfume worth more than $5); label the package PERSONAL USE and attach a list of its contents and their retail value. Do not label the package UNSOLICITED GIFT or your duty-free exemption will drop to $100. Mailed items do not affect your duty-free allowance on your return.

➤ INFORMATION: **U.S. Customs Service** (✉ 1300 Pennsylvania Ave. NW, Washington, DC 20229, www.customs.gov; inquiries ☎ 202/354–1000; complaints c/o ✉ 1300 Pennsylvania Ave. NW, Room 5.4D, Washington, DC 20229; registration of equipment c/o ✉ Resource Management, ☎ 202/354–1000).

DINING

For country-specific dining information, *see* Dining *in* Pleasures and Pastimes at the beginning of each city's chapter. Additional city-specific dining information may also be found at the start of a city's dining listings. The restaurants we list are the cream of the crop in each price category. Unless otherwise noted, the restaurants listed are open daily for lunch and dinner.

RESERVATIONS & DRESS

Reservations are always a good idea: we mention them only when they're essential or not accepted. Book as far ahead as you can, and reconfirm as soon as you arrive. We mention dress only when men are required to wear a jacket or a jacket and tie.

DISABILITIES & ACCESSIBILITY

Provisions for travelers with disabilities in the Czech Republic and Hungary are extremely limited; probably the best solution is to travel with a nondisabled companion. While many

hotels, especially large American or international chains, offer some wheelchair-accessible rooms, special facilities at museums and restaurants and on public transportation are difficult to find. In Poland wheelchairs are available at all airports, and most trains have special seats designated for people with disabilities, but it is wise to notify ahead. In Slovenia a law was passed in 1997 requiring all public buildings and infrastructure, including hotels, to be made fully accessible to people with disabilities.

➤ LOCAL RESOURCES: Czech Republic: **Sdružení zdravotně postižených** (Association of Disabled Persons; ✉ Karlínské nám. 12, Prague 8, ☎ 02/2481–5914, www.czechia.com/szdp). Hungary: **Mozgáskorlátozottak Egyesületeinek Országos Szövetsége** (National Association of People with Mobility Impairments, or MEOSZ; ✉ 1032 Budapest, San Marco u. 76, ☎ 1/388–5529).

LODGING

Most hotels take few or no measures to accommodate travelers with disabilities. Your best bets the best are newer hotels and international chains.

RESERVATIONS

When discussing accessibility with an operator or reservations agent, **ask hard questions.** Are there any stairs, inside *or* out? Are there grab bars next to the toilet *and* in the shower/tub? How wide is the doorway to the room? To the bathroom?

SIGHTS & ATTRACTIONS

Most tourist attractions in the region pose significant problems. Many are historic structures without ramps or other means to improve accessibility. Streets are often cobblestone, and potholes are common.

TRANSPORTATION

A few Czech trains are equipped with carriages for travelers using wheelchairs. Some stations on the Prague metro have elevators, and there are two lines of accessible buses, but the system is light-years from being barrier-free. For information on Prague public transport, call ☎ 02/2264–6055. Elsewhere in the region, public transportation is difficult, if not impossible, for many travelers with disabilities.

➤ COMPLAINTS: **Disability Rights Section** (✉ U.S. Department of Justice, Civil Rights Division, Box 66738, Washington, DC 20035-6738, ☎ 202/514–0301 or 800/514–0301; 202/514–0383 TTY; 800/514–0383 TTY, FAX 202/307–1198, www.usdoj. gov/crt/ada/adahom1.htm) for general complaints. **Aviation Consumer Protection Division** (☞ Air Travel, *above*) for airline-related problems. **Civil Rights Office** (✉ U.S. Department of Transportation, Departmental Office of Civil Rights, S-30, 400 7th St. SW, Room 10215, Washington, DC 20590, ☎ 202/366–4648, FAX 202/366–9371) for problems with surface transportation.

TRAVEL AGENCIES

In the United States, the Americans with Disabilities Act requires that travel firms serve the needs of all travelers. Some agencies specialize in working with people with disabilities.

➤ TRAVELERS WITH MOBILITY PROBLEMS: **Access Adventures** (✉ 206 Chestnut Ridge Rd., Scottsville, NY 14624, ☎ 716/889–9096, dltravel@prodigy.net), run by a former physical-rehabilitation counselor. **Flying Wheels Travel** (✉ 143 W. Bridge St., Box 382, Owatonna, MN 55060, ☎ 507/451–5005 or 800/ 535–6790, FAX 507/451–1685, thq@ll. net, www.flyingwheels.com).

DISCOUNTS & DEALS

Be a smart shopper and **compare all your options** before making decisions. A plane ticket bought with a promotional coupon from travel clubs, coupon books, and direct-mail offers may not be cheaper than the least expensive fare from a discount ticket agency. And always keep in mind that what you get is just as important as what you save.

In Budapest, the **Budapest Card** entitles holders to unlimited travel on public transportation; free admission to many museums and sights; and discounts on various services from participating businesses. The cost (at press time) is 2,800 Ft. for two days, 3,400 Ft. for three days; one card is valid for an adult plus one child under 14. It is available at many tourist offices along with a similar pass called the **Hungary Card,** which gives discounts to museums, sights, and service in the entire country.

DISCOUNT RESERVATIONS

To save money, **look into discount reservations services** with toll-free numbers, which use their buying power to get a better price on hotels, airline tickets, even car rentals. When booking a room, always **call the hotel's local toll-free number** (if one is available) rather than the central reservations number—you'll often get a better price. Always ask about special packages or corporate rates.

When shopping for the best deal on hotels and car rentals, **look for guaranteed exchange rates,** which protect you against a falling dollar. With your rate locked in, you won't pay more, even if the price goes up in the local currency.

➤ AIRLINE TICKETS: ☎ 800/FLY– ASAP.

➤ HOTEL ROOMS: **International Marketing & Travel Concepts** (☎ 800/790–4682, imtc@mindspring. com). **Steigenberger Reservation Service** (☎ 800/223–5652, www. srs-worldhotels.com). **Travel Interlink** (☎ 800/888–5898, www. travelinterlink.com).

PACKAGE DEALS

Don't confuse packages and guided tours. When you buy a package, you travel on your own, just as though you had planned the trip yourself. Fly/drive packages, which combine airfare and car rental, are often a good deal. If you **buy a rail/drive pass,** you may save on train tickets and car rentals. All Eurail- and Europass holders get a discount on Eurostar fares through the Channel Tunnel.

ELECTRICITY

To use your U.S.-purchased electric-powered equipment, **bring a converter**

and adapter. The electrical current in the Czech Republic and Hungary is 220 volts, 50 cycles alternating current (AC); wall outlets generally take plugs with two round prongs.

If your appliances are dual-voltage, you'll need only an adapter. Don't use 110-volt outlets marked FOR SHAVERS ONLY for high-wattage appliances such as blow-dryers. Most laptops operate equally well on 110 and 220 volts and so require only an adapter.

EMBASSIES

For Australian, Canadian, U.S., and U.K. embassy and consulate contact information, *see* the A to Z in each city's chapter. There are no New Zealand embassies or consulates in the region.

EMERGENCIES

For country-specific emergency numbers, *see* Emergencies in the A to Z section at the end of each city's chapter. For medical emergency contacts, *see also* Health, *below.*

GAY & LESBIAN TRAVEL

The **Czech Republic** is one of the most liberal countries in Eastern and Central Europe. Prague fosters a growing gay and lesbian scene, but up-to-date information is not easy to find. You could try visiting one of the gathering places that attract both gays and straights, such as the **Radost FX club** (☞ Prague Nightlife).

Hungary is relatively open-minded, though even in Budapest, the gay population keeps a fairly low profile. Some of Budapest's thermal baths are popular meeting places (*see* Exploring Budapest Chapter 3), as are the city's several gay bars and clubs, which you can find listed in English-language newspapers and the monthly magazine *Mások.*

➤ GAY- & LESBIAN-FRIENDLY TRAVEL AGENCIES: **Different Roads Travel** (✉ 8383 Wilshire Blvd., Suite 902, Beverly Hills, CA 90211, ☎ 323/651–5557 or 800/429–8747, ℻ 323/651–3678, leigh@west.tzell.com). **Kennedy Travel** (✉ 314 Jericho Turnpike, Floral Park, NY 11001, ☎ 516/352–4888 or 800/237–7433, ℻ 516/354–8849, kennedytravel1@yahoo.com,

www.kennedytravel.com). **Now Voyager** (✉ 4406 18th St., San Francisco, CA 94114, ☎ 415/626–1169 or 800/255–6951, ℻ 415/626–8626, www.nowvoyager.com). **Skylink Travel and Tour** (✉ 1006 Mendocino Ave., Santa Rosa, CA 95401, ☎ 707/546–9888 or 800/225–5759, ℻ 707/546–9891, skylinktvl@aol.com, www.skylinktravel.com), serving lesbian travelers.

HEALTH

Tap water may taste bad but is generally drinkable; when it runs rusty out of the tap or the aroma of chlorine is overpowering, it might help to have some iodine tablets or bottled water handy. Throughout the country, bottled water is inexpensive and widely available; it might be a better choice, especially for children, as there is a history of tap water with heavy lead content. Buy bottled water, particularly if staying in an older home or a hotel.

Vegetarians and those on special diets may have a problem with the heavy local cuisine, which is based largely on pork and beef. To prevent your vitamin intake from dropping to danger levels, buy fresh fruits and vegetables at seasonal street markets—regular grocery stores often don't sell them.

No vaccinations are required for entry into either the Czech Republic or Hungary, but selective vaccinations are recommended. Those traveling in forested areas should consider vaccinating themselves against Central European, or tick-borne, encephalitis. Tick-borne Lyme disease is also a risk in the Czech Republic. Schedule vaccinations well in advance of departure because some require several doses, and others may cause uncomfortable side effects.

To avoid problems clearing customs, diabetic travelers carrying needles and syringes should have on hand a letter from their physician confirming their need for insulin injections.

OVER-THE-COUNTER REMEDIES

For recommended pharmacies, *see* the A to Z sections in each city's chapter.

HOLIDAYS

For country-specific holidays, *see* National Holidays in the A to Z section at the end of each city's chapter.

INSURANCE

The most useful travel-insurance plan is a comprehensive policy that includes coverage for trip cancellation and interruption, default, trip delay, and medical expenses (with a waiver for pre-existing conditions).

Without insurance you will lose all or most of your money if you cancel your trip, regardless of the reason. Default insurance covers you if your tour operator, airline, or cruise line goes out of business. Trip-delay covers expenses that arise because of bad weather or mechanical delays. Study the fine print when comparing policies.

When you're traveling internationally, a key component of travel insurance is coverage for medical bills incurred if you get sick on the road. Such expenses are not generally covered by Medicare or private policies. U.K. residents can buy a travel-insurance policy valid for most vacations taken during the year in which it's purchased (but check pre-existing-condition coverage). British and Australian citizens need extra medical coverage when traveling overseas.

Always **buy travel policies directly from the insurance company**; if you buy them from a cruise line, airline, or tour operator that goes out of business you probably will not be covered for the agency or operator's default, a major risk. Before making any purchase, **review your existing health and home-owner's policies** to find what they cover away from home.

➤ TRAVEL INSURERS: In the U.S.: **Access America** (⊠ 6600 W. Broad St., Richmond, VA 23230, ☎ 804/285–3300 or 800/284–8300, FAX 804/673–1586, www.previewtravel.com), **Travel Guard International** (⊠ 1145 Clark St., Stevens Point, WI 54481, ☎ 715/345–0505 or 800/826–1300, FAX 800/955–8785, www.noelgroup.com).

➤ INSURANCE INFORMATION: In the U.K.: **Association of British Insurers** (⊠ 51–55 Gresham St., London EC2V 7HQ, U.K., ☎ 020/7600–3333, FAX 020/7696–8999, info@abi.org.uk, www.abi.org.uk). In Canada: **Voyager Insurance** (⊠ 44 Peel Center Dr., Brampton, Ontario L6T 4M8, Canada, ☎ 905/791–8700, 800/668–4342 in Canada). In Australia: **Insurance Council of Australia** (☎ 03/9614–1077, FAX 03/9614–7924). In New Zealand: **Insurance Council of New Zealand** (⊠ Box 474, Wellington, New Zealand, ☎ 04/472–5230, FAX 04/473–3011, www.icnz.org.nz).

LANGUAGE

For country-specific information about language issues, *see* Language in the A to Z section at the end of each city's chapter.

LODGING

For city-specific lodging information, *see* Lodging *in* Pleasures and Pastimes at the beginning of each city's chapter. Additional city-specific lodging information may also be found at the start of a city's lodging listings. The lodgings we list are the cream of the crop in each price category. We always list the facilities that are available—but we don't specify whether they cost extra: when pricing accommodations, always ask what's included and what costs extra.

APARTMENT & VILLA RENTALS

If you want a home base that's roomy enough for a family and comes with cooking facilities, **consider a furnished rental.** These can save you money, especially if you're traveling with a group. Home-exchange directories sometimes list rentals as well as exchanges.

Rental apartments are common in Hungary. In Budapest, the best bet is to go through an agency; and in the rest of the country, either check with a local tourist information office or, especially in smaller cities, simply walk around until you see a sign outside a house reading *apartman*.

➤ INTERNATIONAL AGENTS: **Hometours International** (⊠ Box 11503, Knoxville, TN 37939, ☎ 865/690–8484 or 800/367–4668, hometours@aol.com,

http://thor.he.net/áhometour/). Inter-
home (⊠ 1990 N.E. 163rd St., Suite
110, N. Miami Beach, FL 33162, ☎
305/940–2299 or 800/882–6864, ℻
305/940–2911, interhomeu@aol.com,
www.interhome.com).

➤ LOCAL AGENTS: Hungary: In Budapest, **Amadeus Apartments** (⊠ IX,
Üllői út 197, H-1091, ☎ 06/309–
422–893); **TRIBUS Welcome Hotel
Service** (⊠ V, Apáczai Csere János u.
1, ☎ 1/318–5776); **Cooptourist** (⊠
XI, Bartók Béla út 4, ☎ 1/466–5349).

B&BS

Although B&Bs of the traditional
English variety aren't prevalent in the
region, there are numerous variations
on the concept available, including
comfortable and elaborately decorated
facilities in Hungary. For further information, *see* B&B Reservation Agencies
in the A to Z sections of the individual
city's chapters.

CAMPING

For information on camping in the
Czech Republic, contact the Czech
Tourist Authority (☞ Visitor Information, *below*). The Prague Information Service can supply a map of the
dozen or so campgrounds in and
around Prague.

For **Hungary,** campground information, reservations, and an informative
map listing all campgrounds can be
obtained from travel agencies and
Tourinform (☞ Visitor Information
in the Hungary A to Z section of
Chapter 3). You may also contact the
**Hungarian Camping and Caravanning
Club** (⊠ VIII, Mária u. 34, Budapest,
☎ 1/267–5255 or 1/267–5256).

HOME EXCHANGES

If you would like to exchange your
home for someone else's, **join a home-
exchange organization,** which will
send you its updated listings of available exchanges for a year and will
include your own listing in at least
one of them. It's up to you to make
specific arrangements.

➤ EXCHANGE CLUBS: **Intervac U.S.** (⊠
Box 590504, San Francisco, CA
94159, ☎ 800/756–4663, ℻ 415/
435–7440, intervacus@aol.com,
www.intervacus.com; $93 per year
includes two catalogues).

HOSTELS

No matter what your age you can
**save on lodging costs by staying at
hostels.** In some 5,000 locations in
more than 70 countries around the
world, Hostelling International (HI),
the umbrella group for a number of
national youth-hostel associations,
offers single-sex, dorm-style beds and,
at many hostels, couples rooms and
family accommodations. Membership
in any HI national hostel association,
open to travelers of all ages, allows
you to stay in HI-affiliated hostels at
member rates (one-year membership
is about $25 for adults; hostels run
about $10–$25 per night). Members
also have priority if the hostel is full;
they're eligible for discounts around
the world, even on rail and bus travel
in some countries.

In Hungary, most hostels are geared
toward the college crowd. Among
several good ones in Budapest are the
friendly, Internet-equipped **Back Pack
Guesthouse** (⊠ XI, Takács Menyhért
u. 33, ☎ 1/385–8946), where rates
range from 1,300 Ft. (8–10 bed
rooms) to 1,900 Ft. (2-bed rooms),
and the **Sirály Youth Hostel** (⊠ XIII,
Margit-sziget (Margaret Island), ☎ 1/
329–3952), situated in the relative
peace, quiet, and clean air of an
island-park on the Danube, where the
per-person rate in 12-bed rooms is
1,400 Ft. For further information,
consult the free annual accommodations directory published by **Tourinform** (☞ Visitor Information in the
Hungary A to Z section of Chapter 3)
or the listings in **Budapest In Your
Pocket,** available at newsstands.

All but one or two Czech hostels are
located in two towns: Prague and
Český Krumlov. They tend to be
either backpacker-happy, party-all-
night places, or affiliated with sports
clubs or colleges. Most accommodation
services in Prague book hostel rooms.
The Prague representative of Hostelling
International is KMC Travel Service,
Karolíny Světlé 30, ☎ 02/2222–1328.
A relatively well-run Prague hostel, with
six local sites and affiliates in Český
Krumlov, Budapest, and Berlin, is
Travellers' Hostel (main location:
Dlouhá 33, ☎ 02/231–1318).

➤ ORGANIZATIONS: **Hostelling International—American Youth Hostels**

(✉ 733 15th St. NW, Suite 840, Washington, DC 20005, ☎ 202/783–6161, FAX 202/783–6171, hiayhserv@hiayh.org, www.hiayh.org). **Hostelling International—Canada** (✉ 400–205 Catherine St., Ottawa, Ontario K2P 1C3, Canada, ☎ 613/237–7884, FAX 613/237–7868, info@hostellingintl.ca, www.hostellingintl.ca). **Youth Hostel Association of England and Wales** (✉ Trevelyan House, 8 St. Stephen's Hill, St. Albans, Hertfordshire AL1 2DY, U.K., ☎ 0870/8708808, FAX 01727/844126, customerservices@yha.org.uk, www.yha.org.uk). **Australian Youth Hostel Association** (✉ 10 Mallett St., Camperdown, NSW 2050, Australia, ☎ 02/9565–1699, FAX 02/9565–1325, www.yha.com.au). **Youth Hostels Association of New Zealand** (✉ Box 436, Christchurch, New Zealand, ☎ 03/379–9970, FAX 03/365–4476, info@yha.org.nz, www.yha.org.nz).

HOTELS

Throughout the past decade the quality of hotels in the Czech Republic and Hungary has improved notably. Many formerly state-run hotels were privatized, much to their benefit. International hotel chains have established a strong presence in the region; while they may not be strong on local character, they do provide a reliably high standard of quality.

Hotels listed throughout the book have private bath unless otherwise noted.

➤ TOLL-FREE NUMBERS: **Best Western** (☎ 800/528–1234, www.bestwestern.com). **Choice** (☎ 800/221–2222, www.hotelchoice.com). **Hilton** (☎ 800/445–8667, www.hilton.com). **Holiday Inn** (☎ 800/465–4329, www.basshotels.com). **Hungarian Hotels** (☎ 800/448–4321). **Hyatt Hotels & Resorts** (☎ 800/233–1234, www.hyatt.com). **Inter-Continental** (☎ 800/327–0200, www.interconti.com). **Marriott** (☎ 800/228–9290, www.marriott.com). **Radisson** (☎ 800/333–3333, www.radisson.com). **Renaissance Hotels & Resorts** (☎ 800/468–3571, www.renaissancehotels.com/).

MAIL & SHIPPING

For country-specific mail information, *see* Mail in the A to Z section at the end of each city's chapter.

MONEY MATTERS

For country-specific money information, *see* Money and Expenses in the A to Z section at the end of each city's chapter.

Prices throughout this guide are given for adults. Substantially reduced fees are almost always available for children, students, and senior citizens. For information on taxes, *see* Taxes, *below.*

ATMS

ATMs are common in Prague and Budapest and more often than not are part of the Cirrus and Plus networks; outside of urban areas, machines are scarce and you should plan to carry enough cash to meet your needs.

CREDIT CARDS

Credit cards are accepted in places that cater regularly to foreign tourists and business travelers. When you leave the beaten path, be prepared to pay cash. Always inquire about credit card policies when booking hotel rooms. Visa and EuroCard/MasterCard are the most commonly accepted credit cards in the region.

It's smart to **write down (and keep separate) the number of each credit card you're carrying** along with the international service phone number that usually appears on the back of the card.

Throughout this guide, the following abbreviations are used: **AE,** American Express; **D,** Discover; **DC,** Diners Club; **MC,** Master Card; and **V,** Visa.

CURRENCY EXCHANGE

You should **change money at banks** for the most favorable exchange rate. Although fees charged for ATM transactions may be higher abroad than at home, Cirrus and Plus exchange rates are excellent, because they are based on wholesale rates offered only by major banks. You often won't do as well at exchange booths in airports or rail and bus stations, in hotels, in restaurants, or in stores, although you may find their hours more convenient. To avoid lines at airport exchange booths, **get a bit of local currency before you leave home.**

➤ EXCHANGE SERVICES: **International Currency Express** (☎ 888/278–6628 for orders, www.foreignmoney.com). **Thomas Cook Currency Services** (☎ 800/287-7362 for telephone orders and retail locations, www.us. thomascook.com).

TRAVELER'S CHECKS

Do you need traveler's checks? It depends on where you're headed. If you're going to rural areas and small towns, go with cash; traveler's checks are best used in cities. Lost or stolen checks can usually be replaced within 24 hours. To ensure a speedy refund, buy your own traveler's checks— don't let someone else pay for them: irregularities like this can cause delays. The person who bought the checks should make the call to request a refund.

PACKING

Don't worry about packing lots of formal clothing. Fashion was all but nonexistent under 40 years of Communist rule, although residents of Budapest and Prague—catching up with their counterparts in other European capitals—are considerably more fashionably dressed than even a few years ago. A sports jacket for men and a dress or pants for women are appropriate for an evening out. Everywhere else, you'll feel comfortable in casual pants or jeans.

The Czech Republic and Hungary enjoy all the extremes of an inland climate, so plan accordingly. In the higher elevations winter can last until April, and even in summer the evenings will be on the cool side.

Many areas are best seen on foot, so take a pair of sturdy walking shoes. High heels will present considerable problems on the cobblestone streets of Prague, and towns in Hungary. If you plan to visit the mountains, make sure your shoes have good traction

and ankle support, as some trails can be quite challenging.

Toiletries and personal-hygiene products have become relatively easy to find, but it's always a good idea to bring necessities when traveling in rural areas. Streetlights are rare, even in city centers, and often interior hallways are unlit, so bring a flashlight.

In your carry-on luggage, **pack an extra pair of eyeglasses or contact lenses** and **enough of any medication you take** to last the entire trip. You may also ask your doctor to write a spare prescription using the drug's generic name, since brand names may vary from country to country. In luggage to be checked, **never pack prescription drugs or valuables.** To avoid customs delays, carry medications in their original packaging. And don't forget to carry with you the addresses of offices that handle refunds of lost traveler's checks.

CHECKING LUGGAGE

How many carry-on bags you can bring with you is up to the airline. Most allow two, but not always, so make sure that everything you carry aboard will fit under your seat or in the overhead bin, and get to the gate early. Note that if you have a seat at the back of the plane, you'll probably board first, while the overhead bins are still empty.

When flying internationally, note that baggage allowances may be determined not by piece but by weight— generally 88 pounds (40 kilograms) in first class, 66 pounds (30 kilograms) in business class, and 44 pounds (20 kilograms) in economy.

Airline liability for baggage is limited to $1,250 per person on flights within the United States. On international flights it amounts to $9.07 per pound or $20 per kilogram for checked baggage (roughly $640 per 70-pound bag) and $400 per passenger for unchecked baggage. You can buy additional coverage at check-in for about $10 per $1,000 of coverage, but it excludes a rather extensive list of items, shown on your airline ticket.

Before departure, **itemize your bags' contents** and their worth, and label the bags with your name, address, and phone number. (If you use your home address, cover it so potential thieves can't see it readily.) Inside each bag, **pack a copy of your itinerary.** At check-in, **make sure that each bag is correctly tagged** with the destination airport's three-letter code. If your bags arrive damaged or fail to arrive at all, file a written report with the airline before leaving the airport.

PASSPORTS & VISAS

When traveling internationally, **carry your passport** even if you don't need one (it's always the best form of I.D.) and **make two photocopies of the data page** (one for someone at home and another for you, carried separately from your passport). If you lose your passport, promptly call the nearest embassy or consulate and the local police.

ENTERING THE CZECH REPUBLIC AND HUNGARY

See the A to Z section at the end of each city's chapter for specific entrance requirements.

PASSPORT OFFICES

The best time to apply for a passport or to renew is in fall and winter. Before any trip, check your passport's expiration date, and, if necessary, renew it as soon as possible.

➤ AUSTRALIAN CITIZENS: **Australian Passport Office** (☎ 131–232, www.dfat.gov.au/passports).

➤ CANADIAN CITIZENS: **Passport Office** (☎ 819/994–3500; 800/567–6868 in Canada, www.dfait-maeci.gc.ca/passport).

➤ NEW ZEALAND CITIZENS: **New Zealand Passport Office** (☎ 04/494–0700, www.passports.govt.nz).

➤ U.K. CITIZENS: **London Passport Office** (☎ 0870/521–0410, www.ukpa.gov.uk) for fees and documentation requirements and to request an emergency passport.

➤ U.S. CITIZENS: **National Passport Information Center** (☎ 900/225–5674; calls are 35¢ per minute for automated service, $1.05 per minute

for operator service; www.travel.state.gov/npicinfo.html).

REST ROOMS

Public rest rooms are more common, and cleaner, than they used to be in the Czech Republic. You nearly always have to pay 2 Kč–10 Kč to the attendant. Restaurant and bar toilets are generally for customers only.

While the rest rooms at Budapest's Ferihegy Airport may sparkle and smell of soap, don't expect the same of those at **Hungarian** train and bus stations—which usually have attendants who collect a fee of about 40 Ft. Pay the attendant on the way in; you will receive toilet tissue in exchange. Since public rest rooms are scarce, you will find yourself entering cafés, bars, or restaurants to use their toilets; when doing so, you should probably order a little something.

SAFETY

Crime rates are still relatively low in the Czech Republic and Hungary, but travelers should beware of pickpockets in crowded areas. In general, always keep your valuables with you. Make sure your wallet is safe in a buttoned pocket, or watch your handbag.

In the **Czech Republic,** except for widely scattered attacks against people of color, violent crime against tourists is extremely rare. Pickpocketing and bill-padding are the most common complaints.

In **Hungary,** pickpocketing and car theft are the main concerns. While a typical rental car is less likely to be stolen, expensive German makes such as Audi, BMW, and Mercedes are hot targets for car thieves.

LOCAL SCAMS

To avoid potential trouble in the Czech Republic: Ask taxi drivers what the approximate fare will be before getting in, and ask for a receipt (*paragon*); carefully look over restaurant bills; be extremely wary of handing your passport to anyone who accosts you with a demand for I.D.; and never exchange money on the street.

SENIOR-CITIZEN TRAVEL

To qualify for age-related discounts, **mention your senior-citizen status up front** when booking hotel reservations (not when checking out), before you're seated in restaurants (not when paying the bill), as well as when renting a car.

➤ EDUCATIONAL PROGRAMS: **Elderhostel** (✉ 75 Federal St., 3rd floor, Boston, MA 02110, ☎ 877/426–8056, ℻ 877/426–2166, www.elderhostel.org). **Interhostel** (✉ University of New Hampshire, 6 Garrison Ave., Durham, NH 03824, ☎ 603/862–1147 or 800/733–9753, ℻ 603/862–1113, learn.dce@unh.edu, www.learn.unh.edu).

STUDENTS IN THE CZECH REPUBLIC AND HUNGARY

For country-specific student and youth travel information, *see* Student and Youth Travel in the A to Z section at the end of each city's chapter.

➤ I.D.S & SERVICES: **Council Travel** (CIEE; ✉ 205 E. 42nd St., 14th floor, New York, NY 10017, ☎ 212/822–2700 or 888/268–6245, ℻ 212/822–2699, info@councilexchanges.org, www.councilexchanges.org) for mail orders only, in the U.S. **Travel Cuts** (✉ 187 College St., Toronto, Ontario M5T 1P7, Canada, ☎ 416/979–2406 or 800/667–2887 in Canada, www.travelcuts.com).

TAXES

Most Eastern and Central European countries have some form of value-added tax (VAT); rebate rules vary by country, but you'll need to present your receipts on departure.

For country-specific tax and VAT information, *see* Customs and Duties and Money and Expenses in the A to Z section at the end of each chapter.

TELEPHONES

For additional country-specific telephone information, *see* Telephones in the A to Z section at the end of each city's chapter.

AREA & COUNTRY CODES

Country and select city codes are as follows: Czech Republic (420), Prague (2); Hungary (36), Budapest (1).

When dialing a Czech or Hungarian number from abroad, drop the initial 0 from the local area code. The country code for the United States is 1 for the United States and Canada, 61 for Australia, 64 for New Zealand, and 44 for the U.K.

LONG-DISTANCE SERVICES

AT&T, MCI, and Sprint access codes make calling long distance relatively convenient, but you may find the local access number blocked in many hotel rooms. First ask the hotel operator to connect you. If the hotel operator balks, ask for an international operator, or dial the international operator yourself. One way to improve your odds of getting connected to your long-distance carrier is to travel with more than one company's calling card (a hotel may block Sprint, for example, but not MCI). If all else fails, call from a pay phone.

➤ ACCESS CODES: **AT&T Direct** (☎ 0042000101 in the Czech Republic; 0080001111 in Hungary; 800/435–0812 for other areas). **MCI World-Phone** (☎ 0042000112 in the Czech Republic; 0680001411 in Hungary). **Sprint International Access** (☎ 0042087187 in the Czech Republic; 0680001877 in Hungary; 800/877–4646 for other areas).

TIME

The Czech Republic and Hungary are on Central European Time (CET), one hour ahead of Greenwich Mean Time and six hours ahead of the eastern time zone of the United States.

TOURS & PACKAGES

Because everything is prearranged on a prepackaged tour or independent vacation, you'll spend less time planning—and often get it all at a good price.

BOOKING WITH AN AGENT

Travel agents are excellent resources. But it's a good idea to collect brochures from several agencies as some agents' suggestions may be influenced by relationships with tour and package firms that reward them for volume sales. If you have a special interest, **find an agent with expertise in that area**; the American Society of

SMART TRAVEL TIPS / THE GOLD GUIDE

Travel Agents (ASTA; ☞ Travel Agencies, *below*) has a database of specialists worldwide.

Make sure your travel agent knows the accommodations and other services of the place they're recommending. Ask about the hotel's location, room size, beds, and whether it has a pool, room service, or programs for children, if you care about these. Has your agent been there in person or sent others whom you can contact?

Do some homework on your own, too: local tourism boards can provide information about lesser-known and small-niche operators, some of which may sell only direct.

BUYER BEWARE

Each year consumers are stranded or lose their money when tour operators—even large ones with excellent reputations—go out of business. So **check out the operator.** Ask several travel agents about its reputation, and try to **book with a company that has a consumer-protection program.** (Look for information in the company's brochure.) In the United States, members of the National Tour Association and the United States Tour Operators Association are required to set aside funds to cover your payments and travel arrangements in the event that the company defaults. It's also a good idea to choose a company that participates in the American Society of Travel Agents' Tour Operator Program (TOP); ASTA will act as mediator in any disputes between you and your tour operator.

Remember that the more your package or tour includes the better you can predict the ultimate cost of your vacation. Make sure you know exactly what is covered, and **beware of hidden costs.** Are taxes, tips, and transfers included? Entertainment and excursions? These can add up.

➤ TOUR-OPERATOR RECOMMENDATIONS: **American Society of Travel Agents** (☞ Travel Agencies, *below*). **National Tour Association** (NTA; ✉ 546 E. Main St., Lexington, KY 40508, ☎ 859/226–4444 or 800/ 682–8886, www.ntaonline.com).

United States Tour Operators Association (USTOA; ✉ 342 Madison Ave., Suite 1522, New York, NY 10173, ☎ 212/599–6599 or 800/468–7862, FAX 212/599–6744, ustoa@aol.com, www.ustoa.com).

GROUP TOURS

The classifications used below represent different price categories. The key difference is usually in accommodations, which run from budget to better, and better-yet to best.

➤ SUPER-DELUXE: **Abercrombie & Kent** (✉ 1520 Kensington Rd., Oak Brook, IL 60521-2141, ☎ 630/954–2944 or 800/323–7308, FAX 630/954–3324). **Travcoa** (✉ Box 2630, 2350 S.E. Bristol St., Newport Beach, CA 92660, ☎ 714/476–2800 or 800/ 992–2003, FAX 714/476–2538).

➤ DELUXE: **Globus** (✉ 5301 S. Federal Circle, Littleton, CO 80123-2980, ☎ 303/797–2800 or 800/221–0090, FAX 303/347–2080). **Maupintour** (✉ 1515 St. Andrews Dr., Lawrence, KS 66047, ☎ 785/843–1211 or 800/255–4266, FAX 785/843–8351). **Tauck Tours** (✉ Box 5027, 276 Post Rd. W, Westport, CT 06881-5027, ☎ 203/226–6911 or 800/468–2825, FAX 203/221–6866).

➤ FIRST-CLASS: **Brendan Tours** (✉ 15137 Califa St., Van Nuys, CA 91411, ☎ 818/785–9696 or 800/ 421–8446, FAX 818/902–9876). **Caravan Tours** (✉ 401 N. Michigan Ave., Chicago, IL 60611, ☎ 312/321–9800 or 800/227–2826, FAX 312/321–9845). **Čedok Travel** (✉ 10 E. 40th St., #3604, New York, NY 10016, ☎ 212/725–0948 or 800/800–8891). **Collette Tours** (✉ 162 Middle St., Pawtucket, RI 02860, ☎ 401/728–3805 or 800/340–5158, FAX 401/728–4745). **DER Travel Services** (✉ 9501 W. Devon Ave., Rosemont, IL 60018, ☎ 800/937–1235, FAX 847/692–4141; 800/282–7474; 800/860–9944 for brochures). **General Tours** (✉ 53 Summer St., Keene, NH 03431, ☎ 603/357–5033 or 800/221–2216, FAX 603/357–4548). **Insight International Tours** (✉ 745 Atlantic Ave., #720, Boston, MA 02111, ☎ 617/482–2000 or 800/582–8380, FAX 617/482–2884 or 800/622–5015). **Trafalgar Tours** (✉ 11 E. 26th St., New York,

NY 10010, ☎ 212/689–8977 or 800/854–0103, FAX 800/457–6644).

➤ BUDGET: **Cosmos** (☞ Globus, *above*). **Trafalgar Tours** (☞ *above*).

PACKAGES

Independent vacation packages are available from major tour operators and airlines. The companies listed below offer vacation packages in a broad price range.

➤ AIR/HOTEL: **Continental Vacations** (☎ 800/634–5555). **DER Travel Services** (☞ Group Tours, *above*). **General Tours** (☞ Group Tours, *above*).

THEME TRIPS

➤ BALLOONING: **Buddy Bombard European Balloon Adventures** (✉ 333 Pershing Way, West Palm Beach, FL 33401, ☎ 561/837–6610 or 800/862–8537, FAX 561/837–6623).

➤ BARGE/RIVER CRUISES: **KD River Cruises of Europe** (✉ 2500 Westchester Ave., Purchase, NY 10577, ☎ 914/696–3600 or 800/346–6525, FAX 914/696–0833).

➤ BEER/WINE: **MIR Corporation** (✉ 85 S. Washington St., #210, Seattle, WA 98104, ☎ 206/624–7289 or 800/424–7289, FAX 206/624–7360).

➤ BICYCLING: **Backroads** (✉ 801 Cedar St., Berkeley, CA 94710-1800, ☎ 510/527–1555 or 800/462–2848, FAX 510/527–1444). **Butterfield & Robinson** (✉ 70 Bond St., Toronto, Ontario, Canada M5B 1X3, ☎ 416/864–1354 or 800/678–1147, FAX 416/864–0541). **Euro-Bike Tours** (✉ Box 990, De Kalb, IL 60115, ☎ 800/321–6060, FAX 815/758–8851). **Uniquely Europe** (✉ 1940 116th Ave. NE, Bellevue, WA 98004, ☎ 425/455–4445 or 800/927–3876, FAX 425/455–2111).

➤ CRUISING: **EuroCruises** (✉ 303 W. 13th St., New York, NY 10014-1207, ☎ 800/688–3876, FAX 212/366–4747).

➤ HISTORY & ART: **IST Cultural Tours** (✉ 225 W. 34th St., New York, NY 10122-0913, ☎ 212/563–1202 or 800/833–2111, FAX 212/594–6953). **Smithsonian Study Tours and Seminars** (✉ 1100 Jefferson Dr. SW, Room 3045, 20560, Washington, DC 20560, ☎ 202/357–4700, FAX 202/633–9250).

➤ NATURAL HISTORY: **Earthwatch** (✉ Box 9104, 680 Mount Auburn St., Watertown, MA 02272, ☎ 617/926–8200 or 800/776–0188, FAX 617/926–8532) for research expeditions. **Questers** (✉ 381 Park Ave. S, New York, NY 10016, ☎ 212/251–0444 or 800/468–8668, FAX 212/251–0890). **Victor Emanuel Nature Tours** (✉ Box 33008, Austin, TX 78764, ☎ 512/328–5221 or 800/328–8368, FAX 512/328–2919).

➤ PERFORMING ARTS: **Dailey-Thorp Travel** (✉ 330 W. 58th St., #610, New York, NY 10019-1817, ☎ 212/307–1555 or 800/998–4677, FAX 212/974–1420).

➤ SINGLES AND YOUNG ADULTS: **Club Europa** (✉ 802 W. Oregon St., Urbana, IL 61801, ☎ 217/344–5863 or 800/331–1882, FAX 217/344–4072). **Contiki Holidays** (✉ 300 Plaza Alicante, #900, Garden Grove, CA 92640, ☎ 714/740–0808 or 800/266–8454, FAX 714/740–0818).

➤ SPAS: **Great Spas of the World** (✉ 55 John St., New York, NY 10038, ☎ 212/267–5500 or 800/772–8463, FAX 212/571–0510). **Spa-Finders** (✉ 91 5th Ave., #301, New York, NY 10003-3039, ☎ 212/924–6800 or 800/255–7727).

➤ TRAIN TOURS: **Abercrombie & Kent** (☞ Group Tours, *above*).

➤ WALKING/HIKING: **Backroads** (☞ Bicycling, *above*). **Himalayan Travel** (✉ 110 Prospect St., Stamford, CT 06901, ☎ 203/359–3711 or 800/225–2380, FAX 203/359–3669). **Mountain Travel-Sobek** (✉ 6420 Fairmount Ave., El Cerrito, CA 94530, ☎ 510/527–8100 or 800/227–2384, FAX 510/525–7710). **Uniquely Europe** (☞ Bicycling, *above*).

TRAIN TRAVEL

Although standards have improved, on the whole they are far short of what is acceptable in the West. Trains are very busy, and it is rare to find one running less than full or almost so. Each country operates its own dining, buffet, and refreshment services. Always crowded, they tend to open and close at the whim of the staff. In Hungary, couchette cars are second class only and can be little more than a hard bunk without springs and adequate bed linen. First class couchettes are also available on Czech trains, and there are two types of second class couchettes. The cheaper have six hard beds per compartment; the slightly more expensive have three beds and a sink and are sex-segregated. Some of the most comfortable trains are the express trains in the Czech Republic and Hungary—they're normally less crowded and more comfortable. (You should make a reservation.)

Although trains can mean hours of sitting on a hard seat in a smoky car, traveling by rail is very inexpensive. Rail networks in the Czech Republic and Hungary are very extensive, though trains can be infuriatingly slow.

For information about fares and schedules and other country-specific train information, *see* Arriving and Departing and Getting Around in the A to Z section at the end of each city's chapter.

CUTTING COSTS

To save money, **look into rail passes.** But be aware that if you don't plan to cover many miles you may come out ahead by buying individual tickets.

You can use the **European East Pass** on the national rail networks of Austria, the Czech Republic, Hungary, Poland, and Slovakia. The pass covers five days of unlimited first-class travel within a one-month period for $199. Additional travel days may be purchased.

You can also combine the East Pass with a national rail pass. A pass for the Czech Republic costs $69 for five days of train travel within a 15-day period—far more than you'd spend on individual tickets. The Hungarian Flexipass costs $64 for five days of unlimited first-class train travel within a 15-day period or $80 for 10 days within a one-month period.

Hungary is one of 17 countries in which you can **use Eurailpasses,** which provide unlimited first-class rail travel, in all of the participating countries, for

the duration of the pass. If you plan to rack up the miles, get a standard pass. These are available for 15 days ($554), 21 days ($718), one month ($890), two months ($1,260), and three months ($1,558).

In addition to standard Eurailpasses, **ask about special rail-pass plans.** Among these are the Eurail Youthpass (for those under age 26), the Eurail Saverpass (which gives a discount for two or more people traveling together), a Eurail Flexipass (which allows a certain number of travel days within a set period), the Euraildrive Pass and the Europass Drive (which combines travel by train and rental car). Whichever pass you choose, remember that you must **purchase your pass before you leave** for Europe.

Many travelers assume that rail passes guarantee them seats on the trains they wish to ride. Not so. You need to **book seats ahead even if you are using a rail pass;** seat reservations are required on some European trains, particularly high-speed trains, and are a good idea on trains that may be crowded—particularly in summer on popular routes. You will also need a reservation if you purchase sleeping accommodations.

➤ INFORMATION AND PASSES: **Rail Europe** (✉ 500 Mamaroneck Ave., Harrison, NY 10528, ☎ 914/682–5172 or 800/438–7245, FAX 800/432–1329; ✉ 2087 Dundas E, Suite 106, Mississauga, Ontario L4X 1M2, ☎ 800/361–7245, FAX 905/602–4198). **DER Travel Services** (✉ 9501 W. Devon Ave., Rosemont, IL 60018, ☎ 800/782–2424, FAX 800/282–7474 for information; 800/860–9944 for brochures). **CIT Tours Corp.** (✉ 15 West 44th Street, 10th Floor, New York, NY 10036, ☎ 212/730–2400; 800/248–7245 in the U.S.; 800/387–0711; 800/361–7799 in Canada).

FROM THE U.K.

There are no direct trains from London. You can take a direct train from Paris via Frankfurt to Prague (daily) or from Berlin via Dresden to Prague (5 times a day). Vienna is a good starting point for Prague. There are three trains a day to Prague from

Vienna's Südbahnhof (South Station) via Brno (5 hours). You should check out times and routes before leaving.

TRAVEL AGENCIES

A good travel agent puts your needs first. Look for an agency that has been in business at least five years, emphasizes customer service, and has someone on staff who specializes in your destination. In addition, **make sure the agency belongs to a professional trade organization.** The American Society of Travel Agents (ASTA), with 27,000 agents in some 170 countries, is the largest and most influential in the field. Operating under the motto "Integrity in Travel," it maintains and enforces a strict code of ethics and will step in to help mediate any agent-client disputes if necessary. ASTA also maintains a Web site that includes a directory of agents. (If a travel agency is also acting as your tour operator, *see* Buyer Beware *in* Tours & Packages, *above*.)

➤ LOCAL AGENT REFERRALS: American Society of Travel Agents (ASTA; ☎ 800/965–2782 24-hr hot line, FAX 703/684–8319, www.astanet.com). Association of British Travel Agents (✉ 68–71 Newman St., London W1P 4AH, U.K., ☎ 020/7637–2444, FAX 020/7637–0713, information@ abta.co.uk, www.abtanet.com). Association of Canadian Travel Agents (✉ 1729 Bank St., Suite 201, Ottawa, Ontario K1V 7Z5, Canada, ☎ 613/237–3657, FAX 613/521–0805, acta.ntl@sympatico.ca). Australian Federation of Travel Agents (✉ Level 3, 309 Pitt St., Sydney 2000, Australia, ☎ 02/9264–3299, FAX 02/ 9264–1085, www.afta.com.au). Travel Agents' Association of New Zealand (✉ Box 1888, Wellington 10033, New Zealand, ☎ 04/499– 0104, FAX 04/499–0827, taanz@ tiasnet.co.nz).

VISITOR INFORMATION

➤ CZECH REPUBLIC: Czech Tourist Authority (in the U.S.: ✉ 1109–1111 Madison Ave., New York, NY 10028, ☎ 212/288–0830, FAX 212/288–0971, www.czechcenter.com; in Canada: ✉ Czech Airlines office, Simpson Tower, 401 Bay St., Suite 1510, Toronto, Ontario M5H 2YA, ☎ 416/363–

3174, FAX 416/363–0239; in the U.K.: ✉ 95 Great Portland St., London W1N 5RA, ☎ 0171/291–9925, FAX 0171/436–8300).

➤ HUNGARY: In the United States and Canada: **Hungarian National Tourist Office** (✉ 150 E. 58th St., New York, NY 10155, ☎ 212/355–0240, FAX 212/207–4103). In Canada: **Hungarian Consulate General Office** (✉ 121 Bloor St. E, Suite 1115, Toronto M4W3M5, Ontario, ☎ 416/923– 8981, FAX 416/923–2732). In the United Kingdom: **Hungarian National Tourist Board** (✉ c/o Embassy of the Republic of Hungary, Commercial Section, 46 Eaton Pl., London, SW1X 8AL, ☎ 0171/823–1032 or 0171/ 823–1055, FAX 0171/823–1459).

➤ U.S. GOVERNMENT ADVISORIES: **U.S. Department of State** (✉ Overseas Citizens Services Office, Room 4811 N.S., 2201 C St. NW, Washington, DC 20520, ☎ 202/647–5225 for interactive hot line, 301/946–4400 for computer bulletin board, FAX 202/ 647–3000 for interactive hot line); enclose with inquiries a self-addressed, stamped, business-size envelope.

WEB SITES

Do check out the World Wide Web when you're planning. You'll find everything from current weather forecasts to virtual tours of famous cities. Fodor's Web site, www.fodors. com, is a great place to start your on-line travels. When you see a 🌐 in this book, go to www.fodors.com/urls for an up-to-date link to that destination's site.

➤ SUGGESTED WEB SITES: Czech Republic: **Czech Tourist Authority** (www.visitczech.cz). Hungary: **Live Budapest** (www.livebudapest.com).

WHEN TO GO

The tourist season generally runs from April or May through October; spring and fall combine good weather with a more bearable level of tourism. The ski season lasts from mid-December through March. Outside the mountain resorts you will encounter few other visitors; you'll have the opportunity to see the region covered in snow, but many of the sights are

SMART TRAVEL TIPS

closed, and it can get very, very cold. If you're not a skier, try visiting the Giant Mountain of Bohemia in late spring or fall; the colors are dazzling, and you'll have the hotels and restaurants pretty much to yourself. Bear in mind that many attractions are closed November through March.

Prague and Budapest are beautiful year-round, but avoid midsummer (especially July and August) and the Christmas and Easter holidays, when the two cities are choked with visitors. July and August, peak vacation season for Hungarians as well as foreign tourists, can be extremely hot and humid; Budapest is stuffy and crowded, and the entire Lake Balaton region is overrun with vacationers.

CLIMATE

The following are the average daily maximum and minimum temperatures for Prague and Budapest.

BUDAPEST

Jan.	34F	1C	May	72F	22C	Sept.	73F	23C
	25	− 4		52	11		54	12
Feb.	39F	4C	June	79F	26C	Oct.	61F	16C
	28	− 2		59	15		45	7
Mar.	50F	10C	July	82F	28C	Nov.	46F	8C
	36	2		61	16		37	3
Apr.	63F	17C	Aug.	81F	27C	Dec.	39F	4C
	25	− 4		61	16		30	− 1

PRAGUE

Jan.	36F	2C	May	66F	19C	Sept.	68F	20C
	25	− 4		46	8		50	10
Feb.	37F	3C	June	72F	22C	Oct.	55F	13C
	27	− 3		52	11		41	5
Mar.	46F	8C	July	75F	24C	Nov.	46F	8C
	32	0		55	13		36	2
Apr.	58F	14C	Aug.	73F	23C	Dec.	37F	3C
	39	4		55	13		28	− 2

➤ FORECASTS: **Weather Channel Connection** (☎ 900/932–8437), 95¢ per minute from a Touch-Tone phone.

1 DESTINATION: PRAGUE AND BUDAPEST

UNDER THE SPELL

Despite our most lyrical fantasies, traveling through Europe has an inescapable element of the predictable. Streams of familiar landmarks and famed artworks are broken by the seemingly endless searches for comfortable hotels, public restrooms, and espressos that cost less than $7. Over a century's worth of tourism industry experience lies behind the glossy brochures and prepackaged souvenirs, and the beaten paths are now beyond well-worn. As the legs tire and the senses numb, the cities themselves begin to take on the look and feel of museums—handsome and well-organized monuments to events that happened long ago.

Then there are Prague and Budapest.

Travelers to these lively, enchanting capitals will be forgiven for wanting to throttle their brothers' friends for steering them toward Vienna or Brussels. Unlike much of Western Europe, Prague and Budapest can easily satiate the castle-and-church set while at the same time inviting adventurous spirits into a whimsical café-and-club party that seems to have been raging since 1878. All this, of course, at prices that still make Germans blush.

Prague and Budapest's intoxicating mixes of beautiful settings, dynamic times, and—not least—cheap and tasty local drink, have convinced thousands of visitors since 1989 to stay just one more week, which became one more month, which turned into years. Prague's over-documented expatriates tend toward goatees and tattoos, bookstores and rock bands, while Budapest's lower-profile expats are more likely to work for an ad agency and belong to a wine society. Both communities have produced useful little touches of home, such as vegetarian restaurants and decent newspapers. The two cities are competing, as they have for a thousand years, for the mantle of Capital of Central Europe, and the cosmopolitanism that goes with it. Since both capitals also compete directly for tourist dollars, locals have become accustomed to (and a bit cynical of) loud foreigners asking for directions or occupying the next barstool. Luckily for hospitality's sake, Czechs and Hungarians love to hunker down over beer and brandy shots with strangers, so if you go out for a polite night on the town you can easily wind up, 36 hours later, with a dozen new friends, a smoking habit, and skeleton keys to a downtown apartment.

It has not always been thus. Prague, during the Communist "normalization" period of the 1970s and '80s, was a miserable place. People lived in legitimate fear of imprisonment for listening to bootleg Velvet Underground tapes, and the nameless, soot-stained shops had few edible goods. Hungary, whose "Goulash communism" was a much less repressive strain, nonetheless suffered from the same lack of funds to maintain buildings or modernize foul factories and automobiles. The once-flourishing 19th-century cafés on Budapest's ring boulevard Nagykörút were shuttered in favor of joyless stand-up coffee shacks.

Both nations briefly and gloriously shook off the shackles during the Soviet era, only to be crushed once again by Warsaw Pact tanks—Hungary in 1956 and Czechoslovakia in 1968. After 51 consecutive years of living under failed 20th-century political systems, Czechs and Hungarians threw long and sweet coming-out parties in 1989–90. When the confetti was finally swept away, the two countries took turns playing poster child for post-communist reform, taking great pains to remind visitors with short memories that the nations were taking their rightful, historic place back in the Western family.

Twelve years into the process, the cities and people have changed seismically. In Prague, the smothering blanket of gray has given way to birthday-cake pastels. Scaffolding and corrugated tin are being rapidly shed from downtown streets and squares, giving an exhilarating sense of rediscovery and renewal to residents and visitors alike. The radio dial is jammed with good stations, although the excellent Radio One, long an independent-minded mix of international and local music, is having its personality sanded away under its new American ownership. Budapest has a rash of modern office buildings and spruced-up promenades; it's also planning to build a national theater and a large business-cum-shopping center at the edge of downtown in 2001. Signs of conspicuous wealth are everywhere, from the new mansions atop the Buda hills to the shiny Mercedes zipping through the crowded streets and the purring of cell phones—in fact, Hungary has more cellular phones per capita than the United States.

For all the cosmetic improvements, Czechs and Hungarians have suffered more this decade than most of us have in a lifetime. Meager pensions have lagged behind the mostly double-digit inflation, factory towns in the countryside have been decimated by unemployment, and the rules and certainties of a half-century of communism have been overturned. Because they enjoyed relative prosperity in the 1980s, Hungarians have had a particularly hard time adjusting; many people find it hard to understand why they need to suffer through the latest austerity program. The pension problem is a bitter example; Hungarian men, on average, die before qualifying for a pension, leaving their widows to struggle with only their own devalued portion. Often these women are reduced to selling bunches of flowers or odd bits of clothing in metro stations.

Crime, too, has gone from nearly nonexistent to pervasive, with Russian thugs setting off pipe bombs in Budapest, and corrupt Czech fund managers embezzling investor money from Prague banks to offshore accounts. Ruling parties in both countries were rocked by political corruption scandals before being tossed out in 1998 elections. These issues loom large, but most travelers need not worry about safety beyond keeping their wallets safe from pickpockets and avoiding restaurants that charge foreigners $100 for a drink.

The dramatic pace of change contributes to a sense of action and possibility too often missing in Western capitals, breathing contemporary life to the centuries of drama written on every meandering downtown street. It is here, mere steps off the beaten tourist paths, where the hidden spirits that seem to govern Prague and Budapest reveal themselves, transcending and even laughing at the political and social shifts of the moment.

Prague's spirit is clever and romantic, with a decidedly dark sense of humor. The easily walkable Malá Strana (Lesser Quarter), Staré Město (Old Town), and Nové Město (New Town) are all haunted alleyways and curves, some leading to hidden 13th-century churches, some coming to abrupt stops, others emptying into exuberant squares or regal gardens. Gaiety and paranoia forge an uneasy truce, neither keeping the upper hand for long. Czechs themselves are just as likely to snarl at you (especially if you set foot inside a restaurant or neighborhood shop), as invite you to their countryside cottage for a week of picking mushrooms and drinking three-day-old wine, called *burčak*.

This duality is crammed side-by-side into ever-smaller living quarters. Just off Wenceslas Square you can find the world's most frivolous Cubist lamp standing next to the solemn Gothic heights of the 14th-century Church of Our Lady of the Snows—and to complete the absurd picture, there's a Japanese bonsai garden in the church's backyard. The spooky St. Vitus Cathedral is a wonderful testament to architectural potluck, with one of its dark 13th-century spires topped by a goofy 18th-century onion dome, while snarling Gothic gargoyles glower above Art Nouveau stained glass.

Because the city has miraculously avoided war damage over the centuries, the streets themselves are a vivid history lesson. Walk through the sad but re-emergent Jewish Quarter, and imagine how Hitler planned on "preserving" this neighborhood as a monument to the "decadent" Jewish culture he was busy annihilating. See the terrific statue of Protestant revolutionary Jan Hus on Old Town Square, imagine how his followers were executed in that very space for insisting that the laity be allowed to take Communion with the same wine reserved for the priests, and then visit any Hussite cathedral and notice the symbolic wine goblet carved above the front door. Go to a performance of *The Bartered Bride* inside the lush, gilded National Theater, and imagine how Bedřich Smetana's opera must have been received here at the height of the 19th-century National Revival, when Czechs flouted their German masters by constructing the theater entirely from private donations. (Note too, the ridiculous juxtaposition of the Communist New Theater monstrosity right next door.)

Visits to the National Gallery, the stunningly restored Art Nouveau Municipal

House, and the cavernous new Museum of Modern Art will tell you much of what you need to know about Czech history and art, from the empire years of King Charles IV to the mad alchemy of Rudolf II to the exuberant but unsteady days of the interwar First Republic. You can get a feel for Prague's artistic magnetism—past and present—by catching a film, a reading, or a live band. The city is weird, inhabited by ghosts, tangled with mysterious, narrow streets—a legendary source of inspiration. But for true immersion, nothing beats stepping into any one of a thousand neighborhood pubs, drinking the best beer in the world for 50 cents a pint, watching as the dour locals suddenly spring to life when someone breaks out a guitar, and then stumbling back out into the world to watch the sun rise over a mercifully empty Charles Bridge.

Budapest, unlike Prague, is haunted by memories of more recent grandeur, specifically the Austro-Hungarian empire era of 1867–1918. The major streets are grand and broad, suitable for victory marches, and the city's dividing river is the wide, impressive Danube, a stronger presence than Prague's winsome Vltava. The city itself is almost twice as large as Prague, and shares none of the Czech capital's cloying, pastel-frosting cutesiness. Some buildings are still pockmarked with bullet holes from the 1956 uprising and the extensive battles that ripped the city apart in World War II.

The historical wounds seem fresher, more immediate here than in Prague. Besides the tragedy of 1956, residents still invoke the 1918 Treaty of Trianon, which lopped off two-thirds of prewar Hungary's territory. There is an oft-remarked melancholia in the Hungarian people, which pop psychologists attribute to being on the wrong side of seven consecutive wars, or speaking a language everyone else on earth finds incomprehensible.

But visitors expecting a mopey lot grumbling over 19th-century maps are in for a shocker. Hungarians are a hyper-smart, multilingual, and deeply sensual people who enjoy the finer things in life, from Turkish baths to good red wine to coffee cakes drenched in chocolate. Hospitality knows no limits (though one must be careful about scam artists), and people seem to have an uncanny knack for knowing exactly what foreigners want. There is a

whiff of decadence and chaos in the air, a happy remnant from the hated 1541–1686 Ottoman occupation. Hungarians seem to have picked up only the nicer of the Balkan habits, such as promenading each evening down the riverside *korzó* and other pedestrian zones.

Indeed, the country truly serves as a European crossroads between East and West, North and South. On the streets, it is common to hear Russian, Arabic, Serbo-Croatian, English, and German. Roman ruins lie next to Turkish mosques across the river from the largest synagogue in Europe. There are excellent French, Greek, Italian, Turkish, Mexican, Irish, and Japanese restaurants, and of course the blood-red Hungarian eateries with Gypsy violinists wearing folk vests. But unlike that of Prague, Budapest's arts and culture scene is still a bit hesitant, trying to weigh the past while incorporating a flood of imported entertainment.

Elegant monuments to Hungary's romanticized failures can be found throughout the city, from the new, understated statue of 1956 leader Imre Nagy looking toward the Parliament building to the riverside memorial to 1848 hero Sándor Petőfi, a young poet who accurately prophesied his own revolutionary death. Many buildings tell long, complicated stories of their own, such as the unheralded Mai Manó Photo Gallery at 20 Nagymező utca, a street known as the once and future "Hungarian Broadway." This Art Nouveau structure was commissioned in 1894 by court photographer Manó Mai, who used it as a studio for his portrait sittings of luminaries such as Franz Joseph I and composer Béla Bartók. After Mai's death, the building became a decadent cabaret called the Arizona, complete with revolving hydraulic stages and naked girls on chandeliers. The club was a favorite of international royalty and government officials, but during World War II its Jewish owners were murdered by occupying German soldiers. During Communism the building fell into disrepair, but now a small photography gallery has taken root, and the managers have ambitious plans to revamp the entire space, adding a café, exhibition rooms, and a library. The building is taking center stage in the projected rejuvenation of the theaters along the run-down avenue, which itself is a cornerstone of the city's dramatic overhaul.

As post-communism rolls toward its second decade, Prague and Budapest have emerged as the political and cultural epicenters of the former Eastern bloc. Prague has reawakened in its role as capital of Bohemia, becoming the favored European tour date for inventive rock and pop acts (including repeat performers such as Sonic Youth, Bob Dylan, and the Rolling Stones) and inspiring untold thousands of wild young souls to pursue their artistic and entrepreneurial dreams. Budapest attracts multinational companies with equal success, even luring some European headquarters away from nearby Vienna. Hungary is blazing most trails in Central European economic reform, and Budapest's activist mayor is more than halfway through an ambitious renewal plan aiming to restore the city's salon culture to its pre–World War I splendor.

Hungary and the Czech Republic are quickly distancing themselves from their Communist past; soon they will have their own stars on the European Union flag, and the best Hungarian wines and Czech beers will be sold for prices depressingly familiar to travelers from the West. Before the window closes, though, Prague and Budapest will continue to seduce, infuriate, and even ensnare those daring enough to visit.

— Matt Welch

WHAT'S WHERE

Prague and Environs

Planted firmly in the heart of Central Europe—Prague is some 320 kilometers (200 miles) north*west* of Vienna—the Czech Republic is culturally and historically more closely linked to Western, particularly Germanic, culture than any of its former East-bloc brethren. The capital city of **Prague** sits on the Vltava (Moldau) River, roughly in the middle of Bohemian territory. A stunning city of human dimensions, Prague offers the traveler a lesson in almost all the major architectural styles of Western European history; relatively unscathed by major wars, most of Prague's buildings are remarkably well preserved. The five main historic districts echo what were once five separate towns: Hradčany (Castle Area), Malá Strana (Lesser Quarter), Staré Město (Old Town), Nové Město (New Town), and Josefov (the Jewish Quarter). The stunning Karlův Most (Charles Bridge) links the Old Town and Lesser Quarter, while the Pražský Hrad (Prague Castle) overlooks the city from its hilltop west of the river.

Prague is planted in the heart of **Bohemia,** an area where the history of internal conflict, invasions, and religious revolts is almost palpable. Southern Bohemia is dotted with several stunning walled towns retaining much of their medieval appearance, many of which played important roles in the Hussite religious wars of the 15th century. The two most notable towns are Tábor and Český Krumlov. Western Bohemia, especially the far western hills near the German border, remains justly famous for its mineral springs and **spa towns,** in particular Karlovy Vary, Mariánské Lázně, and Františkový Lázně. These elegant towns are just a couple of hours away from the capital.

Budapest and Environs

Sandwiched between Slovakia and Romania, Hungary was the Austro-Hungarian Empire's eastern frontier, the geographical link between the Slavic regions of Central Europe and the Black Sea region's amalgam of Orthodox and Islamic cultures. The capital, **Budapest,** crouches on the Danube, just an hour from Bratislava in Slovakia and two-and-a-half hours from Vienna. Like Prague, Budapest is an amalgam of once-separate towns—Óbuda, Buda, and Pest were joined in the 19th century. Buda, on the Danube's western bank, is quite hilly; most of its major sights are clustered on the Várhegy (Castle Hill). Pest, on the eastern side of the river, is flat and laced with wide avenues and circular *körúts* (ring roads).

Just north of Budapest, the Danube River forms a gentle, heart-shape curve along which lie the romantic and historic towns of the region called the Danube Bend. Southwest of Budapest are the vineyards, historic villages, and popular, developed summer resorts around **Lake Balaton,** the largest lake in Central Europe. The towns along the northern shore of the lake are often less developed and thus, more attractive—these include the spa town of Balatonfüred and the abbey-crowned village of Tihany.

NEW AND NOTEWORTHY

Prague

One tangible impact of the Czech Republic's recent economic reforms has been an acceleration in the pace of architectural renovations. Many hotels, old private houses, and churches are installing new fixtures and applying a fresh coat of paint. This is most noticeable in Prague, but everywhere, castles, palaces, and dusty old museums are spiffing themselves up and throwing open their doors to visitors. The fiscal shocks of 1997, a year when the Czech crown lost more than 20 percent of its value against the U.S. dollar, could not shut the doors on several **major museum projects** planned for Prague for 1998. These include the private Mucha Museum, the Prague Municipal House's collection of 20th-century Czech art, and the long-awaited reopening of the Prague Castle Picture Gallery.

The number of **hotels and restaurants** keeps pace with the growing number of visitors. It has become easier to find mid-range hotels, and the luxury Kempinski and Four Seasons hotels will open in 2001. From Bosnian to Argentine, the range of dishes emerging from the city's restaurant kitchens is unprecedented. Two one-time rarities—a real espresso and a dry martini—are now commonplace.

Prague's **cultural life** continues to thrive, and the city in particular is a dream for classical-music lovers and opera fans. The annual mid-May–early June Prague Spring Music Festival, which even before the collapse of the Communist government was one of the great events on the European calendar, is attracting record numbers of music lovers. The less-hyped Prague Autumn festival has begun to bring in equally strong performers and orchestras. Major events set for 2001 include the opening of a new museum of Czech modern art on Kampa Island, and a huge summer exhibition, "The Glory of Baroque Prague." The Asian art museum in suburban Zbraslav is a welcome addition to the city's cultural offerings.

Budapest

Two years into **NATO membership** and expected to join the European Union by around mid-decade (the pundits differ on the probable timing), Hungary continues to strengthen both its international position and its internal assets. The triple excitement of the year 2000—which coincided with the **Magyar Millennium,** the 1,000th anniversary of Hungary's founding as a state, and marked a decade as a multi-party democracy—is still in the air. Following through on the celebratory restorations in honor of another recent national anniversary in 1996—the 1,100th anniversary of the Magyar settlement of the Carpathian Basin—much restoration work on important sites nationwide was completed in the year 2000, and more is underway.

Grand old **Budapest** is seeing more and more development, from private restoration of crumbling buildings to city-funded projects, such as the increase in pedestrian-only zones. Political tensions between the governments of capital and country may have stalled construction of a fourth metro line, but Hungary's overall stability and continued attraction of foreign investment have fostered ongoing revitalization. Indeed, theater and café culture seems no worse for politics (the bleaker days of Communism prepared it well). Even while many Hungarians can hardly afford going out to eat, an emerging middle class has gradually reimbued Budapest with confidence unseen since perhaps the heady days of the Austro-Hungarian empire a century ago.

Slowly but surely, Hungary continues to **improve its infrastructure,** helping it fill its increasingly important role as a link between Eastern and Western Europe. Over the next several years, major highways will continue to be upgraded and extended; the airport in Budapest has seen major expansion in the past few years. Last but not least, the once-antiquated telephone system (which goes partly to explain why cell phones are ringing just about everywhere) is being overhauled. While progress is certainly apparent, travelers should note that in Hungary, silence at the other end of the line is still usually assumed to be a broken connection as opposed to a crank call.

The contours of the political playing field are coming into focus as the May 2002 elections approach. The main parties at Hungary's helm—the center-right FIDESZ (Alliance of Young Democrats–Hungarian Civic Party), led by Prime Minister Viktor Orbán; and the junior governing partner, the more right-wing Smallholders—are gearing to face off against the MSZP (Hungarian Socialist Party), which they barely managed to oust from power in the 1998 elections along with the Free Democrats. What with its vast resources and nostalgia in many voters for the "certainties" of the past, the MSZP, whose leadership includes mostly former Communists, remains a formidable force.

At press time, Hungary's annual inflation rate had dropped under 10% from the 25% of five years ago, and with continued significant devaluation of the forint, exchange rates keep improving for visitors from North America and Great Britain. Although Hungary remains a bargain compared with Western Europe, strictly rock-bottom prices are a thing of the past as restaurant and hotel rates creep upward to compensate for the nation's shrinking currency.

FODOR'S CHOICE

Dining

Prague

★ **V Zátiši.** In one of the city's oldest and calmest squares—the restaurant's name means "still life"—this refined dining room offers tantalizing international specialties and wonderful service. *$$$$*

★ **Lobkovická.** This atmospheric, 17th-century restaurant has an imaginative menu and an enticing roster of Moravian wines. *$$$*

★ **Kavárna Slavia.** To lap up some of the artistic scene, come to this Art Deco café; the views of the Prague Castle and the National Theater aren't too shabby either. *$*

Budapest

★ **Gundel.** Established at the turn of the 20th century, Budapest's most famous restaurant continues its legacy of Old World grandeur and elegant cuisine. *$$$$*

★ **Művészinas.** The chef at this romantic, bustling bistro in downtown Pest has a flair for taking typical Hungarian dishes to new heights. *$$$*

★ **Kisbuda Gyöngye.** This intimate setting is the place to look for a *liba lakodalmas* (goose wedding feast)—a roast goose leg, goose liver, and goose cracklings. *$$$*

★ **Lou Lou.** This restaurant has been buzzing for years, having struck a mouth-watering balance between Hungarian and Continental influences. At press time it was about to relocate, so check with the tourist office to track it down. *$$$*

★ **Náncsi Néni.** It's a bit out of the way, but that hasn't deterred the crowds from this warm restaurant—garlic and paprika hang from the ceiling and jars of home-pickled vegetables line the walls. These will hopefully sharpen your appetite, as the plates are loaded with excellent Hungarian home-cooking. *$$*

Lodging

Prague

★ **Dům U Červeného Lva.** Just five minutes from Prague Castle's front gates, this immaculate hotel has striking details, such as the painted-beam ceilings. *$$$$*

★ **Palace.** The soft pinks and greens of the room decor, the classic Continental restaurant, and the location near Wenceslas Square make this a great combination of elegance and convenience. *$$$$*

★ **Savoy.** From the Jugendstil facade to the afternoon tea in the library, this small hotel is all about luxury. *$$$$*

★ **Romantik Hotel U Raka.** There are just six rooms in this 18th century building, so plan way ahead to snare a spot. It's just behind the Loreto Church, so you'll have a wonderful base for exploring the city. *$$$*

★ **Pension Louda.** While this pension is a good 20 minutes away from the city center, the south-facing rooms have stunning views of Prague. *$*

Budapest

★ **Kempinski Hotel Corvinus Budapest.** Sleek, modern, and luxurious, this hotel oozes solicitousness. The large, sparkling bathrooms are the city's best. *$$$$*

★ **Danubius Hotel Gellért.** This grand 1918 Art Nouveau hotel on the Danube at the foot of Gellért Hill is the pride of Budapest. Housing an extensive, elegant complex of marble bathing facilities fed by ancient curative springs, it is also one of Europe's most famous Old World spas. *$$$$*

★ **Victoria.** You can see the Parliament building and the twinkling city lights from every room of this small hotel smack on the Danube. *$$*

★ **Kulturinov.** Set on one of historic Castle Hill's most famous cobblestone squares, this neo-Baroque castle houses budget accommodations in a priceless location. *$*

Museums and Religious Buildings

Prague

★ **Chrám svatého Mikuláše (St. Nicholas Church).** With its dynamic curves, dramatic statues, and remarkable dome, this church embodies the height of high Baroque.

★ **Chrám svatého Víta (St. Vitus Cathedral).** Soaring above the castle walls and dominating the city at its feet, St. Vitus Cathedral is among the most beautiful sights in Europe. Its stained-glass windows are particularly brilliant.

★ **Kostel Panny Marie před Týnem (Týn Church).** The exterior of this 15th-century cathedral, with its twin gold-tipped, jet-black spires, is a sterling example of Prague Gothic.

★ **Národní galérie (National Gallery).** Spread among a half-dozen branches around the city, the National Gallery's collections span most major periods of European art, from medieval and Baroque masters to a vast constructivist gallery of 20th-century Czech and European works.

★ **Strahovský klášter (Strahov Monastery).** Now a museum of national literature, this monastery is known for its collection of early Czech manuscripts and the striking fresco on the ceiling of its Philosophical Hall.

★ **Židovské muzeum v Praze (Prague Jewish Museum).** Actually a collection of several must-see sights and exhibits, the Jewish Museum includes the Old Jewish Cemetery, crowded with tombstones, and several historic synagogues.

Budapest

★ **Mátyás Templom (Matthias Church).** Castle Hill's soaring Gothic church is colorfully ornate inside with lavishly frescoed Byzantine pillars.

★ **Nagy Zsinagóga (Great Synagogue).** This giant Byzantine-Moorish beauty (Europe's largest synagogue) underwent a massive restoration four decades after being ravaged by Hungarian and German Nazis during World War II.

★ **Néprajzi Múzeum (Museum of Ethnography).** A majestic 1890s structure across from the Parliament building—the lavish marble entrance hall alone is worth a visit—houses an impressive exhibit on Hungary's historic folk traditions.

★ **Szent István Bazilika (St. Stephen's Basilica).** Inside this massive neo-Renaissance beauty, the capital's biggest church, is a rich collection of mosaics and statuary, as well as the mummified right hand of Hungary's first king and patron saint, St. Stephen.

★ **Szépművészeti Múzeum (Museum of Fine Arts).** Hungary's best collection of fine art includes esteemed works by Dutch and Spanish old masters, as well as exhibits on major Hungarian artists.

FESTIVALS AND SEASONAL EVENTS

Prague

➤ DECEMBER: **Christmas fairs and programs** take place in towns and cities throughout the country.

➤ JANUARY: Prague hosts the **FebioFest International Film, Television and Video Festival.**

➤ MARCH: Another film festival, **Days of European Film,** comes to the capital.

➤ APRIL: Eastertime brings two festivals of sacred music: **Musica Ecumenica** and **Musica Sacra Praga.** English-language and world authors appear at the **Prague Writers' Festival.**

➤ MAY: Events both athletic and artistic fill the calendar; there's the **Prague Spring International Music Festival** as well as the **Prague Marathon.** Major writers from around the world present readings during the **Prague Writers' Festival.**

➤ JUNE: The international dance festival **Tanec Praha** and the **Respect** ethnic-music fest hit town.

➤ JULY: The **Open Air Opera Festival** begins at the Lichtenstein Palace.

➤ AUGUST: Prague's **Verdi Festival** is staged at the State Opera.

➤ SEPTEMBER: The **Prague Autumn International Music Festival** brings major orchestras and soloists to town, and

music in the city's churches, chapels, and synagogues highlights the **St. Wenceslas Celebrations.**

➤ OCTOBER: The capital continues its run of cultural events, including an **International Jazz Festival,** the **Dance Theater Festival,** and a grab bag of alternative arts performances, **Next Wave.**

➤ NOVEMBER: The **Czech Press Photo exhibition** focuses on visual arts, and the **Musica Iudaica** festival on Jewish music.

Budapest

For contact information about most of these festivals, *see* the city or town's Nightlife and the Arts section or inquire at the Budapest Tourinform office or the local visitor information center.

➤ DECEMBER: Budapest's **New Year's Eve** festivities include a gala in the beautiful, neo-Renaissance Opera House.

➤ MID-MARCH TO EARLY APRIL: The season's first and biggest arts festival, the **Budapest Spring Festival,** showcases Hungary's best opera, music, theater, fine arts, and dance, as well as visiting foreign artists. Other towns—including Kecskemét, Szentendre, and Szombathely—also participate.

➤ LATE JUNE–EARLY JULY: The **World Music Festival** in Budapest, held in early July, has several days of world music concerts by local and international artists. The **International Puppet Festival** draws puppeteers from Hungary and abroad to Sárospatak from July 1–4 every two years, next in 2002.

➤ AUGUST: Toward mid-month, Budapest hosts a **Formula 1** car race, while the weeklong **BudaFest** opera and ballet festival takes place mid-month at the opera house after the opera season ends. **St. Stephen's Day** (August 20) is a major national holiday. **Youth Culture Festival** is held in mid-August on Óbuda Island. Young people swarm over the island, sometimes camping out for the week, to catch performances by bands ranging from international (and aging) heavy-metal groups to folk musicians. The weeklong **Jewish Summer Festival,** held in late August and early September, features cantors, classical concerts, a kosher cabaret, films, and theater and dance performances, in Budapest and sometimes elsewhere.

➤ SEPTEMBER: A **wine festival** in the capital celebrates the autumn grape harvest.

2 PRAGUE

The "hundred-spired" capital city of Prague—one of the world's best-preserved architectural cityscapes—offers world-class cultural performances and increasingly distinctive dining and shopping. In the countryside beyond, medieval castles perch quietly near lost-in-time Baroque and Renaissance villages.

By Mark Baker

Updated by Ky
Krauthamer

A VICTIM OF ENFORCED OBSCURITY throughout much of the 20th century, the Czech Republic, encompassing the provinces of Bohemia and Moravia, is once again in the spotlight. In 1989, in a world where revolution was synonymous with violence, and in a country where truth was quashed by the tanks of Eastern-bloc socialism, Václav Havel's sonorous voice proclaimed the victory of the "Velvet Revolution" to enthusiastic crowds on Wenceslas Square and preached the value of "living in truth." Recording the dramatic events of the time, television cameras panned across Prague's glorious skyline and fired the world's imagination with the image of political renewal superimposed on somber Gothic and voluptuous Baroque.

Travelers have rediscovered the country, and Bohemians and Moravians have rediscovered the world. The stagnant "normalization" of the last two decades under Communist rule gave way in the 1990s to a new dynamism and international outlook. Visitors now encounter enthusiasm, and such conveniences as English-language newspapers and attentive service. Not that the Czech Republic has joined the ranks of "Western" countries. It remains the poor relation compared with its Central European neighbors Germany and Austria, with the average Czech worker's wage standing at around $350 a month. This makes the signs of modernity even more remarkable. Nowadays there are cybercafés and cell phones to help visitors stay in touch with the outer world. It's all happening fastest in Prague, but the pace of change is accelerating everywhere. In the small towns and villages where so many Czechs still live, however, you may struggle with a creeping sensation of melancholy and neglect—or, putting a positive spin on it, you may enjoy the slower, more relaxed tempo.

The experience of visiting the Czech Republic still involves stepping back in time. Even in Prague, now deluged by tourists two-thirds of the year, the sense of history—stretching back through centuries of wars, empires, and monuments to everyday life—remains uncluttered by the trappings of modernity. The peculiar melancholy of Central Europe still lurks in narrow streets and forgotten corners. Crumbling facades, dilapidated palaces, and treacherous cobbled streets both shock and enchant the visitor used to a world where what remains of history has been spruced up for tourist eyes.

The arrival of designer boutiques, chain restaurants, and shopping malls does mean that the country has lost some of the "feel" it had just a few years ago. Although the dark side of freedom—rising unemployment and corruption—began to hit home in the late 1990s, the Czechs continued to move toward harmonization with Western ways. The country joined the NATO alliance in 1999 and will become a European Union member state, perhaps as early as 2003. Yet the process goes slowly. Economic and social integration into the "common European home," which in the postrevolutionary euphoria seemed possible within a few years, must now be measured in decades.

The strange, old-world, and at times frustratingly bureaucratic, atmosphere of the Czech Republic is not all a product of the Communist era. Many of the everyday rituals are actually remnants of the Hapsburg Empire and are also to be found, perhaps to a lesser degree, in Vienna and Budapest. The *šatna* (coat room), for example, plays a vivid role in any visit to a restaurant or theater at any time of year other than summer. Coats must be given with a few coins to the attendant, usually an old lady with a sharp eye for ignorant or disobedient tourists.

The key to enjoying Prague is to relax. There is no point in demanding high levels of service or quality. And for the budget-conscious traveler, this is Central Europe at its most beautiful, at prices that are several times lower than those of Austria and Germany.

In the years since November 17, 1989, when Prague's students took to the streets to help bring down the 40-year-old Communist regime, the city has enjoyed an exhilarating cultural renaissance. Amid Prague's cobblestone streets and gold-tip spires, new galleries, cafés, and clubs teem with young Czechs (the middle-aged are generally too busy trying to make a living) and members of the city's colony of "expatriates." New shops and, perhaps most noticeably, scads of new restaurants have opened, expanding the city's culinary reach far beyond the traditional roast pork and dumplings. Many have something to learn in the way of presentation and service, but Praguers still marvel at a variety that was unthinkable not so many years ago.

The arts and theater are also thriving in the "new" Prague. Young playwrights, some writing in English, regularly stage their own works. Weekly poetry readings are standing room only. Classical music maintains its famous standards, while rock, jazz, and dance clubs are jammed nightly. The arts of the new era—nonverbal theater, "installation" art, world music—are as trendy in Prague as in any European capital, but possess a distinctive Czech flavor.

All of this frenetic activity plays well against a stunning backdrop of towering churches and centuries-old bridges and alleyways. Prague achieved much of its present glory in the 14th century, during the long reign of Charles IV, king of Bohemia and Moravia and Holy Roman Emperor. It was Charles who established a university in the city and laid out the New Town, charting Prague's growth.

During the 15th century, the city's development was hampered by the Hussite Wars, a series of crusades launched by the Holy Roman Empire to subdue the fiercely independent Czech noblemen. The Czechs were eventually defeated in 1620 at the Battle of White Mountain (Bílá Hora) near Prague and were ruled by the Hapsburg family for the next 300 years. Under the Hapsburgs, Prague became a German-speaking city and an important administrative center, but it was forced to play second fiddle to the monarchy's capital, Vienna. Much of the Lesser Quarter, on the left bank of the Vltava, was built up at this time, becoming home to Austrian nobility and its Baroque tastes.

Prague regained its status as a national capital in 1918, with the creation of the modern Czechoslovak state, and quickly asserted itself in the interwar period as a vital cultural center. Although the city escaped World War II essentially intact, Czechoslovakia fell under the political and cultural domination of the Soviet Union until the 1989 popular uprisings. The election of dissident playwright Václav Havel to the post of national president set the stage for the city's renaissance, which has since proceeded at a dizzying, quite Bohemian rate.

Pleasures and Pastimes

Boating and Sailing

The country's main boating area is the enormous series of dams and reservoirs along the Vltava south of Prague. The most popular reservoir is Slapy, an hour's drive due south of the capital, where it is possible to rent small paddleboats or relax and swim on a hot day. Rowboats are available for rent along Prague's Vltava in summertime.

Dining

The quality of restaurant cuisine and service in the Czech Republic remains uneven. The exception is found in Prague, where dozens of restaurants compete for an increasingly discriminating clientele. The traditional dishes—roast pork or duck with dumplings, or broiled meat with sauce—can be light and tasty when well prepared. Grilled pond trout appears on most menus and is often the tastiest item available. An annoying "cover charge" (20 Kč–50 Kč in expensive places) usually makes its way onto restaurant bills, seemingly to subsidize the salt and pepper shakers. You should discreetly check the bill, since a few unscrupulous proprietors still overcharge foreigners.

Restaurants generally fall into three categories. A *pivnice* or *hospoda* (beer hall) usually offers a simple, inexpensive menu of goulash or pork with dumplings. The atmosphere tends to be friendly and casual, and you can expect to share a table. More attractive, and more expensive, are the *vinárna* (wine cellar) and the *restaurace* (restaurant), which serve a full range of dishes. Wine cellars, some occupying Romanesque basements, can be a real treat.

Ignoring the familiar fast-food outlets that are now a common sight, the quickest and cheapest dining option is the *lahůdky* (snack bar or deli). The *kavárna* (café) and *čajovna* (tea house) are ever more popular—and welcome—additions to the dining scene.

Lunch, usually eaten between noon and 2, is the main meal for Czechs and the best deal. Many restaurants put out a special luncheon menu (*denní lístek*), with more appetizing selections at better prices. If you don't see it, ask your waiter. Dinner is usually served from 5 until 9 or 10, but don't wait too long to eat. Most Czechs eat only a light meal in the evening. Also, restaurant cooks frequently knock off early on slow nights, and the later you arrive, the more likely it is that the kitchen will be closed. In general, dinner menus do not differ substantially from lunch offerings, except the prices are higher.

CATEGORY	PRAGUE*	OTHER AREAS*
$$$$	over $40	over $30
$$$	$20–$40	$15–$30
$$	$10–$20	$7–$15
$	under $10	under $7

per person for a three-course meal, excluding wine and tip

Lodging

The number of hotels and pensions has increased dramatically throughout the Czech Republic, in step with the influx of tourists. Finding a suitable room should pose no problem, although it is highly recommended that you book ahead during the peak tourist season (nationwide, July and August; in Prague, April through October and the Christmas, New Year, and Easter holidays). Hotel prices, in general, remain high. This is especially true in Prague and in the spa towns of western Bohemia. Some Prague hotels reduce rates slightly in July and August, when many European travelers prefer to head for the beaches. Better value can often be found at private pensions and with individual home-owners offering rooms to let. In the outlying towns, the best strategy is to inquire at the local tourist information office or simply fan out around the town and look for room-for-rent signs on houses (usually in German: ZIMMER FREI or PRIVATZIMMER).

Most of the old-fashioned hotels away from the major tourist centers, invariably situated on a town's main square, have been modernized and now provide private bathrooms in most or all rooms and a higher comfort level throughout. Newer hotels, often impersonal concrete boxes, tend to be found on the outskirts of towns; charming, older buildings in the center of town, newly transformed into hotels and pensions, are often the best choice. Bare-bones hostels are a popular means of circumventing Prague's summer lodging crunch; many now stay open all year.

Czech hotels set their own star ratings, which more or less match the international star system. Often you can book rooms—both at hotels and in private homes—through visitor bureaus. Otherwise, try calling or writing the hotel directly. Keep in mind that in many hotels, except at the deluxe level, a "double" bed means two singles that can be pushed together. (Single-mattress double beds are generally not available.)

At certain times, such as Easter and during festivals, prices can jump 15%–25%. As a rule, always ask the price before taking a room. Your best bet for lodging in the $ price range will usually be a private room. Unless otherwise noted, breakfast is included in the rate.

As for camping, there are hundreds of sites for tents and trailers throughout the country, but most are open only in summer (May to mid-September), although a number of campsites in and around Prague have year-round operation. You can get a map from the Prague Information Service of all the sites, with addresses, opening times, and facilities. Camping outside official sites is prohibited. Campgrounds generally have hot water and toilets.

CATEGORY	PRAGUE*	OTHER AREAS*
$$$$	over $200	over $100
$$$	$100–$200	$50–$100
$$	$50–$100	$25–$50
$	under $50	under $25

*All prices are for a standard double room during peak season, including breakfast.

☙ following the text of a review is your signal that the property has a Web site, where you will find details and, usually, images; for a link, visit www.fodors.com/urls.

Shopping

In Prague, Karlovy Vary, and elsewhere in Bohemia, look for elegant and unusual crystal and porcelain. Bohemia is also renowned for the quality and deep red color of its garnets; keep an eye out for beautiful garnet rings and brooches. You can also find excellent ceramics, especially in Moravia, as well as other folk artifacts, such as printed textiles, lace, hand-knit sweaters, and painted eggs. There are attractive crafts stores throughout the Czech Republic. Karlovy Vary is blessed with a variety of unique items to buy, including the strange pipelike drinking mugs used in the spas; vases left to petrify in the mineral-laden water; and Becherovka, a tasty herbal aperitif that makes a nice gift to take home.

Wine and Beer

Czechs are reputed to drink more beer per capita than any people on earth; small wonder, as many connoisseurs rank Bohemian lager-style beer as the best in the world. This cool, crisp brew was invented in Plzeň in 1842, although Czech beer had already been brewed for centuries prior to that time. Aside from the world-famous Plzeňský Prazdroj (Pilsner Urquell) and milder Budvar (the original Budweiser) brands, some typical beers are the slightly bitter Krušovice; fruity Radegast; and the sweeter, Prague-brewed Staropramen. *Světlé pivo*, or golden beer, is most common, although many pubs also serve *černé* (dark), which is often slightly sweeter than the light variety.

Czechs also produce quite drinkable wines: peppy, fruity whites and mild, versatile reds. Southern Moravia, with comparatively warm summers and rich soil, grows the bulk of the wine harvest. Look for the Mikulov and Znojmo regional designations. Favorite white varietals are *Müller-Thurgau,* with a fine muscat bouquet and light flavor, and *Neuburské,* yellow-green in color and with a dry, smoky bouquet. *Rulandské bílé,* a semidry Burgundy-like white, has a flowery bouquet and full-bodied flavor. Belying the notion that northerly climes are more auspicious for white than red grapes, northern Bohemia's scant few hundred acres of vineyards produce reliable reds and the occasional jewel. *Frankovka* is fiery red and slightly acidic, while the cherry red *Rulandské červené* is an excellent, drier choice. *Vavřinecké* is dark and slightly sweet.

EXPLORING PRAGUE

The spine of the city is the River Vltava (also known by its German name, Moldau), which runs through the city from south to north with a single sharp curve to the east. Prague originally comprised five independent towns, represented today by its main historic districts: Hradčany (Castle Area), Malá Strana (Lesser Quarter), Staré Město (Old Town), Nové Město (New Town), and Josefov (the Jewish Quarter).

Hradčany, the seat of Czech royalty for hundreds of years, has as its center the Pražský hrad (Prague Castle), which overlooks the city from its hilltop west of the Vltava. Steps lead down from Hradčany to the Lesser Quarter, an area dense with ornate mansions built by 17th- and 18th-century nobility.

Karlův most (Charles Bridge) connects the Lesser Quarter with the Old Town. Just a few blocks east of the bridge is the district's focal point, Staroměstské náměstí (Old Town Square). The Old Town is bounded by the curving Vltava and three large commercial avenues: Revoluční to the east, Na Příkopě to the southeast, and Národní třída to the south. North of Old Town Square, the diminutive Jewish Quarter fans out around the wide avenue called Pařížská.

Beyond the Old Town to the south is the New Town, a highly commercial area that includes the city's largest square, Karlovo náměstí (Charles Square). Roughly 1 km (½ mi) farther south is Vyšehrad, an ancient castle high above the river.

On a promontory to the east of Václavské náměstí (Wenceslas Square) stretches Vinohrady, once the favored neighborhood of well-to-do Czechs. Bordering Vinohrady are the crumbling neighborhoods of Žižkov to the north and Nusle to the south. On the west bank of the Vltava lie many older residential neighborhoods and several sprawling parks. About 3 km (2 mi) from the center in every direction, Communist-era housing projects begin their unsightly sprawl.

Numbers in the text correspond to numbers in the margin and on the Prague map.

Great Itineraries

IF YOU HAVE 1–2 DAYS

Even during such a short stay, you can get a strong taste of Prague's historical richness and buzzing energy. Start at the top with the hilltop Pražský hrad (Prague Castle), visiting the soaring, Gothic Chrám svatého Víta (St. Vitus's Cathedral) and the Královský palác (Royal Palace) and drinking in views of the city. To get to or from the castle, walk along Nerudova ulice, a steep street lined with burgher's homes—and little restaurants if you need a break. Cross over the river to the

Prague

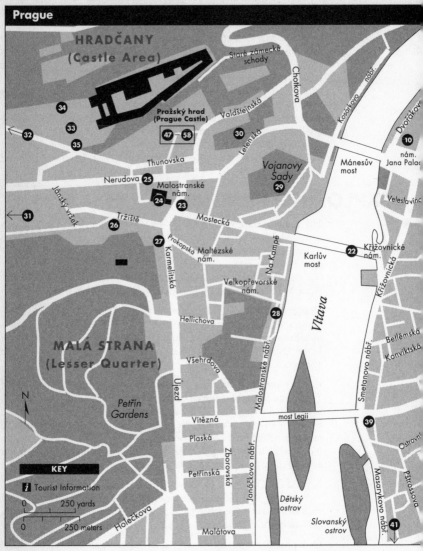

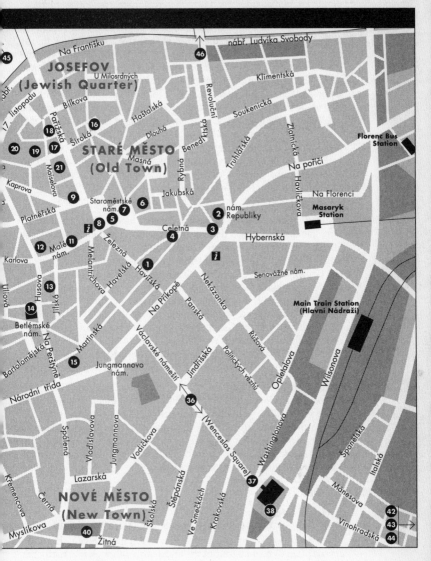

nábř. Ludvíka Svobody

Na Františku

JOSEFOV
(Jewish Quarter)

U Milosrdných

Klimentská

Bílkova

Soukenická

Haštalská

Dlouhá

Pařížská

Široká

STARÉ MĚSTO
(Old Town)

Masná

Kaprova

Maiselova

Platnéřská

Staroměstské
nám.

Jakubská

nám.
Republiky

Celetná

Hybernská

Malé
nám.

Železná

Karlova

Husova

Jilská

Melantrichova

Havelská

Havířská

Na Příkopě

Panská

Senovážné nám.

Betlémské
nám.

Martinská

Václavské náměstí

Jindřišská

Politických vězňů

Růžova

Wilsonova

Bartolomějská

Na Perštýně

Jungmannovo
nám.

[Wenceslas Square]

Washingtonova

Opletalova

Národní třída

Spálená

Vladislavova

Jungmannova

Vodičkova

Lazarská

Štěpánská

 Škólská

Ve Smečkách

Krakovská

NOVÉ MĚSTO
(New Town)

Myslíkova

Žitná

17. listopadu

Revoluční

Benediktská

Rybná

Truhlářská

Na poříčí

Na Florenci

Zlatnická

Havlíčkova

Hálská

Mánesova

Vinohradská

Špankská

Kremencova

Černá

Nekázanka

Na Florenci

Benedikt

Bílkova

Florenc Bus
Station

Masaryk
Station

Main Train Station
(Hlavní Nádraží)

Staré Město (Old Town) and the very center of historic Prague: Staroměstské náměstí (Old Town Square). Try to time your visit to coincide with the hourly performance of the astronomical clock on the Staroměstská radnice (Old Town Hall); you can also visit the Gothic-on-the-outside, Baroque-on-the-inside Kostel Panny Marie před Týnem (Týn Church). Stretching southeast of the Old Town is Václavské náměstí (Wenceslas Square), actually a long avenue humming with activity—be sure to duck into some of the arcades that branch off the boulevard. In the evening, go back towards the river for the unforgettable view from the statue-lined Karlův most (Charles Bridge). If you have another morning here, head to the Josefov (Jewish quarter) early, before the crowds of tourists pack its tiny streets. You can also dip into the Malá Strana (Lesser Quarter) to see the voluptuous Baroque curves of Chrám svatého Mikuláše (St. Nicholas Church).

IF YOU HAVE 3–5 DAYS

With a few extra days, you can devote more time to the historic quarters, spending most of a day taking in the castle and later visiting the Strahovský klášter (Strahov Monastery) and Národní galerie (National Gallery) in the castle district. You could also duck into one of the city's beautiful gardens, such as the Vrtbovská zahrada (Vrtba Garden), or take a ride on one of the many sightseeing boats that ply the Vltava River. If you're interested in modern architecture, head to the Nové Město (New Town), where you can see the "Fred and Ginger" building by Frank Gehry and Vlado Milunić as well as several Cubist buildings. For indoor modern art, head to either the Galerie hl. města Prahy (Prague City Gallery) or the Galerie Rudolfinum, both in the Old Town, or check out the Veletržní palác (Trade Fair Palace) gallery.

IF YOU HAVE 5–7 DAYS

Besides the explorations described above, take a quick trip out to the spa towns in Western Bohemia. The rich, famous, and curious flocked here in the 19th century, and you can walk through the colonnades and sip the waters that drew everyone from Chopin to Mark Twain to Karl Marx. The classic resort hotels in Karlovy Vary or Mariánské Lázně are tempting places to overnight.

Staré Město (Old Town)

A Good Walk

Ever-hopping Wenceslas Square (☞ Nové Město [New Town] and Vyšehrad, *below*), convenient to hotels and transportation, is an excellent place to begin a tour of the Old Town, although it actually lies within the New Town. To begin the approach to the Old Town proper, start at the lower end of the square, walk past the tall, Art Deco Koruna complex, and turn right onto the handsome pedestrian zone of **Na Příkopě.** Turn left onto Havířská ulice and follow this small alley to the glittering green-and-cream splendor of the 18th-century theater called the **Stavovské divadlo** ①.

Return to Na Příkopě, turn left, and continue to the end of the street. On weekdays between 8 AM and 5 PM, it's well worth taking a peek at the stunning interior of the Živnostenská banka (Merchant's Bank), at No. 20.

Na Příkopě ends abruptly at náměstí Republiky (Republic Square), an important New Town transportation hub (with a metro stop). The severe depression-era facade of the Česká Národní banka (at Na Příkopě 30) makes the building look more like a fortress than the nation's central bank. Close by stands a stately tower, the **Prašná brána,** its fes-

tive Gothic spires looming above the square. Adjacent to this dignified building, the **Obecní dům** ② concert hall looks decidedly decadent.

Walk through the arch at the base of the Prašná brána and down the
formal **Celetná ulice** ③, the first leg of the so-called Royal Way. Monar-
chs favored this route primarily because the houses along Celetná
were among the city's finest, providing a suitable backdrop to the coronation procession. The pink U Sixtu (Sixt House), at Celetná 2, sports
one of the street's handsomest, if restrained, Baroque facades. Baroque
influence is even visible in the Cubist department store **Dům U černé
Matky Boží** ④, now a museum.

Staroměstské náměstí ⑤, at the end of Celetná, is dazzling, thanks partly
to the double-spired **Kostel Panny Marie před Týnem** ⑥, which rises
over the square from behind a row of patrician houses. To the immediate left of this church, at No. 13, is Dům U Kamenného zvonu
(House at the Stone Bell), a Baroque town house that has been stripped
down to its original Gothic elements.

Next door stands the gorgeous pink-and-ocher **Palác Kinských**. At
this end of the square, you can't help noticing the expressive **Jan Hus
monument** ⑦. Just beyond is the Gothic **Staroměstská radnice** ⑧,
which, with its impressive 200 ft tower, gives the square its sense of
importance. As the hour approaches, join the crowds milling below
the tower's 15th-century astronomical clock for a brief but spooky spectacle taken straight from the Middle Ages, every hour on the hour.

The square's second church, the Baroque **Kostel svatého Mikuláše** ⑨,
is not to be confused with the Lesser Quarter's Chrám svatého Mikuláše
on the other side of the river (☞ Karlův most [Charles Bridge] and Malá
Strana [Lesser Quarter], *below*). For a small detour, head down Kaprova
street to the **Rudolfinum** ⑩ concert hall and gallery; across the street
is the Uměleckoprůmyslové muzeum (Museum of Decorative Arts). Both
are notable neo-Renaissance buildings.

Returning to Staroměstské náměstí, you'll find the **Franz Kafka Exposition**
adjoining Kostel svatého Mikuláše on náměstí Franze Kafky, a little
square that used to be part of U Radnice street. Continue along U Radnice proper just a few yards until you come to **Malé náměstí** ⑪, a mini-
square with arcades on one side. Look for tiny Karlova ulice, which
begins in the southwest corner of the square, and take another quick
right to stay on it (watch the signs—this medieval street seems designed
to confound the visitor). At the České muzeum výtvarných umění
(Czech Museum of Fine Arts), pause and inspect the exotic **Clam-Gallas palác** ⑫, behind you at Husova 20. You'll recognize it easily: look
for the Titans in the doorway holding up what must be a very heavy
Baroque facade. Head the other way down Husova for a glimpse of
ecstatic Baroque stuffed inside somber Gothic at the **Kostel svatého
Jiljí** ⑬, at No. 8.

Continue walking along Husova to Na Perštýně and turn right at tiny
Betlémská ulice. The alley opens up onto a quiet square, Betlémské
náměstí, and upon the most revered of all Hussite churches in Prague,
the **Betlémská kaple** ⑭.

Return to Na Perštýně and continue walking to the right. As you near
the back of the buildings of the busy Národní třída (National Boulevard), turn left at Martinská ulice. At the end of the street, the forlorn
but majestic church **Kostel svatého Martina ve zdi** ⑮ stands like a postwar ruin. Walk around the church to the left and through a little archway of apartments onto the bustling Národní třída. To the left, a

five-minute walk away, lies Wenceslas Square and the starting point of the walk.

Wenceslas Square and Old Town Square are busy with activity around-the-clock almost all year round. If you're in search of a little peace and quiet, you will find the streets at their most subdued on early week-end mornings or right after a sudden downpour. The streets in this walk-ing tour are reasonably close together and can be covered in half a day. Remember to be in the Old Town Square just before the hour if you want to see the astronomical clock in action.

Sights to See

⓮ **Betlémská kaple** (Bethlehem Chapel). The church's elegant simplicity is in stark contrast to the diverting Gothic and Baroque of the rest of the city. The original structure dates from the end of the 14th century, and the Czech religious reformer Jan Hus was a regular preacher here from 1402 until his exile in 1412. After the Thirty Years' War the church fell into the hands of the Jesuits and was finally demolished in 1786. Excavations carried out after World War I uncovered the original por-tal and three windows, and the entire church was reconstructed dur-ing the 1950s. Although little remains of the first church, some remnants of Hus's teachings can still be read on the inside walls. ⊠ *Betlémské nám. 5.* ☒ *30 Kč.* ۞ *Daily 10–5.*

❸ **Celetná ulice.** Most of this street's facades indicate the buildings are from the 17th or 18th century, but appearances are deceiving: many of the houses in fact have foundations dating from the 12th century. U **Sixtu** (Sixt House), at Celetná 2, dates from the 12th century—its Romanesque vaults are still visible in the cellar. The house is being con-verted into a luxury hotel, due to open in 2001.

⓬ **Clam-Gallas palác** (Clam-Gallas Palace). The beige-and-brown palace dates from 1713–1729 and is the work of Johann Bernhard Fischer von Er-lach, the famed Viennese architectural virtuoso of the day. Enter the building for a glimpse of the finely carved staircase, the work of the mas-ter himself, and of the Italian frescoes featuring Apollo that surround it. The building now houses the municipal archives and is rarely open to vis-itors (so walk in as if you have business there). ⊠ *Husova 20.*

❹ **Dům U černé Matky Boží** (House of the Black Madonna). In the sec-ond decade of the 20th century, young Czech architects boldly applied Cubism's radical reworking of visual space to structures. Adding a de-cided jolt to the architectural styles along Celetná, this Cubist build-ing, designed by Josef Gočár, is unflinchingly modern yet topped with an almost Baroque tile roof. It now houses a permanent exhibit of Czech Cubist design and hosts temporary art shows. ⊠ *Celetná 34,* ☎ *02/ 2421–1732.* ☒ *35 Kč.* ۞ *Tues.–Sun. 10–6.*

Franz Kafka Exposition. Kafka came into the world on July 3, 1883, in a house next to the Kostel svatého Mikuláše (Church of St. Nicholas). For years the writer was only grudgingly acknowledged by the Com-munist cultural bureaucrats, reflecting the traditionally ambiguous at-titude of the Czech government toward his work. The Communists were always too uncomfortable with Kafka's themes of bureaucracy and alien-ation to sing his praises loudly, if at all. As a German and a Jew, more-over, Kafka could easily be dismissed as standing outside the mainstream of Czech literature. Following the 1989 revolution, however, Kafka's popularity soared, and his works are now widely available in Czech. Only the portal of the original house remains; inside the building is a fascinating little exhibit (mostly photographs) on Kafka's life, with commentary in English. ⊠ *Nám. Franze Kafky 3 (formerly U Radnice 5).* ☒ *50 Kč.* ☉ *Tues.–Fri. 10–6, Sat. 10–5.*

❼ Jan Hus monument. Few memorials have elicited as much controversy as this one, which was dedicated in July 1915, exactly 500 years after Hus was burned at the stake in Constance, Germany. Some maintain that the monument's Secessionist style (the inscription seems to come right from turn-of-the-20th-century Vienna) clashes with the Gothic and Baroque of the square. Others dispute the romantic depiction of Hus, who appears here in flowing garb as tall and bearded. The real Hus, historians maintain, was short and had a baby face. Still, no one can take issue with the influence of this fiery preacher, whose ability to transform doctrinal disputes, both literally and metaphorically, into the language of the common man made him into a religious and national symbol for the Czechs. ⊠ *Staroměstské nám.*

Klášter svaté Anežky České (St. Agnes's Convent). Situated near the river between Pařížská and Revoluční streets, this peaceful complex has Prague's first buildings in the Gothic style, built from the 1230s to the 1280s. The convent is to be home to the National Gallery's marvelous collection of Czech Gothic art, which was scheduled to be moved here from the Klášter svatého Jiří in Prague Castle (☞ *below*) at the end of 2000. Check the status of this maneuver at a visitor bureau or any gallery branch. ⊠ *U Milosrdných 17,* ☎ *02/2481–0628.* ☒ *90 Kč.* ☉ *Tues.–Sun. 10–6.*

★ ❻ Kostel Panny Marie před Týnem (Church of the Virgin Mary Before Týn). The exterior of the church is one of the best examples of Prague Gothic and is in part the work of Peter Parler, architect of the Charles Bridge and Chrám svatého Víta (St. Vitus's Cathedral). Construction of its twin black-spire towers was begun later, by King Jiří of Poděbrad in 1461, during the heyday of the Hussites. Jiří had a gilded chalice, the symbol of the Hussites, proudly displayed on the front gable between the two towers. Following the defeat of the Czech Protestants by the Catholic Hapsburgs, the chalice was removed and eventually replaced by a Madonna. As a final blow, the chalice was melted down and made into the Madonna's glimmering halo (you still can see it by walking into the center of the square and looking up between the spires). The entrance to the church is through the arcades on Old Town Square, under the house at No. 604.

Much of the interior, including the tall nave, was rebuilt in the Baroque style in the 17th century. Some Gothic pieces remain, however: look to the left of the main altar for a beautifully preserved set of early Gothic carvings. The main altar itself was painted by Karel Škréta, a luminary of the Czech Baroque. Before leaving the church, look for the grave marker (tucked away to the right of the main altar) of the great Danish astronomer Tycho Brahe, who came to Prague as "Imperial Mathematicus" in 1599 under Rudolf II. As a scientist, Tycho had a place in history that is assured: Johannes Kepler (another resident of the Prague court) used Tycho's observations to formulate his laws of planetary motion. But it is myth that has endeared Tycho to the hearts of Prague residents. The robust Dane, who was apparently fond of duels, lost part of his nose in one (take a closer look at the marker). He quickly had a wax nose fashioned for everyday use but preferred to parade around on holidays and festive occasions sporting a bright silver one. ⊠ *Staroměstské nám., between Celetná and Týnská.* ☉ *Hours vary.*

⓭ Kostel svatého Jiljí (Church of St. Giles). This was another important outpost of Czech Protestantism in the 16th century. The exterior is a powerful example of Gothic architecture, including the buttresses and a characteristic portal. The interior, as in many important Czech churches, is Baroque, with a design by Johann Bernhard Fischer von Erlach and sweeping frescoes by Václav Reiner. The interior can be viewed during the day from the vestibule or at the evening concerts held several times a week. ⊠ *Husova 8.*

⑮ Kostel svatého Martina ve zdi (Church of St. Martin-in-the-Wall). It was here in 1414 that Holy Communion was first given to the Bohemian laity in the form of both bread and wine, in defiance of the Catholic custom of the time, which dictated that only bread was to be offered to the masses, with wine reserved for the priests and clergy. From then on, the chalice came to symbolize the Hussite movement. The church is open for evening concerts, held several times each week. ⊠ *Martinská ul.*

❾ Kostel svatého Mikuláše (Church of St. Nicholas). Designed in the 18th century by Prague's own master of late Baroque, Kilian Ignaz Dientzenhofer, this church is probably less successful in capturing the style's lyric exuberance than its namesake across town, the Chrám svatého Mikuláše. Still, Dientzenhofer utilized the limited space to create a well-balanced structure. The interior is compact, with a beautiful but small chandelier and an enormous black organ that seems to overwhelm the rear of the church. The church hosts almost continuous afternoon and evening tourist concerts. ⊠ *Staroměstské nám. Apr.–Oct., Mon. noon–4, Tues.–Sat. 10–4, Sun. noon–3; Nov.–Mar., Tues.–Fri. and Sun. 10–noon (Wed. until 4).*

⑪ Malé náměstí (Small Square). Note the iron fountain dating from around 1560 in the center of the square. The colorfully painted house at No. 3, originally a hardware store, is not as old as it looks, but here and there you can find authentic Gothic portals and Renaissance sgraffiti that betray the square's true age.

Na Příkopě. The name means "At the Moat" and harks back to the time when the street was indeed a moat separating the Old Town from the New Town. Today the pedestrian zone Na Příkopě is prime shopping territory. At No. 19 an oversize new building, one of the worst excesses of the 1990s in Prague, houses a Marks & Spencer store. Have a look at the chic, hard-edged black-and-white Černá Růže (Black Rose) arcade at No. 12.

❷ Obecní dům (Municipal House). The city's Art Nouveau showpiece still fills the role it had when it was completed in 1911: it's a center for concerts, rotating art exhibits, and café society. The mature Art Nouveau style recalls the lengths the Czech middle classes went to at the turn of the 20th century to imitate Paris, then the epitome of style and glamour. Much of the interior bears the work of Art Nouveau master Alfons Mucha, Max Švabinský, and other leading Czech artists. Mucha decorated the Hall of the Lord Mayor upstairs with impressive, magical frescoes depicting Czech history; unfortunately it's not open to the public. The beautiful **Smetanova síň** (Smetana Hall), which hosts concerts by the Prague Symphony Orchestra as well as international guests, is on the second floor. The ground-floor café is touristy, but a lovely sight with its glimmering chandeliers and exquisite woodwork. There's also a beer hall in the cellar with passable beer and mediocre food and superbly executed ceramic murals on the walls. ⊠ *Nám. Republiky 5,* ☎ *02/2200–2100.* ☺ *Information center and box office daily 10–6.*

NEED A
BREAK?

If you prefer subtle elegance, head around the corner to the café at the **Hotel Paříž** (⊠ U Obecního domu 1, ☎ 02/2422–2151), a Jugendstil jewel tucked away on a relatively quiet street.

Palác Kinských (Kinský Palace). This exuberant building, built in 1765 from Kilian Ignaz Dientzenhofer's design, is considered one of Prague's finest late-Baroque structures. With its exaggerated pink overlay and numerous statues, the facade looks extreme when contrasted with the more staid Baroque elements of other nearby buildings. (The interior, however, was "modernized" under Communism.) The palace once housed a German school—where Franz Kafka was a student for nine misery-laden years—and presently contains the National Gallery's graphics collection. At press time exhibitions were scheduled to reopen by the end of 2000 following reconstruction of the interior. It was from this building that Communist leader Klement Gottwald, flanked by his Slovak comrade Vladimír Clementis, first addressed the crowds after seizing power in February 1948—an event recounted in the first chapter of Milan Kundera's novel *The Book of Laughter and Forgetting.* ⊠ *Staroměstské nám. 12.*

Prašná brána (Powder Tower). Construction of the tower, which replaced one of the city's 13 original gates, was begun by King Vladislav II of Jagiello in 1475. At the time, the kings of Bohemia maintained their royal residence next door, on the site of the current Obecní dům (☞ *above*), and the tower was intended to be the grandest gate of all. But Vladislav was Polish and thus heartily disliked by the rebellious Czech citizens of Prague. Nine years after he assumed power, fearing for his life, he moved the royal court across the river to Prague Castle. Work on the tower was abandoned, and the half-finished structure was used for storing gunpowder—hence its odd name—until the end of the 17th century. The oldest part of the tower is the base. The golden spires were not added until the end of the 19th century. Climb to the top for a striking view of the Old Town and Prague Castle in the distance. ⊠ *Nám. Republiky.* 🎫 *20 Kč.* ☉ *Apr.–Oct., daily 9–6.*

❿ Rudolfinum. Thanks to a thorough makeover and exterior sandblasting, this neo-Renaissance monument designed by Josef Zítek and Josef Schulz presents the cleanest, brightest stonework in the city. Completed in 1884 and named for then–Hapsburg Crown Prince Rudolf, the rather low-slung sandstone building was meant to be a combination concert hall and exhibition gallery. After 1918 it was converted into the parliament of the newly independent Czechoslovakia until German invaders reinstated the concert hall in 1939. Czech writer Jiří Weil's novel *Mendelssohn Is on the Roof* tells of the cruel farce that ensued when officials ordered the removal of the Jewish composer's statue from the roof balustrade. Now the Czech Philharmonic has its home base here. The 1,200-seat **Dvořákova síň** (Dvořák Hall) has superb acoustics (the box office faces 17. listopadu). ⊠ *Nám. Jana Palacha,* ☎ *02/2489–3111.*

Behind Dvořák Hall is a set of large exhibition rooms, the **Galerie Rudolfinum**, an innovative, state-supported gallery for rotating shows of contemporary art. Four or five large shows are mounted here annually, showcasing excellent Czech work along with international artists such as photographer Cindy Sherman. ⊠ *Alšovo nábř. 12,* ☎ *02/2489–3205.* 🎫 *40 Kč.* ☉ *Tues.–Sun. 10–6.*

★ ❽ Staroměstská radnice (Old Town Hall). This is one of Prague's magnets: hundreds of people gravitate to it to see the hour struck by the mechanical figures of the **astronomical clock**. Just before the hour, look to the upper part of the clock, where a skeleton begins by tolling a death knell and turning an hourglass upside down. The Twelve Apostles parade momentarily, and then a cockerel flaps its wings and crows, piercing the air as the hour finally strikes. To the right of the skeleton, the dreaded Turk nods his head, seemingly hinting at another invasion like those of the 16th and 17th centuries. This small spectacle doesn't clue viewers in to the way this 15th-century marvel indicates the time—by the season, the zodiac sign, and the positions of the sun and moon. The calendar under the clock dates from the mid 19th century.

The Old Town Hall served as the center of administration for the Old Town beginning in 1338, when King John of Luxembourg first granted the city council the right to a permanent location. The impressive 200 ft **Town Hall Tower**, where the clock is mounted, was first built in the 14th century and given its current late-Gothic appearance around 1500 by the master Matyáš Rejsek. For a rare view of the Old Town and its maze of crooked streets and alleyways, climb the ramp or ride the elevator to the top of the tower.

If you walk around the hall to the left, you'll see it's actually a series of houses jutting into the square; they were purchased over the years and successively added to the complex. On the other side, jagged stonework reveals where a large, neo-Gothic wing once adjoined the tower until it was destroyed during fighting between townspeople and Nazi troops in May 1945.

Guided tours (most guides speak English, and English texts are on hand) of the Old Town Hall depart from the main desk inside. However, the only notable features are the fine Renaissance ceilings, the Gothic Council Room, and the Gothic chapel, where you can see the clock's apostles up close. ⊠ *Staroměstské nám.* ☎ *Tower 30 Kč, tours 30 Kč each.* ☉ *Tues.–Sun. 9–6, Mon. 11–6 (until 5, Oct.–Apr.).*

★ ❺ **Staroměstské náměstí** (Old Town Square). There are places that, on first glimpse, stop you dead in your tracks in sheer wonder. Old Town Square is one such place. Long the heart of the Old Town, the square grew to its present proportions when the city's original marketplace was moved away from the river in the 12th century. Its shape and appearance have changed little over the years. During the day the square has a festive atmosphere as musicians vie for the favor of onlookers and artists display renditions of Prague street scenes. At night, the gaudily lit towers of the Church of the Virgin Mary Before Týn rise ominously over the glowing Baroque facades. The crowds thin out, and the ghosts of the square's stormy past return.

During the 15th century the square was the focal point of conflict between Czech Hussites and German Catholics. In 1422 the radical Hussite preacher Jan Želivský was executed here for his part in storming the New Town's town hall three years earlier (☞ Karlovo náměstí *in* Nové Město [New Town] and Vyšehrad, *below*). In the 1419 uprising, three Catholic consuls and seven German citizens were thrown out the window—the first of Prague's many famous defenestrations. Within a few years, the Hussites had taken over the town, expelled the Germans, and set up their own administration.

Twenty-seven white crosses set flat in the paving stones in the square, at the Old Town Hall's base, mark the spot where 27 Bohemian noblemen were killed by the Hapsburgs in 1621 during the dark days following the defeat of the Czechs at the Battle of White Mountain. The grotesque spectacle, designed to quash any further national or religious opposition, took some five hours to complete, as the men were put to the sword or hanged one by one.

One of the square's most interesting houses, at No. 3, juts out into the small extension leading into Malé náměstí. This is the house called U **Minuty,** with its 16th-century Renaissance sgraffiti of biblical and classical motifs. The young Franz Kafka lived here in the 1890s.

❶ **Stavovské divadlo** (Estates Theater). Built in the 1780s in the classical style, this handsome theater was for many years a beacon of Czech-
language culture in a city long dominated by the German variety. It is
probably best known as the site of the world premiere of Mozart's opera
Don Giovanni in October 1787, with the composer himself conducting. Prague audiences were quick to acknowledge Mozart's genius: the
opera was an instant hit here, though it flopped nearly everywhere else
in Europe. Mozart wrote most of the opera's second act in Prague at
the Villa Bertramka (☞ Karlův most [Charles Bridge] and Malá Strana
[Lesser Quarter], *below*), where he was a frequent guest. ⊠ *Ovocný
trh 1,* ☎ *02/2421–5001 (box office).*

Josefov (Jewish Quarter)

Prague's Jews survived centuries of discrimination, but two unrelated
events of modern times have left their historic ghetto little more than
a collection of museums. Around 1900, city officials decided for hy-
gienic purposes to raze the minuscule neighborhood—it had ceased to
be a true ghetto with the political reforms of 1848–49, and by this time
the majority of its residents were poor Gentiles—and pave over its
crooked streets. Only some of the synagogues, the town hall, and the
cemetery survived this early attempt at urban renewal. The second event
was the Holocaust. Under Nazi occupation, a staggering percentage
of the city's Jews were deported or murdered in concentration camps.
Of the 35,000 Jews living in Prague before World War II, only about
1,200 returned to resettle the city after the war. The community is still
tiny. Only a scant few Jews, mostly elderly, live in the "ghetto" today.

Treasures and artifacts of the ghetto are now the property of the
Židovské muzeum v Praze (Prague Jewish Museum; ☎ 02/231–7191),
which includes the Old Jewish Cemetery and collections installed in
four surviving synagogues and the Ceremony Hall. (The Staronová
synagóga, or Old-New Synagogue, a functioning house of worship, technically does not belong to the museum, but the Prague Jewish Community oversees both.) The museum was founded in 1906, but traces
the vast majority of its holdings to the Nazis' destruction of 150 Jewish communities in Bohemia and Moravia. Dedicated museum workers, nearly all of whom were to die at Nazi hands, gathered and
cataloged the stolen artifacts under German supervision. Exhibitions
were even held during the war. A ticket good for all museum sites may
be purchased at any of the synagogues but the Old-New Synagogue;
single-site tickets apply only at the Old-New Synagogue and during
occasional exhibits at the Spanish Synagogue. All museum sites are closed
Saturday and Jewish holidays.

A Good Walk

To reach the Jewish Quarter, leave Old Town Square via handsome
Pařížská ulice, centerpiece of the urban renewal effort, and head north
toward the river. The festive atmosphere changes suddenly as you enter
the area of the ghetto. The buildings are lower here; the mood is hushed.
Take a right on Široká and stroll two blocks down to the recently restored **Španělská synagóga** ⑯. Head back the other way, past Pařížská,
turn right on Maiselova, and you'll come to the **Židovská radnice** ⑰, home
to the Jewish Community Center. Adjoining it on Červená is the 16th-
century High Synagogue. Across the street, at Červená 2, you see the
Staronová synagóga ⑱, the oldest surviving synagogue in Prague.

Go west on the little street U starého hřbitova. The main museum ticket
office is at the **Klausová synagóga** at No. 3A. Next door, separated
from the synagogue by the exit gate of the Old Jewish Cemetery, is the

former building of the Jewish Burial Society, **Obřadní síň,** which exhibits traditional Jewish funeral objects.

Return to Maiselova and follow it to Široká. Turn right to find the **Pinkasova synagóga** ⑲, a handsome Gothic structure. Here also is the entrance to the Jewish ghetto's most astonishing sight, the **Starý židovský hřbitov** ⑳.

Return to Maiselova once more and turn right in the direction of the Old Town. Look in at the displays of Czech Jewish history in the **Maiselova synagóga** ㉑.

TIMING

The Jewish Quarter is one of the most popular visitor destinations in Prague, especially in the height of summer, when its tiny streets are jammed to bursting with tourists almost all the time. The best time for a quieter visit is early morning when the museums and cemetery first open. The area itself is very compact, and a fairly thorough tour should only take half a day.

Sights to See

Klausová synagóga (Klausen Synagogue). This Baroque former synagogue was built at the end of the 17th century in the place of three small buildings (a synagogue, school, and ritual bath) that were destroyed in a fire that devastated the ghetto in 1689. Inside, displays of Czech Jewish traditions emphasize celebrations and daily life. ⊠ *U starého hřbitova 3A.* 🎫 *Combined ticket to museum sites and Old-New Synagogue, 480 Kč; museum sites only, 280 Kč.* ☉ *Apr.–Oct., Sun.–Fri. 9–6; Nov.–Mar., Sun.–Fri. 9–4:30.*

㉑ **Maiselova synagóga** (Maisel Synagogue). Here, the history of Czech Jews from the 10th to the 18th century is illustrated with the aid of some of the Prague Jewish Museum's most precious objects, including silver Torah shields and pointers, spice boxes, and candelabra; historic tombstones; and fine ceremonial textiles, including some donated by Mordechai Maisel to the synagogue he founded. The richest items come from the late 16th and early 17th century—a prosperous era for Prague's Jews. ⊠ *Maiselova 10.* 🎫 *Combined ticket to museum sites and Old-New Synagogue, 480 Kč; museum sites only, 280 Kč.* ☉ *Apr.–Oct., Sun.–Fri. 9–6; Nov.–Mar., Sun.–Fri. 9–4:30.*

Obřadní síň (Ceremony Hall). In this neo-Romanesque building, the focus is on rather grim subjects: Jewish funeral paraphernalia, old gravestones, and medical instruments. Special attention is paid to the activities of the Jewish Burial Society through many fine objects and paintings. ⊠ *U starého hřbitova 3A.* 🎫 *Combined ticket to museum sites and Old-New Synagogue, 480 Kč; museum sites only, 280 Kč.* ☉ *Apr.–Oct., Sun.–Fri. 9–6; Nov.–Mar., Sun.–Fri. 9–4:30.*

⑲ **Pinkasova synagóga** (Pinkas Synagogue). This synagogue has two particularly moving testimonies to the appalling crimes perpetrated against the Jews during World War II. One tribute astounds by sheer numbers: The inside walls are covered with nearly 80,000 names of Bohemian and Moravian Jews murdered by the Nazis. Among them are the names of the paternal grandparents of U.S. Secretary of State Madeleine Albright, who learned of their fate only in 1997. There is also an exhibition of drawings made by children at the Nazi concentration camp Terezín. The Nazis used the camp for propaganda purposes to demonstrate their "humanity" toward the Jews, and prisoners were given relative freedom to lead "normal" lives. However, transports to death camps in Poland began in earnest in 1944, and many thousands of Terezín prisoners, including many of these children, eventually perished. ⊠ *Enter from Široká 3.* ☎ *Combined ticket to museum sites and Old-New Synagogue, 480 Kč; museum sites only, 280 Kč.* ☉ *Apr.–Oct., Sun.–Fri. 9–6; Nov.–Mar., Sun.–Fri. 9–4:30.*

★ ⑯ **Španělská synagóga** (Spanish Synagogue). A domed Moorish-style synagogue was built in 1868 on the site of the Altschul, the city's oldest synagogue. Here, the historical exposition that begins in the Maisel Synagogue (☞ *above*) continues, taking the story up to the post–World War II period. The displays are not that compelling, but the building's painstakingly restored interior definitely is. ⊠ *Vězeňská 1.* ☎ *Combined ticket to museum sites and Old-New Synagogue, 480 Kč; museum sites only, 280 Kč.* ☉ *Apr.–Oct., Sun.–Fri. 9–6; Nov.–Mar., Sun.–Fri. 9–4:30.*

★ ⑱ **Staronová synagóga** (Old-New Synagogue, or Altneuschul). Dating from the mid 13th century, this is one of the most important works of early Gothic in Prague. The odd name recalls the legend that the synagogue was built on the site of an ancient Jewish temple and that stones from the temple were used to build the present structure. The oldest part of the synagogue is the entrance, with its vault supported by two pillars. The synagogue has not only survived fires and the razing of the ghetto at the end of the last century but also emerged from the Nazi occupation intact; it is still in active use. As the oldest synagogue in Europe that still serves its original function, it is a living storehouse of Bohemian Jewish life. Note that men are required to cover their heads inside and that during services men and women sit apart. ⊠ *Červená 2.* ☎ *Combined ticket to Old-New Synagogue and museum sites, 480 Kč; Old-New Synagogue only, 200 Kč.* ☉ *Apr.–Oct., Sun.–Thurs. 9–6; Nov.–Mar., Sun.–Thurs. 9–4:30; closes 2–3 hrs early on Fri.*

★ ⑳ **Starý židovský hřbitov** (Old Jewish Cemetery). This unforgettably melancholy sight not far from the busy city was, from the 15th century to 1787, the final resting place for all Jews living in Prague. The confined space forced graves to be piled one on top of the other. Tilted at crazy angles, the 12,000 visible tombstones are but a fraction of countless thousands more buried below. Walk the path amid the gravestones; the relief symbols you see represent the names and professions of the deceased. The oldest marked grave belongs to the poet Avigdor Kara, who died in 1439; the grave is not accessible from the pathway, but the original tombstone can be seen in the Maisel Synagogue. The best-known marker is that of Jehuda ben Bezalel, the famed Rabbi Loew (died 1609), a chief rabbi of Prague and profound scholar who is credited with creating the mythical Golem. Even today, small scraps of paper bearing wishes are stuffed into the cracks of the rabbi's tomb in the hope he will grant them. Loew's grave lies near the exit. ⊠ *Široká 3.* ☎ *Combined ticket to museum sites and Old-New Synagogue, 480 Kč; museum sites only, 280 Kč.* ☉ *Apr.–Oct., Sun.–Fri. 9–6; Nov.–Mar., Sun.–Fri. 9–4:30.* ✎

⑰ **Židovská radnice** (Jewish Town Hall). The hall was the creation of Mordechai Maisel, an influential Jewish leader at the end of the 16th century. It was restored in the 18th century and given its clock and bell tower at that time. A second clock, with Hebrew numbers, keeps time counterclockwise. Now home to the Jewish Community Center, the building also houses a kosher restaurant, Shalom. ⊠ *Maiselova 18.*

Karlův most (Charles Bridge) and Malá Strana (Lesser Quarter)

One of Prague's most exquisite neighborhoods, the Lesser Quarter (or Little Town) was established in 1257 and for years was home to the merchants and craftsmen who served the royal court. The Lesser Quarter is not for the methodical traveler. Its charm lies in the tiny lanes, the sudden blasts of bombastic architecture, and the soul-stirring views that emerge for a second before disappearing behind the sloping roofs.

A Good Walk

Begin your tour on the Old Town side of **Karlův most** ㉒, which you can reach by foot in about 10 minutes from the Old Town Square. Rising above it is the majestic **Staroměstská mostecká věž.** The climb of 138 steps is worth the effort for the view you get of the Old Town and, across the river, of the Lesser Quarter and Prague Castle.

It's worth pausing to take a closer look at some of the statues as you walk across Karlův most toward the Lesser Quarter. You'll see Kampa Island below you, separated from the mainland by an arm of the Vltava known as Čertovka (Devil's Stream).

By now you are almost at the end of the bridge. In front of you is the striking conjunction of the two Malá Strana bridge towers, one Gothic, the other Romanesque. Together they frame the Baroque flamboyance of Chrám svatého Mikuláše in the distance. At night this is an absolutely wondrous sight.

Walk under the gateway of the towers into the little uphill street called Mostecká. You have now entered the Lesser Quarter. Follow Mostecká up to the rectangular **Malostranské náměstí** ㉓, now the district's traffic hub rather than its heart. In the middle of the square stands **Chrám svatého Mikuláše** ㉔.

Nerudova ulice ㉕ runs up from the square toward Prague Castle. Lined with gorgeous houses (and in recent years an ever-larger number of places to spend money), it's sometimes burdened with the moniker "Prague's most beautiful street." A tiny passageway at No. 13, on the left-hand side as you go up, leads to Tržiště ulice and the **Schönbornský palác** ㉖, once Franz Kafka's home, now the embassy of the United States. Tržiště winds down to the quarter's traffic-plagued main street, Karmelitská, where the famous Infant Jesus of Prague resides in the **Kostel Panny Marie vítězné.** A few doors away, closer to Tržiště, is a quiet oasis, the **Vrtbovská zahrada** ㉗. Tiny Prokopská ulice leads off of Karmelitská, past the former Church of St. Procopius (now converted, oddly, into an apartment block), and into Maltézské náměstí (Maltese Square), a characteristically noble compound. The square next door, **Velkopřevorské náměstí,** boasts even grander palaces.

A tiny bridge at the cramped square's lower end takes you across the creeklike Čertovka to the island of **Kampa** ㉘ and its broad lawns, cafés, and river views. Winding your way underneath Karlův most and along the street U lužického semináře brings you to a quiet walled garden, **Vojanovy sady** ㉙. To the northwest, hiding off busy Letenská ulice near the Malostranská metro station, is **Zahrada Valdštejnského paláce** ㉚, a more formal garden with an unbeatable view of Prague Castle looming above.

TIMING

The area is at its best in the evening, when the softer light hides the crumbling facades and brings you into a world of glimmering beauty. The basic walk described here could take as little as half a day—longer if you'd like to explore the area's lovely nooks and crannies.

Sights To See

★ ㉔   **Chrám svatého Mikuláše** (Church of St. Nicholas). With its dynamic curves, this church is one of the purest and most ambitious examples of high Baroque. The celebrated architect Christoph Dientzenhofer began the Jesuit church in 1704 on the site of one of the more active Hussite churches of 15th-century Prague. Work on the building was taken over by his son Kilian Ignaz Dientzenhofer, who built the dome and presbytery. Anselmo Lurago completed the whole in 1755 by adding the bell tower. The juxtaposition of the broad, full-bodied dome with the slender bell tower is one of the many striking architectural contrasts that mark the Prague skyline. Inside, the vast pink-and-green space is impossible to take in with a single glance. Every corner bristles with movement, guiding the eye first to the dramatic statues, then to the hectic frescoes, and on to the shining faux-marble pillars. Many of the statues are the work of Ignaz Platzer, and in fact they constitute his last blaze of success. Platzer's workshop was forced to declare bankruptcy when the centralizing and secularizing reforms of Joseph II toward the end of the 18th century brought an end to the flamboyant Baroque era. ⊠ *Malostranské nám.* 🎫 *30 Kč.* ☉ *Daily 9–4.*

㉘ Kampa. Prague's largest island is cut off from the "mainland" by the narrow Čertovka streamlet. The name Čertovka, or Devil's Stream, reputedly refers to a cranky old lady who once lived on Maltese Square (given the river's present filthy state, the name is certainly appropriate). The unusually well-kept lawns of the **Kampa Gardens** that occupy much of the island are one of the few places in Prague where sitting on the grass is openly tolerated. If it's a warm day, spread out a blanket and bask for a while in the sunshine. The row of benches that lines the river is also a popular spot from which to contemplate the city. At night this stretch along the river is especially romantic.

★ ㉒ Karlův most (Charles Bridge). The view from the foot of the bridge on the Old Town side is nothing short of breathtaking, encompassing the towers and domes of the Lesser Quarter and the soaring spires of St. Vitus's Cathedral to the northwest. This heavenly vision changes subtly in perspective as you walk across the bridge, attended by the host of Baroque saints that decorate the bridge's peaceful Gothic stones. At night its drama is spellbinding: St. Vitus's Cathedral lit in a ghostly green, the castle in monumental yellow, and the Church of St. Nicholas in a voluptuous pink, all viewed through the menacing silhouettes of the bowed statues and the Gothic towers. If you do nothing else in Prague, you must visit the Charles Bridge at night. During the day the pedestrian bridge buzzes with activity. Street musicians vie with artisans hawking jewelry, paintings, and glass for the hearts and wallets of the passing multitude. At night the crowds thin out a little, the musicians multiply, and the bridge becomes a long block party—nearly everyone brings a bottle.

When the Přemyslid princes set up residence in Prague in the 10th century, there was a ford across the Vltava at this point—a vital link along one of Europe's major trading routes. After several wooden bridges and the first stone bridge had washed away in floods, Charles IV appointed the 27-year-old German Peter Parler, the architect of St. Vitus's Cathedral, to build a new structure in 1357. After 1620, following the defeat of Czech Protestants by Catholic Hapsburgs at the Battle of White Mountain, the bridge became a symbol of the Counter-Reformation's vigorous re-Catholicization efforts. The many Baroque statues that began to appear in the late 17th century, commissioned by Catholics, eventually came to symbolize the totality of the Austrian (hence Catholic) triumph. The Czech writer Milan Kundera sees the statues from this perspective: "The thousands of saints looking out from all sides, threatening you, following you, hypnotizing you, are the raging hordes of occupiers who invaded Bohemia 350 years ago to tear the people's faith and language from their hearts."

The religious conflict is less obvious nowadays, leaving only the artistic tension between Baroque and Gothic that gives the bridge its allure. It's worth pausing to take a closer look at some of the statues as you walk toward the Lesser Quarter. The third on the right, a bronze crucifix from the mid 17th century, is the oldest of all. It is mounted on the location of a wooden cross destroyed in a battle with the Swedes (the golden Hebrew inscription was reputedly financed by a Jew accused of defiling the cross). Eighth on the right, the statue of St. John of Nepomuk, designed by Johann Brokoff in 1683, begins the Baroque lineup of saints. On the left-hand side, sticking out from the bridge between the 9th and 10th statues (the latter has a wonderfully expressive vanquished Satan), stands a Roland (Bruncvík) statue. This knightly figure, bearing the coat of arms of the Old Town, was once a reminder that this part of the bridge belonged to the Old Town before Prague became a unified city in 1784.

In the eyes of most art historians, the most valuable statue is the 12th on the left, near the Lesser Quarter end. Mathias Braun's statue of St. Luitgarde depicts the blind saint kissing Christ's wounds. The most compelling grouping, however, is the second from the end on the left, a work of Ferdinand Maxmilian Brokoff (son of Johann) from 1714. Here the saints are incidental; the main attraction is the Turk, his face expressing extreme boredom at guarding the Christians imprisoned in the cage at his side. When the statue was erected, just 31 years after the second Turkish siege of Vienna, it scandalized the Prague public, who smeared it with mud. A half-dozen of the 30 bridge sculptures are 19th-century replacements for originals damaged in wars or sunk in a 1784 flood. All but a couple of the bridge's surviving Baroque statues, including St. Luitgarde and the Turk, have been replaced by modern copies. The 17th- and 18th-century originals are in safer quarters, protected from Prague's acidic air. Several, including St. Luitgarde, can be viewed in the Lapidarium museum at the Výstaviště exhibition grounds in Prague 7; a few more occupy a man-made cavern at Vyšehrad (☞ Nové Město [New Town] and Vyšehrad, *below*).

★ **Kostel Panny Marie vítězné** (Church of Our Lady Victorious). This comfortably ramshackle church on the Lesser Quarter's main street is the unlikely home of one of Prague's best-known religious artifacts, the *Pražské Jezulátko* (Infant Jesus of Prague). Originally brought to Prague from Spain in the 16th century, this tiny porcelain doll (now bathed in neon lighting) is renowned worldwide for showering miracles on anyone willing to kneel before it and pray. Nuns from a nearby convent arrive at dawn each day to change the infant's clothes; pieces of the doll's extensive wardrobe have been sent by believers from around the world. ✉ *Karmelitská 9A.* 🎟 *Free.* ☉ *Mon.–Sat. 10–5:30, Sun. 1–5.*

Ledeburská zahrada (Ledeburg Garden). Rows of steeply banked Baroque gardens rise behind the palaces of Valdštejnská ulice. This one makes a pleasant spot for a rest amid shady arbors and niches. The garden, with its frescoes and statuary, was restored with support from a fund headed by Czech president Václav Havel and Charles, Prince of Wales. ✉ *Entrance at Valdštejnské nám. 3; also from the south gardens of Prague Castle in summer.* 🎟 *25 Kč.* ☉ *Daily 10–6.*

㉓ **Malostranské náměstí** (Lesser Quarter Square). The arcaded houses on the east and south sides of the square, dating from the 16th and 17th centuries, exhibit a mix of Baroque and Renaissance elements. The Czech Parliament resides partly in the gaudy yellow-and-green palace on the square's north side, partly in the street behind the palace, Sněmovní. The huge bulk of the Church of St. Nicholas divides the lower, busier section—buzzing with restaurants, street vendors, clubs, and shops—from the quieter upper part.

㉕ **Nerudova ulice.** This steep little street used to be the last leg of the Royal Way walked by the king before his coronation, and it is still the best way to get to Prague Castle. It was named for the 19th-century Czech journalist and poet Jan Neruda (after whom Chilean poet Pablo Neruda renamed himself). Until Joseph II's administrative reforms in the late 18th century, house numbering was unknown in Prague. Each house bore a name, depicted on the facade, and these are particularly prominent on Nerudova ulice. House No. 6, U červeného orla (At the Red Eagle), proudly displays a faded painting of a red eagle. No. 12 is known as U tří housliček (At the Three Fiddles). In the early 18th century, three generations of the Edlinger violin-making family lived here. Joseph II's scheme numbered each house according to its position in its "town" (here the Lesser Quarter) rather than its sequence on the street. The red plates record the original house numbers; the blue ones are the numbers used in addresses today. To confuse the tourist, many architectural guides refer to the old, red-number plates.

Two palaces break the unity of the burghers' houses on Nerudova ulice. Both were designed by the adventurous Baroque architect Giovanni Santini, one of the Italian builders most in demand by wealthy nobles of the early 18th century. The **Morzin Palace,** on the left at No. 5, is now the Romanian Embassy. The fascinating facade, with an allegory of night and day, was created in 1713 and is the work of Ferdinand Brokoff of Charles Bridge statue fame. Across the street at No. 20 is the **Thun-Hohenstein Palace,** now the Italian Embassy. The gateway with two enormous eagles (the emblem of the Kolovrat family, who owned the building at the time) is the work of the other great Charles Bridge statue sculptor, Mathias Braun. Santini himself lived at No. 14, the **Valkoun House.**

The archway at Nerudova 13 hides one of the many winding passageways that give the Lesser Quarter its enchantingly ghostly character at night. Higher up the street at No. 33 is the **Bretfeld Palace,** a rococo house on the corner of Jánský vršek. The relief of St. Nicholas on the facade is the work of Ignaz Platzer, a sculptor known for his classic and rococo work, but the building is valued more for its historical associations than for its architecture: this is where Mozart, his lyricist partner Lorenzo da Ponte, and the aging but still infamous philanderer and music lover Casanova stayed at the time of the world premiere of *Don Giovanni* in 1787.

NEED A BREAK?
Nerudova ulice is filled with little restaurants and snack bars and offers something for everyone. **U zeleného čaje** (✉ Nerudova 19) is a fragrant little tearoom offering herbal and fruit teas as well as light salads and sweets. **U Kocoura** (✉ Nerudova 2) is a traditional pub that hasn't caved in to touristic niceties.

㉖ **Schönbornský palác** (Schönborn Palace). Franz Kafka had an apartment in this massive Baroque building at the top of Tržiště ulice in mid-1917, after moving from Zlatá ulička, or Golden Lane (☞ Pražský hrad [Prague Castle], *below*). The U.S. Embassy now occupies this prime location. If you look through the gates, you can see the beautiful formal gardens rising up to the Petřín hill. They are unfortunately not open to the public, but can be glimpsed from the neighboring garden, Vrtbovská zahrada (☞ *below*). ✉ Tržiště at Vlašská.

Staroměstská mostecká věž (Old Town Bridge Tower). This was where Peter Parler, the architect of St. Vitus's Cathedral and eventually the

Charles Bridge, began his bridge building. The carved facades he designed for the sides of the tower were destroyed by Swedish soldiers in 1648, at the end of the Thirty Years' War. The sculptures facing the Old Town, however, are still intact (although some are recent copies); they depict an old and gout-ridden Charles IV with his son, who later became Wenceslas IV. Above them are two of Bohemia's patron saints, Adalbert of Prague and Sigismund. Inside the tower is a small exhibit of antique musical instruments. 🎫 *20 Kč.* ☉ *Daily 10–5 (until 7 in summer).*

Velkopřevorské náměstí (Grand Priory Square). This square lies just south of the Charles Bridge, next to the Čertovka. The Grand Prior's Palace fronting the square is considered one of the finest Baroque buildings in the Lesser Quarter, though it is now part of the Embassy of the Knights of Malta and no longer open to the public. Opposite is the flamboyant orange-and-white stucco facade of the Buquoy Palace, built in 1719 by Giovanni Santini and the present home of the French Embassy. The so-called **John Lennon Peace Wall**, leading to a bridge over the Čertovka, was once a kind of monument to youthful rebellion, emblazoned with a large painted head of the former Beatle, lyrics from his songs, and other messages of peace. It has lost much social significance, not to mention attractiveness, since the years around the 1989 revolution when graffiti actually meant something in Prague.

㉙ Vojanovy sady (Vojan Park). Once the gardens of the Monastery of the Discalced Carmelites, later taken over by the Order of the English Virgins, and now part of the Ministry of Finance, this walled garden, with its weeping willows, fruit trees, and benches, makes another peaceful haven in summer. Exhibitions of modern sculptures are often held here, contrasting sharply with the two Baroque chapels and the graceful Ignaz Platzer statue of John of Nepomuk standing on a fish at the entrance. The park is surrounded by the high walls of the old monastery and new Ministry of Finance buildings, with only an occasional glimpse of a tower or spire to remind you that you're in Prague. ✉ *U lužického semináře, between Letenská ul. and Míšeňská ul.* ☉ *Nov.–Mar., daily 8–5; Apr.–Oct., daily 8–7.*

★ ㉗ Vrtbovská zahrada (Vrtba Garden). An unobtrusive door on noisy Karmelitská hides the entranceway to a fascinating oasis that also has one of the best views over the Lesser Quarter. The street door opens onto the intimate courtyard of the Vrtbovský palác (Vrtba Palace), which is now private housing. Two Renaissance wings flank the courtyard; the left one was built in 1575, the right one in 1591. The owner of the latter house was one of the 27 Bohemian nobles executed by the Hapsburgs in 1621 before the Old Town Hall. The house was given as confiscated property to Count Sezima of Vrtba, who bought the neighboring property and turned the buildings into a late-Renaissance palace. The Vrtba Garden, created a century later, reopened in summer 1998 after an excruciatingly long renovation. This is the most elegant of the Lesser Quarter's public gardens, built in five levels rising behind the courtyard in a wave of statuary-bedecked staircases and formal terraces to reach a seashell-decorated pavilion at the top. (The fenced-off garden immediately behind and above belongs to the U.S. Embassy.) The powerful stone figure of Atlas that caps the entranceway in the courtyard and most of the other classically derived statues are from the workshop of Mathias Braun, perhaps the best of the Czech Baroque sculptors. ✉ *Karmelitská 25.* 🎫 *20 Kč.* ☉ *Apr.–Oct., daily 10–6.*

OFF THE
BEATEN PATH

VILLA BERTRAMKA – Mozart fans won't want to pass up a visit to this villa, where the great composer lived during a couple of his visits to Prague. The small, well-organized W. A. Mozart Museum is packed with memorabilia, including a flyer for a performance of *Don Giovanni* in 1788, only months after the opera's world premiere at the Estates Theater. Also on hand is one of the master's pianos. Take Tram No. 12 from Karmelitská south (or ride Metro Line B) to the Anděl metro station, then transfer to Tram No. 4, 7, 9, or 10 and ride to the first stop (Bertramka). A 10-minute walk, following the signs, brings you to the villa. ⊠ *Mozartova ul. 169, Prague 5 (Smíchov),* ☎ *02/540–012.* 🖼 *90 Kč.* ⊙ *Apr.–Oct., daily 9:30–6; Nov.–Mar., daily 9:30–5.*

★ ㉚ **Zahrada Valdštejnského paláce** (Wallenstein Palace Gardens). Albrecht von Wallenstein, onetime owner of the house and gardens, began a meteoric military career in 1622 when the Austrian emperor Ferdinand II retained him to save the empire from the Swedes and Protestants during the Thirty Years' War. Wallenstein, wealthy by marriage, offered to raise 20,000 men at his own cost and lead them personally. Ferdinand II accepted and showered Wallenstein with confiscated land and titles. Wallenstein's first acquisition was this enormous area. Having knocked down 23 houses, a brick factory, and three gardens, in 1623 he began to build his magnificent palace with its idiosyncratic high-walled gardens and superb, vaulted Renaissance *sala terrena* (room opening onto a garden). Walking around the formal paths, you'll come across numerous statues, an unusual fountain with a woman spouting water from her breasts, and a lava-stone grotto along the wall. Most of the palace itself now serves the Czech Senate as meeting chamber and offices. The palace's cavernous former *Jízdárna*, or riding school, now hosts occasional art exhibitions. ⊠ *Garden entrance: Letenská 10.* 🖼 *Garden free.* ⊙ *Garden May–Sept., daily 9–7; Mar. 21–Apr. 30, and Oct., daily 10–6.*

Hradčany (Castle Area)

To the west of Prague Castle is the residential Hradčany (Castle Area), the town that during the early 14th century emerged out of a collection of monasteries and churches. The concentration of history packed into Prague Castle and Hradčany challenges visitors not versed in the ups and downs of Bohemian kings, religious uprisings, wars, and oppression. The picturesque area surrounding Prague Castle, with its breathtaking vistas of the Old Town and the Lesser Quarter, is ideal for just wandering. But the castle itself, with its convoluted history and architecture, is difficult to appreciate fully without investing a little more time.

A Good Walk

Begin on Nerudova ulice (☞ Karlův most [Charles Bridge] and Malá Strana [Lesser Quarter], *above*), which runs east–west a few hundred yards south of Prague Castle. At the western (upper) end of the street, look for a flight of stone steps guarded by two saintly statues. Take the stairs up to Loretánská ulice, and take in panoramic views of the Church of St. Nicholas and the Lesser Quarter. At the top of the steps, turn left and walk a couple hundred yards until you come to a dusty elongated square named Pohořelec (Scene of Fire), which suffered tragic fires in 1420, 1541, and 1741. Go through the inconspicuous gateway at No. 8 and up the steps, and you'll find yourself in the courtyard of one of the city's richest monasteries, the **Strahovský klášter** ㉛.

Retrace your steps to Loretánské náměstí, the square at the head of Loretánská ulice that is flanked by the feminine curves of the Baroque church **Loreta** ㉜. Across the road, the 29 half pillars of the Černínský palác (Černín Palace) now mask the Czech Ministry of Foreign Affairs. At the bottom of Loretánské náměstí, a little lane trails to the left into the area known as **Nový Svět**; the name means "New World," though the district is as old-world as they come. Turn right onto the street Nový Svět. Around the corner you get a tantalizing view of the cathedral through the trees. Walk down the winding Kanovnická ulice past the Austrian Embassy and the dignified but melancholy Kostel svatého Jana Nepomuckého (Church of St. John of Nepomuk). At the top of the street on the left, the rounded, Renaissance corner house, Martinický palác, catches the eye with its detailed sgraffiti decorations. Martinický palác opens onto **Hradčanské náměstí** ㉝ with its grandiose gathering of Renaissance and Baroque palaces. To the left of the bright yellow Arcibiskupský palác (Archbishop's Palace) on the square is an alleyway leading down to the **Národní galerie** ㉞ and its collections of European art. Across the square, the handsome sgraffito sweep of **Schwarzenberský palác** ㉟ beckons; this is the building you saw from the back side at the beginning of the tour.

TIMING

To do justice to the subtle charms of Hradčany, allow at least an hour just for ambling and admiring the passing buildings and views of the city. The Strahovský klášter halls need about a half hour to take in, more if you tour the small picture gallery there, and the Loreta and its treasures need at least that length of time. The Národní galerie in the Šternberský palác deserves at least a couple of hours. Keep in mind that several places are not open on Monday.

Sights to See

㉝ **Hradčanské náměstí** (Hradčany Square). With its fabulous mixture of Baroque and Renaissance housing, topped by the castle itself, the square had a prominent role (disguised, ironically, as Vienna) in the film *Amadeus,* directed by the then-exiled Czech director Miloš Forman. The house at No. 7 was the set for Mozart's residence, where the composer was haunted by the masked figure he thought was his father. Forman used the flamboyant rococo **Arcibiskupský palác** (Archbishop's Palace), on the left as you face the castle, as the Viennese archbishop's palace. The plush interior, shown off in the film, is open to the public only on Maundy Thursday. No. 11 was home for a brief time after World War II to a little girl named Marie Jana Korbelová, who would grow up to be U.S. Secretary of State Madeleine Albright.

㉜ **Loreta** (Loreto Church). The church's seductive lines were a conscious move on the part of Counter-Reformation Jesuits in the 17th century who wanted to build up the cult of Mary and attract the largely Protestant Bohemians back to the church. According to legend, angels had carried Mary's house from Nazareth and dropped it in a patch of laurel trees in Ancona, Italy. Known as *Loreto* (from the Latin for laurel), it immediately became a center of pilgrimage. The Prague Loreto was one of many symbolic reenactments of this scene across Europe, and it worked: pilgrims came in droves. The graceful facade, with its voluptuous tower, was built in 1720 by Kilian Ignaz Dientzenhofer, the architect of the two St. Nicholas churches in Prague. Most spectacular of all is a small exhibition upstairs displaying the religious treasures presented to Mary in thanks for various services, including a monstrance studded with 6,500 diamonds. ✉ *Loretánské nám. 7,* 🎟 *80 Kč (priests, monks, and nuns admitted free).* ☉ *Tues.–Sun. 9–12:15 and 1–4:30.*

★ ㉞ **Národní galerie** (National Gallery). Housed in the 18th-century **Šternberský palác** (Sternberg Palace), this collection, though impressive, is limited compared to German and Austrian holdings. During the time when Berlin, Dresden, and Vienna were building up superlative old-master galleries, Prague languished, neglected by her Viennese rulers—

one reason why the city's museums lag behind. On the first floor there's an exhibition of icons, Italian religious art from the 3rd to 14th century, and early Dutch Renaissance masters. Up a second flight of steps is an assortment of paintings by Cranach, Holbein, Dürer, Van Dyck, El Greco, Rembrandt, and Rubens. Other branches of the National Gallery are scattered around town. ⊠ *Hradčanské nám. 15,* ☎ *02/2051–4634.* ⬛ *90 Kč.* ☉ *Tues.–Sun. 10–6.* ⬥

Nový Svět. This picturesque, winding little alley, with facades from the 17th and 18th centuries, once housed Prague's poorest residents; now many of the homes are used as artists' studios. The last house on the street, No. 1, was the home of the Danish-born astronomer Tycho Brahe. Living so close to the Loreto, so the story goes, Tycho was constantly disturbed during his nightly stargazing by the church bells. He ended up complaining to his patron, Emperor Rudolf II, who instructed the Capuchin monks to finish their services before the first star appeared in the sky.

㉟ Schwarzenberský palác (Schwarzenberg Palace). This boxy palace with its extravagant sgraffito facade contains the **Vojenské historické muzeum** (Military History Museum), one of the largest of its kind in Europe. A dim, old-fashioned collection, it concentrates on pre-20th-century Czech military history. Of more general interest are the jousting tournaments held in the courtyard in summer. ⊠ *Hradčanské nám. 2.* ⬛ *20 Kč.* ☉ *Apr.–Oct., Tues.–Sun. 10–6.*

★ ㉛ Strahovský klášter (Strahov Monastery). Founded by the Premonstratensian order in 1140, the monastery remained in its hands until 1952, when the Communists suppressed all religious orders and turned the entire complex into the **Památník národního písemnictví** (Museum of National Literature). The major building of interest is the **Strahov Library**, with its collection of early Czech manuscripts, the 10th-century Strahov New Testament, and the collected works of famed Danish astronomer Tycho Brahe. Also of note is the late-18th-century **Philosophical Hall.** Engulfing its ceilings is a startling sky blue fresco that depicts an unusual cast of characters, including Socrates' nagging wife Xanthippe, Greek astronomer Thales with his trusty telescope, and a collection of Greek philosophers mingling with Descartes, Diderot, and Voltaire. Also on the premises is the order's small art gallery, highlighted by late-Gothic altars and paintings from Rudolf II's time. You can arrange for a tour in English with several days' advance notice. ⊠ *Strahovské nádvoří 1/132,* ☎ *02/2051–6671 (tour arrangements).* ⬛ *Gallery 25 Kč, library tour 20 Kč.* ☉ *Gallery Tues.–Sun. 9–noon and 12:30–5. Library daily 9–noon and 1–5.* ⬥

OFF THE BEATEN PATH

PETŘÍN – For a superb view of the city—from a mostly undiscovered, tourist-free perch—stroll over from the Strahov Monastery along the paths toward Prague's own miniature version of the Eiffel Tower. You'll find yourself in a hilltop park, laced with footpaths, with several buildings clustered together near the tower—just keep going gradually upward until you reach the tower's base. The tower and its breathtaking view, the mirror maze (*bludiště*) in a small structure near the tower's base, and the seemingly abandoned svatý Vavřinec (St. Lawrence) church are beautifully peaceful and well worth an afternoon's wandering. You can also walk up from Karmelitská ulice or Újezd down in the Lesser Quarter or ride the funicular railway from U lanové dráhy ulice, off Újezd. Regular public-transportation tickets are valid. For the descent, take the funicular or meander on foot down through the stations of the cross on the pathways leading back to the Lesser Quarter.

Pražský Hrad (Prague Castle)

*Numbers in the text correspond to numbers in the margin and on the
Prague Castle (Pražský hrad) map.*

Despite its monolithic presence, the Prague Castle is a collection of buildings dating from the 10th to the 20th century, all linked by internal
courtyards. The most important structures are **Chrám svatého Víta** ㊾,
clearly visible soaring above the castle walls, and the **Královský palác** ㊾,
the official residence of kings and presidents and still the center of political power in the Czech Republic. The castle is compact and easy to
navigate. Be forewarned: in summer, Chrám svatého Víta and Zlatá
ulička take the brunt of the heavy sightseeing traffic, although all of
the castle is hugely popular.

TIMING

The castle is at its mysterious best in early morning and late evening,
and it is incomparable when it snows. The cathedral deserves an hour,
as does the Královský palác, while you can easily spend an entire day
taking in the museums, the views of the city, and the hidden nooks of
the castle. Remember that some sights, such as the Lobkovický palác
and the National Gallery branch at Klášter svatého Jiří, are not open
on Monday.

Sights to See

㊿ **Bazilika svatého Jiří** (St. George's Basilica). This church was originally
built in the 10th century by Prince Vratislav I, the father of Prince (and
St.) Wenceslas. It was dedicated to St. George (of dragon fame), who
it was believed would be more agreeable to the still largely pagan people. The outside was remodeled during early Baroque times, although
the striking rusty red color is in keeping with the look of the Romanesque
edifice. The interior looks more or less as it did in the 12th century and
is the best-preserved Romanesque relic in the country. The effect is at once
barnlike and peaceful, the warm golden yellow of the stone walls and the
small arched windows exuding a sense of enduring harmony. The house-
shape painted tomb at the front of the church holds the remains of the
founder, Vratislav I. Up the steps, in a chapel to the right, is the tomb Peter
Parler designed for St. Ludmila, the grandmother of St. Wenceslas. ⊠ *Nám.
U sv. Jiří.* ✉ *For admission information, see Informační středisko, below.*
☼ *Apr.–Oct., daily 9–5; Nov.–Mar., daily 9–4.*

★ ㊾ **Chrám svatého Víta** (St. Vitus's Cathedral). With its graceful, soaring
towers, this Gothic cathedral—among the most beautiful in Europe—
is the spiritual heart not only of Prague Castle, but of the entire country. It has a long and complicated history, beginning in the 10th century
and continuing to its completion in 1929. If you want to hear its history in depth, English-speaking guided tours of the cathedral and the
Královský palác (☞ *below*) can be arranged at the information office
across from the cathedral entrance.

Once you enter the cathedral, pause to take in the vast but delicate beauty
of the Gothic and neo-Gothic interior glowing in the colorful light that
filters through the startlingly brilliant stained-glass windows. This
western third of the structure, including the facade and the two towers you can see from outside, was not completed until 1929, following the initiative of the Union for the Completion of the Cathedral, set
up in the last days of the 19th century. Don't let the neo-Gothic illu-
sion keep you from examining this new section. The six stained-glass
windows to your left and right and the large rose window behind are
modern masterpieces. Take a good look at the third window up on the
left. The familiar Art Nouveau flamboyance, depicting the blessing of
Sts. Cyril and Methodius (9th-century missionaries to the Slavs and

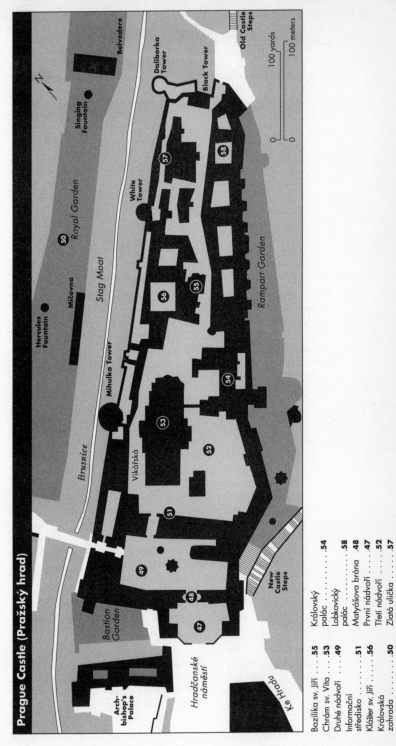

Prague Castle (Pražský hrad)

37

Archbishop's Palace

Belvedere

Hercules Fountain

Royal Garden

Singing Fountain

Míčovna

Stag Moat

Brusnice

Mihulka Tower

White Tower

Daliborka Tower

Black Tower

Old Castle Steps

Vikářská

Rampart Garden

Bastion Garden

Hradčanské náměstí

Ke Hradu

New Castle Steps

0 · · · 100 yards
0 · · · 100 meters

N

47 · 48 · 49 · 50 · 51 · 52 · 53 · 54 · 55 · 56 · 57 · 58

Bazilika sv. Jiří **55**
Chrám sv. Víta **53**
Druhé nádvoří . . . **49**
Informační
středisko **51**
Klášter sv. Jiří **56**
Královská
zahrada **50**

Královský
palác **54**
Lobkovický
palác **58**
Matyášova brána . . **48**
První nádvoří **47**
Třetí nádvoří **52**
Zlatá ulička **57**

creators of the Cyrillic alphabet), is the work of the Czech father of the style, Alfons Mucha. He achieved the subtle coloring by painting rather than staining the glass.

If you walk halfway up the right-hand aisle, you will find the **Svatováclavská kaple** (Chapel of St. Wenceslas). With a tomb holding the saint's remains, walls covered in semi-precious stones, and paintings depicting the life of Wenceslas, this square chapel is the ancient heart of the cathedral. Stylistically, it represents a high point of the dense, richly decorated though rather gloomy Gothic favored by Charles IV and his successors. Wenceslas (the "good king" of Christmas-carol fame) was a determined Christian in an era of widespread paganism. Around 925, as prince of Bohemia, he founded a rotunda church dedicated to St. Vitus on this site. But the prince's brother, Boleslav, was impatient to take power, and he ambushed Wenceslas in 929 (or 935 according to some experts) near a church at Stará Boleslav, northeast of Prague. Wenceslas was originally buried in that church, but his grave produced so many miracles that he rapidly became a symbol of piety for the common people, something that greatly irritated the new Prince Boleslav. Boleslav was finally forced to honor his brother by reburying the body in the St. Vitus Rotunda. Shortly afterward, Wenceslas was canonized.

The rotunda was replaced by a Romanesque basilica in the late 11th century. Work was begun on the existing building in 1344. For the first few years the chief architect was the Frenchman Mathias d'Arras, but after his death in 1352 the work was continued by the 22-year-old German architect Peter Parler, who went on to build the Charles Bridge and many other Prague treasures.

The small door in the back of the chapel leads to the **Korunní komora** (Crown Chamber), the repository of the Bohemian crown jewels. It remains locked with seven keys held by seven different people and is definitely not open to the public.

A little beyond the Chapel of St. Wenceslas on the same side, stairs lead down to the underground **royal crypt,** interesting primarily for the information it provides about the cathedral's history. As you descend the stairs, you'll see parts of the old Romanesque basilica and portions of the foundations of the rotunda. Moving around into the second room, you'll find a rather eclectic group of royal remains ensconced in new sarcophagi dating from the 1930s. In the center is Charles IV, who died in 1378. Rudolf II, patron of Renaissance Prague, is entombed at the rear in the original tin coffin. To his right is Maria Amalia, the only child of Empress Maria Theresa to reside in Prague. Ascending the wooden steps back into the cathedral, you'll come to the white-marble **Kralovské mausoleum** (Royal Mausoleum), atop which lie stone statues of the first two Hapsburg kings to rule in Bohemia, Ferdinand I and Maximilian II, and of Ferdinand's consort, Anne Jagiello.

The cathedral's **Kralovské oratorium** (Royal Oratory) was used by the kings and their families when attending mass. Built in 1493, the work is a perfect example of late Gothic, laced on the outside with a stone network of gnarled branches very similar in pattern to the ceiling vaulting in the Královský palác (☞ *below*). The oratory is connected to the palace by an elevated covered walkway, which you can see from outside.

A few more steps toward the east end, you can't fail to catch sight of the ornate silver **sarcophagus of St. John of Nepomuk.** According to legend, when Nepomuk's body was exhumed in 1721 to be reinterred, the tongue was found to be still intact and pumping with blood. This strange tale served a highly political purpose. The Catholic Church and the Hapsburgs were seeking a new folk hero to replace the Protestant forerunner Jan Hus, whom they despised. The 14th-century priest Nepomuk, killed during a power struggle with King Václav IV, was sainted and reburied a few years later with great ceremony in the 3,700-pound silver tomb, replete with angels and cherubim; the tongue was enshrined in its own reliquary.

The eight chapels around the back of the cathedral are the work of the original architect, Mathias d'Arras. A number of old tombstones, including some badly worn grave markers of medieval royalty, can be seen within, amid furnishings from later periods. Opposite the wooden relief, depicting the looting of the cathedral by Protestants in 1619, is the **Valdštejnská kaple** (Wallenstein Chapel). Since the last century, the chapel has housed the Gothic tombstones of its two architects, d'Arras and Peter Parler, who died in 1352 and 1399, respectively. If you look up to the balcony, you can just make out the busts of these two men, designed by Parler's workshop. The other busts around the triforium depict royalty and other VIPs of the time.

The Hussite wars in the 15th century put an end to the first phase of the cathedral's construction. During the short era of illusory peace before the Thirty Years' War, the massive south tower was completed, but lack of money quashed any idea of finishing the building, and the cathedral was closed by a wall built across from the Chapel of St. Wenceslas. Not until the 20th century was the western side of the cathedral, with its two towers, completed in the spirit of Parler's conception.

A key element of the cathedral's teeming, rich exterior decoration is the **Last Judgment mosaic** above the ceremonial entrance, called the Golden Portal, on the south side. The use of mosaic is quite rare in countries north of the Alps; this work, dating from the 1370s, is made of 1 million glass and stone chunks. It's currently undergoing an extensive, desperately needed restoration led by the Getty Conservation Institute. The central field shows Christ in glory, adored by Charles IV and his consort, Elizabeth of Pomerania, as well as several saints; the risen dead and attendant angels are on the left; and on the right the flames of Hell lick around the figure of Satan. ⊠ *St. Vitus's Cathedral.* 🖼 *Western section free; chapels, crypt, and tower accessible with castle-wide ticket (see Informační středisko, below).* ☉ *Apr.–Oct., daily 9–5; Nov.–Mar., daily 9–4.*

🈺 **Druhé nádvoří** (Second Courtyard). Empress Maria Theresa's court architect, Nicolò Pacassi, received the imperial approval to remake the castle in the 1760s, as it was badly damaged by Prussian shelling during the Seven Years' War in 1757. The Second Courtyard was the main victim of Pacassi's attempts at imparting classical grandeur to what had been a picturesque collection of Gothic and Renaissance styles. Except for the view of the spires of St. Vitus's Cathedral, the exterior courtyard offers little for the eye to feast upon. This courtyard also houses the rather gaudy **Kaple svatého Kříže** (Chapel of the Holy Cross), with decorations from the 18th and 19th centuries.

Built in the late 16th and early 17th century, the Second Courtyard was originally part of a reconstruction program commissioned by Rudolf II, under whom Prague enjoyed a period of unparalleled cultural development. Once the Prague court was established, the emperor gathered around him some of the world's best craftsmen, artists, and scientists, including the brilliant astronomers Johannes Kepler and Tycho Brahe.

Rudolf also amassed a large and famed collection of fine and decorative art, scientific instruments, philosophic and alchemical books, natural wonders, coins, and everything else under the sun. The bulk of the collection was looted by the Swedes during the Thirty Years' War, removed to Vienna when the imperial capital returned there after Rudolf's death, or auctioned off during the 18th century. Artworks that survived the turmoil, for the most part acquired after Rudolf's time, are displayed in the **Obrazárna** (Picture Gallery), on the left side of the courtyard as you face St. Vitus's. In rooms elegantly redecorated by the official castle architect, Bořek Šípek, there are good Renaissance, Mannerist, and Baroque paintings that hint at the luxurious tastes of Rudolf's court. Across the passageway by the gallery entrance is the **Císařská konírna** (Imperial Stable), where temporary exhibitions are held. The passageway forms the northern entrance to the castle and leads out over a luxurious ravine known as the **Jelení příkop** (Stag Moat), which can be entered (from April through October) either here or at the lower end via the metal catwalk off Chotkova ulice. ⊠ *Obrazárna: Second Courtyard.* 🎟 *100 Kč.* ☉ *Daily 10–6.*

🟢 **Informační středisko** (Castle Information Office). This is the place to come for entrance tickets, guided tours, headphones for listening to recorded tours in English, tickets to cultural events held at the castle, and money changing. Tickets are valid for three consecutive days and allow admission to the older parts of St. Vitus's Cathedral, Královský palác, St. George's Basilica (but not the adjacent National Gallery exhibition), and a medieval bastion called Mihulka with an exhibition on alchemy. These sights may be visited only with the three-day ticket; the 20th-century section of the cathedral is free. Buy tickets to other castle sights at the door. If you just want to walk through the castle grounds, note that the gates close at midnight from April through October and at 11 PM the rest of the year, while the gardens are open from April through October only. ⊠ *Třetí nádvoří, across from the entrance to St. Vitus's Cathedral,* ☎ *02/2437–3368.* 🎟 *3-day tickets 120 Kč; English-language guided tours 300 Kč for up to 5 people, 60 Kč per additional person (advance booking recommended); grounds and gardens free.* ☉ *Apr.–Oct., daily 9–5; Nov.–Mar., daily 9–4.*

🟢 **Klášter svatého Jiří** (St. George's Convent). The first convent in Bohemia was founded here in 973 next to the even older St. George's Basilica (☞ *above*). The National Gallery collections of Czech Mannerist and Baroque art are housed here. The highlights include the voluptuous work of Rudolf II's court painters, the giant Baroque religious statuary, and some fine paintings by Karel Škréta and Petr Brandl. At press time the National Gallery's medieval Czech art collection was set to move from here to another monastery, the Klášter svaté Anežky České in the Old Town (☞ *above*), in November 2000. It's worth seeking out, for this fascinating trove contains some of the most memorable artworks made in northern Europe during the high- and late-Gothic periods, by influential Bohemian painters such as Master Theodoric and the Master of the Třeboň Altar. ⊠ *Nám. U sv. Jiří,* ☎ *02/5732–0536.* 🎟 *90 Kč.* ☉ *Tues.–Sun. 10–6.*

🟢 **Královská zahrada** (Royal Garden). This peaceful swath of greenery affords an unusually lovely view of St. Vitus's Cathedral and the castle's walls and bastions. Originally laid out in the 16th century, it endured devastation in war, neglect in times of peace, and many redesigns, reaching its present parklike form early this century. Luckily, its Renaissance treasures survive. One of these is the long, narrow **Míčovna** (Ball Game Hall), built by Bonifaz Wohlmut in 1568, its garden front completely covered by a dense tangle of allegorical sgraffiti.

The **Královský letohrádek** (Royal Summer Palace, also known as the Belvedere), at the garden's eastern end, deserves its usual description as one of the most beautiful Renaissance structures north of the Alps. Italian architects began it; Wohlmut finished it off in the 1560s with a copper roof like an upturned boat's keel riding above the graceful arcades of the ground floor. During the 18th and 19th centuries, military engineers tested artillery in the interior, which had already lost its rich furnishings to Swedish soldiers during their siege of the city in 1648. The Renaissance-style *giardinetto* (little garden) adjoining the summer palace centers on another masterwork, the Italian-designed, Czech-cast Singing Fountain, which resonates to the sound of falling water. ⊠ *Garden entrances from U Prašného mostu ul. and Mariánské hradby ul. near Chotkovy Park.* 🕮 *Free.* ☉ *Apr.–Oct., daily 10–5:45.*

54 **Královský palác** (Royal Palace). The palace is an accumulation of the styles and add-ons of many centuries. The best way to grasp its size is from within the **Vladislavský sál** (Vladislav Hall), the largest secular Gothic interior space in Central Europe. The enormous hall was completed in 1493 by Benedikt Ried, who was to late–Bohemian Gothic what Peter Parler was to the earlier version. The room imparts a sense of space and light, softened by the sensuous lines of the vaulted ceilings and brought to a dignified close by the simple oblong form of the early Renaissance windows. In its heyday, the hall was the site of jousting tournaments, festive markets, banquets, and coronations. In more recent times, it has been used to inaugurate presidents, from the Communist Klement Gottwald in 1948 to Václav Havel in 1989, 1993, and 1998.

From the front of the hall, turn right into the rooms of the **Česká kancelář** (Bohemian Chancellery). This wing was built by the same Benedikt Ried only 10 years after the hall was completed, but it shows a much stronger Renaissance influence. Pass through the Renaissance portal into the last chamber of the chancellery. This room was the site of the second defenestration of Prague, in 1618, an event that marked the beginning of the Bohemian rebellion and, ultimately, the Thirty Years' War. This peculiarly Bohemian method of expressing protest (throwing someone out a window) had first been used in 1419 in the New Town Hall, during the lead-up to the Hussite wars. Two hundred years later the same conflict was reexpressed in terms of Hapsburg-backed Catholics versus Bohemian Protestants. Rudolf II had reached an uneasy agreement with the Bohemian nobles, allowing them religious freedom in exchange for financial support. But his next-but-one successor, Ferdinand II, was a rabid opponent of Protestantism and disregarded Rudolf's tolerant "Letter of Majesty." Enraged, the Protestant nobles stormed the castle and chancellery and threw two Catholic officials and their secretary, for good measure, out the window. Legend has it they landed on a mound of horse dung and escaped unharmed, an event the Jesuits interpreted as a miracle. The square window in question is on the left as you enter the room.

At the back of the Vladislav Hall, a staircase leads up to a gallery of the **Kaple všech svatých** (All Saints' Chapel). Little remains of Peter Parler's original work, but the church contains some fine works of art. The large room to the left of the staircase is the **Stará sněmovna** (council chamber), where the Bohemian nobles met with the king in a kind of prototype parliament. The descent from Vladislav Hall toward what remains of the **Romanský palác** (Romanesque Palace) is by way of a wide, shallow set of steps. This **Jezdecké schody** (Riders' Staircase) was the entranceway for knights who came for the jousting tournaments. ⊠ *Royal Palace, Třetí nádvoří.* 🕮 *For admission information, see Informační středisko, above.* ☉ *Apr.–Oct., daily 9–5; Nov.–Mar., daily 9–4.*

⑤⑧ Lobkovický palác (Lobkowicz Palace). From the beginning of the 17th century until the 1940s, this building was the residence of the powerful Catholic Lobkowicz family. It was supposedly to this house that the two defenestrated officials escaped after landing on the dung hill in 1618. During the 1970s the building was restored to its early Baroque appearance and now houses the National Museum's permanent exhibition on Czech history. If you want to get a chronological understanding of Czech history from the beginnings of the Great Moravian Empire in the 9th century to the Czech national uprising in 1848, this is the place. Copies of the crown jewels are on display here, but it is the rich collection of illuminated Bibles, old musical instruments, coins, weapons, royal decrees, paintings, and statues that makes the museum well worth visiting. Detailed information on the exhibits is available in English. ⊠ *Jiřská ul.* ☎ *40 Kč.* ☉ *Tues.–Sun. 9–5.*

㊽ Matyášova brána (Matthias Gate). Built in 1614, the stone gate once stood alone in front of the moats and bridges that surrounded the castle. Under the Hapsburgs, the gate survived by being grafted as a relief onto the palace building. As you go through it, notice the ceremonial white-marble entrance halls on either side that lead up to President Václav Havel's reception rooms (which are only rarely open to the public).

㊼ První nádvoří (First Courtyard). The main entrance to Prague Castle from Hradčanské náměstí is a little disappointing. Going through the wrought-iron gate, guarded at ground level by Czech soldiers and from above by the ferocious *Battling Titans* (a copy of Ignaz Platzer's original 18th-century work), you'll enter this courtyard, built on the site of old moats and gates that once separated the castle from the surrounding buildings and thus protected the vulnerable western flank. The courtyard is one of the more recent additions to the castle, designed by Maria Theresa's court architect, Nicolò Pacassi, in the 1760s. Today it forms part of the presidential office complex. Pacassi's reconstruction was intended to unify the eclectic collection of buildings that made up the castle, but the effect of his work is somewhat flat.

㊾ Třetí nádvoří (Third Courtyard). The contrast between the cool, dark interior of St. Vitus's Cathedral (☞ *above*) and the brightly colored Pacassi facades of the Third Courtyard just outside is startling. The courtyard's clean lines are the work of Slovenian architect Jože Plečnik in the 1930s, but the modern look is a deception. Plečnik's paving was intended to cover an underground world of house foundations, streets, and walls dating from the 9th through 12th centuries and rediscovered when the cathedral was completed. (You can see a few archways through a grating in a wall of the cathedral.) Plečnik added a few eclectic features to catch the eye: a granite obelisk to commemorate the fallen of the First World War, a black-marble pedestal for the Gothic statue of St. George (a copy of the National Gallery's original statue), the inconspicuous entrance to his Bull Staircase leading down to the south garden, and the peculiar golden ball topping the eagle fountain near the eastern end of the courtyard.

㊹ Zlatá ulička (Golden Lane). An enchanting collection of tiny, ancient, brightly colored houses crouches under the fortification wall, looking remarkably like a set for *Snow White and the Seven Dwarfs*. Legend has it that these were the lodgings of the international group of alchemists whom Rudolf II brought to the court to produce gold. The truth is a little less romantic: the houses were built during the 16th century for the castle guards, who supplemented their income by practicing various crafts outside the jurisdiction of the powerful guilds. By the early 20th century, Golden Lane had become the home of poor artists and writers. Franz Kafka, who lived at No. 22 in 1916 and 1917, described the house on first sight as "so small, so dirty, impossible to live in and lacking everything necessary." But he soon came to love the place. As he wrote to his fiancée: "Life here is something special . . . to close out the world not just by shutting the door to a room or apartment but to the whole house, to step out into the snow of the silent lane." The lane now houses tiny stores selling books, music, and crafts.

Within the walls above Golden Lane, there is a timber-roof **corridor** lined with replica suits of armor and weapons (some of it for sale), mock torture chambers, and the like. At the far end of the lane is the private **Muzeum hraček** (Toy Museum). The building once belonged to a high royal official called the Supreme Burgrave. ⊠ *Corridor: enter between No. 23 and No. 24. Toy Museum: enter from Jiřská ul.* 🎫 *Corridor free, Toy Museum 40 Kč.* ☉ *Corridor Tues.–Sun. 10–6, Mon. 1–6; Toy Museum daily 9:30–5:30.*

Nové Město (New Town) and Vyšehrad

To this day, Charles IV's building projects are tightly woven into the daily lives of Praguers. His most extensive scheme, the New Town, is still such a lively, vibrant area you may hardly realize that its streets, Gothic churches, and squares were planned as far back as 1348. With Prague fast outstripping its Old Town parameters, Charles IV extended the city's fortifications. A high wall surrounded the newly developed 2½ square km (1½ square mi) area south and east of the Old Town, tripling the walled territory on the Vltava's right bank. The wall extended south to link with the fortifications of the citadel called Vyšehrad. In the mid 19th century, new building in the New Town boomed in a welter of Romantic and neo-Renaissance styles, particularly on Wenceslas Square and avenues such as Vodičkova, Na Poříčí, and Spálená. One of the most important structures was the Národní divadlo (National Theater), meant to symbolize in stone the revival of the Czechs' history, language, and sense of national pride. Both preceding and following Czechoslovak independence in 1918, modernist architecture entered the mix, particularly on the outer fringes of the Old Town and in the New Town. One of modernism's most unexpected products was Cubist architecture, a form unique to Prague, which produced four notable examples at the foot of ancient Vyšehrad.

A Good Walk

Václavské náměstí ㊱, marked by the **Statue of St. Wenceslas** ㊲, is a long, gently sloping boulevard rather than a square in the usual sense. It is bounded at the top (the southern end) by the **Národní muzeum** ㊳ and at the bottom by the pedestrian shopping areas of Národní třída and Na Příkopě. Today Václavské náměstí has Prague's liveliest street scene. Don't miss the dense maze of arcades tucked away from the street in buildings that line both sides. You'll find an odd assortment of cafés, shops, ice cream parlors, and movie houses, all seemingly unfazed by the passage of time. One eye-catching building on the square is the Hotel Europa, at No. 25, a riot of Art Nouveau that recalls the glamorous world of turn-of-the-20th-century Prague. Work by the Czech artist whose name is synonymous with Art Nouveau is on show just a block off the square, via Jindřišská, at the **Mucha Museum.**

From the foot of square, head down 28. řijna to Jungmannovo náměstí, a small square named for the linguist and patriot Josef Jungmann (1773–1847). In the courtyard off the square at No. 18, have a look at the Kostel Panny Marie Sněžné (Church of the Virgin Mary of the Snows). Building ceased during the Hussite wars, leaving a very high, foreshortened church that never grew into the monumental structure planned by Charles IV. Beyond it lies a quiet sanctuary: the walled

Františkánská zahrada (Franciscan Gardens). A busy shopping street, Národní třída, extends from Jungmannovo náměstí about ¾ km (½ mi) to the river and the **Národní divadlo** ㊳. From the theater, follow the embankment, Masarykovo nábřeží, south toward Vyšehrad. Note the Art Nouveau architecture of No. 32, the amazingly eclectic design by Kamil Hilbert at No. 26, and the tile-decorated Hlahol building at No. 16. Opposite, on a narrow island, is a 19th century, yellow-and-white ballroom-restaurant, Žofín.

Straddling an arm of the river at Myslíkova ulice are the modern Galerie Mánes (1928–1930) and its attendant 15th-century water tower, where, from a lookout on the sixth floor, Communist-era secret police used to observe Václav Havel's apartment at Rašínovo nábřeží 78. This building, still part-owned by the president, and the adjoining **Tančící dům** are on the far side of a square named Jiráskovo náměstí after the historical novelist Alois Jirásek. From this square, Resslova ulice leads uphill four blocks to a much larger, parklike square, **Karlovo náměstí** ㊵.

If you have the energy to continue on toward Vyšehrad, a convenient place to rejoin the riverfront is Palackého náměstí via Na Moráni street at the southern end of Karlovo náměstí. The square has a (melo)dramatic monument to the 19th-century historian František Palacký, "awakener of the nation," and the view from here of the Benedictine Klášter Emauzy is lovely. The houses grow less attractive south of here, so you may wish to hop a tram (No. 3, 16, or 17 at the stop on Rašínovo nábřeží) and ride one stop to Výtoň, at the base of the **Vyšehrad** ㊶ citadel. Walk under the railroad bridge on Rašínovo nábřeží to find the closest of four nearby **Cubist buildings.** Another lies just a minute's walk farther along the embankment; two more are on Neklanova, a couple of minutes' walk "inland" on Vnislavova. To get up to the fortress, make a hard left onto Vratislavova (the street right before Neklanova), an ancient road that runs tortuously up into the heart of Vyšehrad.

It's about 2¼ km (1½ mi) between Národní divadlo and Vyšehrad. Note that Tram No. 17 travels the length of the embankment, if you'd like to make a quicker trip between the two points.

TIMING

You might want to divide the walk into two parts, first taking in the busy New Town between Václavské náměstí and Karlovo náměstí, then doing Vyšehrad and the Cubist houses as a side trip. A leisurely stroll from the Národní divadlo to Vyšehrad may easily absorb two hours, as may an exploration of Karlovo náměstí and the Klášter Emauzy. Vyšehrad is open every day, year-round, and the views are stunning on a clear day or evening, but keep in mind that there is little shade along the river walk on hot afternoons.

Sights to See

Cubist buildings. Born of zealous modernism, Prague's Cubist architecture followed a great Czech tradition in that it fully embraced new ideas while adapting them to existing artistic and social contexts. Between 1912 and 1914, Josef Chochol (1880–1956) designed several of the city's dozen or so Cubist projects. His apartment house **Neklanova 30**, on the corner of Neklanova and Přemyslova, is a masterpiece in dingy concrete. The pyramidal, kaleidoscopic window mouldings and roof cornices are completely novel while making an expressive link to Baroque forms; the faceted corner balcony column elegantly alludes to Gothic forerunners. On the same street, at **Neklanova 2**, is another apartment house attributed to Chochol; like the building at Neklanova 30, it uses pyramidal shapes and the suggestion of Gothic columns.

Chochol's **villa**, on the embankment at Libušina 3, has an undulating effect created by smoothly articulated forms. The wall and gate around the back of the house use triangular moldings and metal grating to create an effect of controlled energy. The **three-family house**, about 100 yards away from the villa at Rašínovo nábřeží 6–10, was completed slightly earlier, when Chochol's Cubist style was still developing. Here, the design is touched with Baroque and neoclassical influence, with a mansard roof and end gables.

40 **Karlovo náměstí** (Charles Square). This square began life as a cattle market, a function chosen by Charles IV when he established the New Town in 1348. The horse market (now Wenceslas Square) quickly overtook it as a livestock-trading center, and an untidy collection of shacks accumulated here until the mid-1800s, when it became a green park named for its patron.

Novoměstská radnice (New Town Hall), at the northern edge of the square, has a late-Gothic tower similar to that of the Old Town Hall and three tall Renaissance gables. The first defenestration of Prague occurred here on July 30, 1419, when a mob of townspeople, followers of the martyred religious reformer Jan Hus, hurled Catholic town councillors out the windows. Historical exhibitions and contemporary art shows are held here regularly (admission prices vary), and you can climb the tower for a view of the New Town. ⊠ *Karlovo nám. at Vodičkova, Prague 2.* ▤ *Tower 20 Kč.* ☉ *Tower June–Sept., Tues.– Sun. 10–6.*

Just south of the square lies another of Charles IV's gifts to the city, the Benedictine **Klášter Emauzy** (Emmaus Monastery). It is often called Na Slovanech, literally "At the Slavs'," in reference to its purpose when established in 1347: the emperor invited Croatian monks here to celebrate mass in Old Slavonic and thus cultivate religion among the Slavs in a city largely controlled by Germans. A faded but substantially complete cycle of biblical scenes by Charles's court artists lines the four cloister walls. The frescoes, and especially the abbey church, suffered heavy damage from a February 14, 1945, raid by Allied bombers that may have mistaken Prague for Dresden, 121 km (75 mi) away. The church lost its spires, and the interior remains a blackened shell. Some years after the war, two curving concrete "spires" were set atop the church. ⊠ *Vyšehradská 49 (cloister entrance on the left at the rear of the church).* ▤ *10 Kč.* ☉ *Weekdays 8–6 or earlier depending on daylight.*

Mucha Museum. For decades it was almost impossible to find an Alfons Mucha original in the homeland of this famous Czech artist, until, in 1998, this private museum opened with nearly 100 works from his long career. What you'd expect to see is here—the theater posters of actress Sarah Bernhardt; the magazine covers; the luscious, sinuous Art Nouveau designs—and there are also paintings, photographs taken in Mucha's studio (one shows Paul Gauguin playing the piano in his underwear), and even Czechoslovak banknotes designed by the artist. ⊠ *Panská 7 (1 block off Wenceslas Square, across from the Palace Hotel),* ☎ *02/628–4162.* ▤ *120 Kč.* ☉ *Daily 10–6.*

39 **Národní divadlo** (National Theater). The idea for a Czech national theater began during the revolutionary decade of the 1840s. In a telling display of national pride, donations to fund the plan poured in from all over the country, from people of every socioeconomic stratum. The cornerstone was laid in 1868, and the "National Theater generation" who built the neo-Renaissance structure became the architectural and artistic establishment for decades to come. Its designer, Josef Zítek (1832–1909), was the leading neo-Renaissance architect in Bohemia. The nearly finished interior was gutted by a fire in 1881, and Zítek's onetime student Josef Schulz (1840–1917) saw the reconstruction through to completion two years later. Statues representing Drama and Opera rise above the riverfront side entrances; two gigantic chariots flank figures of Apollo and the nine Muses above the main facade. The performance space itself is filled with gilding, voluptuous plaster figures and plush upholstery. Next door is the modern (1970s–1980s) Nová scéna (New Stage), where the popular Magic Lantern black-light shows are staged. The Národní divadlo is one of the best places to see a performance; ticket prices start as low as 30 Kč. ⊠ *Národní třída 2,* ☎ *02/2490–1448.*

🕸 **Národní muzeum** (National Museum). This imposing structure, designed by Prague architect Josef Schulz and built between 1885 and 1890, does not come into its own until it is bathed in nighttime lighting. By day the grandiose edifice seems an inappropriate venue for a musty collection of stones and bones, minerals, and coins. This museum is only for dedicated fans of the genre. ⊠ *Václavské nám. 68,* ☎ *02/2449–7111.* 🎫 *70 Kč.* ☉ *May–Sept., daily 10–6; Oct.–Apr., daily 9–5; closed 1st Tues. of month.*

🕸 **Statue of St. Wenceslas.** Josef Václav Myslbek's huge equestrian grouping of St. Wenceslas with other Czech patron saints around him is a traditional meeting place at times of great national peril or rejoicing. In 1939, Praguers gathered to oppose Hitler's takeover of Bohemia and Moravia. It was here also, in 1969, that the student Jan Palach set himself on fire to protest the bloody invasion of his country by the Soviet Union and other Warsaw Pact countries in August of the previous year. The invasion ended the "Prague Spring," a cultural and political movement emphasizing free expression, which was supported by Alexander Dubček, the popular leader at the time. Although Dubček never intended to dismantle Communist authority completely, his political and economic reforms proved too daring for fellow comrades in the rest of Eastern Europe. In the months following the invasion, conservatives loyal to the Soviet Union were installed in all influential positions. The subsequent two decades were a period of cultural stagnation. Hundreds of thousands of Czechs and Slovaks left the country, a few became dissidents, and many more resigned themselves to lives of minimal expectations and small pleasures. ⊠ *Václavské náměstí.*

Tančící dům (Dancing House). This whimsical building was partnered into life in 1996 by architect Frank Gehry (of Guggenheim Museum in Bilbao fame) and his Croatian-Czech collaborator Vlado Milunic. A wasp-waisted glass-and-steel tower sways into the main structure as though they were a couple on the dance floor—a "Fred and Ginger" effect that gave the wacky, yet somehow appropriate, building its nickname. A French restaurant occupies the top floors (☞ *La Perle de Prague in* Dining, *below*), and there is a café at street level. ⊠ *Rašínovo nábř. 80.*

🕸 **Václavské náměstí** (Wenceslas Square). You may recognize this spot from your television set, for it was here that some 500,000 students and citizens gathered in the heady days of November 1989 to protest the policies of the former Communist regime. The government capitulated after a week of demonstrations, without a shot fired or the loss of a single life, bringing to power the first democratic government in 40 years (under playwright-president Václav Havel). Today this peaceful transfer of power is half-ironically referred to as the "Velvet" or "Gentle" Revolution (*něžná revoluce*). It was only fitting that the 1989 revolution should take place on Wenceslas Square: throughout much of Czech history, the square has served as the focal point for popular discontent. The long "square" was first laid out by Charles IV in 1348 as a horse market at the center of the New Town.

At No. 25, the **Hotel Europa** is an Art Nouveau gem, with elegant stained glass and mosaics in the café and restaurant. The terrace is an excellent spot for people-watching.

㊶ Vyšehrad. Bedřich Smetana's symphonic poem *Vyšehrad* opens with four bardic harp chords that seem to echo the legends surrounding this ancient fortress. Today, the flat-top bluff standing over the right bank of the Vltava is a green, tree-dotted expanse showing few signs that splendid medieval monuments once made it a landmark to rival Prague Castle. With its neo-Gothic spires, **Kapitulní kostel svatých Petra a Pavla** (Chapter Church of Sts. Peter and Paul) dominates the plateau as it has since the 11th century. Next to the church lies the burial ground of the nation's revered cultural figures. Most of the buildings still standing are from the 19th century, but scattered among them are a few older structures and some foundation stones of the medieval palaces. Surrounding the ruins are gargantuan, excellently preserved brick fortifications built from the 17th to the mid 19th century; their broad tops allow strollers to take in sweeping vistas up- and downriver.

The historical father of Vyšehrad, the "High Castle," is Vratislav II (ruled 1061–1092), a Přemyslid duke who became first king of Bohemia. He made the fortified hilltop his capital, but, under subsequent rulers, it fell into disuse until the 14th century, when Charles IV transformed the site into an ensemble of palaces, the Gothicized main church, battlements, and a massive gatehouse called *Špička*, whose scant remains are on V pevnosti ulice. By the 17th century, royalty had long since departed, and most of the structures they built were crumbling. Vyšehrad was turned into a fortress.

Vyšehrad's place in the modern Czech imagination is largely thanks to the National Revivalists of the 19th century, particularly writer Alois Jirásek (1851–1930), who mined medieval chronicles for legends and facts to glorify the early Czechs. In his rendition, Vyšehrad was the court of the prophetess-ruler Libuše, who had a vision of her husband-to-be, the ploughman Přemysl—father of the Přemyslid line—and of "a city whose glory shall reach the heavens" called Praha. (In truth, the Czechs first came to Vyšehrad around the beginning of the 900s, slightly later than the building of Prague Castle.)

A concrete result of the National Revival was the establishment of the **Hřbitov** (cemetery) in the 1860s—it peopled the fortress with the remains of luminaries from the arts and sciences. The grave of Smetana faces the Slavín, a mausoleum for more than 50 honored men and women including Alfons Mucha, sculptor Jan Štursa, inventor František Křižík, and the opera diva Ema Destinnová. All are guarded by a winged genius who hovers above the inscription AČ ZEMŘELI, JEŠTĚ MLUVÍ ("Although they have died, they yet speak"). Antonín Dvořák (1841–1904) rests in the arcade along the north wall of the cemetery. Among the many writers buried here are Jan Neruda, Božena Němcová, Karel Čapek, and the Romantic poet Karel Hynek Mácha, whose grave was visited by students on their momentous November 17, 1989, protest march.

Traces of the citadel's distant past do remain. A heavily restored **Romanesque rotunda,** built by Vratislav II, stands on the east side of the compound. Foundations and a few embossed floor tiles from the late-10th-century **Basilika svatého Vavřince** (St. Lawrence Basilica) are in a structure on Soběslavova street (if it is locked, you can ask for the key at the refreshment stand just to the left of the basilica entrance; admission is 5 Kč). Part of the medieval fortifications stand next to the surprisingly confined foundation mounds of a medieval palace overlooking a ruined watchtower called Libuše's Bath. A nearby plot of grass hosts a statue of Libuše and her consort Přemysl, one of four large sculpted images of couples from Czech legend by J. V. Myslbek (1848–1922), the sculptor of the St. Wenceslas monument.

The military history of the fortress and the city is covered in a small exposition inside the **Cihelná brána** (Brick Gate). The gate is also the entrance to the casemates—a long, dark passageway within the walls that ends at a dank hall used to store several original, pollution-scarred Charles Bridge sculptures. A guided tour into the casemates and the statue storage room starts at the military history exhibit. ⊠ *Entrances on Vratislavova ul. and V pevnosti ul. Information center: V pevnosti. ⊠ Casemates tour 20 Kč, military exhibit 10 Kč. ☉ Grounds daily. Casemates, military history exhibit, St. Lawrence Basilica Apr.–Oct., daily 9:30–5:30; Nov.–Mar., daily 9:30–4:30. Cemetery Apr.–Oct., daily 8–6; Nov.–Mar., daily 8–4. Metro: Vyšehrad.*

Vinohrady

From Riegrovy Park and its sweeping view of the city from above the National Museum, the eclectic apartment houses and villas of the elegant residential neighborhood called Vinohrady extend eastward and southward. The pastel-tint ranks of turn-of-the-20th-century apartment houses—many crumbling after years of neglect—are slowly but unstoppably being transformed into upscale flats, slick offices, eternally packed new restaurants, and a range of shops unthinkable only a half decade ago. Much of the development lies on or near Vinohradská, the main street, which extends from the top of Wenceslas Square to a belt of enormous cemeteries about 3 km (2 mi) eastward. Yet the flavor of daily life persists: smoky old pubs still ply their trade on the quiet side streets; the stately theater, Divadlo na Vinohradech, keeps putting on excellent shows as it has for decades; and on the squares and in the parks nearly everyone still practices Prague's favorite form of outdoor exercise—walking the dog.

㊷ Kostel Nejsvětějšího Srdce Páně (Church of the Most Sacred Heart). If you've had your fill of Romanesque, Gothic, and Baroque, take the metro to the Jiřího z Poděbrad station (Line A) for a look at a startling Art Deco edifice. Designed in 1927 by Slovenian architect Jože Plečnik (the same architect commissioned to update Prague Castle), the church resembles a luxury ocean liner more than a place of worship. The effect was conscious: during the 1920s and 1930s, the avant-garde imitated mammoth objects of modern technology. Plečnik used many modern elements on the inside. Notice the hanging speakers, seemingly designed to bring the word of God directly to the ears of each worshiper. You may be able to find someone at the back entrance of the church who will let you walk up the long ramp into the fascinating glass clock tower. ⊠ *Nám. Jiřího z Poděbrad. ☉ Daily 10–5.*

㊸ Nový židovský hřbitov (New Jewish Cemetery). Tens of thousands of Czechs find eternal rest in Vinohrady's cemeteries. In this, the newest of the city's half-dozen Jewish burial grounds, you'll find the modest **tombstone of Franz Kafka**, which seems grossly inadequate to Kafka's stature but oddly in proportion to his own modest ambitions. The cemetery is usually open, although guards sometimes inexplicably seal off the grounds. Men may be required to wear a yarmulke (you can buy one here). Turn right at the main cemetery gate and follow the wall for about 100 yards. Kafka's thin, white tombstone lies at the front of section 21. City maps may label the cemetery *Židovské hřbitovy.* ⊠ *Vinohradská at Jana Želivského.* 🖾 *Free.* ☉ *June–Aug., Sun.–Thurs. 9–5, Fri. 9–1; Sept.–May, Sun.–Thurs. 9–4, Fri. 9–1. Metro: Vyšehrad.*

㊹ Pavilon. This gorgeous, turn-of-the-20th-century, neo-Renaissance, three-story market hall is one of the most attractive sites in Vinohrady. It used to be a major old-style market, a vast space filled with stalls selling all manner of foodstuffs plus the requisite grimy pub. After being spiffed up several years ago, it mutated into an upscale shopping mall. Off the tourist track, Pavilon is a good place to watch Praguers—those who can afford its shops' gleaming designer pens and Italian shoes—ostentatiously drinking in *la dolce vita,* cell phones in hand. ⊠ *Vinohradská 50,* ☎ *02/2209–7111.* ☉ *Mon.–Sat. 8:30 AM–9 PM, Sun. noon–6.*

NEED A BREAK?	A symbol of this bucolic neighborhood's intellectual leanings, the literary café **Literární kavárna G + G** (⊠ Čerchovská 4, ☎ 02/627–3332) serves coffees and light desserts in a well-lit and welcoming shop brimming with books, newspapers, and magazines (most in Czech). It's a block east of Riegrovy Park, or two blocks off Vinohradská via U Kanálky. Several nights a week, the café hosts readings as well as intimate concerts of folk, jazz, or Romany (Gypsy) music.

Letná and Holešovice

From above the Vltava's left bank, the large, grassy plateau called Letná gives you one of the classic views of the Old Town and the many bridges crossing the river. (To get to Letná from the Old Town, take Pařížská street north, cross the Čechův Bridge, and climb the stairs.) Beer gardens, tennis, and Frisbee attract people of all ages, while amateur soccer players emulate the professionals of Prague's top team, Sparta, which plays in the stadium just across the road. A 10-minute walk from Letná, down into the residential neighborhood of Holešovice, brings you to a massive, gray-blue building whose cool exterior gives no hint of the treasures of Czech and French modern art that line its corridors. Just north along Dukelských hrdinů street is Stromovka—a royal hunting preserve turned gracious park.

Numbers in the margin correspond to numbers on the Exploring Prague map.

㊺ Letenské sady (Letna Park). Come to this large, shady park for an unforgettable view of Prague's bridges. From the enormous cement pedestal at the center of the park, the largest statue of Stalin in Eastern Europe once beckoned to citizens on the Old Town Square far below. The statue was ripped down in the 1960s, when Stalinism was finally discredited. On sunny Sundays expatriates often meet up here to play ultimate Frisbee.

㊻ Veletržní palác (Trade Fair Palace). The National Gallery's **Sbírka moderního a soucasného umění** (Collection of Modern and Contemporary Art) has become a keystone in the city's visual-arts scene since its opening in 1995, despite unclear leadership. Touring the vast spaces of this 1920s Constructivist exposition hall and its comprehensive collection of 20th-century Czech art is the best way to see how Czechs surfed the forefront of the avant-garde wave until the cultural freeze following the Communist takeover in 1948, which threw the visual arts into gloom and introspection. (Most of the collections languished in storage for decades, either because some cultural commissar forbade their public display or because there was no exhibition space.) Also on display are works by Western European, mostly French, artists from Delacroix to the present. Especially noteworthy are the early Cubist paintings by Picasso and Braque. The 19th-century Czech art collection of the National Gallery was installed in the palace in the summer of 2000. Watch the papers and posters for information on traveling shows and temporary exhibits by young Czech artists. ⊠ *Dukelských hrdinů 47*, ☎ *02/2430–1111*. ◪ *90 Kč.* ☉ *Tues.–Sun. 10–6 (Thurs. until 9).*

DINING

Dining choices in Prague have increased greatly in the past decade as hundreds of new places have opened to meet the soaring demand from tourists and locals alike. These days, out-and-out rip-offs have almost disappeared, but before paying up at the end of a meal it's a good idea to take a close look at the added cover charge on your bill. Also keep an eye out for a large fee tacked on to a credit card bill. In pubs and neighborhood restaurants, ask if there is a *denní lístek* (daily menu) of cheaper and often fresher selections, but note that many places provide daily menus for the midday meal only. Special local dishes worth making a beeline for include *cibulačka* (onion soup), *kulajda* (potato soup with sour cream), *svíčková* (beef sirloin in cream sauce), and *ovocné knedlíky* (fruit dumplings, often listed under "meatless dishes").

The crush of visitors has placed tremendous strain on the more popular restaurants. The upshot: reservations are an excellent idea, especially for dinner during peak tourist periods. If you don't have reservations, try arriving a little before standard meal times: 11:30 AM for lunch or 5:30 PM for dinner.

For a cheaper and quicker alternative to the sit-down establishments listed below, try a light meal at one of the city's growing number of street stands or fast-food places. Look for stands offering *párky* (hot dogs) or the fattier *klobásy* (grilled sausages served with bread and mustard). For more exotic fare, try the very good vegetarian cooking at **Country Life** (⊠ Melantrichova 15, in the Old Town, ☎ 02/2421–3366). Chic new cafés and bakeries spring up all the time. **Vzpomínky na Afriku** (⊠ Rybná at Jakubská, near the Kotva department store) has the widest selection of gourmet coffees in town, served at the single table or to go.

Staré Město (Old Town)

$$$$ ✕ **Bellevue.** The first choice for visiting dignitaries and businesspeople blessed with expense accounts, Bellevue has creative, freshly prepared cuisine, more nouvelle than Bohemian—and the elegant setting not far from Charles Bridge doesn't hurt. Look for the lamb carpaccio with fresh rosemary, garlic, and extra-virgin olive oil, or the wild berries marinated in port and cognac, served with vanilla-and-walnut ice cream. Window seats have stunning views of Prague Castle. The Sunday jazz brunch is a winner, too. ⊠ *Smetanovo nábř. 18*, ☎ *02/2222–1449. AE, MC, V.*

$$$$ ✕ **Jewel of India.** Although generally Asian cooking of any stripe is not Prague's forte, here is a sumptuous spot well worth seeking out for northern Indian tandooris and other moderately spiced specialties, including some delicious vegetarian dishes. ⊠ *Pařížská 20*, ☎ *02/ 2481–1010. AE, MC, V. Metro: Staroměstská.*

$$$$ ✕ **V Zátiší.** White walls and casual grace accentuate the subtle flavors
   ★   of smoked salmon, plaice, beef Wellington, and other non-Czech specialties. Here, as at most of the city's better establishments, the wine list has expanded in recent years and now includes most of the great wine-producing regions, though good Moravian vintages are still kept

on hand. In behavior unusual for the city, the benign waiters fairly fall over each other to serve diners. ⊠ *Liliová 1 at Betlémské nám.,* ☎ *02/ 2222–2025. AE, MC, V.* 🐾

$$$ ✕ **Barock.** Call it chic or call it pretentious, Barock exemplifies the revolution in Prague's dining and social life since those uncool Communists decamped. Thai and Japanese dishes predominate, and there are other Asian choices and international standards. Although eating isn't the main point here—being seen is—the fish dishes and sushi won't let you down. ⊠ *Pařížská 24,* ☎ *02/232–9221. AE, DC, MC, V.*

$$ ✕ **Chez Marcel.** At this authentic French bistro on a quiet street, you can get a little taste of that *other* riverside capital. French owned and operated, Chez Marcel has a smallish but reliable menu listing pâtés, salads, rabbit and chicken, and some of the best steaks in Prague. The specials board usually has some tempting choices, such as salmon, beef daube, or foie gras. ⊠ *Haštalská 12,* ☎ *02/231–5676. No credit cards.*

$ ✕ **Kavárna Slavia.** This legendary hangout for the best and brightest
★ in Czech arts—from composer Bedřich Smetana and poet Jaroslav Seifert to then-dissident Václav Havel—reopened after being held hostage in absurd real-estate wrangles for most of the 1990s. Its Art Deco decor is a perfect backdrop for people watching, and the vistas (the river and Prague Castle on one side, the National Theater on the other) are a compelling reason to linger for hours over a coffee—although it's not the best brew in town. The Slavia is a café to its core, but you can also get a light meal, such as a small salad with Balkan cheese, an open-face sandwich, or breakfast in the form of scrambled eggs (don't even think about toast). And despite what the old-guard coat-check lady will tell you on your way in, it is not obligatory to check your coat with her. ⊠ *Smetanovo nábř. 1012/2,* ☎ *02/2422–0957. AE, MC, V.*

$ ✕ **Lotos.** Banana ragout with polenta and broccoli strudel are two favorites at what is undoubtedly the best of the city's scant selection of all-vegetarian restaurants. Blond-wood tables and billowing tie-dye fabric set an informal yet elegant atmosphere. The salads and soups are wonderful. ⊠ *Platnéřská 13,* ☎ *02/232–2390. MC, V.*

$ ✕ **Pizzeria Rugantino.** Bright and spacious, this buzzing pizzeria serves up thin-crust pies; big, healthy salads; and good Italian bread. It can get quite loud when full, which is most nights. ⊠ *Dušní 4,* ☎ *02/231– 8172. No credit cards. No lunch Sun.*

Malá Strana (Lesser Quarter)

$$$$ ✕ **Circle Line.** Now moved out of the cellar into two elegant dining rooms, one done up in blue and the other in pink, Circle Line maintains its high standards with such dishes as fallow deer with spaetzle, pike perch, and yellowfin tuna carpaccio. The service can't be faulted. There are creative seasonal specials such as the warm foie gras with cherries, but be sure to save room for the chocolate plate for dessert. Brunch is served daily until 6 PM. ⊠ *Malostranské nám. 12,* ☎ *02/5753– 0022. AE, MC, V.*

$$$$ ✕ **Pasha.** This inviting Middle Eastern spot at the foot of Prague Castle hits just the right notes of luxury and easiness. The à la carte menu includes luscious *adana kebab* (skewer of minced lamb), pilaf, and shish kebab. Baklava served with fresh mint tea makes a splendid dessert. ⊠ *Letenská 1,* ☎ *02/549–773. AE, MC, V. Closed Mon.*

$$$ ✕ **Lobkovická.** This dignified *vinárna* (wine hall) set inside a 17th-cen-
★ tury town palace serves innovative, imaginative dishes by Prague standards. Chicken breast with crabmeat and curry sauce is an excellent main dish and typical of the kitchen's approach to sauces and spices. Deep red carpeting sets the perfect mood for enjoying bottles of Moravian wine. ⊠ *Vlašská 17,* ☎ *02/530–185 or 02/5753–2511. AE, MC, V.*

Prague Dining and Lodging

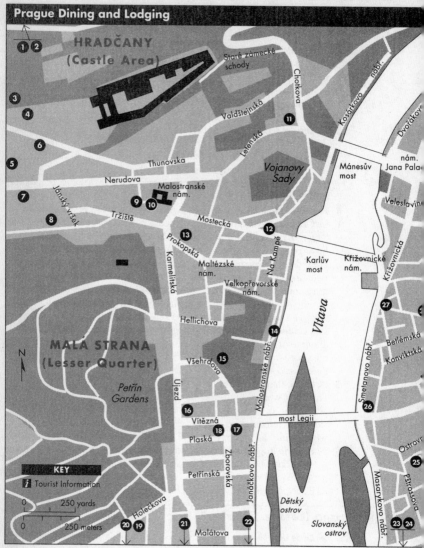

Dining

Barock	**32**
Bella Napoli	**55**
Bellevue	**27**
Bohemia Bagel	**16**
Café Savoy	**17**
Chez Marcel	**34**
Circle Line	**9**
Dolly Bell	**23**
Fakhreldine	**56**
Fromin	**51**
Jewel of India	**31**
Kavárna Slavia	**26**

La Crêperie	**39**
La Perle de Prague	**24**
Lobkovická	**8**
Lotos	**30**
Mailsi	**47**
Myslivna	**59**
Novoměstský pivovar	**54**
Pasha	**11**
Pizzeria Coloseum	**52**
Pizzeria Rugantino	**33**

Radost FX Café	**58**
Rybářský klub	**14**
The Sushi Bar	**18**
U Maltézských rytířů	**13**
U Mecenáše	**10**
U Počtů	**38**
U Ševce Matouše	**6**
U Zlaté hrušky	**4**
Universal	**25**
V Krakovské	**57**
V Zátiší	**28**

Lodging

Apollo	**36**
Astra	**60**
Axa	**42**
Balkan	**22**
Bern	**48**
Central	**44**
City Hotel Moran	**53**
Diplomat	**1**
Dům U Červeného lva	**7**

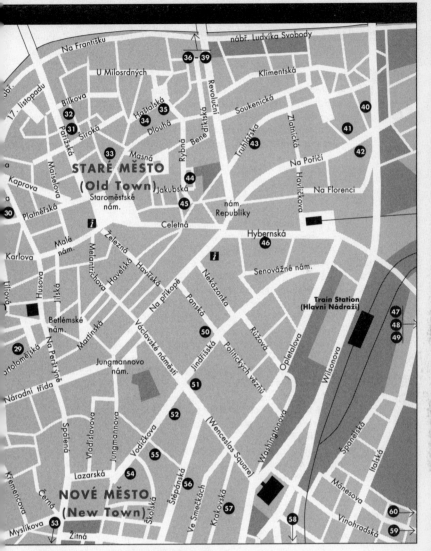

Na Františku

nábř. Ludvíka Svobody

36 – 39

U Milosrdných

Klimentská

Bílkova

Hastalská

Soukenická

32

35

Revoluční

Dlouhá

Benediktská

17. listopadu

31

Široká

34

Zlatnická

40

Pařížská

Masná

Rybná

Bene

Truhlářská

41

33

STARÉ MĚSTO
(Old Town)

Jakubská

44

Na Poříčí

42

Maiselova

Kaprova

Staroměstské
nám.

45

nám.
Republiky

Na Florenci

30

Platnéřská

Celetná

i

Hybernská

Malá
nám.

Železná

46

Karlova

Melantrichova

Havelská

Havířská

i

Senovážné nám.

Husova

Jilská

Na příkopě

Panská

Nekázanka

Train Station
(Hlavní Nádraží)

47

Lilová

Betlémské
nám.

Martinská

Václavské náměstí

Růžová

48

49

29

Na Perštýně

Jungmannovo
nám.

Jindřišská

Politických vězňů

Opletalova

Wilsonova

rtolomějská

Martinská

50

Národní třída

51

Španělská

Spálena

Vladislavova

Jungmannova

52

Wenceslas Square

Washingtonova

Italská

Vodičkova

55

Lazarská

54

Šepánská

Krakovská

Mánesova

NOVÉ MĚSTO
(New Town)

56

Ve Smečkách

57

60

Kremencova

Černá

Školská

58

Vinohradská

59

Myslíkova

53

Žitná

$$$ ✕ **The Sushi Bar.** This chic little joint with the wacky whale sculpture floating overhead could have been transported straight from San Francisco. Given Prague's distance from the sea, the selection of sushi and sashimi is excellent. For the same reason, call ahead to check when the fresh seafood is due (it's delivered twice a week), or stick to the broiled salmon or tempura dishes. ⊠ *Zborovská 49,* ☎ *0603/244–882. DC, MC, V.*

$$$ ✕ **U Maltézských rytířů.** The tongue-twisting name means "At the Knights of Malta," a reference to the Catholic order whose embassy is nearby. The upstairs dining room and bar are cozy, but ask for a table in the deep cellar—then ask the proprietress to regale you with yarns about this ancient house. They've dropped some old favorites from the menu, but still offer good steaks, game, and fish. ⊠ *Prokopská 10,* ☎ *02/5753–3666. AE, MC, V.*

$$$ ✕ **U Mecenáše.** A fetching Renaissance inn from the 17th century, with dark, high-back benches in the front room and cozy, elegant sofas and chairs in back, this is a place to splurge. From the aperitifs to the specialty steaks or beef Wellington and the cognac (swirled lovingly in oversize glasses), the presentation is seamless. ⊠ *Malostranské nám. 10,* ☎ *02/5753–1631. AE, MC, V.*

$$ ✕ **Rybářský klub.** The "Fishing Club" restaurant shares its building
★   with a real fishing club's headquarters, and it's a great place to try a wide variety of freshwater fish. The friendly staff serves perch, eel, barbel, and the esteemed pike perch at picnic-style tables or by the water in summer. ⊠ *U Sovových mlýnů 1, Kampa Island,* ☎ *02/530–223. MC, V.*

$ ✕ **Bohemia Bagel.** It's not New York, but the friendly, North American–owned Bohemia Bagel still serves up a plentiful assortment of fresh bagels, from raisin-walnut to "supreme," with all kinds of toppings. Their thick soups are among the best in Prague for the price, and the bottomless cups of coffee are a further draw. ⊠ *Újezd 16,* ☎ *02/531–002. No credit cards.*

$ ✕ **Café Savoy.** Opened in 1887 as a grand café, the Savoy lasted only a few years before the long, airy room was divided up to be made into shops. In 1992 the café was reborn, and best of all, the painted and stuccoed ceiling that had long been covered over was restored. It's best for coffee, a drink, or a fine apple strudel; typical meat dishes such as pork steak with horseradish are also available. ⊠ *Vítězná 5,* ☎ *no phone. AE, DC, MC, V.*

Hradčany

$$$$ ✕ **U Zlaté hrušky.** At this fetching little rococo house perched on one of Prague's prettiest cobblestone streets, slide into one of the cozy dark-wood booths and let the cheerful staff advise on wines and specials. Among the regular offerings are a superb leg of venison with pears and millet gnocchi and an excellent appetizer of duck liver in wine sauce. After dinner, stroll to the castle for an unforgettable panorama. ⊠ *Nový Svět 3,* ☎ *02/2051–4778. AE, MC, V.*

$$ ✕ **U Ševce Matouše.** Steaks are the raison d'être at this former shoemaker's shop, where a gold shoe still hangs from the ceiling of the arcade outside to guide patrons into the vaulted dining room. Appetizers are hit-and-miss; stick with the dozen or so tenderloins and filet mignons. ⊠ *Loretánské nám. 4,* ☎ *02/2051–4536. MC, V.*

Nové Město (New Town) and Vyšehrad

$$$$ ✕ **La Perle de Prague.** Delicious Parisian cooking awaits at the top of the curvaceous "Fred and Ginger" building. The interior of the main room is washed with soft tones of lilac and sea green. This room also has smallish windows—typical of architect Frank Gehry's designs—and rather cheesy nude photographs, but the semiprivate dining room at the very top has a riveting view over the river. Try the red snapper Provençal, freshwater *candát* (pike perch), or tournedos of beef Béarnaise. Make reservations as early as you can. This is also a good reason to unpack your tie. ⊠ *Rašínovo nábř. 80*, ☎ *02/2198–4160. AE, DC, MC, V. Closed Sun. No lunch Mon.*

$$$ ✕ **Fakhreldine.** This elegant Lebanese restaurant, now at a more central location, offers an excellent range of authentic dishes, such as *kibbey bisayniyeh* (lamb and ground pine-nut patty), *warakinab* (stuffed grape leaves), and three kinds of baklava. For a moderately priced meal, try several *meze* (appetizers)—hummus and garlic yogurt, perhaps—instead of a main course. ⊠ *Štěpánská 32*, ☎ *02/2223–2617. AE, DC, MC, V. Closed Sun.*

$$ ✕ **Bella Napoli.** The decor may be a little much, but the food is gen-
★ uine and the price-to-quality ratio hard to beat. Close your eyes to the alabaster Venus de Milos astride shopping-mall fountains and head straight for the antipasto bar, which will distract you with fresh olives, eggplant, squid, and mozzarella. For your main course, go with any of a dozen superb pasta dishes or splurge with shrimp or chicken parmigiana. ⊠ *V Jámě 8*, ☎ *02/2223–2933. No credit cards.*

$$ ✕ **Dolly Bell.** This restaurant's whimsical design, with upside-down tables hanging from the ceiling, provides a clever counterpoint to the extensive selection of well-prepared Yugoslav dishes. There's an emphasis on meat and seafood—try the corn bread (polenta) with Balkan cheese, *čevapčiči* (pork sausage), and *tufahija* (baked apple with a smooth nut filling). ⊠ *Neklanova 20*, ☎ *02/298–815. DC, MC, V.*

$$ ✕ **Fromin.** Come dressed to the teeth—flourishing your mobile phone, preferably—for dinner at this cavernous, postmodern loft high above Wenceslas Square. The food is better than average, with entrées unusual for hereabouts, such as turkey steak with rosemary, lamb cutlets, and fresh tuna steaks. The upstairs café is quiet in the mornings; at 10 PM it becomes a disco whose doorman will turn away unstylishly dressed guests. ⊠ *Václavské nám. 21*, ☎ *02/2423–2319. AE, MC, V.*

$ ✕ **Novoměstský pivovar.** It's easy to lose your way in this crowded microbrewery-restaurant with its maze of rooms, some painted in mock-medieval style, others covered with murals of Prague street scenes. *Vepřové koleno* (pork knuckle) is a favorite dish. The beer is the cloudy, fruity "fermented" style. ⊠ *Vodičkova 20*, ☎ *02/2223–1662. AE, MC, V.*

$ ✕ **Pizzeria Coloseum.** An early entry in the burgeoning pizza-and-pasta trade, this one has kept its popularity due largely to its position right off Wenceslas Square. Location doesn't have everything to do with it, though; the pizzas have a wonderfully thin, crisp crust, and the pasta with Gorgonzola sauce will have you blessing Italian cows. Long picnic tables make this an ideal spot for an informal lunch or dinner. There's a salad bar, too. ⊠ *Vodičkova 32*, ☎ *02/2421–4914. AE, MC, V.*

$ ✕ **Radost FX Café.** Colorful and campy in design, this lively café is a street-level adjunct to the popular Radost dance club. It's a vegetarian heaven for both Czechs and expatriates: the creative specials of a Mexican or Italian persuasion are tasty, and filling enough to satisfy carnivores. If you suddenly find yourself craving a brownie, this is the place to get a fudge fix. Another plus: it's open until around 3 AM. ⊠ *Bělehradská 120*, ☎ *02/2425–4776. No credit cards.*

$ ✕ **Universal.** A pioneer in the neighborhood behind the National Theater that's fast becoming a trendy dining ghetto, Universal serves up satisfying French- and Indian-influenced main courses, giant side orders of scalloped potatoes, and luscious lemon tarts or chocolate mousse—all at ridiculously low prices. ⊠ *V Jirchářích 6*, ☎ *02/2491–8182. No credit cards.*

$ ✗ **V Krakovské.** At this clean, proper pub close to the major tourist sights, the food is traditional and hearty. This is the place to try *svíčková na smetaně* (thinly sliced sirloin beef in cream sauce) paired with an effervescent pilsner beer. ✉ *Krakovská 20,* ☎ *02/2221–0204. No credit cards.*

Vinohrady

$$ ✗ **Myslivna.** The name means "Hunting Lodge," and the cooks at this neighborhood eatery certainly know their way around venison, quail, and boar. Attentive staff can advise on wines: try Vavřinecké, a hearty red that holds its own with any beast. The stuffed quail and the leg of venison with walnuts get high marks. A cab from the city center to Myslivna should cost under 200 Kč. ✉ *Jagellonská 21,* ☎ *02/627–0209. AE, MC, V.*

Letná and Holešovice

$ ✗ **La Crêperie.** Run by a Czech-French couple, this creperie near the Veletržní palác (Trade Fair Palace) serves all manner of crepes, both sweet and savory. (It may take at least three or four to satisfy a hearty appetite.) Make sure to leave room for the dessert crepe with cinnamon-apple purée layered with lemon cream. The wine list offers both French and Hungarian vintages. ✉ *Janovského 4, Holešovice,* ☎ *02/ 878–040. No credit cards.*

$ ✗ **U Počtů.** This is a charmingly old-fashioned neighborhood eatery with comparatively skilled service. Garlic soup and chicken livers in wine sauce are flawlessly rendered, and the grilled trout is delicious. ✉ *Milady Horákové 47, Letná,* ☎ *02/3337–1419. AE, MC, V.*

Žižkov

$ ✗ **Mailsi.** Funky paintings of Arabian Nights–type scenes in a low-ceil-
★   ing cellar make for a casual, cheerful setting at this Pakistani restaurant. Chicken is done especially well here—the *murgh vindaloo* may well be the spiciest dish in Prague, and the thin-sliced marinated chicken (*murgh tikka*) appetizer is a favorite. Take Tram 5, 9, or 26 to the Lipanská stop, then walk one block uphill. ✉ *Lipanská 1,* ☎ *02/9005–9706 or 0603/466–626. No credit cards.*

LODGING

A slow rise in lodging standards continues, but at all but the most expensive hotels standards lag behind those of Germany and Austria—as do prices. In most of the $$$$ and $$$ hotels, you can expect to find a restaurant and an exchange bureau on or near the premises. During the peak season reservations are absolutely imperative; for the remainder of the year they are highly recommended. Many hotels in Prague go by a three-season system: the lowest rates are charged from December through February, excluding Christmas (at some hotels) and New Year's (at all hotels), when high-season rates are charged; the middle season includes March, November, and often July and August; and spring and fall bring the highest rates. Easter sees higher-than-high-season rates, and some hotels up the price for other holidays and trade fairs. It always pays to ask first.

A private room or apartment can be a cheaper and more interesting alternative to a hotel. You'll find agencies offering such accommodations all over Prague, including at the main train station (Hlavní nádraží), Holešovice station (Nádraží Holešovice), and at Ruzyně Airport. These bureaus normally are staffed with people who can speak some English, and most can book rooms in hotels and pensions as well as private accommodations. Rates for private rooms start at around $15 per person per night and can go much higher for better-quality rooms. In general, there is no fee, but you may need to try several bureaus to find the accommodation you want. Ask to see a photo of the room before accepting it, and be sure to pinpoint its location on a map—you don't want to wind up in an inconveniently distant location. You may be approached by (usually) men in the stations hawking rooms, and while these deals aren't always rip-offs, you should be wary of them. **Prague Information Service** (☞ Visitor Information *in* Prague A to Z, *below*) arranges lodging from all of its central offices, including the branch in the main train station, which is in the booth marked TURISTICKÉ INFORMACE on the left side of the main hall as you exit the station.

The bluntly named **Accommodation Service** (⊠ Haštalská 7, ☎ 02/231–0202 or 0602/210–515, ⅇ 02/231–6640) is a small but efficient agency that specializes in Old Town apartments at about 2,000 Kč for either one or two people and also arranges less costly rooms farther from the center. It's open daily between April and October from 9 to 7 and from November to March 9 to 1 and 2 to 6 (Sunday 9 to 1). Another helpful agency is **Hello Ltd.** (⊠ Senovážné nám. 3, ☎ ⅇ 02/2421–2647 or 02/2421–4212), open daily 9 AM–9 PM (weekdays 8–7 in the off-season); it's a 10-minute walk from the main train station. Both these agencies provide car or minivan transfers from the airport and train stations.

Staré Město (Old Town)

$$$$ 🏨 **Grand Hotel Bohemia.** This beautifully refurbished Art Nouveau town palace sits across the street from Obecní dům (Municipal House), near the Prašná brána (Powder Tower). During the Communist era it was a nameless, secure hideaway for ranking foreign party members. Once restored to private hands, the Austrian owners opted for a muted, modern decor in the rooms but left the sumptuous Boccaccio ballroom in its faux-rococo glory. In the rooms, sweeping, long drapes frame spectacular views of the Old Town. Each room's amenities include a fax, trouser press, and answering machine. ⊠ *Králodvorská 4, 110 00 Prague 1,* ☎ *02/2480–4111,* ⅇ *02/232–9545. 73 rooms, 5 suites. Restaurant, bar, café, in-room safes, minibars, no-smoking floor, meeting rooms. AE, DC, MC, V.* 🐾

$$$ 🏨 **Maximilian.** Oversize beds, classic French cherry-wood furniture, and thick drapes make for a relaxing stay in this luxurious hotel. A relatively new property (opened in 1995), it's located on a peaceful square, well away from traffic, noise, and crowds, yet within easy walking distance of Old Town Square and Pařížská Street. There are fax machines and satellite TVs in every room. ⊠ *Haštalská 14, 110 00 Prague 1,* ☎ *02/2180–6111,* ⅇ *02/2180–6110. 72 rooms. Breakfast room, in-room safes, minibars, meeting rooms, no-smoking rooms, parking (fee). AE, DC, MC, V.*

$$ 🏨 **Central.** This hotel lives up to its name, with a site on a relatively quiet side street near Celetná ulice and náměstí Republiky (Republic Square). Recent "improvements" raised prices more than the quality level, leaving the hallways as drab and the rooms as sparely furnished as ever (most lack TVs), but it remains perhaps the least expensive full-service hotel in the Old Town. ⊠ *Rybná 8, 110 00 Prague 1,* ☎ *02/2481–2041,* ⅇ *02/232–8404. 62 rooms, 4 suites. Restaurant. AE, DC, MC, V.*

$ 🏨 **Pension Unitas.** Now operated by the Christian charity Unitas, the spartan rooms of this former convent used to serve as interrogation cells for the Communist secret police. (Václav Havel was once a "guest.") Today conditions are much more comfortable, though the ambience is more that of a hostel than a pension. There's a common (but clean) bathroom on each floor. You'll need to reserve well in advance, even in the off-season. No smoking is allowed. Note that there is an adjacent three-star hotel, Cloister Inn, using the same location and phone number; when calling, specify the pension. ⊠ *Bartolomějská 9, 110 00 Prague 1,* ☎ *02/232–7700,* 𝖥𝖠𝖷 *02/232–7709. 40 rooms, none with bath. Restaurant. No credit cards.*

Malá Strana (Lesser Quarter)

$$$ 🏨 **Dům U Červeného lva.** On the Lesser Quarter's main, historic thor-
★   oughfare, a five-minute walk from Prague Castle's front gates, the "Baroque House at the Red Lion" is an intimate, immaculately kept hotel. Guest rooms have parquet floors, 17th-century painted-beam ceilings, superb antiques, and all-white bathrooms with brass fixtures. The two top-floor rooms can double as a suite. Note that there is no elevator, and the stairs are steep. ⊠ *Nerudova 41, 118 00 Prague 1.* ☎ *02/5753–3832 or 02/5753–3833,* 𝖥𝖠𝖷 *02/5753–2746. 5 rooms, 3 suites. 2 restaurants, bar, in-room safes, minibars. AE, DC, MC, V.* ☙

$$$ 🏨 **Kampa.** This early Baroque armory turned hotel is tucked away on
★   an abundantly picturesque street at the southern end of the Lesser Quarter, just off Kampa Island. The bucolic setting and comparatively low rates make the hotel one of the city's better bargains. Note the late-Gothic vaulting in the massive dining room. ⊠ *Všehrdova 16, 118 00 Prague 1,* ☎ *02/5732–0508 or 02/5732–0404,* 𝖥𝖠𝖷 *02/5732–0262. 85 rooms. Restaurant, minibars. AE, MC, V.*

$$$ 🏨 **U Tří Pštrosů.** The location could not be better: a romantic corner just a stone's throw from the river and within arms' reach of the Charles Bridge. The airy rooms of the centuries-old building still have their original oak-beam ceilings and antique furniture, and many have views over the river. Massive walls keep out the noise of the crowds on the bridge. An excellent in-house restaurant serves traditional Czech dishes to guests and nonguests alike. Rates drop slightly in July and August—probably because there's no air-conditioning, though the building's thick walls help keep it cool. ⊠ *Dražického nám. 12, 118 00 Prague 1,* ☎ *02/5753–2410,* 𝖥𝖠𝖷 *02/5753–3217. 14 rooms, 4 suites. Restaurant. AE, DC, MC, V.* ☙

Hradčany

$$$$ 🏨 **Savoy.** A restrained yellow Jugendstil facade conceals one of the city's
★   most luxurious small hotels. The former budget hotel was gutted and lavishly refurbished in the mid-1990s. A harmonious maroon-and-mahogany color scheme carries through the public spaces and the rooms, some of which are furnished in purely modern style while others have a rococo look. The Restaurant Hradčany is one of the city's best hotel dining rooms. The only drawback: although Prague Castle is just up the road, none of the rooms have a view of it. ⊠ *Keplerova 6, 118 00 Prague 6,* ☎ *02/2430–2430,* 𝖥𝖠𝖷 *02/2430–2128. 55 rooms, 6 suites. Restaurant, café, in-room safes, minibars, sauna, exercise room, meeting rooms. AE, DC, MC, V.* ☙

$$$ 🏨 **Romantik Hotel U Raka.** This private guest house, since 1997 a mem-
★   ber of the Romantik Hotels & Restaurants organization, has a quiet location on the ancient, winding streets of Nový Svět, just behind the Loreto Church and a 10-minute walk from Prague Castle. One side of the 18th-century building presents a rare example of half-timbering, and the rooms sustain the country feel with heavy furniture reminiscent of a Czech farmhouse. There are only six rooms, but if you can get a reservation (try at least a month in advance), you will have a wonderful base for exploring Prague. ⊠ *Černínská 10/93, 118 00 Prague*

1, ☎ 02/2051–1100, FAX 02/2051–0511. *5 rooms, 1 suite. Breakfast room. AE, MC, V.* ✎

Nové Město (New Town)

$$$$ 🏨 **Palace.** For the well-heeled, this is Prague's most coveted address—
★ a muted, pistachio green Art Nouveau building perched on a busy corner only a block from Wenceslas Square. The hotel's spacious, well-appointed rooms, each with a white-marble bathroom, are dressed in velvety pinks and greens cribbed straight from an Alfons Mucha print. The hotel's restaurant is pure Continental, from the classic garnishes to the creamy sauces. Two rooms are set aside for travelers with disabilities. Children 12 and under stay for free. ✉ *Panská 12, 111 21 Prague 1,* ☎ *02/2409–3111,* FAX *02/2422–1240. 114 rooms, 10 suites. 2 restaurants, in-room safes, minibars, 2 no-smoking floors, sauna. AE, DC, MC, V.* ✎

$$$ 🏨 **Axa.** Funky and functional, this 1932 high-rise was once a mainstay of the budget-hotel crowd. Over the years, the rooms have certainly improved; however, the lobby and public areas are still decidedly tacky, with plastic flowers, lots of mirrors, and glaring lights. There are scores of free weights in Axa's gym, making it one of the best in Prague. ✉ *Na Poříčí 40, 113 03 Prague 1,* ☎ *02/2481–2580,* FAX *02/ 232–2172. 126 rooms, 6 suites. Restaurant, bar, pool, sauna, health club. AE, DC, MC, V.* ✎

$$$ 🏨 **City Hotel Moran.** This renovated 19th-century town house has a bright, inviting lobby and equally bright and clean rooms that are modern, if slightly bland. Some upper-floor rooms have good views of Prague Castle. ✉ *Na Moráni 15, 120 00 Prague 2,* ☎ *02/2491–5208,* FAX *02/ 2492–0625. 57 rooms. Restaurant. AE, DC, MC, V.*

$$$ 🏨 **Meteor Plaza.** This Best Western hotel combines modern conveniences with historical ambience (Empress Maria Theresa's son, Joseph II, stayed here when he was passing through in the 18th century). The setting is ideal: a Baroque building that is only five minutes on foot from downtown. To get a sense of the hotel's age, visit the original 14th-century wine cellar. Rates drop markedly in midsummer and even more in winter. ✉ *Hybernská 6, 110 00 Prague 1,* ☎ *02/2419–2111,* FAX *02/2421–3005. 90 rooms, 6 suites. Restaurant, exercise room, parking (fee). AE, DC, MC, V.* ✎

$$$ 🏨 **Opera.** Once the lodging of choice for divas performing at the nearby Státní opera (State Theater), the Opera greatly declined under the Communists. The mid-1990s saw the grand fin-de-siècle facade rejuvenated with a perky pink-and-white exterior paint job. This exuberance is strictly on the outside, though, and the room decor is modern and easy on the eyes. In the off-season a double room can be had for around 2,500 Kč. ✉ *Těšnov 13, 110 00 Prague 1,* ☎ *02/231–5609,* FAX *02/231–1477. 64 rooms. Restaurant, bar, minibars. AE, DC, MC, V.*

$$ 🏨 **Harmony.** This is one of the renovated, formerly state-owned standbys. A stern 1930s facade clashes with the bright, 1990s interior, but cheerful receptionists, comfortably casual rooms, and an easy 10-minute walk to the Old Town compensate for the aesthetic flaws. Ask for a room away from the bustle of one of Prague's busiest streets. ✉ *Na Poříčí 31, 110 00 Prague 1,* ☎ *02/232–0016,* FAX *02/231–0009. 60 rooms. 2 restaurants. AE, DC, MC, V.*

$$ 🏨 **Salvator.** An efficiently run establishment just outside the Old Town, this pension offers more comforts than most in its class, including satellite TV and minibars in most rooms, and a combination breakfast room and bar with a billiard table. Rooms are pristine if plain, with the standard narrow beds; those without private bath also lack TVs but are a good value nonetheless. ✉ *Truhlářská 10, 110 00 Prague 1,* ☎ *02/*

231–2234, FAX *02/231–6355. 28 rooms, 16 with bath, 7 suites. Break-*
fast room, parking (fee). AE (5% fee). Metro: Náměstí Republiky.

Smíchov

$$$ ⚏ **Kinsky Garden.** You could walk the mile or so from this hotel to
Prague Castle entirely on the tree-lined paths of Petřín, the hilly park
that starts across the street. Opened in 1997, the hotel takes its name
from a garden established by Count Rudolf Kinsky in 1825 on the south-
ern side of Petřín. The public spaces and some rooms are not spacious,
but everything is tasteful and comfortable. Try to get a room on one of
the upper floors for a view of the park. The management and restaurant
are Italian. ⊠ *Holečkova 7, 150 00 Prague 5,* ☎ *02/5731–1173,* FAX *02/
5731–1184. 60 rooms. Restaurant, bar, meeting room. AE, DC, MC, V.*

$$ ⚏ **Mepro.** Standard rooms and service and a reasonably central location make this small hotel worth considering. The Smíchov neighborhood
offers a good range of restaurants (including the U Mikuláše Dačického
wine tavern, across the street from the hotel) and nice strolls along the
river or up the Petřín hill. ⊠ *Viktora Huga 3, 150 00 Prague 5,* ☎ *02/
548–549,* FAX *02/571–2380. 26 rooms. Snack bar. AE, MC, V.*

$$ ⚏ **Petr.** Set in a quiet part of Smíchov, just a few minutes' stroll from
the Lesser Quarter, this is an excellent value. As a "garni" hotel, it does
not have a full-service restaurant, but it does serve breakfast (included
in the price). The rooms are simply but adequately furnished. It's a 10-
minute walk from metro Anděl (Line B). ⊠ *Drtinova 17, 150 00
Prague 5,* ☎ *02/5731–4068,* FAX *02/5731–4072. 37 rooms, 2 suites.
AE, MC, V.*

$ ⚏ **Balkan.** Still holding its own as the city center's lone bare-bones bud-
get hotel, the spartan Balkan is on a busy street not far from the Lesser
Quarter and the Národní divadlo (National Theater). Breakfast is served
for 85 Kč. ⊠ *Svornosti 28, 150 00 Prague 5,* ☎ FAX *02/5732–7180, 02/
5732–2150, or 02/5732–5583. 24 rooms. Restaurant. AE (5% fee).*

Žižkov

$$ ⚏ **Bern.** The cream-color Bern is a comfortable alternative to staying
in the city center. Although rather far out, it is situated on several city
bus routes into the New and Old Towns; buses run frequently even on
evenings and weekends, and the trip takes 10–15 minutes. ⊠ *Koněvova
28, 130 00 Prague 3,* ☎ FAX *02/697–5807 or 02/697–4420. 26 rooms with
shower. Restaurant, bar, air-conditioning, minibars. AE, DC, MC, V.*

$$ ⚏ **Olšanka.** The main calling card of this boxy modern hotel is its out-
standing 50-meter swimming pool and modern sports center, which
includes a pair of tennis courts and aerobics classes. Rooms are clean
and, though basic, have the most important hotel amenities. There's
also a relaxing sauna with certain nights reserved for men, women, or
both. (Note that the sports facilities may be closed in August.) The neigh-
borhood is nondescript, but the Old Town is only 10 minutes away
by direct tram. ⊠ *Táboritská 23, 130 87 Prague 3,* ☎ *02/6709–2202,*
FAX *02/2271–3315. 200 rooms. Restaurant, bar, pool, health club,
meeting rooms. AE, MC, V.*

Eastern Suburbs

$$ ⚏ **Astra.** The location best serves drivers coming into town from the
east, although the nearby metro station makes this modern hotel easy
to reach from the center. The neighborhood is quiet, if ordinary, and
the rooms are more comfortable than most in this price range. ⊠
Mukařovská 1740/18, 100 00 Prague 10, ☎ *02/781–3595,* FAX *02/781–
0765. 43 rooms, 10 suites. Restaurant, nightclub. AE, DC, MC, V. Metro:*

Skalka (Line A), then walk south on Na padesátém about 5 mins to Mukařovská.

$ 🏨 **Apollo.** This is a standard, no-frills, square-box hotel where clean rooms come at a fair price. Its primary flaw is its location: roughly 20 minutes away by metro and tram from the city center. ⊠ *Kubišova 23, 182 00 Prague 8,* ☎ *02/688–0628,* FAX *02/688–4570. 35 rooms. MC, V. Metro: Nádraží Holešovice (Line C), then Tram 5, 14, or 17 to the Hercovka stop.*

$ 🏨 **Pension Louda.** The friendly owners of this family-run guest house go
★ out of their way to make you feel welcome. The large, spotless rooms are an exceptional bargain, and although the place is in the suburbs, the hilltop site offers a stunning view of greater Prague from the south-facing rooms. ⊠ *Kubišova 10, 182 00 Prague 8,* ☎ *02/688–1491,* FAX *02/688–1488. 9 rooms. Sauna, exercise room. No credit cards. Metro: Nádraží Holešovice (Line C), then Tram 5, 14, or 17 to the Hercovka stop.*

Western Suburbs

$$$$ 🏨 **Diplomat.** This sprawling complex opened in 1990 and remains popular with business travelers thanks to its location between the airport and downtown. From the hotel, you can easily reach the city center by metro. The modern rooms may not exude much character, but they are tastefully furnished and quite comfortable. You can drive a miniature racing car at the indoor track next door. ⊠ *Evropská 15, 160 00 Prague 6,* ☎ *02/2439–4111,* FAX *02/2439–4215. 369 rooms, 13 suites. 2 restaurants, bar, café, 2 no-smoking floors, sauna, exercise room, nightclub, meeting room, parking (fee). AE, DC, MC, V. Metro: Dejvická (Line A).*

$ 🏨 **Penzion Sprint.** Straightforward rooms, most of which have their own bathroom (however tiny), make the Sprint a fine choice. This pension is located on a quiet residential street, next to a large track and soccer field, in the outskirts of Prague about 20 minutes from the airport. Tram 18 rumbles directly to the Old Town from the Batérie stop just two blocks away. ⊠ *Cukrovárnická 62, 160 00 Prague 6,* ☎ *02/312–3338,* FAX *02/312–1797. 21 rooms, 6 with bath. AE, MC, V.*

NIGHTLIFE AND THE ARTS

The fraternal twins of the performing arts and nightlife continue to enjoy an exhilarating growth spurt in Prague, and the number of concerts, plays, musicals, and clubs keeps rising. Some venues in the city center pitch themselves to tourists, but there are dozens of places where you can join the local crowds for music, dancing, or the rituals of beer and conversation. For details of cultural and nightlife events, look for the English-language newspaper the *Prague Post* or one of the multilingual monthly guides available at hotels, tourist offices, and newsstands.

Nightlife

Cabaret
For adult stage entertainment (with some nudity) try the **Varieté Praga** (⊠ Vodičkova 30, ☎ 02/2421–5945).

Discos
Dance clubs come and go regularly. The longtime favorite is **Radost FX** (⊠ Bělehradská 120, ☎ 02/2251–3144), with imported and home-grown DJs playing the latest house, hip-hop, and dance music. **Karlovy Lázně** (⊠ Novotného lávka), near the Charles Bridge, is a four-story dance palace with everything from Czech oldies to ambient chill-out

sounds. **La Habana** (✉ Míšeňská 12, ☎ 02/5731–5104), is the place
to show off your moves to recorded salsa and merengue music.

Jazz Clubs

Jazz gained notoriety under the Communists as a subtle form of protest,
and the city still has some great jazz clubs, featuring everything from
swing to blues and modern. The listed clubs have a cover charge. **Re-
duta** (✉ Národní 20, ☎ 02/2491–2246) features a full program of local
and international musicians. **AghaRTA** (✉ Krakovská 5, ☎ 02/2221–
1275) offers a variety of jazz acts in an intimate space. Music starts
around 9 PM, but come earlier to get a seat. **Jazz Club Železná** (✉ Železná
16, ☎ 02/2421–2541) mixes its jazz acts with world music. **Jazz Club
U staré paní** (✉ Michalská 9, ☎ 02/264–920) has a rotating list of
tried-and-true Czech bands.

Pubs, Bars, and Lounges

Bars and lounges are not traditional Prague fixtures, but bars catering
to a young crowd have elbowed their way in over the past few years.
Still, most social life of the drinking variety takes place in pubs (*pivnice*
or *hospody*), which are liberally sprinkled throughout the city's neighborhoods. Tourists are welcome to join in the evening ritual of sitting
around large tables and talking, smoking, and drinking beer. Before
venturing in, however, it's best to familiarize yourself with a few points
of pub etiquette: Always ask if a chair is free before sitting down (*Je
tu volno?*). To order a beer (*pivo*), do not wave the waiter down or
shout across the room; he will usually assume you want beer—most
pubs serve one brand—and bring it over to you without asking. He
will also bring subsequent rounds to the table without asking. To
refuse, just shake your head or say no thanks (*ne, děkuju*). At the end
of the evening, usually around 10:30 or 11, the waiter will come to
tally the bill. There are plenty of popular pubs in the city center, all of
which can get impossibly crowded. **U Medvídků** (✉ Na Perštýně 7, ☎
02/2421–1916) was a brewery at least as long ago as the 15th century.
Beer is no longer made on the premises; rather, they serve draft Budvar shipped from České Budějovice. **U svatého Tomáše** (✉ Letenská
12, ☎ 02/5732–0101) brewed beer for Augustinian monks starting in
1358. Now they serve commercially produced beer in a tourist-friendly
mock-medieval hall in the Lesser Quarter. **U Zlatého Tygra** (✉ Husova
17, ☎ 02/2222–1111) is famed as one of the three best Prague pubs
for Pilsner Urquell, the original and perhaps the greatest of the pilsners.
It also used to be a hangout for such raffish types as the writer Bohumil Hrabal, who died in 1997.

One of the oddest phenomena of Prague's post-1989 renaissance is the
sight of travelers and tour groups from the United States, Britain, Australia, and even Japan descending on this city to experience the life of—
American expatriates. There are a handful of bars guaranteed to ooze
Yanks and other native English speakers. The **James Joyce Pub** (✉ Liliová 10, ☎ 02/2424–8793) is authentically Irish (it has Irish owners),
with Guinness on tap and excellent food of the fish-and-chips persuasion.
U Malého Glena (✉ Karmelitská 23, ☎ 02/535–8115) offers a popular bar and a stage for local and expat jazz, blues, and folk.

Rock Clubs

Prague's rock, alternative, and world-music scene is thriving. The cavernous **Palác Akropolis** (✉ Kubelíkova 27, ☎ 02/2271–2287), in the
Žižkov neighborhood, has top Czech acts and major international
world-music performers; as the name suggests, the space has an Acrop-
olis theme. Hard-rock enthusiasts should check out the **Rock Café** (✉
Národní 20, ☎ 02/2491–4416). You can also slouch into the **Lucerna
Music Bar** (✉ Vodičkova 36, ☎ 02/2421–7108) to catch popular

Czech rock and funk bands and visiting acts. For dance tracks, hip locals congregate at **Roxy** (⊠ Dlouhá 33, ☎ 02/2481–0951). **Malostranská Beseda** (⊠ Malostranské nám. 21, ☎ 02/539–024) is a dependable bet for sometimes bizarre but always good musical acts from around the country.

The Arts

Prague's cultural flair is legendary, and performances are sometimes booked far in advance by all sorts of Praguers. The concierge at your hotel may be able to reserve tickets for you. Otherwise, for the cheapest tickets go directly to the theater box office a few days in advance or immediately before a performance. Ticket agencies may charge higher prices than box offices do. **Ticketpro** (main branch: ⊠ Salvátorská 10, ☎ 02/2481–4020 or 02/1051), with outlets all over town, accepts major credit cards. Another big agency is **Bohemia Ticket International** (⊠ Na Příkopě 16, ☎ 02/2421–5031, or Malé nám. 13, ☎ 02/2422–7832). You can also purchase tickets at **American Express** (☞ Travel Agencies *in* Prague A to Z, *below*).

Film

If a film was made in the United States or Britain, the chances are good that it will be shown with Czech subtitles rather than dubbed. (Film titles, however, are usually translated into Czech, so your only clue to the movie's country of origin may be the poster used in advertisements.) Movies in the original language are normally indicated with the note *českými titulky* (with Czech subtitles). Many downtown cinemas cluster near Wenceslas Square. One of the largest is **Blaník** (⊠ Václavské nám. 56, ☎ 02/2221–0110). **Lucerna** (⊠ Vodičkova 36, ☎ 02/2421–6972) is a classic picture palace in the shopping arcade of the same name. **Praha** (⊠ Václavské nám. 17, ☎ 02/262–035) shows first-run features in the main hall and second-run films in a smaller screening room. Another central cinema with multiple screens is **Světozor** (⊠ Vodičkova 39, ☎ 02/2494–7566). Prague's English-language publications carry film reviews and full timetables.

Music

Classical concerts are held all over the city throughout the year. One of the best orchestral venues is the resplendent Art Nouveau **Smetana Hall** (⊠ Obecní dům, nám. Republiky 5, ☎ 02/2200–2100), home of the excellent Prague Symphony Orchestra and major venue for the annual Prague Spring music festival. **Dvořák Hall** (⊠ Rudolfinum, nám. Jana Palacha, ☎ 02/2489–3111) is home to one of Central Europe's best orchestras, the Czech Philharmonic, led since 1998 by the Russian pianist-conductor Vladimir Ashkenazy. Frequent guest conductor Sir Charles Mackerras is a leading proponent of modern Czech music.

Performances also are held regularly at many of the city's **palaces and churches,** including the Garden on the Ramparts below Prague Castle (where the music comes with a view); both Churches of St. Nicholas; the Church of Sts. Simon and Jude on Dušní in the Old Town; the Church of St. James on Malá Štupartská, near Old Town Square; the Zrcadlová kaple (Mirror Chapel) in the Klementinum on Mariánské náměstí in the Old Town; and the Lobkowicz Palace at Prague Castle. If you're an organ-music buff, you'll most likely have your pick of recitals held in Prague's historic halls and churches. Popular programs are offered at the Church of St. Nicholas in the Lesser Quarter and the Church of St. James, where the organ plays amid a complement of Baroque statuary. Classical ensembles are the most common finds, and the standard of performance ranges from adequate to superb, though the programs tend to take few risks. Serious fans of Baroque music may have the opportunity to hear works of little-known Bohemian composers at these concerts. Some of the best chamber ensembles are the Talich Chamber Orchestra, the Prague Chamber Philharmonic (also known as the Prague Philharmonia), the Wihan Quartet, the Czech Trio, and the Agon contemporary music group.

Concerts at the **Villa Bertramka** (⊠ Mozartova 169, in Smíchov, ☎ 02/540–012) emphasize the music of Mozart and his contemporaries.

Opera and Ballet

The Czech Republic has a strong operatic tradition. A great venue for a night at the opera is the plush **Národní divadlo** (National Theater; ⊠ Národní třída 2, ☎ 02/2490–1448). Performances at the **Statní Opera Praha** (State Opera House; ⊠ Wilsonova 4, ☎ 02/265–353), near the top of Wenceslas Square, can also be excellent. Unlike during the Communist period, operas are almost always sung in their original tongue, and the repertoire offers plenty of Italian favorites as well as the Czech national composers Janaček, Dvořák, and Smetana. (Czech operas are supertitled in English.) These two theaters also often stage ballets. The historic **Stavovské divadlo** (Estates Theater; ⊠ Ovocný trh 1, ☎ 02/2421–5001), where *Don Giovanni* premiered in the 18th century, plays host to a mix of operas and dramatic works. Appropriate attire is recommended for all venues; the National and Estates theaters instituted a "no jeans" rule in 1998. Ticket prices have risen, but are still quite reasonable at 300 Kč–500 Kč (slightly more at the Estates Theater).

Puppet Shows

This traditional form of Czech popular entertainment has been given new life thanks to the productions mounted at the **Národní divadlo marionet** (National Marionette Theater; ⊠ Žatecká 1, ☎ 02/232–2536; in season, shows are also performed at Celetná 13). Children and adults alike can enjoy the hilarity and pathos of famous operas adapted for non-human "singers." The company's bread and butter is a production of Mozart's *Don Giovanni*.

Theater

A dozen or so professional theater companies play in Prague to ever-packed houses. Visiting the theater is a vital activity in Czech society, and the language barrier can't obscure the players' artistry. Nonverbal theater also abounds: not only tourist-friendly mime and "Black Light Theater"—a melding of live acting, mime, video, and stage trickery—but also serious (or incomprehensible) productions by top local and foreign troupes. The famous **Laterna Magika** (Magic Lantern) puts on a multimedia extravaganza in the National Theater's ugly modern hall (⊠ Národní třída 4, ☎ 02/2491–4129). The popular **Archa Theater** (⊠ Na Poříčí 26, ☎ 02/232–8800) offers avant-garde and experimental theater, music, and dance and has hosted world-class visiting ensembles such as the Royal Shakespeare Company. Several English-language theater groups operate sporadically. For complete listings, pick up a copy of the *Prague Post*.

OUTDOOR ACTIVITIES AND SPORTS

Boats

Rowboats and paddle boats can be rented on Slovanský ostrov, the island in the Vltava just south of the National Theater.

Fitness Clubs

Some luxury hotels have well-equipped fitness centers with swimming pools. The **Corinthia Towers** (⊠ Kongresova 1, Prague 4, ☎ 02/6119–

1111) is south of the center, near the Vyšehrad metro station. The more centrally located **Hilton** (⊠ Pobřežní 1, Prague 8, ☎ 02/2484–1111, Metro: Florenc) has full fitness facilities and tennis courts. Excellent and much less costly facilities can be found at the **Hotel Axa** (⊠ Na Poříčí 40, ☎ 02/2481–2580).

Golf

Prague's only course is a nine-holer located in the western suburbs at the **Hotel Golf** (⊠ Plzeňská 215, ☎ 02/5721–5185). Take a taxi to the hotel or Tram 4, 7, or 9 from metro station Anděl to the Hotel Golf stop. **Praha Karlštejn Golf Club** offers a more challenging course with a view of the famous Karlštejn Castle. It's 30 km (18 mi) southwest of Prague, just across the Berounka River from the castle.

Jogging

The best place for jogging is **Stromovka,** a large, flat park adjacent to the Výstaviště fairgrounds in Prague 7 (take Tram 5, 12, or 17 to the Výstaviště stop). Closer to the center, another popular park is **Letenské sady** (Letna Park), the park east of the Royal Garden at Prague Castle, across Chotkova street (☞ Letná and Holešovice *in* Exploring Prague, *above*). For safety's sake, unaccompanied women should avoid the more remote corners of this park.

Spectator Sports

Prague plays host to a wide variety of spectator sports, including world-class ice hockey, soccer, and tennis. The best place to find out what's going on (and where) is the weekly sports page of the *Prague Post,* or you can inquire at your hotel.

Soccer

National and international matches are played regularly at the home of Prague's Sparta team, Sparta Stadium in Letná, behind Letna Park. To reach the stadium, take Tram 1, 25, or 26 to the Sparta stop.

Swimming

The best public swimming pool in Prague is at the **Podolí Swimming Stadium** in Podolí, which you can get to from the city center in 15 minutes or less by taking Tram 3 or 17 to the Kublov stop. The indoor pool is 50 meters long, and the complex also includes two open-air pools, a sauna, a steam bath, and a wild-ride water slide. (A word of warning: Podolí, for all its attractions, is notorious as a local hot spot of petty thievery. Don't entrust any valuables to the lockers—it's best either to check them in the safe with the *vrátnice* [superintendent], or better yet, don't bring them at all.) The pools at the **Hilton** and **Hotel Axa** (☞ Fitness Clubs, *above*) are smaller but more conveniently located.

Tennis

There are public tennis courts at the **Strahov Stadium** in Břevnov. Take Bus 176 from Karlovo náměstí in the New Town, or Bus 143 from the Dejvická metro station (Line A), to the Stadion Strahov stop. The **Hilton** (☞ Fitness Clubs, *above*) has two public indoor courts.

SHOPPING

Despite the relative shortage of quality clothes—Prague has a long way to go before it can match shopping meccas Paris and Rome—the capital is a great place to pick up gifts and souvenirs. Bohemian crystal and porcelain deservedly enjoy a worldwide reputation for quality, and plenty of shops offer excellent bargains. The local market for antiques and art is still relatively undeveloped, although dozens of antiquarian bookstores harbor some excellent finds, particularly German and Czech books and graphics.

Shopping Districts

The major shopping areas are **Na Příkopě,** which runs from the foot of Wenceslas Square to náměstí Republiky (Republic Square), and the area around **Old Town Square.** The Old Town streets **Pařížská ulice** and **Karlova ulice** are dotted with boutiques and antiques shops. In the Lesser Quarter, try **Nerudova ulice,** the street that runs up to Hradčany.

Department Stores

Prague's department stores are not always well stocked and often have everything except the one item you're looking for, but a stroll through one may yield some interesting finds and bargains. **Bílá Labuť'** (⊠ Na Poříčí 23, ☎ 02/2481–1364) has a decent selection, but the overall shabbiness harkens back to socialist times. **Kotva** (⊠ Nám. Republiky 8, ☎ 02/2480–1111) is comparatively upscale, with a nice stationery shop and a basement supermarket with wine and cheese aisles. The centrally located **Tesco** (⊠ Národní třída 26, ☎ 02/2200–3111) is generally the best place for one-stop shopping. It has same-day film developing, a newsstand that stocks English-language newspapers and magazines, American-brand toiletries, a supermarket with Western groceries (if you're dying for corn chips, you'll find them here), and a multilingual staff.

Street Markets

For fruits and vegetables, the best street market in central Prague is on **Havelská ulice** in the Old Town. You'll need to arrive early in the day if you want something a bit more exotic than tomatoes and cucumbers. The biggest market for nonfood items is the flea market in **Holešovice,** north of the city center, although there isn't really much of interest here outside of cheap tobacco and electronics products. Take the metro (Line C) to the Vltavská station and then catch any tram heading east (running to the left as you exit the metro station). Exit at the first stop and follow the crowds.

Specialty Stores

Antiques

For antiques connoisseurs, Prague can be a bit of a letdown. Even in comparison with other former Communist capitals such as Budapest, the choice of antiques in Prague can seem depressingly slim, as the city lacks large stores with a diverse selection of goods. The typical Prague *starožitnosti* (antiques shop) tends to be a small, one-room jumble of old glass and bric-a-brac. The good ones distinguish themselves by focusing on one particular specialty.

On the pricey end of the scale is the Prague affiliate of the Austrian **Dorotheum** auction house (⊠ Ovocný trh 2, ☎ 02/2422–2001) in the Old Town. It is an elegant pawnshop that specializes in small things: jewelry, porcelain knickknacks, and standing clocks, as well as the odd military sword. The small **JHB Starožitnosti** (⊠ Panská 1, ☎ 02/261–425) in the New Town is the place for old clocks: everything from rococo to Empire standing clocks and Bavarian cuckoo clocks. The shop also has a wide array of antique pocket watches. **Nostalgie Antique** (⊠ Jánský Vršek 8, ☎ 02/5753–0049) specializes in old textiles and jewelry. Most of the textiles are pre–World War II and include clothing, table linens, curtains, hats, and laces. **Papillio** (⊠ Týn 1, ☎ 02/2489–5454), in the elaborately refurbished medieval courtyard behind the

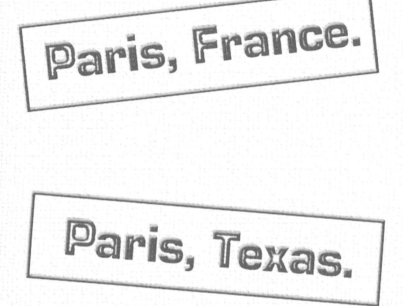

Paris, France.

Paris, Texas.

When it Comes to Getting Local Currency at an ATM, Same Thing.

Whether you're in Yosemite or Yemen, using your Visa® card or ATM card with the PLUS symbol is the easiest and most convenient way to get local currency.

For example, let's say you're in France. When you make a withdrawal, using your secured PIN, it's dispensed in francs, but is debited from your account in U.S. dollars.

This makes it easy to take advantage of favorable exchange rates. And if you need help finding one of Visa's 627,000 ATMs in 127 countries worldwide, visit **visa.com/pd/atm**. We'll make finding an ATM as easy as finding the Eiffel Tower, the Pyramids or even the Grand Canyon.

It's Everywhere You Want To Be®

SEE THE WORLD
IN FULL COLOR

Fodor's Exploring Guides bring all the great sights vividly to life with hundreds of photographs, fascinating historical background, and colorful anecdotes. Detailed maps and practical information keep you headed in the right direction.

Pair a **Fodor's** Exploring Guide with your trusted Gold Guide for a complete planning package.

Church of the Virgin Mary Before Týn, is probably one of the best antiques shops in Prague, offering furniture, paintings, and especially museum-quality antique glass. Here you can find colorful Biedermeier goblets by Moser and wonderful Loetz vases. **Zlatnictví Vomáčka** (✉ Náprstkova 9, ☎ 02/2222–2017) is a cluttered shop that redeems itself with its selection of old jewelry in a broad price range, including rare Art Nouveau rings and antique garnet brooches. In the shop's affiliate next door, jewelry is repaired, cleaned, and made to order.

Art Galleries

The best galleries in Prague are quirky and eclectic affairs, places to sift through artworks rather than browse at arms' length. Many galleries are also slightly off the beaten track and away from the main tourist thoroughfares. Prague's as-yet-untouristed Nový Svět neighborhood is something of a miniature artist's quarter and home to two of Prague's more interesting galleries. One is **Galerie Gambra** (✉ Černínská 5, ☎ 02/2051–4527), owned by the surrealist animator Jan Švankmajer. The space was originally Švankmajer's kitchen, where dissident surrealists used to gather and trade ideas; now the gallery displays Švankmajer's bizarre collages as well as his wife's anthropomorphic ceramics. Books and magazines focusing on Czech surrealist art are also for sale. **Galerie Nový Svět** (✉ Nový Svět 5, ☎ 02/2051–4611) displays interesting paintings and drawings by somewhat obscure Czech artists, as well as ceramics, glass, and art books. At the higher end is **Galerie Peithner-Lichtenfels** (✉ Michalská 12, ☎ 02/2422–7680) in the Old Town, which specializes in modern Czech art. Paintings, prints, and drawings crowd the walls and are propped against glass cases and window sills. Comb through works by Czech Cubists, currently fetching high prices at international auctions.

Galerie Litera (✉ Karlinske nám. 13, Prague 8, ☎ 02/231–7195) is in Karlín, a neighborhood rarely set foot in by tourists—it's not rough but pretty seedy. (It's northeast of the city center; get off the metro at Florenc and walk five minutes up Sokolovská.) Most of the gallery space is given over to temporary shows of unique, high-quality graphics. There are also some lovely ceramics as well as a refined selection of antiquarian art books.

Books and Prints

Like its antiques shops, Prague's rare book shops, or *antikvariáts*, were once part of a massive state-owned consortium that, since privatization, has split up and diversified. Now most shops tend to cultivate their own specialties. Some have a small English-language section with a motley blend of potboilers, academic texts, classics, and tattered paperbacks. Books in German, on the other hand, are abundant.

Antikvariát Karel Křenek (✉ Celetná 31, ☎ 02/231–4734), near the Prašná brána (Powder Tower) in the Old Town, specializes in books with a humanist slant. It has a good selection of modern graphics and prides itself on its avant-garde periodicals and journals from the 1920s and 1930s. It also has a small collection of English books. **Antikvariát Makovský & Gregor** (✉ Kaprova 9, ☎ 02/232–8335) is a great all-around bookstore as attested by the constant traffic of liberal-arts students from nearby Charles University. It's particularly fun to hunt around in the art section, where you could turn up the *Memoirs of Casanova* with illustrations by Aubrey Beardsley or a book on Leni Riefenstahl's mountaineering movies. If you'd just like a good read, be sure to check out the **Globe Bookstore and Coffeehouse** (✉ Pšstrossova 6, ☎ 02/2491–7230), a longtime magnet for the local English-speaking community, in its new, more central site.

U Karlova Mostu (✉ Karlova 2, ☎ 02/2222–0286) is the preeminent Prague bookstore. In a suitably bookish location opposite the Klementinum, it's the place to go if you are looking for that elusive 15th-century manuscript. In addition to housing ancient books too precious to be leafed through, the store has a good selection of books on local subjects, a small foreign-language section, and a host of prints, maps, drawings, and paintings. For new books in English, try **Anagram Books** (✉ Týn 4, ☎ 02/2489–5737). There's also a great selection around the corner at **Big Ben Bookshop** (✉ Malá Štupartská 5, ☎ 02/2482–6565).

Food & Wine
Specialty food and beverage stores are slowly catching on in Prague. **Fruits de France** (✉ Jindřišská 9 and Bělehradská 94, ☎ 02/9000–0339) charges Western prices for Prague's freshest fruits and vegetables, imported directly from France. **Cellarius** (✉ Lucerna Passage [Wenceslas Square between Vodičkova and Štěpánská streets], ☎ 02/2421–0979) has a wide choice of Moravian and Bohemian wines and spirits, as well as products from more recognized wine-making lands.

Fun Things for Children
Nearly every stationery store has beautiful watercolor and colored-chalk sets available at rock-bottom prices. The Czechs are also master illustrators, and the books they've made for young "pre-readers" are some of the world's loveliest. For delightful Czech-made wooden toys and wind-up trains, cars, and animals, look in at **Hračky** (✉ Pohořelec 24, ☎ 0604/757–214). For the child with a theatrical bent, a marionette—they range from finger-size to nearly child-size—can be a wonder (☞ Marionettes, *below*). For older children and teens, it's worth considering a Czech or Eastern European watch, telescope, or set of binoculars. The quality–price ratio is unbeatable.

Glass
Glass has traditionally been Bohemia's biggest export, and it was one of the few products manufactured during Communist times that managed to retain an artistically innovative spirit. Today Prague has plenty of shops selling Bohemian glass, much of it tourist kitsch. A good spot is the stylish **Galerie A** (✉ Na Perštýně 10, ☎ 02/261–334), which stocks Art Nouveau, Biedermeier, and medieval replica glass in Art Deco vitrines from the 1920s. Much more contemporary and decidedly less practical are the art-glass offerings at **Galerie 'Z'** (✉ U lužického semináře 7, ☎ 02/9005–5188), which sells limited-edition mold-melted and blown glass, and its sister shop, **Galerie Mozart** (✉ Uhelnýtrh 11, ☎ 02/2421–1127), off Národní třída, which also has glass sculptures and some colorful vases and bowls. **Moser** (✉ Na Příkopě 12, ☎ 02/2421–1293), the opulent flagship store of the world-famous Karlovy Vary glassmaker, offers the widest selection of traditional glass. Even if you're not in the market to buy, stop by the store simply to look at the elegant wood-paneled salesrooms on the second floor. The staff will gladly pack goods for traveling.

Home Design
Czech design is wonderfully rich both in quality and imagination, emphasizing old-fashioned craftsmanship while often taking an offbeat, even humorous approach. Strained relations between Czech designers and producers have reined in the potential selection, but there are nevertheless a handful of places showcasing Czech work. **Fast** (✉ Sázavská 32, Vinohrady, ☎ 02/2425–0538) is a little bit off the beaten track but worth the trek. Besides ultramodern furniture, there are ingenious (and more portable) pens, binders, and other office and home accoutrements. **Arzenal** (✉ Valentinská 11, ☎ 02/2481–4099) is a design shop that of-

fers Japanese and Thai food in addition to vases and chairs; it exclusively sells work by Bořek Šípek, President Havel's official designer. **Galerie Bydlení** (✉ Truhlářská 20, ☎ 02/231–7743) is a father-and-son operation focusing exclusively on Czech-made furniture.

Jewelry
Alfons Mucha is perhaps most famous for his whiplash Art Nouveau posters, but he also designed furniture, lamps, clothing, and jewelry. **Art Décoratif** (✉ U Obecního domu, ☎ 02/2200–2350), right next door to the Art Nouveau Obecní Dům, sells Mucha-inspired designs—the jewelry is especially remarkable. The Old Town's **Granát** (✉ Dlouhá 30, ☎ 02/231–5612) has a comprehensive selection of garnet jewelry, plus contemporary and traditional pieces set in gold and silver. **Halada** (✉ Karlova 25, ☎ 02/2421–8643) offers sleek, Czech-designed silver jewelry; an affiliate shop at Na Příkopě 16 specializes in gold, diamonds, and pearls.

Marionettes
Marionettes have a long tradition in Bohemia, going back to the times when traveling troupes used to entertain children with morality plays on town squares. Now, although the art form survives, it has become yet another tourist lure, and you'll continually stumble across stalls selling almost identical marionettes. The marionettes at **Manhartský Dům** (✉ Celetná 17, ☎ 02/2480–9156) are the real thing. These puppets—knights, princesses, and cloven-hoofed devils—are made by the same artists who supply professional puppeteers. Prices may be higher than for the usual stuff on the street, but the craftsmanship is well worth it. Secondhand and antique marionettes are surprisingly hard to find. One place to look is **Antikva Ing. Bürger** (✉ Betlémské nám. 8, in the courtyard, ☎ 02/269–9148).

Musical Instruments
Hudební nástroje Kliment (✉ Jungmannova nám. 17, ☎ 02/2421–3966) carries a complete range of quality musical instruments at reasonable prices. **Capriccio** (✉ Újezd 15, ☎ 02/532507) has sheet music of all kinds.

Sports Equipment
Kotva (☞ Department Stores, *above*) has a good selection of sports gear and clothing. For quality hiking and camping equipment, try **Hudy Sport** (✉ Na Perštýně 14, ☎ 02/2421–8600).

SIDE TRIPS TO BOHEMIAN SPA TOWNS

Until World War II, western Bohemia was the playground of Central Europe's rich and famous. Its three well-known spas, Karlovy Vary, Mariánské Lázně, and Františkovy Lázně (better known by their German names, Karlsbad, Marienbad, and Franzensbad, respectively), were the annual haunts of everybody who was anybody: Johann Wolfgang von Goethe, Ludwig van Beethoven, Karl Marx, and England's King Edward VII, to name but a few. Although strictly "proletarianized" in the Communist era, the spas still exude a nostalgic aura of a more elegant past and, unlike most of Bohemia, offer a basic tourist infrastructure that makes dining and lodging a pleasure.

Karlovy Vary
★ ㊾ *132 km (79 mi) due west of Prague on Rte. 6 (E48).*

Karlovy Vary, better known outside the Czech Republic by its German name, Karlsbad, is the most famous Bohemian spa. It is named for Emperor Charles IV, who allegedly happened upon the springs in 1358

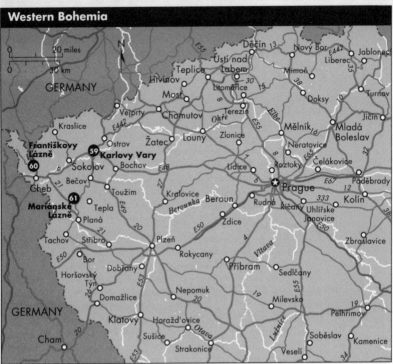

Western Bohemia

while on a hunting expedition. As the story goes, the emperor's hound—chasing a harried stag—fell into a boiling spring and was scalded. Charles had the water tested and, familiar with spas in Italy, ordered baths to be established in the village of Vary. The spa reached its heyday in the 19th century, when royalty came here from all over Europe for treatment. The long list of those who "took the cure" includes Peter the Great, Goethe (no fewer than 13 times, according to a plaque on one house by the main spring), Schiller, Beethoven, and Chopin. Even Karl Marx, when he wasn't decrying wealth and privilege, spent time at the resort; he wrote some of *Das Kapital* here between 1874 and 1876.

After decades of neglect under the Communists that left many buildings crumbling behind their beautiful facades, the town leaders today face the daunting task of carving out a new role for Karlovy Vary, since few Czechs can afford to set aside weeks or months at a time for a leisurely cure. To raise some quick cash, many sanatoriums have turned to offering short-term accommodations to foreign visitors (at rather expensive rates). By the week or by the hour, "classical" spa procedures, laser treatments, plastic surgery, and even acupuncture are purveyed to German clients or to large numbers of Russians who have bought property in town in the last few years. For most visitors, though, it's enough simply to stroll the streets and parks and allow the eyes to feast awhile on the splendors of the past.

Whether you're arriving by bus, train, or car, your first view of the town on the approach from Prague will be of the ugly new section on the banks of the Ohře River. Don't despair: continue along the main road—following the signs to the Grandhotel Pupp—until you reach the lovely main street of the older spa area, situated gently astride the banks of the little Teplá ("Warm") River. (Drivers, note that driving through or parking in the main spa area is allowed only with a permit obtainable from your hotel.) The walk from the new town to the spa area is about 20 minutes. The **Historická čtvrt** (Historic District) is still largely intact. Tall 19th-century houses, boasting decorative and often eccentric facades, line the spa's proud riverside streets. Throughout you'll see colonnades full of people sipping the spa's hot sulfuric water from odd pipe-shape drinking cups. At night the streets fill with steam escaping from cracks in the earth, giving the town a slightly macabre feel.

Karlovy Vary's jarringly modern **Vřídelní kolonáda** (Vřídlo Colonnade) is built around the spring of the same name, the town's hottest and most dramatic gusher. The Vřídlo is indeed unique, shooting its scalding water to a height of some 40 ft. Walk inside the arcade to watch the hundreds of patients here take the famed Karlsbad drinking cure. They promenade somnambulistically up and down, eyes glazed, clutching drinking glasses filled periodically at one of the five "sources." The waters are said to be especially effective against diseases of the digestive and urinary tracts. They're also good for gout (which probably explains the spa's former popularity with royals!). If you want to join the crowds and take a sip, you can buy your own spouted cup from vendors within the colonnade.

To the right of the Vřídlo Colonnade are steps up to the white **Kostel Mařĭ Magdaleny** (Church of Mary Magdalene). Designed by Kilian Ignaz Dientzenhofer (architect of the two Churches of St. Nicholas in Prague), this church is the best of the few Baroque buildings still standing in Karlovy Vary. ⊠ *Moravská ul.,* ☎ *no phone.* ☺ *Daily 9–6.*

The spa's centerpiece is just a couple minutes' walk along the river, back in the direction of the new town. The neo-Renaissance pillared hall **Mlýnská kolonáda** (Mill Colonnade), built from 1871 to 1881, has four springs: Rusalka, Libussa, Prince Wenceslas, and Millpond.

If you continue down the valley, you'll soon arrive at the very elegant **Sadová kolonáda** (Park Colonnade), a white, wrought iron construction. It was built in 1882 by the Viennese architectural duo of Fellner and Helmer, who sprinkled the Austro-Hungarian Empire with many such edifices during the late 19th century and who also designed the town's theater, the quaint wooden Tržní kolonáda (Market Colonnade) next to the Vřídlo Colonnade, and one of the old bathhouses.

The 20th century emerges at its most disturbing a little farther along the valley across the river, in the form of the huge, bunkerlike **Thermal Hotel,** built in the late 1960s. Although the building is a monstrosity, the view of Karlovy Vary from the rooftop pool is nothing short of spectacular. (The pool is open from 8 AM to 8 PM.) Even if you don't feel like a swim, it's worth taking the winding road up to the baths for the view. ⊠ *I.P. Pavlova.*

From the Market Colonnade, a steep street called **Zámecký vrch** leads up to some other sights. A five-minute walk brings you to the redbrick Victorian **Kostel svatého Lukáše** (St. Luke's Church), at the intersection of Zámecký vrch and Petra Velikého, once used by the local English community. A few blocks farther along Petra Velikého street, you'll come to the splendid Russian Orthodox church **Kostel svatých Petra a Pavla** (Church of Sts. Peter and Paul). Return to the Victorian church and take a sharp right uphill on the redbrick road. Then turn left onto a footpath through the woods, following the signs to **Jelení skok** (Stag's Leap). After a while you'll see steps leading up to a bronze statue of a deer looking over the cliffs, the symbol of Karlovy Vary. From here a winding path leads up to **Altán Jelení skok,** a little red gazebo opening onto a fabulous panorama.

NEED A
BREAK?

Reward yourself for making the climb to Stag's Leap with a light meal at the nearby restaurant **Jelení skok.** You may have to pay an entrance fee if there is a live band (but you'll also get the opportunity to polka). If you don't want to walk up, you can drive up a signposted road from the Victorian church.

It's not necessary to walk for one of the best views of the town. Above Stag's Leap is an observation tower, **rozhledna Diana,** accessible by funicular from behind the Grandhotel Pupp (☞ Dining and Lodging, *below*). There's an elevator to the top of the tower.

The town's most exclusive shopping clusters around the Grandhotel Pupp and back toward town along the river on Stará louka. Here too is the **Elefant,** one of the last of a dying breed of sophisticated coffeehouses. This kind of elegant café is now a rarity, but happily the café as an institution is making a real comeback in the Czech Republic. ⊠ *Stará louka 30*

Dining and Lodging

$$$ ✕ **Embassy.** This cozy, sophisticated wine restaurant, conveniently located near the Grandhotel Pupp, serves an innovative menu by local standards. Tagliatelle with smoked salmon in cream sauce makes an excellent main course, as does roast duck with cabbage and dumplings. The wine list features Czech varieties like the dry whites Rulandské bílé and Ryzlink Rýnský (the latter being the domestic version of the Riesling grape) and some pricey imports. ⊠ *Nová louka 21,* ☎ *017/ 322–1161. AE, DC, MC, V.*

$$ ✕ **Karel IV.** Its location atop an old castle tower not far from the Market Colonnade gives diners the best view in town. Good renditions of traditional Czech standbys—*bramborák* (potato pancake) and chicken breast with peaches—are served in small, secluded dining areas that are particularly intimate after sunset. ⊠ *Zámecký vrch 2,* ☎ *017/322– 7255. AE, MC, V.*

$$$$ 🏨 **Dvořák.** Consider a splurge here if you're longing for Western stan-
★ dards of service and convenience. Opened in late 1990, this Austrian-owned hotel occupies three renovated town houses that are just a five-minute walk from the main spas. If possible, request a room with a bay-window view of the town. Spa treatments here run to about $750 per person per week in the high season. ⊠ *Nová louka 11, 360 21,* ☎ *017/322–4145,* 🖷 *017/322–2814. 76 rooms, 3 suites. Restaurant, café, pool, beauty salon, massage, sauna, exercise room, casino. AE, DC, MC, V.*❧

$$$–$$$$ 🏨 **Grandhotel Pupp.** This enormous hotel with a 215-year history is
★ one of Karlovy Vary's landmarks—it's also one of Central Europe's most famous resorts. Standards and service slipped under the Communists (when the hotel was known as the Moskva), but the highly professional management has more than made up for the decades of neglect. Some guest rooms are furnished in 18th-century period style. The vast public rooms exude the very best taste, circa 1913, when the present building was completed. Every July, the Pupp becomes a temporary home base for international movie stars who come to the Karlovy Vary International Film Festival. (The adjacent Parkhotel Pupp, under the same management, is an affordable alternative to the Grandhotel.) Breakfast costs 375 Kč extra. ⊠ *Mírové nám. 2, 360 91,* ☎ *017/310–9111,* 🖷 *017/310–9620 or 017/322–4032. Grandhotel: 75 rooms, 34 suites. Parkhotel: 108 rooms, 6 suites. 4 restaurants, lounge, sauna, exercise room, casino, 2 nightclubs, parking (fee). AE, DC, MC, V.*❧

$$$ 🏨 **Elwa.** Renovations have successfully integrated modern comforts into this older, elegant spa resort located midway between the old and new towns. Modern features include clean, comfortable rooms with con-

temporary furnishings such as overstuffed chairs. There's also an on-site fitness center. The spa specializes in digestive diseases. ⊠ *Zahradní 29, 360 01,* ☎ *017/322–8472,* ⊠ *017/322–8473. 10 rooms, 7 suites. Restaurant, bar, beauty salon, health club. AE, MC, V.*

$$$ ⊞ **Růže.** More than adequately comfortable and well-priced given its location smack in the center of the spa district, this is a good choice for travelers who prefer a hotel to a pension or private room. ⊠ *I.P. Pavlova 1, 360 01,* ☎ ⊠ *017/322–1846 or 017/322–1853. 20 rooms. Restaurant. AE, V.*

Nightlife and the Arts

In Karlovy Vary, the upscale action centers on the two nightclubs and the casino of the **Grandhotel Pupp** (☞ Dining and Lodging, *above*). **Club Propaganda** (⊠ Jaltská 7, ☎ 017/323–3792) is Karlovy Vary's best venue for live rock and new music. The Karlovy Vary Symphony Orchestra plays regularly at **Lázně III** (⊠ Mlýnské nábř. 5, ☎ 017/322–5641).

Outdoor Activities and Sports

Karlovy Vary's warm open-air public pool on top of the **Thermal Hotel** (⊠ I.P. Pavlova) offers the unique experience of swimming comfortably even in the coolest weather; the view over the town is outstanding. Marked **hiking trails** snake across the beech-and-pine-covered hills that surround the town on three sides. The **Karlovy Vary Golf Club** is just out of town on the road to Prague.

Shopping

In western Bohemia, Karlovy Vary is best known to glass enthusiasts as the home of **Moser** (⊠ Tržiště 7, ☎ 017/323–5303), one of the world's leading producers of crystal and decorative glassware. A number of outlets for lesser-known, although also high-quality, makers of glass and porcelain can be found along Stará louka. For excellent buys in porcelain, try **Karlovarský porcelán** (⊠ Tržiště 27, ☎ 017/322–5660).

A cheaper but nonetheless unique gift from Karlovy Vary would be a bottle of the ubiquitous bittersweet (and potent) **Becherovka,** a liqueur produced by the town's own Jan Becher distillery. Another neat gift would be one of the pipe-shape ceramic drinking cups used to take the drinking cure at spas; you can find them at the colonnades. You can also buy boxes of tasty *oplatky* (wafers), sometimes covered with chocolate, at shops in all of the spa towns.

Františkovy Lázně

⑥⓪ *6 km (4 mi) from Cheb, 40 km (25 mi) west of Karlovy Vary.*

Františkovy Lázně, or Franzensbad, the smallest of the three main Bohemian spas, isn't really in the same league as the other two (Karlovy Vary and Mariánské Lázně). Built on a more modest scale at the start of the 19th century, the town's ubiquitous kaiser-yellow buildings have been spruced up after their neglect under the previous regime and now present cheerful facades, almost too bright for the few strollers. The poorly kept parks and the formal yet human-scale neoclassical architecture retain much of their former charm. Overall, a pleasing torpor reigns in Františkovy Lázně. There is no town to speak of, just **Národní ulice,** the main street, which leads down into the spa park. The waters, whose healing properties were already known in the 16th century, are used primarily for treating heart problems—and infertility, hence the large number of young women wandering the grounds.

The most interesting sight in town may be the small **Lázeňský muzeum** (Spa Museum), just off Národní ulice. There is a wonderful collection of spa-related antiques, including copper bathtubs and a turn-of-the-20th-century exercise bike called a Velotrab. The guest books provide an insight into the cosmopolitan world of pre–World War I Central Europe. The book for 1812 contains the entry "Ludwig van Beethoven, composer from Vienna." ⊠ *Ul. Doktora Pohoreckého 8,* ☎ *0166/542–344.* 🖼 *20 Kč.* ⊙ *Tues.–Fri. 10–5, weekends 10–4 (usually closed mid-Dec.–mid-Jan.).*

The main spring, **Františkův pramen,** is under a little gazebo filled with brass pipes. The colonnade to the left was decorated with a bust of Lenin that was replaced in 1990 by a memorial to the American liberation of the town in April 1945. The oval neo-Classical temple just beyond the spring (amazingly, *not* painted yellow and white) is the **Glauberova dvorana** (Glauber Pavilion), where several springs bubble up into glass cases. ⊠ *Národní ul.*

NEED A BREAK?	Only insipid pop music (the scourge of eating and drinking places everywhere in the country) interrupts the cheerful atmosphere of the little café of the **Slovan** (☞ Dining and Lodging, *below*) on Národní. The tiny gallery and lively frescoes make it a great spot for cake, coffee, or drinks.

Dining and Lodging

Most of the establishments in town do a big trade in spa patients, who generally stay for several weeks. Spa treatments usually require a medical check and cost substantially more than the normal room charge. Walk-in treatment can be arranged at some hotels or at the information center (☞ Visitor Information *in* Bohemian Spa Towns A to Z, *below*). Signs around town advertise massage therapy and other treatments for casual visitors.

$$ ✕🖼 **Slovan.** This gracious place is the perfect complement to this relaxed little town. The eccentricity of the original turn-of-the-20th-century design survived a thorough renovation during the 1970s. The airy rooms are clean and comfortable, and some have a balcony overlooking the main street. The main-floor restaurant serves above-average Czech dishes such as tasty *svíčková* (beef sirloin in a citrusy cream sauce) and roast duck. ⊠ *Národní 5, 351 01,* ☎ *0166/542–841,* 🖷 *0166/542–843. 25 rooms, 19 with bath. Restaurant, bar, café. AE, MC, V.*

$$$ 🖼 **Tři Lilie.** Reopened in 1995 after an expensive refitting, the "Three Lilies," which once accommodated the likes of Goethe and Metternich, immediately reestablished itself as the most comfortable spa hotel in town. It is thoroughly elegant, from guest rooms to brasserie. ⊠ *Národní 3,* ☎ 🖷 *0166/542–415. 31 rooms. Restaurant, brasserie, café. AE, MC, V.*

$$ 🖼 **Centrum.** Rooms in this barnlike building are well appointed if a bit sterile. Still, it is among the best-run hotels in town and only a short walk from the main park and central spas. ⊠ *Anglická 392, 351 01,* ☎ *0166/543–156,* 🖷 *0166/543–157. 30 rooms. Restaurant, bar. AE, MC, V.*

Mariánské Lázně

★ ❻① *47 km (29 mi) south of Karlovy Vary.*

Your expectations of what a spa resort should be may come nearest to fulfillment here. It's far larger and more active than Františkovy Lázně and greener and quieter than Karlovy Vary (☞ *above*). This was the spa favored by Britain's Edward VII. Goethe and Chopin also repaired here frequently. Mark Twain, on a visit to the spa in 1892, labeled the town a "health factory" and couldn't get over how new everything looked. Indeed, at that time everything was new. The sanatoriums, most built during the 19th century in a confident, outrageous mixture of "neo" styles, fan out impressively around a finely groomed oblong park. Cure takers and curiosity seekers alike parade through the Empire-style Cross Spring pavilion and the long colonnade near the top of the park. Buy a spouted drinking cup (available at the colonnades) and join the rest of the sippers taking the drinking cure. Be forewarned, though: the waters from the Rudolph, Ambrose, and Caroline springs, though harmless, all have a noticeable diuretic effect. For this reason they're used extensively in treating disorders of the kidney and bladder. For information on spa treatments, inquire at the main **spa offices** (✉ Masarykova 22, ☎ 0165/623–061). Walk-in treatment can be arranged at the **Nové Lázně** (New Spa; ✉ Reitenbergerova 53, ☎ 0165/ 644–111).

A stay in Mariánské Lázně can be healthful even without special treatment. Special walking trails of all difficulty levels surround the resort in all directions. The best advice is simply to put on comfortable shoes, buy a hiking map, and head out. One of the country's few golf courses lies about 3 km (2 mi) to the east of town. Hotels can also help to arrange special activities, such as tennis and horseback riding. For the less intrepid, a simple stroll around the gardens, with a few deep breaths of the town's famous air, is enough to restore a healthy sense of perspective.

Dining and Lodging

The best place to look for private lodgings is along Paleckého ulice and Hlavní třída, south of the main spa area. Private accommodations can also be found in the neighboring villages of Zádub and Závišín in the woods to the east of town.

$$ ✕ **Filip.** This bustling wine bar is where locals come to find relief from the sometimes large horde of tourists. There's a tasty selection of traditional Czech dishes—mainly pork, grilled meats, and steaks. ✉ *Poštovní 96,* ☎ *0165/626–161. No credit cards.*

$$ ✕ **Koliba.** This combination hunting lodge and wine tavern, set in the
★ woods roughly 10 minutes on foot from the spas, is an excellent alternative to the hotel restaurants in town. Grilled meats and shish kebabs, plus tankards of Moravian wine (try the dry, cherry red Rulandské červené), are served with traditional gusto while fiddlers play rousing Moravian tunes. ✉ *Dusíkova 592, in the direction of Karlovy Vary,* ☎ *0165/625–169. V.*

$$$$ 🏨 **Excelsior.** This lovely older hotel is on the main street and is convenient to the spas and colonnade. Rooms have traditional cherry-wood furniture and marble bathrooms, and the views over the town are enchanting. The staff is friendly and multilingual. While the food in the restaurant is only average, the romantic setting provides adequate compensation. ✉ *Hlavní třída 121, 353 01,* ☎ *0165/622–705,* FAX *0165/625–346. 64 rooms. Restaurant, café, massage, sauna. AE, DC, MC, V.*

$$$ 🏨 **Bohemia.** At this gracious, century-old hotel, beautiful crystal chan-
★ deliers in the main hall set the stage for a comfortable and elegant stay. The crisp beige-and-white rooms let you spread out and *really* unpack; they're spacious and high ceilinged. (If you want to indulge, request one of the enormous suites overlooking the park). The helpful staff can arrange spa treatments and horseback riding. ✉ *Hlavní třída 100, 353 01,* ☎ *0165/623–251,* FAX *0165/622–943. 73 rooms, 4 suites. Restaurant, café, lounge. AE, MC, V.*

$$$ 🏨 **Hotel Golf.** Book in advance to secure a room at this stately villa situated 3½ km (2 mi) out of town on the road to Karlovy Vary. The large, open rooms are cheery and modern. The restaurant on the main floor is excellent, but the big draw is the 18-hole golf course on the premises, one of the few in the Czech Republic. The course was opened in 1905 by King Edward VII. ⊠ *Zádub 55, 353 01,* ☎ *0165/622–651 or 0165/622–652,* FAX *0165/622–655. 25 rooms. Restaurant, pool, 18-hole golf course, tennis court, nightclub. AE, DC, MC, V.*

Nightlife and the Arts
The West Bohemian Symphony Orchestra performs regularly in the New Spa (Nové Lázně, ☞ *above*). The town's annual Chopin festival each August brings in pianists from around Europe to perform the Polish composer's works.

The Bohemian Spa Towns A to Z

Arriving and Departing
Prague is the main gateway to the Bohemian spa towns (☞ Arriving and Departing *in* Prague A to Z, *below*). Major trains from Nuremberg and Munich stop at some of the spa towns. It is also an easy drive across the border from Bavaria on the E48 to Cheb and from there to any of the spas.

Getting Around
Good, if slow, train service links all the major towns west of Prague. The best stretches are from Františkovy Lázně to Prague via Plzeň. The Prague–Karlovy Vary run takes far longer than it should—more than three hours by the shortest route. Frequent bus service between Prague and Karlovy Vary, by contrast, makes the journey in only about two hours each way. If you're driving, you can take the E48 directly from Prague to Karlovy Vary. Roads in the area tend to be in good condition, though they can sometimes be quite narrow.

Contacts and Resources
EMERGENCIES
Police (☎ 158). **Ambulance** (☎ 155). **Breakdowns** (☎ 1054; Yellow Angels ☎ 1230; Autoklub Bohemia Assistance [ABA] ☎ 1240).

GUIDED TOURS
Most of Prague's tour operators offer excursions to Karlovy Vary; inquire at the Prague Information Service or American Express. **Čedok** (☎ 02/2419–7111) offers one-day and longer tours covering western Bohemia's major sights, as well as curative vacations at many Czech spas.

TRAVEL AGENCIES
Karlovy Vary (⊠ American Express representative, Vřídelní 51, ☎ 017/323–0368).

VISITOR INFORMATION
Cheb (⊠ Nám. Krále Jiřího z Poděbrad 33, ☎ 0166/434–385 or 422–705). **Františkovy Lázně** (⊠ Tři Lilie Travel Agency, Národní 3, ☎ 0166/542–430). **Karlovy Vary** (⊠ Kur-Info, Vřídelní kolonáda [Vřídlo Colonnade], ☎ 017/322–4097, or Nám. Dr. M. Horákové 18 [near the bus station], ☎ 017/322–2833). **Mariánské Lázně** (⊠ Cultural and Information Center, Hlavní 47, ☎ 0165/625–892 or 0165/622–474). **Plzeň** (⊠ Nám. Republiky 41, ☎ 019/703–2750).

PRAGUE A TO Z

Arriving and Departing

By Bus

The Czech complex of regional bus lines known collectively as **ČSAD** operates its dense network from the sprawling Florenc station on Křižíkova (Metro: Florenc, Line B or C). For information about routes and schedules call ☎ 02/1034, consult the confusingly displayed timetables posted at the station, or visit the information window in the lower level lobby, open daily from 6 AM to 9 PM. One of several Web sites with bus and train information in English can be found at idos.datis.cdrail.cz.

By Car

Prague is well served by major roads and highways from anywhere in the country. On arriving in the city, simply follow the signs to CENTRUM (city center). During the day, traffic can be stop-and-go. Pay particular attention to the trams, which have the right-of-way in every situation. Avoid, when possible, driving in the congested and labyrinthine Old Town.

By Plane

Ruzyně Airport, 20 km (12 mi) northwest of the downtown area, is small but easily negotiated. Construction of a new terminal contiguous with the existing one has eased traffic flow.

ČSA (the Czech national carrier) offers direct flights all over the world from Ruzyně. Major airlines with offices in Prague are **Air Canada** (☎ 02/2489–2730); **Air France** (☎ 02/2422–7164); **Alitalia** (☎ 02/2419–4150); **American Airlines** (☎ 02/9623–6673); **British Airways** (☎ 02/2211–4444); **British Midland** (☎ 02/2481–0180); **ČSA** (☎ 02/2010–4310); **Delta** (☎ 02/2494–7332); **KLM** (☎ 02/2422–8678); **Lufthansa** (☎ 02/2481–1007); **SAS** (☎ 02/2481–1007); and **Swissair** (☎ 02/2481–2111).

Between the Airport and Downtown: The **Cedaz** minibus shuttle links the airport with náměstí Republiky (Republic Square, just off the Old Town). It runs hourly, more often at peak periods, between 6 AM and 9:30 PM daily and makes an intermediate stop at the Dejvická metro station. The one-way fare is 90 Kč. The minibus also serves many hotels for 360 Kč, which is less than the taxi fare in most cases. Regular municipal bus service (Bus 119) connects the airport and the Dejvická station; the fare is 12 Kč (15 Kč if purchased from the driver), and the ticket is transferable to trams or the metro. From Dejvická you can take the metro to the city center. To reach Wenceslas Square, get off at the Můstek station.

Taxis offer the easiest and most convenient way of getting downtown. The trip is a straight shot down Evropská Boulevard and takes approximately 20 minutes. The road is not usually busy, but anticipate an additional 20 minutes during rush hour (7 AM–9 AM and 3 PM–6 PM). The ride should cost 500 Kč–700 Kč.

By Train

International trains arrive at and depart from either of two stations: The main station, **Hlavní nádraží** (✉ Wilsonova ulice) is about 500 yards east of Wenceslas Square on Opletalova or Washingtonova street. Then there's the suburban **Nádraží Holešovice** (✉ about 2 km [1 mi] north of the city center). This is an unending source of confusion—always make certain you know which station your train is using. Note also that trains arriving from the west usually stop at Smíchov station, on the west bank of the Vltava, before continuing to the main station. Prague's other central train station, **Masarykovo nádraží** (⊠ Hybernská 13), serves mostly local trains but has an international ticket window that is often much less crowded than those at the main station. For train times, consult timetables in a station or get in line at the **information office** (☎ 02/2422–4200) upstairs at the main station (for domestic trains; open daily 3 AM–11:45 PM) or downstairs near the exits under the ČD Centrum sign (open daily 6 AM–7:30 PM). The main Čedok office (☞ Visitor Information, *below*) also provides train information and issues tickets.

Wenceslas Square is a convenient five-minute walk from the main station (best not undertaken late at night), or you can take the subway (Line C) one stop in the Háje direction to Muzeum. A taxi ride from the main station to the center should cost about 100 Kč, but the station cabbies are known for overcharging. To reach the city center from Nádraží Holešovice, take the metro (Line C) four stops to Muzeum; a taxi ride should cost roughly 200 Kč–250 Kč.

Getting Around

To see Prague properly, there is no alternative to walking. And the walking couldn't be more pleasant—most of it along the beautiful bridges and cobblestone streets of the city's historic core. Before venturing out, however, be sure you have a good map. The city is divided into 10 administrative districts; Prague 1 and part of Prague 2 lie entirely within the historic center, and the castle area is bordered by Prague 6 and Prague 7.

By Bus and Tram

Prague's extensive bus and streetcar network allows for fast, efficient travel throughout the city. Tickets are the same as those used for the metro, although you validate them at machines inside the bus or tram. Tickets (*jízdenky*) can be bought at hotels, some newsstands, and from dispensing machines in the metro stations. The basic, transferable ticket costs 12 Kč. It permits one hour's travel throughout the metro, tram, and bus network between 5 AM and 8 PM on weekdays, or 90 minutes' travel at other times. Single-ride tickets cost 8 Kč and allow one 15-minute ride on a tram or bus, without transfer, or a metro journey of up to four stations lasting less than 30 minutes (transfer between lines is allowed). You can also buy a one-day pass allowing unlimited use of the system for 70 Kč, a three-day pass for 180 Kč, a seven-day pass for 250 Kč, or a 15-day pass for 280 Kč. The passes can be purchased at the main metro stations, from ticket machines, and at some newsstands in the center. A pass is not valid until stamped in the orange machines in metro stations or aboard trams *and* the required information is entered on the back (there are instructions in English). A refurbished old tram, No. 91, travels through the Old Town and Lesser Quarter on summer weekends. The metro shuts down at midnight, but Trams 50–59 and Buses 500 and above run all night. Night trams run at 40-minute intervals, and all routes intersect at the corner of Lazarská and Spálená streets in the New Town near the Národní třída metro station.

By Car

Traveling by car is the easiest and most flexible way of seeing the Czech Republic—other than Prague. If you intend to visit only the capital, you can do without a car. The city center is congested and difficult to navigate, and you'll save yourself a lot of hassle by sticking to public transportation.

A permit is required to drive on expressways and other four-lane highways. They cost 100 Kč for 10 days, 200 Kč for one month, and 800

Kč for one year, and are sold at border crossings, some service stations, and all post offices.

In case of an accident or breakdown, *see* Emergencies, *below*.

PARKING

Parking is permitted in the center of town on a growing number of streets with parking meters or in the few small lots within walking distance of the historic center—but parking spaces are scarce. A meter with a green stripe lets you park up to six hours; an orange-stripe meter gives you two. (Use change in the meters.) A sign with a blue circle outlined in red with a diagonal red slash indicates a no-parking zone. Avoid the blue-marked spaces, which are reserved for local residents. Violaters may find a "boot" immobilizing their vehicle.

There's an underground lot at náměstí Jana Palacha, near Old Town Square. There are also park-and-ride (P+R) lots at some suburban metro stations, including Skalka (Line A), Zličín and Černý Most (Line B), and Nádraží Holešovice and Opatov (Line C).

ROAD CONDITIONS

The Prague city center is mostly a snarl of traffic, one-way streets, and tram lines. If you plan to drive outside the capital, there are few four-lane highways, but most of the roads are in reasonably good shape, and traffic is usually light. Roads can be poorly marked, however, so before you start out, buy one of the inexpensive multilingual auto atlases available at any bookstore.

RULES OF THE ROAD

The Czech Republic follows the usual Continental rules of the road. A right turn on red is permitted only when indicated by a green arrow. Signposts with yellow diamonds indicate a main road where drivers have the right of way. The speed limit is 130 kph (78 mph) on four-lane highways, 90 kph (56 mph) on open roads, and 50 kph (30 mph) in built-up areas. Seat belts are compulsory, and drinking before driving is absolutely prohibited. Passengers under 12 years of age, or less than 150 cm (5 ft) in height, must ride in the back seat.

By Subway

Prague's subway system, the metro, is clean and reliable; the stations are marked with an inconspicuous M sign. Trains run daily from 5 AM to midnight. Validate your ticket at an orange machine before descending the escalator. Trains are patrolled often; the fine for riding without a valid ticket is 200 Kč. Beware of pickpockets, who often operate in large groups on crowded trams and metro cars.

By Taxi

Dishonest taxi drivers are the shame of the nation. Luckily you probably won't need to rely on taxis for trips within the city center (it's usually easier to walk or take the subway). Typical scams include drivers doctoring the meter or simply failing to turn the meter on and then demanding an exorbitant sum at the end of the ride. In an honest cab, the meter starts at 25 Kč and increases by 17 Kč per km (½ mi) or 4 Kč per minute at rest. (The Airport Cars taxis operating from, but not to, the airport have a monopoly and charge slightly higher rates.) Most rides within town should cost no more than 80 Kč–150 Kč. To minimize the chances of getting ripped off, avoid taxi stands in Wenceslas Square, Old Town Square, and other heavily touristed areas. The best alternative is to phone for a taxi in advance. Two reputable firms are **AAA Taxi** (☎ 02/1080) and **Profitaxi** (☎ 02/1035). Many firms have English-speaking operators.

Prague Metro

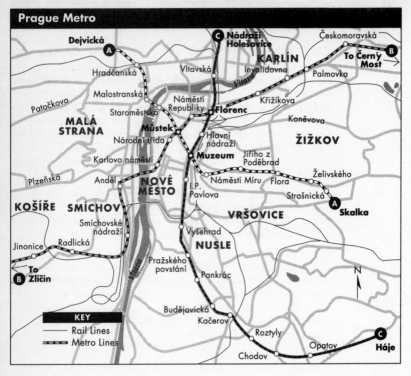

Contacts and Resources

Car Rentals

The following rental agencies are based in Prague:

Alamo (⊠ Hilton Hotel, ☎ 02/2484–2407, or Ruzyně Airport, ☎ 02/2011–3676). **Avis** (⊠ Klimentská 46 and Ruzyně Airport, ☎ 02/2185–1225). **Budget** (⊠ Hotel Inter-Continental, nám. Curieových 5, ☎ 02/231–9595, or Ruzyně Airport, ☎ 02/2011–3253). **Hertz** (⊠ Karlovo nám. 28, ☎ 02/2223–1010, or Ruzyně Airport, ☎ 02/312–0717). **Thrifty** (⊠ Washingtonova 9, ☎ 02/2421–1587, or Ruzyně Airport, ☎ 02/2011–4370).

Customs and Duties

VALUE ADDED TAX (VAT)

Value added tax reimbursements are available for items over 1,000 Kč exported within 30 days of purchase and certified by customs officials. You can pick up a reimbursement form at the customs office, travel agency, and some shops. As you must get the reimbursement directly from the retailer, most people use an intermidiary agency—VatMax is the only one which covers retailers nationwide. They reimburse you at the border, but take up to 30% commission, depending on the value of your purchase.

Embassies

U.S. Embassy (⊠ Tržiště 15, Lesser Quarter, ☎ 02/5753–0663). **U.K. Embassy** (⊠ Thunovská 14, Lesser Quarter, ☎ 02/5753–0278). **Canadian Embassy** (⊠ Mickiewiczova 6, Hradčany, ☎ 02/7210–1800). There are no Australian or New Zealand embassies.

Emergencies

Federal Police (☎ 158). **Prague city police** (156). **Ambulance** (☎ 155). **Medical emergencies: Lékařská služba první pomoci** (district first-aid clinic; ✉ Downtown: Palackého 5, ☎ 02/2494–9181); **Na Homolce Hospital** (✉ Roentgenova 2, Prague 5, ☎ 02/5727–2146 weekdays [foreigners' department]; 02/5721–1111; 02/5727–2191); **First Medical Clinic of Prague** (✉ Tylovo nám. 3/15, Prague 2, ☎ 02/2425–1319); **American Medical Center** (✉ Janovského 48, Prague 7, ☎ 02/807–756 for 24 hr service). Be prepared to pay in cash for medical treatment, whether you are insured or not. **Dentist** (✉ Palackého 5, ☎ 02/2494–6981 for 24-hr emergency service).

Lost credit cards: American Express (☎ 02/2421–9978); **Diners Club** (☎ 02/6731–4485); **MasterCard** (☎ 02/2424–8110); **Visa** (☎ 02/2412–5353).

English-Language Bookstores

In the city center nearly every bookstore (☞ Shopping, *above*) carries a few guidebooks and paperbacks. Street vendors on Wenceslas Square and Na Příkopě carry leading foreign newspapers and periodicals. For hiking maps and auto atlases, try the downstairs level of the **Jan Kanzelsberger bookshop** (✉ Václavské nám. 42, ☎ 02/2421–7335) on Wenceslas Square.

Guided Tours

Čedok (☞ Visitor Information, *below*) offers a three-and-a-half-hour "Grand City Tour," a combination bus and walking venture that covers all the major sights with commentary in English. It departs daily at 9:30 AM year-round, and also at 2 PM from April through October, from opposite the Prašná brána (Powder Tower) on Republic Square, near the main Čedok office. The price is about 750 Kč. "Historic Prague on Foot" is a slower-paced, three-hour walking tour for 400 Kč. From April through October, it departs Republic Square on Wednesday, Friday, and Sunday at 9:30 AM; in the off-season, it departs Friday at 9:30 AM. More tours are offered, especially in summer, and the schedules may well vary according to demand. You can also contact Čedok's main office to arrange a personalized walking tour. Times and itineraries are negotiable; prices start at around 500 Kč per hour.

Very similar tours by other operators also depart daily from Republic Square, Národní třída near Jungmannovo náměstí, and Wenceslas Square. Prices are generally a couple hundred crowns less than for Čedok's tours. Themed walking tours are very popular as well. You can choose medieval architecture, "Velvet Revolution walks," visits to Communist monuments, and any number of pub crawls. Each year, four or five small operators do these tours, which generally last a couple of hours and cost 200 Kč–300 Kč. Inquire at Prague Information Service (☞ Visitor Information, *below*) or a major ticket agency for the current season's offerings.

Late-Night Pharmacies

There are two 24-hour pharmacies close to the city's center: **Lékárna U Anděla** (✉ Štefánikova 6, Prague 5, ☎ 02/537–039 or 02/5732–0918); and **Lékárna** (✉ Belgická 37, Prague 2, ☎ 02/2251–9731).

Language

Czech, a Slavic language closely related to Slovak and Polish, is the official language of the Czech Republic. Learning English is popular among young people, but German is still the most useful language for tourists, especially outside Prague.

Mail
POSTAL RATES

In 2000, postcards to the United States and Canada cost 8 Kč; letters up to 20 grams in weight, 13 Kč. Postcards to Great Britain cost 7 Kč; letters, 9 Kč. You can buy stamps at post offices, hotels, and shops that sell postcards.

RECEIVING MAIL

If you don't know where you'll be staying, American Express mail service is a great convenience, available at no charge to anyone holding an American Express credit card or carrying American Express traveler's checks. The **American Express office** (Václavské nám. 56) is on Wenceslas Square in central Prague. You can also have mail held *poste restante* (general delivery) at post offices in major towns, but the letters should be marked *Pošta 1,* to designate the city's main post office. The poste restante window in Prague is at the **main post office** (✉ Jindřišská ul. 14). You will be asked for identification when you collect your mail.

Money and Expenses
COSTS

With inflation down to manageable levels, the Czech Republic is still generally a bargain by Western standards. Prague remains the exception. Hotel prices in particular are often higher than the facilities would warrant. Nevertheless, you can still find bargain private accommodations. The prices at tourist resorts outside the capital are lower and, in the outlying areas and off the beaten track, very low. It is an unfortunate fact that many venues such as museums, castles, and certain clubs charge a higher entrance fee for foreigners than they charge for Czechs. A few hotels still follow this practice, too. Venue staff can be quite militant about defending this policy, which is legally acceptable in the Czech Republic, and protesting such discrimination when it happens will usually get you nowhere.

CURRENCY

The unit of currency in the Czech Republic is the koruna, or crown (Kč), which is divided into 100 haléřů, or hellers. There are (little-used) coins of 10, 20, and 50 hellers; coins of 1, 2, 5, 10, 20, and (rarely) 50 Kč; and notes of 50, 100, 200, 500, 1,000, 2,000, and 5,000 Kč. Notes of 1,000 Kč and up may not always be accepted for small purchases.

Try to avoid exchanging money at hotels or private exchange booths, including the ubiquitous Chequepoint and Exact Change booths. They routinely take commissions of 8%–10%. The best places to exchange are at bank counters, where the commissions average 1%–3%, or at ATMs. The koruna is fully convertible, which means it can be purchased outside the country and exchanged into other currencies.

At press time the exchange rate was around 35 Kč to the U.S. dollar, 24 Kč to the Canadian dollar, and 56 Kč to the pound sterling.

SAMPLE PRICES

A cup of coffee, about 30 Kč; public museum or castle entrance, 20 Kč–150 Kč; private museum entrance, up to 450 Kč; a good theater seat, up to 500 Kč; a cinema seat, 60 Kč–100 Kč; ½ liter (pint) of Czech beer, 15 Kč–50 Kč; a 2-km (1-mi) taxi ride, 60 Kč–200 Kč; a bottle of Moravian wine in a good restaurant, 140 Kč–400 Kč; a glass (2 deciliters or 7 ounces) of wine, 35 Kč–60 Kč.

National Holidays

January 1; Easter Monday; May 1 (Labor Day); May 8 (Liberation Day); July 5 (Sts. Cyril and Methodius); July 6 (Jan Hus); October 28 (Czech National Day); and December 24, 25, and 26.

Opening and Closing Times

Though hours vary, most banks are open weekdays 8–5. Private exchange offices usually have longer hours. Museums are usually open daily except Monday 9–5 or 10–6; they tend to stop selling tickets an hour before closing time. It used to be that many sights outside the large towns, including most castles, were open daily except Monday only from May through September and in April and October were open only on weekends. Lately the trend is toward a longer season, although off-season hours may change capriciously. Stores are open weekdays 9–6. Some grocery stores open at 6 AM. Department stores often stay open until 7 PM. Outside Prague, most stores close for the weekend at noon on Saturday, although you can usually find a grocery open nights and weekends.

Passports and Visas

United States, Canadian, and British citizens need only a valid passport to visit the Czech Republic as tourists. U.S. citizens may stay for 30 days without a visa; British and Canadian citizens, six months. A new law effective Jan. 1, 2000, may raise additional bureaucratic obstacles in the path of those wishing to stay longer. Those interested in working or living in the Czech Republic are advised to contact the Czech embassy or consulate in their home country well in advance of their trip.

Student and Youth Travel

CKM (⊠ Jindřišská 28, ☎ 02/2423–0218) and **GTS** (⊠ Ve Smečkách 27, ☎ 02/9622–4300) provide information on travel bargains within the Czech Republic and abroad to students, travelers under 26, and teachers. **KMC** (Young Travelers' Club; ⊠ Karoliny Světlé 30, ☎ 02/2222–1328) issues IYH cards (150 Kč for those under 26, 200 Kč for others) and books hostel beds throughout the country.

Telephones

The country code for the Czech Republic is 420. When dialing a number in the Czech Republic from abroad, drop the initial zero from the regional area code. Prefixes 0601 to 0606 denote mobile phones; when dialing these numbers, no regional area code is needed.

INTERNATIONAL CALLS

You can reach an English-speaking operator in the United States through one of these toll-free operators: **AT&T** (☎ 00–420–00101); **MCI** (☎ 00–420–00112); or **Sprint** (☎ 00–420–87187). To Canada, dial **CanadaDirect** (☎ 00–420–00151). To the United Kingdom, dial **BT Direct** (☎ 00–420–04401). The operator will connect your collect or credit-card call at the carrier's standard rates. In Prague, many phone booths allow direct international dialing. With the prepaid **X Card** (300 Kč–1,000 Kč), rates to the U.S. are roughly 22 Kč per minute; a call to the U.K. costs about 14 Kč per minute. If you can't find a booth, the telephone office of the **main post office** (Jindřišská 14), open 24 hours, is the best place to try. Once inside, follow signs for TELEGRAF/TELEFAX. The international dialing code is 00. For calls to the United States, Canada, or the United Kingdom, dial the **international operator** (☎ 133004). For inquiries, dial **international directory assistance** (☎ 1181). Otherwise, ask the receptionist at any hotel to put a call through for you, though beware: the more expensive the hotel, the more expensive the call will be.

LOCAL CALLS

Coin-operated pay phones are hard to find. Most newer public phones operate only with a special telephone card, available from post offices and newsstands in denominations of 150 Kč and up. A short call within Prague costs 4 Kč from a coin-operated phone or the equivalent of 3 Kč (1 unit) from a card-operated phone. The dial tone is a series of alternating short and long buzzes.

Tipping

Service is usually not included in restaurant bills. Round the bill up to the next multiple of 10 (if the bill comes to 83 Kč, for example, give the waiter 90 Kč); 10% is considered appropriate in all but the most expensive places. Tip porters who bring bags to your rooms 40 Kč total. For room service, a 20 Kč tip is enough. In taxis, round the bill up by 10%. Give tour guides and helpful concierges between 50 Kč and 100 Kč for services rendered.

Travel Agencies

American Express (⊠ Václavské nám. 56, ☎ 02/2421–9992, or Mostecká 12, ☎ 02/5731–3636). **Thomas Cook** (⊠ Národní třída 28, ☎ 02/2110–5276).

For bus tickets to just about anywhere in Europe, try **Bohemia Tour** (⊠ Zlatnická 7, ☎ 02/231–3925) or Čedok's main office (☞ Visitor Information, *below*).

Visitor Information

There are four central offices of the municipal **Prague Information Service** (PIS). The **Old Town Hall branch** (⊠ Staroměstská radnice [Old Town Hall], ☎ 02/2448–2018) is open weekdays 9 to 6 and weekends 9 to 5. The **Na Příkopě office** (⊠ Na Příkopě 20, ☎ 02/264–020), just a few doors down from Čedok's main office, is open weekdays 9 to 6 and Saturday 9 to 3. The **Hlavní nádraží branch** (⊠ Hlavní nádraží, lower hall, ☎ 02/2423–9258) is open from April to October, weekdays 9 to 7 and weekends 9 to 4, and from November to March, weekdays 9 to 6 and Saturday 9 to 3. The **Charles Bridge tower office** (⊠ Malostranská mostecká věž, ☎ 02/536–010), in the tower on the Lesser Quarter end of Charles Bridge, is open April through October only. PIS locates lodging, offers city maps and general tourist information, sells tickets to cultural events, and arranges group and individual tours.

Čedok (⊠ Main office: Na Příkopě 18, ☎ 02/2419–7111, FAX 02/232–1656), the ubiquitous travel agency, provides general tourist information and city maps. Čedok will also exchange money, book accommodations, arrange guided tours, and book passage on airlines, buses, and trains. You can pay for Čedok services, including booking rail tickets, with any major credit card. Note limited weekend hours. The main office is open weekdays from 8:30 to 6 and Saturday 9–1.

The **Czech Tourist Authority** (⊠ Staroměstské nám. 6, ☎ FAX 02/2481–0411) on Old Town Square can provide information on tourism outside Prague but does not sell tickets or book accommodations.

To find out what's on and to get the latest tips for shopping, dining, and entertainment, consult Prague's weekly English-language newspaper, the *Prague Post.* It prints comprehensive entertainment listings and can be bought at most downtown newsstands as well as in major North American and European cities. The monthly *Culture in Prague,* available at newsstands and tourist offices for 40 Kč, provides a good overview of major cultural events.

3   BUDAPEST

Revitalization continues full-swing in Hungary as the Communist legacy fades into 20th-century history. Budapest offers breathtaking Old World grandeur and thriving cultural life—a must-stop on any trip to Central Europe. Hearty meals spiced with rich red paprika, the generosity and warmth of the Magyar soul: These and more sustain visitors in this land of vital spirit and beauty.

By Alan Levy
and Julie
Tomasz

Updated by
Paul Olchváry

HUNGARY SITS AT THE CROSSROADS of Central Europe, having retained its own identity by absorbing countless invasions and foreign occupations. Its industrious, resilient people have a history of brave but unfortunate uprisings: against the Turks in the 17th century, the Hapsburgs in 1848, and the Soviet Union in 1956. Each has resulted in a period of readjustment, a return to politics as the art of the possible.

A year into the new millennium much indeed seems possible. The economy continues to improve as European Union (EU) membership is on the near horizon. Hungary joined NATO in 1999. While this momentum was essentially spurred by the collapse of the one-party state in 1990, the lot of most Hungarians had improved even in the 1960s and '70s. Communist Party leader János Kádár remained relatively popular at home and abroad, allowing Hungary to expand and improve ties with the West. The bubble began to burst in the 1980s, however, when the economy stagnated and inflation swelled. The peaceful transition to democracy began when young reformers in the party shunted aside the aging Kádár in 1988 and began speaking openly about multiparty democracy, a market economy, and a break from Moscow—daring ideas at the time.

Events unfolded quickly, and by spring 1990, as the Iron Curtain fell, Hungary held its first free elections in more than 40 years. A center-right government took office, sweeping away the Communists and their renamed successor party, the Socialists. Ironically, four years later, in the next elections, Hungarians chose none other than the Hungarian Socialist Party, which ruled in coalition with the Free Democrats until ousted again in the 1998 elections. Voting the center-right FIDESZ party, led by 35-year-old Viktor Orbán, into power, the nation chose a new generation to take it into the new millennium. At press time the Socialists were once again seen as the government's most formidable rival in the next elections (2002)—this time vying for the chance to lead Hungary into the EU. *Plus ça change . . .*

Because Hungary is a small, agriculturally oriented country, visitors are often surprised by its grandeur and Old World charm, especially in the capital, Budapest, which bustles with life as never before. Hungarians spare visitors bureaucratic hassles at the border and airport. Entry is easy and quick for Westerners, most of whom do not need visas.

Situated on both banks of the Danube, Budapest unites the colorful hills of Buda and the wide, businesslike boulevards of Pest. Though it was the site of a Roman outpost during the 1st century, the city was not officially created until 1873, when the towns of Óbuda, Pest, and Buda united. Since then, Budapest has been the cultural, political, intellectual, and commercial heart of Hungary; for the 20% of the nation's population who live in the capital, anywhere else is simply *vidék* ("the country").

Budapest has suffered many ravages in the course of its long history. It was totally destroyed by the Mongols in 1241, captured by the Turks in 1541, and nearly destroyed again by Soviet troops in 1945. But this bustling industrial and cultural center survived as the capital of the People's Republic of Hungary after the war—and then, as the 1980s drew to a close, it became one of the Eastern Bloc's few thriving bastions of capitalism. Today, judging by the city's flourishing cafés and restaurants, markets and bars, the stagnation enforced by the Communists seems a thing of the very distant past.

Much of the charm of a visit to Budapest lies in unexpected glimpses into shadowy courtyards and in long vistas down sunlit cobbled streets. Although some 30,000 buildings were destroyed during World War II and in the 1956 Revolution, the past lingers on in the often crumbling architectural details of the antique structures that remain.

Hungarians are known for their hospitality and love talking to foreigners, although their unusual language can be a challenge. Today, however, everyone seems to be learning English, especially young people. But what all Hungarians share is a deep love of music, and the calendar is studded with it, from Budapest's famous opera to its annual spring music festival. And at many restaurants Gypsy violinists serenade you during your evening meal.

Pleasures and Pastimes

Dining

Through the lean postwar years the Hungarian kitchen lost none of its spice and sparkle. Meats, rich sauces, and creamy desserts predominate, but the more health-conscious will also find salads, even out of season. (Strict vegetarians should note, however, that even meatless dishes are usually cooked with lard [*zsír*].) In addition to the ubiquitous dishes most foreigners are familiar with, such as chunky beef *gulyás* (goulash) and *paprikás csirke* (chicken paprika) served with *galuska* (little pinched dumplings), traditional Hungarian classics include fiery *halászlé* (fish soup), scarlet with hot paprika; *fogas* (pike perch) from Lake Balaton; and goose liver, duck, and veal specialties. Lake Balaton is the major source of fish in Hungary, particularly for *süllő*, a kind of perch. Hungarians are also very fond of carp (*ponty*), catfish (*harcsa*), and eel (*angolna*), which are often stewed in a garlic-and-tomato sauce.

Portions are large, so don't plan to eat more than one main Hungarian meal a day. Desserts are lavish, and every inn seems to have its house *torta* (cake), though *rétes* (strudels), *Somlói galuska* (a steamed sponge cake soaked in chocolate sauce and whipped cream), and *palacsinta* (stuffed crepes) are ubiquitous. Traditional rétes fillings are *mák* (sugary poppy seeds), *meggy* (sour cherry), and *túró* (sweetened cottage cheese); palacsintas always come rolled with *dió* (sweet ground walnuts), *túró*, or *lekvár* (jam)—often *sárgabarack* (apricot).

In major cities, there is a good selection of restaurants, from the grander establishments that echo the imperial past of the Hapsburg era to the less expensive, rustic spots favored by locals. In addition to trying out the standard *vendéglő* or *étterem* (restaurants), you can eat at a *bisztró étel bár* (sit-down snack bar), a *büfé* (snack counter), an *eszpresszó* (café), or a *söröző* (pub). And no matter how strict your diet, don't pass up a visit to at least one *cukrászda* (pastry shop). Our dining choices focus primarily on Hungarian and Continental cuisine; if you find yourself longing for something farther afield, from pizza to Chinese to Greek to American-style fast food, you can find it aplenty in the larger cities.

Although prices are steadily increasing, there are plenty of good, affordable restaurants offering a variety of Hungarian dishes. Even in Budapest, eating out can provide you with some of the best value for the money of any European capital. In almost all restaurants, an inexpensive prix-fixe lunch called a *menü* is available, usually for as little as 400 Ft. It includes soup or salad, an entrée, and a dessert. One caveat: Some of the more touristy restaurants sometimes follow the international practice of embellishing tourists' bills; it doesn't hurt to check the prices discreetly before ordering and the total before paying. Budapest made international news in 1998 for a flagrant overcharging incident; authorities have since cracked down on the guilty establishments. Also note that most restaurants have a fine-print policy of charging for each slice of bread consumed from the bread basket.

Hungarians eat early—you risk offhand service and cold food after 9 PM. Lunch, the main meal for many, is served from noon to 2. At most moderately priced and inexpensive restaurants, casual but neat dress is acceptable.

CATEGORY	COST*
$$$$	over $11
$$$	$8–$11
$$	$5–$8
$	under $5
*per person for a three-course meal, excluding wine and tip	

Folk Art

Hungary's centuries-old traditions of handmade, often regionally specific folk art are still beautifully alive. Intricately carved wooden boxes, vibrantly colorful embroidered tablecloths and shirts, matte-black pottery pitchers, delicately woven lace collars, ceramic plates splashed with painted flowers and birds, and decorative heavy leather whips are among the favorite handcrafted pieces a visitor can purchase. You'll find them in folk-art stores around the country but can purchase them directly from the artisans at crafts fairs and from peddlers on the streets. Dolls dressed in national costume are also popular souvenirs.

Lodging

Outside Budapest there are few very expensive hotels, so you will improve your chances of having a memorable lodging experience by arranging a stay in one of the alternative options noted below. For specific recommendations or information about how to book lodging in these accommodations, see the lodging and information sections throughout the chapter.

Bought back from the government over the last several years, more and more of Hungary's magnificent, centuries-old castles and mansions are being restored and opened as country resorts; a night or two in one of these majestic old places makes for an unusual and romantic (but not always luxurious) lodging experience. Northern Hungary has some of the best.

Guest houses, also called *panziók* (pensions), provide simple accommodations—well suited to people on a budget. Like B&Bs, most are run by couples or families and offer simple breakfast facilities and usually have private bathrooms; they're generally outside the city or town center. Arrangements can be made directly with the panzió or through local tourist offices and travel agents abroad. Another good budget option is renting a room in a private home. In the provinces it is safe to accept rooms offered to you directly; they will almost always be clean and in a relatively good neighborhood, and the prospective landlord will probably not cheat you. Look for signs reading SZOBA KIADÓ (or the German ZIMMER FREI). Reservations and referrals can also be made by any tourist office, and if you go that route, you have someone to complain to if things don't work out.

Village tourism is a growing trend in Hungary, affording visitors a chance to sink into life in tiny, typical villages around the country. The Hungarian Tourist Board's *Village Tourism* publication provides descriptions and color photos of many of the village homes now open to guests, either by renting a home or as an overnight guest. Apartments in Budapest and cottages at Lake Balaton are available for short- and long-term rental and can make the most economic lodging for families—particularly for those who prefer to cook their own meals. Rates and reservations can be obtained from tourist offices in Hungary and abroad. Also consult the free annual accommodations directory published by **Tourinform** (☞ Visitor Information *in* Budapest A to Z, *below*); published in five languages, it lists basic information about hotels, pensions, bungalows, and tourist hostels throughout the country. A separate brochure lists the country's campgrounds.

For single rooms with bath, count on paying about 80% of the double-room rate. During the off-season (in Budapest, September through March; at Lake Balaton, September through May), rates can drop considerably. Prices at Lake Balaton tend to be significantly higher than those in the rest of the countryside. Note that most large hotels require payment in hard currency—either U.S. dollars or Deutschemarks. As the slated 2002 adoption of the Euro as a common currency in many Western European countries nears, however, ever more hotels now listing their rates in Deutschemarks will be doing so in Euros.

CATEGORY	BUDAPEST*	OTHER AREAS*
$$$$	over $200	over $70
$$$	$140–$200	$50–$70
$$	$80–$140	$30–$50
$	under $80	under $30

*All prices are for a standard double room with bath and breakfast during peak season (June through August).

🐾 following the text of a review is your signal that the property has a Web site, where you will find details and, usually, images; for a link, visit www.fodors.com/urls.

Porcelain

Among the most sought-after items in Hungary are the exquisite hand-painted Herend and Zsolnay porcelain. Unfortunately, the prices on all makes of porcelain have risen considerably in the last few years. For guaranteed authenticity, make your purchases at the specific Herend and Zsolnay stores in major cities, or at the factories themselves in Herend and Pécs, respectively.

Spas and Thermal Baths

Several thousand years ago, the first settlers of the area that is now Budapest chose their home because of its abundance of hot springs. Centuries later, the Romans and the Turks built baths and developed cultures based on medicinal bathing. Now there are more than 1,000 medicinal hot springs bubbling up around the country. Budapest alone has some 14 historic working baths, which attract ailing patients with medical prescriptions for specific water cures as well as "recreational" bathers—locals and tourists alike—wanting to soak in the relaxing waters, try some of the many massages and treatments, and experience the architectural beauty of the bathhouses themselves.

For most, a visit to a bath involves soaking in several thermal pools of varying temperatures and curative contents—perhaps throwing in a game of aquatic chess—relaxing in a steam room or sauna, and getting a brisk, if not brutal, massage (average cost: 800 Ft. for 15 minutes). Many bath facilities are single-sex or have certain days set aside for men or women only, and most people walk around nude or with miniature loincloths, provided at the door. Men should be aware that some men-only baths have a strong gay clientele.

In addition to the ancient beauties there are newer, modern baths open to the public at many spa hotels. They lack the charm and aesthetic appeal of their older peers but provide the latest treatments in sparkling facilities. Of the areas outside Budapest covered in this guidebook, Debrecen, Hévíz, and Eger are famous spa towns with popular bath facilities. For more information, page through the "Hungary: Land of Spas" brochure published by the Hungarian Tourist Board, available free from most tourist offices.

Wine, Beer, and Spirits

Hungary tempts wine connoisseurs with its important wine regions, especially Villány, near Pécs, in the south; Eger and Tokaj in the north; and the northern shore of Lake Balaton. Szürkebarát and especially Olaszrizling are common white table wines; Tokay, one of the great wines of the world, can be heavy, dark, and sweet, and its most famous variety is drunk as an aperitif or a dessert wine. It's expensive, especially by Hungarian standards, so it's usually reserved for special occasions.

The gourmet red table wine of Hungary, Egri Bikavér (Bull's Blood of Eger, usually with *el toro* himself on the label), is the best buy and the safest bet with all foods. Villány produces superb reds and the best rosés; the most adventurous reds—with sometimes successful links to both Austrian and Californian wine making and viticulture—are from the Sopron area.

Before- and after-dinner drinks tend toward schnapps, most notably *Barack-pálinka,* an apricot brandy. A plum brandy called *Kosher szilva-pálinka,* bottled under rabbinical supervision, is the very best of the brandies available in stores. *Vilmos körte-pálinka,* a pear variety, is almost as good. Note that any bottle under 1,000 Ft. or so probably contains more ethyl alcohol than pure fruit brandy. Unicum, Hungary's national liqueur, is a dark, thick, and potent herbal bitter that could be likened to Germany's Jägermeister. Its chubby green bottle makes it a good souvenir to take home.

Major Hungarian beers are Dreher, Kőbányai, and Aranyászok, and several good foreign beers are produced in Hungary under license.

EXPLORING BUDAPEST

The principal sights of the city fall roughly into three areas, each of which can be comfortably covered on foot. The Budapest hills are best explored by public transportation. Note that street names have been changed in the past several years to purge all reminders of the Communist regime. Underneath the new names, the old ones sometimes remain, canceled out by a big red slash. Also note that a Roman-numeral prefix listed before an address refers to one of Budapest's 22 districts. Districts V, VI, and VII are in downtown Pest; I includes Castle Hill, the main tourist district of Buda.

Numbers in the text correspond to numbers in the margin and on the Exploring Budapest and Castle Hill (Várhegy) maps.

Great Itineraries

IF YOU HAVE 1–2 DAYS

A whistle-stop visit should start at Várhegy (Castle Hill), where you can walk along cobblestone streets lined with Baroque, Gothic, and Renaissance houses and visit the Királyi Palota (Royal Palace). Zip down the hill for a soak or massage at one of the beautiful baths, such as those at the Gellért Hotel, and then cross to the Pest side of the river for a walk along the *korzó* (promenade) up towards the lovely Széchenyi lánchíd (Chain Bridge). If you're determined to shop, Váci utca is your best bet—the pedestrian-only street is unabashedly touristy, but there's a wealth of shops selling everything from paprika to crystal. Vörösmarty tér (Vörösmarty Square) is a good place to find a café and take a break. With extra time, you could visit Szent István Bazilika (St. Stephen's Basilica) and then walk up the grand avenue Andrássy út to Hősök tere (Heroes' Square). If at all possible, catch a performance at the neo-Renaissance Operaház (Opera House).

IF YOU HAVE 3–5 DAYS

Take time to thoroughly explore the museums, squares, and religious buildings on Castle Hill, including Mátyás templom (Matthias Church), the Budapesti Történeti Múzeum (Budapest History Museum), and quiet, tree-lined Tóth Árpád sétány promenade. (This could easily take a full day and a half.) Spend a couple of afternoons in Budapest's other wonderful museums, such as the Magyar Nemzeti Múzeum (Hungarian National Museum), where you can see the epic Hungarian history exhibit and sundry treasures (but to see the Crown of St. Stephen, which used to be here, visit the Parliament building, where it's in safekeeping until at least August 20, 2001); the Szépművészeti Múzeum (Museum of Fine Arts), which has Hungary's finest collection of European art, or the Néprajzi Múzeum (Museum of Ethnography) and its detailed exhibit on Hungarian folk cuture. You could also visit Europe's largest synagogue, the Nagy Zsinagóga (Great Synagogue). If it's a sunny afternoon and you can't bear to be indoors, head to Margit-sziget (Margaret Island). If you enjoy classical music, try to nip in to a performance at the Liszt Ferenc Zeneakadémia (Franz Liszt Academy of Music).

IF YOU HAVE 5–7 DAYS

After spending a few days exploring the city as described above, take a trip to the north shore of Lake Balaton. Here you can swim, hike up the vineyard-covered slopes of Mount Badacsony, do some wine tasting, and have incredible fresh fish for dinner. Tihany is a good place to spend the night; in the morning you can wander its twisting streets and visit its hilltop abbey. Alternatively, you could spend the night in the busy spa town of Balatonfüred.

Várhegy (Castle Hill)

Most of the major sights of Buda are on Várhegy (Castle Hill), a long, narrow plateau laced with cobblestone streets, clustered with beautifully preserved Baroque, Gothic, and Renaissance houses, and crowned by the magnificent Royal Palace. The area is theoretically banned to private cars (except for those of neighborhood residents and Hilton Hotel guests), but the streets manage to be lined bumper to bumper with Trabants and Mercedes all the same—sometimes the only visual element to verify you're not in a fairy tale. As in all of Budapest, thriving urban new has taken up residence in historic old; international corporate offices, diplomatic residences, restaurants, and boutiques occupy many of its landmark buildings. But these are still the exceptions, as families occupy most flats and homes. The most striking example, perhaps, is the Hilton Hotel on Hess András tér, which has ingeniously incorporated remains of Castle Hill's oldest church (a tower and one wall), built by Dominican friars in the 13th century.

A GOOD WALK

Castle Hill's cobblestone streets and numerous museums are made to be explored on foot: Plan to spend about a day here. Most of the transportation options for getting to Castle Hill deposit you on Szent György tér or Dísz tér. It's impossible not to find Castle Hill, but it is possible to be confused about how to get on top of it. If you're already on the

92

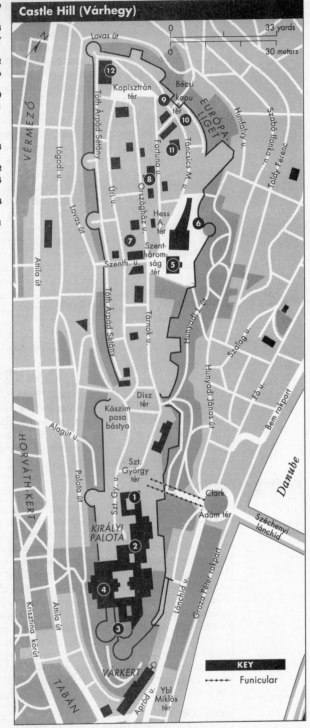

Castle Hill (Várhegy)

Buda side of the river, you can take the Castle bus—*Várbusz*—from the Moszkva tér metro station, northwest of Castle Hill. If you're starting out from Pest, you can take a taxi or Bus 16 from Erzsébet tér or, the most scenic alternative, cross the Széchenyi Lánchíd (Chain Bridge) on foot to Clark Ádám tér and ride the *Sikló* (funicular) up Castle Hill (☞ Clark Ádám tér, *below*).

Begin your exploration by walking slightly farther south to visit the **Királyi Palota** at the southern end of the hill. Of the palace's several major museums, the **Magyar Nemzeti Galéria** ② and the **Budapesti Történeti Múzeum** ③ are particularly interesting. From here, you can cover the rest of the area by walking north along its handful of cobbled streets. From Dísz tér, start with Tárnok utca, whose houses and usually open courtyards offer glimpses of how Hungarians have integrated contemporary life into Gothic, Renaissance, and Baroque settings; of particular interest are the houses at No. 16, now the Aranyhordó restaurant, and at No. 18, the 15th-century Arany Sas Patika (Golden Eagle Pharmacy Museum), with a naïf Madonna and child in an overhead niche. This tiny museum displays instruments, prescriptions, books, and other artifacts from 16th- and 17th-century pharmacies. Modern commerce is also integrated into Tárnok utca's historic homes; you'll encounter numerous folk souvenir shops and tiny boutiques lining the street. Tárnok utca funnels into Szentháromság tér, home of **Mátyás templom** ⑤ and, just behind it, the **Halászbástya** ⑥.

After exploring them, double back to Dísz tér and set out northward again on Úri utca, which runs parallel to Tárnok utca; this long street is lined with beautiful, genteel homes. The funny little Telefónia Museum, at No. 49, is worth a stop, as is the **Budavári Labirintus** ⑦, at No. 9. At the end of Úri utca you'll reach Kapisztrán tér. From here, you can walk south again on a parallel street, Országház utca (Parliament Street), the main thoroughfare of 18th-century Buda; it takes its name from the building at No. 28, which was the seat of Parliament from 1790 to 1807. You'll end up back at Szentháromság tér, with just two streets remaining to explore.

You can stroll down little Fortuna utca, named for the 18th-century Fortuna Inn, which now houses the **Magyar Kereskedelmi és Vendéglátóipari Múzeum** ⑧. At the end of Fortuna utca you'll reach **Bécsi kapu tér** ⑨, opening to Moszkva tér just below. Go back south on the last of the district's streets, Táncsics Mihály utca, stopping at the **Középkori Zsidó Imaház** ⑩ and the **Zenetörténeti Múzeum** ⑪. Next door, at No. 9, is the Baroque house (formerly the Royal Mint) where rebel writer Táncsics Mihály was imprisoned in the dungeons and freed by the people on the Day of Revolution, March 15, 1848. You'll find yourself in front of the Hilton Hotel, back at Hess András tér, bordering Szentháromság tér. Those whose feet haven't protested yet can finish off their tour of Castle Hill by doubling back to the northern end and strolling south back to Dísz tér on **Tóth Árpád sétány,** the romantic, tree-lined promenade along the Buda side of the hill.

TIMING

Castle Hill is small enough to cover in one day, but perusing its major museums and several tiny exhibits will require more time.

Sights to See

❾ Bécsi kapu tér (Vienna Gate Square). Marking the northern entrance to Castle Hill, the stone gateway (rebuilt in 1936) called Vienna Gate opens toward Vienna—or, closer at hand, Moszkva tér a few short blocks below. The square named after it has some fine Baroque and rococo houses but is dominated by the enormous neo-Romanesque (1913–1917) headquarters of the **Országos Levéltár** (Hungarian National Archives), which resembles a cathedral-like shrine to paperwork.

❸ Budapesti Történeti Múzeum (Budapest History Museum). The palace's Baroque southern wing (E) contains the Budapest History Museum, displaying a fascinating permanent exhibit of modern Budapest history from Buda's liberation from the Turks in 1686 through the 1970s. Viewing the vintage 19th- and 20th-century photos and videos of the castle, the Széchenyi Lánchíd, and other Budapest monuments—and seeing them as the backdrop to the horrors of World War II and the 1956 Revolution—helps to put your later sightseeing in context; while you're browsing, peek out one of the windows overlooking the Danube and Pest and let it start seeping in.

Through historical documents, objects, and art, other permanent exhibits depict the medieval history of the Buda fortress and the capital as a whole. This is the best place to view remains of the medieval Royal Palace and other archaeological excavations. Some of the artifacts unearthed during excavations are in the vestibule in the basement; others are still among the remains of medieval structures. Down in the cellars are the original medieval vaults of the palace; portraits of King Matthias and his second wife, Beatrice of Aragon; and many late-14th-century statues that probably adorned the Renaissance palace. ⊠ *Royal Palace (Wing E), Szt. György tér 2,* ☎ *1/375–7533.* ⊡ *400 Ft.* ☉ *Mar.–mid-May and mid-Sept.–Oct., Wed.–Mon. 10–6; mid-May–mid-Sept., daily 10–6; Nov.–Feb., Wed.–Mon. 10–4.*

❼ Budavári Labirintus (Labyrinth of Buda Castle). Used as a wine cellar during the 16th and 17th centuries and then as an air-raid shelter during World War II, the labyrinth—entered at Úri utca 9 below an early 18th-century house—can be explored with a tour or, if you dare, on your own. There are some English-language brochures available. ⊠ *Úri u. 9,* ☎ *1/375–6858.* ⊡ *800 Ft.* ☉ *Daily 9:30–7:30.*

NEED A BREAK?	For a light snack, pastry, and coffee, **Café Miro** (⊠ Úri u. 30, ☎ 1/375–5458) is a fresh, hip alternative to the Old World Budapest cafés.

⑫ Hadtörténeti Múzeum (Museum of Military History). Fittingly, this museum is lodged in a former barracks, on the northwestern corner of Kapisztrán tér. The exhibits, which include collections of uniforms and military regalia, trace the military history of Hungary from the original Magyar conquest in the 9th century through the period of Ottoman rule to the mid-20th century. You can arrange an English-language tour in advance for around 1,000 Ft. ⊠ *I, Tóth Árpád sétány 40,* ☎ *1/356–9522.* ⊡ *270 Ft.* ☉ *Apr.–Sept., Tues.–Sun. 10–6; Oct.–Mar., Tues.–Sun. 10–4.*

★ ❻ Halászbástya (Fishermen's Bastion). The wondrous porch overlooking the Danube and Pest is the neo-Romanesque Fishermen's Bastion, a merry cluster of white stone towers, arches, and columns above a modern bronze statue of St. Stephen, Hungary's first king. Medieval fishwives once peddled their wares here, but the site is now home to souvenirs, crafts, and music.

Kapisztrán tér (Capistrano Square). Castle Hill's northernmost square was named after St. John of Capistrano, an Italian friar who in 1456 recruited a crusading army to fight the Turks who were threatening Hungary. There's a statue of this honored Franciscan on the northwest corner; also here are the **Museum of Military History** (☞ *above*) and the remains of the 12th-century Gothic **Mária Magdolna templom** (Church of St. Mary Magdalene). Its *torony* (tower), completed in 1496, is the only part left standing; the rest of the church was destroyed by air raids during World War II.

★ **Királyi Palota** (Royal Palace, commonly called Buda Castle). During a seven-week siege at the end of 1944, the entire Castle Hill district of palaces, mansions, and churches was turned into one vast ruin. The final German stand was in the Royal Palace, which was utterly gutted by fire; by the end of the siege its walls were reduced to rubble, and just a few scarred pillars and blackened statues protruded from the wreckage. The destruction was incalculable, yet it gave archaeologists and art historians an opportunity to discover the medieval buildings that once stood on the site of this Baroque and neo-Baroque palace. Fortunately, details of the edifices of the kings of the Árpád and Anjou dynasties, of the Holy Roman Emperor Sigismund, and of the great 15th-century king Matthias Corvinus had been preserved in some 80 medieval reports, travelogues, books, and itineraries that were subsequently used to reconstruct the complex.

The postwar rebuilding was slow and painstaking. In some places debris more than 20 ft deep had to be removed. Freed from mounds of rubble, the foundation walls and medieval castle walls were completed, and the ramparts surrounding the medieval royal residence were re-created as close to their original shape and size as possible. Out of this herculean labor emerged the Royal Palace of today, a vast cultural center and museum complex (☞ Budapesti Történeti Múzeum, *above, and* Ludwig Múzeum, Magyar Nemzeti Galéria, *and* Országos Széchenyi Könyvtár, *below*).

🔟 **Középkori Zsidó Imaház** (Medieval Synagogue). The excavated one-room Medieval Synagogue is now used as a museum. On display are objects relating to the Jewish community, including religious inscriptions, frescoes, and tombstones dating to the 15th century. ✉ *Táncsics Mihály u. 26,* ☎ *1/375–7533 (ext. 243).* 🎟 *120 Ft.* ☉ *May–Oct., Tues.–Fri. 10–2, weekends 10–6.*

❶ **Ludwig Múzeum.** This collection of more than 200 pieces of Hungarian and contemporary international art, including works by Picasso and Lichtenstein, occupies the castle's northern wing. ✉ *Royal Palace (Wing A), Dísz tér 17,* ☎ *1/375–7533.* 🎟 *300 Ft., free Tues.* ☉ *Tues.– Sun. 10–6.*

❽ **Magyar Kereskedelmi és Vendéglátóipari Múzeum** (Hungarian Museum of Commerce and Catering). The 18th-century Fortuna Inn now serves visitors in a different way—as the Catering Museum. Displays in a permanent exhibit show the city as a tourist destination from 1870 to the 1930s; you can see, for example, what a room at the Gellért Hotel, still operating today, would have looked like in 1918. The Commerce Museum, just across the courtyard, chronicles the history of Hungarian commerce from the late 19th century to 1947, when the new, Communist regime "liberated" the economy into socialism. The four-room exhibit includes everything from an antique chocolate-and-caramel vending machine to early shoe-polish advertisements. You can rent an English-language recorded tour for 300 Ft. ✉ *Fortuna u. 4,* ☎ *1/375–6249.* 🎟 *120 Ft., free Fri.* ☉ *Wed.–Fri. 10–5, weekends 10–6.*

❷ **Magyar Nemzeti Galéria** (Hungarian National Gallery). The immense center block of the Royal Palace (made up of Wings B, C, and D) exhibits a wide range of Hungarian fine art, from medieval ecclesiastical paintings and statues, through Gothic, Renaissance, and Baroque art, to a rich collection of 19th- and 20th-century works. Especially notable are the works of the romantic painter Mihály Munkácsy, the impressionist Pál Szinyei Merse, and the surrealist Mihály Tivadar

Kosztka Csontváry, whom Picasso much admired. There is also a large collection of modern Hungarian sculpture. There are labels and commentary in English for both permanent and temporary exhibits. If you contact the museum in advance, you can book a tour for up to five people with an English-speaking guide. ⊠ *Royal Palace (entrance in Wing C), Dísz tér 17,* ☏ *1/375–7533.* ▣ *Gallery 400 Ft.; tour 1,000 Ft.* ☉ *Mid-Mar.–Oct., Tues.–Sun. 10–6; Nov.–mid-Jan., Tues.–Sun. 10–4; mid-Jan.–mid-Mar., Tues.–Fri. 10–4, weekends 10–6).*

★ ❺ **Mátyás templom** (Matthias Church). The Gothic Matthias Church is officially the Buda Church of Our Lady but better known by the name of the 15th century's "just king" of Hungary, who was married here twice. It is sometimes called the Coronation Church, because the last two kings of Hungary were crowned here: the Hapsburg emperor Franz Joseph in 1867 and his grandnephew Karl IV in 1916. Originally built for the city's German population in the mid-13th century, the church has endured many alterations and assaults. For almost 150 years it was the main mosque of the Turkish overlords—and the predominant impact of its festive pillars is decidedly Byzantine. Badly damaged during the recapture of Buda in 1686, it was completely rebuilt between 1873 and 1896 by Frigyes Schulek, who gave it an asymmetrical western front, with one high and one low spire, and a fine rose window; the south porch is from the 14th century.

The **Szentháromság Kápolna** (Trinity Chapel) holds an *encolpion,* an enameled casket containing a miniature copy of the Gospel to be worn on the chest; it belonged to the 12th-century king Béla III and his wife, Anne of Chatillon. Their burial crowns and a cross, scepter, and rings found in their excavated graves are also displayed here. The church's **treasury** contains Renaissance and Baroque chalices, monstrances, and vestments. High Mass is celebrated every Sunday at 10 AM, sometimes with full orchestra and choir—and often with major soloists; get here early if you want a seat. During the summer there are usually organ recitals on Friday at 8 PM. Tourists are asked to remain at the back of the church during weddings and services (it's least intrusive to come after 9 AM weekdays and between 1 and 5 PM Sunday and holidays). ⊠ *I, Szentháromság tér 2,* ☏ *1/355–5657.* ☉ *Daily 7 AM–7:30 PM.* ▣ *Church free, except during concerts; treasury 200 Ft.* ☉ *Treasury daily 9:30–5:30.*

❹ **Országos Széchenyi Könyvtár** (Széchenyi National Library). The western wing (F) of the Royal Palace is home to the National Library, which houses more than 2 million volumes. Its archives include well-preserved medieval codices, manuscripts, and historic correspondence. This is not a lending library, but the reading rooms are open to the public (though you must show a passport), and even the most valuable materials can be viewed on microfilm. Small, temporary exhibits on rare books and documents are usually on display; the hours and admission fees for these are quite variable. Note that the entire library closes for one month every summer, usually in July or August. ⊠ *Royal Palace (Wing F). To arrange a tour with an English-speaking guide,* ☏ *1/224–3745.* ▣ *300 Ft.* ☉ *Reading rooms Mon. 1–9, Tues.–Sat. 9–9; exhibits Mon. 1–6, Tues.–Sat. 10–6.*

Statue of Prince Eugene of Savoy. In front of the Royal Palace, facing the Danube by the entrance to Wing C, stands an equestrian statue of Prince Eugene of Savoy, a commander of the army that liberated Hungary from the Turks at the end of the 17th century. From here there is a superb view across the river to Pest. ⊠ *By entrance to Royal Palace, Wing C.*

Szentháromság tér (Holy Trinity Square). This square is named for its Baroque **Trinity Column**, erected in 1712–1713 as a gesture of thanksgiving by survivors of a plague. The column stands in front of the famous Gothic Matthias Church (☞ *above*), its large pedestal a perfect seat from which to watch the wedding spectacles that take over the church on spring and summer weekends: From morning 'til night, frilly engaged pairs flow in one after the other and, after a brief transformation inside, back out onto the square.

★ **Tóth Árpád sétány** (Árpád Tóth Promenade). This romantic, tree-lined promenade along the Buda side of the hill is often mistakenly overlooked by sightseers. Beginning at the Museum of Military History (☞ *above*), the promenade takes you "behind the scenes" along the back sides of the matte-pastel Baroque houses you saw on Úri utca, with their regal arched windows and wrought-iron gates. On a late spring afternoon, the fragrance of the cherry trees and the sweeping view of the quiet Buda neighborhoods below may be enough to revive even the most weary. ⊠ *I, from Kapisztrán tér to Szent György u.*

Úri utca (Úri Street). Running parallel to Tárnok utca, Úri utca has been less commercialized by boutiques and other shops; the longest and oldest street in the castle district, it is lined with many stately houses, all worth special attention for their delicately carved details. Both gateways of the Baroque palace at **Nos. 48–50** are articulated by Gothic niches. The **Telefónia Múzeum** (Telephone Museum), at No. 49, is an endearing little museum entered through a central courtyard shared with the local district police station. Although vintage telephone systems are still in use all over the country, both the oldest and most recent products of telecommunication—from the 1882 wooden box with hose attachment to the latest digital marvels—can be observed and tested here. *Telefónia Múzeum:* ⊠ *Úri u. 49,* ☎ *1/201–8188.* 🖅 *About 100 Ft.* ☉ *Apr.–Oct., Tues.–Sun. 10–4.*

Várszínház (Castle Theater). Once a Franciscan church, this was transformed into a more secular royal venue in 1787 under the supervision of courtier Farkas Kempelen. The first theatrical performance in Hungarian was held here in 1790. Heavily damaged during World War II, the theater was rebuilt and reopened in 1978. While the building retains its original late-Baroque-style facade, the interior was renovated with marble and concrete. It is now used as the studio theater of the National Theater and occasionally for classical recitals, and there is usually a historical exhibition in its foyer—usually theater-related, such as a display of costumes. ⊠ *Színház u. 1–3,* ☎ *1/375–8649.*

⑪ **Zenetörténeti Múzeum** (Museum of Music History). This handsome gray-and-pearl-stone 18th-century palace is where Beethoven allegedly stayed in 1800 when he came to Buda to conduct his works. Now a museum, it displays rare manuscripts and old instruments downstairs in its permanent collection and temporary exhibits upstairs in a small, sunlit hall. The museum also often hosts intimate classical recitals. ⊠ *Táncsics Mihály u. 7,* ☎ *1/214–6770 (ext. 250).* 🖅 *About 200 Ft.* ☉ *Mid-Nov.–late-Dec. and first 2 wks of Mar., Tues.–Sun. 10–5; mid-Mar.–mid-Nov., Tues.–Sun. 10–6.*

Tabán and Gellért-hegy (Tabán and Gellért Hill)

Spreading below Castle Hill is the old quarter called Tabán (from the Turkish word for "armory"). A onetime suburb of Buda, it was known at the end of the 17th century as Little Serbia (*Rác*) because so many Serbian refugees settled here after fleeing from the Turks. It later became a district of vineyards and small taverns. Though most of the small

98

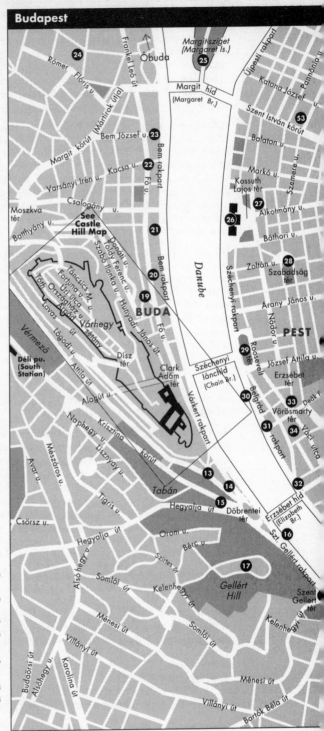

houses characteristic of this district have been demolished—mainly in the interest of easing traffic—a few traditional buildings remain.

Gellért-hegy (Gellért Hill), 761 ft high, is the most beautiful natural formation on the Buda bank. It takes its name from St. Gellért (Gerard) of Csanad, a Venetian bishop who came to Hungary in the 11th century and, legend has it, was rolled off the top of the hill in a cart by pagans. The walk up can be tough, but take solace from the cluster of hot springs at the foot of the hill, which soothe and cure bathers at the Rác, Rudas, and Gellért baths.

Numbers in the text correspond to numbers in the margin and on the Exploring Budapest map.

A Good Walk

From the **Semmelweis Orvostörténeti Múzeum** ⑬, walk around the corner to Szarvas tér and a few yards toward the river to the **Tabán plébánia-templom** ⑭. Walking south on Attila út and crossing to the other side of Hegyalja út, you'll be at the foot of Gellért Hill. From here, take a deep breath and climb the paths and stairs to the **Citadella** ⑰ fortress at the top of the hill (about 30 minutes). After taking in the views and exploring the area, you can descend and treat yourself to a soak or a swim at the **Gellért Szálloda és Thermál Fürdő** ⑱ at the southeastern foot of the hill. On foot, take the paths down the southeastern side of the hill. You can also take Bus 27 down the back of the hill to Móricz Zsigmond körtér and walk back toward the Gellért on busy Bartók Béla út, or take Tram 47, 49, 18, or 19 a couple of stops to Szent Gellért tér.

TIMING

The Citadella and Szabadság szobor are lit in golden lights every night, but the entire Gellért-hegy is at its scenic best every year on August 20, when it forms the backdrop to the spectacular St. Stephen's Day fireworks display.

Sights to See

★ ⑰ **Citadella.** The fortress atop the hill was a much-hated sight for Hungarians. They called it the Gellért Bastille, for it was erected, on the site of an earlier wooden observatory, by the Austrian army as a lookout after the 1848–1849 War of Independence. But no matter what its history may be, the views here are breathtaking. Its transformation into a tourist site during the 1960s improved its image, with the addition of cafés, a beer garden, wine cellars, and a hostel. In its inner wall is a small graphic exhibition (with some relics) of Budapest's 2,000-year history. ☒ XI, Citadella sétány, ☎ No phone. ⌧ Free. ☉ Fortress: daily, 24 hrs; amenities hrs vary.

Erzsébet híd (Elizabeth Bridge). This bridge was named for Empress Elizabeth (1837–1898), called Sissi, of whom the Hungarians were particularly fond. The beautiful but unhappy wife of Franz Joseph, she was stabbed to death in 1898 by an anarchist while boarding a boat on Lake Geneva. The bridge was built between 1897 and 1903; at the time, it was the longest single-span suspension bridge in Europe.

★ ⑱ **Gellért Szálloda és Thermál Fürdő** (Gellért Hotel and Thermal Baths). At the foot of Gellért Hill, are these beautiful art-nouveau establishments. The Danubius Hotel Gellért (☞ Lodging, *below*) is the oldest spa hotel in Hungary, with hot springs that have supplied curative baths for nearly 2,000 years. It is the most popular among tourists, as you don't need reservations, it's quite easy to communicate, and there's a wealth of treatments—including chamomile steam baths, salt-vapor in-halations, and hot mud packs. Many of these treatments require a doc-tor's prescription; they will accept prescriptions from foreign doctors. Men and women have separate steam and sauna rooms; both the in-door pool and the outdoor wave pool are coed (☞ Outdoor Activi-ties and Sports, *below*). ⊠ *XI, Gellért tér 1,* ☎ *1/466–6166 (baths).* 🔁 *Indoor baths and steam rooms 750 Ft. per 1½ hrs; indoor and pool 1,500 Ft. per day.* 🕙 *Baths weekdays 6 AM–6 PM, weekends 6:30–4 (May–Sept. until 7). May–Sept. weekend massage only until 1 PM. Wave pool May–Sept., daily 6 AM–6 PM.*

⑮ Rác Fürdő (Rác Baths). The bright-yellow building tucked away at the foot of Gellért Hill near the Elizabeth Bridge houses these baths, built during the reign of King Zsigmond in the early 15th century and re-built by Miklós Ybl in the mid-19th century. Its waters contain alka-line salts and other minerals; you can also get a massage. Women can bathe on Monday, Wednesday, and Friday; men on Tuesday, Thurs-day, and Saturday (☞ Outdoor Activities and Sports, *below*). These baths are particularly popular with the gay community. ⊠ *I, Hadnagy u. 8–10,* ☎ *1/356–1322.* 🔁 *550 Ft.* 🕙 *Mon.-Sat. 6:30–6.*

⑯ Rudas Fürdő (Rudas Baths). This bath is on the riverbank, the origi-nal Turkish pool making its interior possibly the most dramatically beau-tiful of Budapest's baths. A high, dome roof admits pinpricks of bluish-green light into the dark, circular stone hall with its austere columns and arches. Fed by eight springs with a year-round tempera-ture of 44°C (111°F), the Rudas's highly fluoridated waters have been known for 1,000 years. The facility is open to men only (it does not have a large gay following); a less interesting outer swimming pool is open to both sexes (☞ Outdoor Activities and Sports, *below*). Mas-sages are available. ⊠ *I, Döbrentei tér 9,* ☎ *1/356–1322.* 🔁 *650 Ft.* 🕙 *Weekdays 6 AM–6 PM, weekends 6–noon.*

⑬ Semmelweis Orvostörténeti Múzeum (Semmelweis Museum of Medi-cal History). This splendid Baroque house was the birthplace of Ignác Semmelweis (1818–1865), the Hungarian physician who proved the contagiousness of puerperal (childbed) fever. It's now a museum that traces the history of healing. Semmelweis's grave is in the garden. ⊠ *Apród u. 1–3,* ☎ *1/375–3533.* 🔁 *150 Ft.* 🕙 *Tues.-Sun. 10:30–5:30.*

Szabadság szobor (Liberation Monument). Visible from many parts of the city, this 130-ft-high memorial, which starts just below the southern edge of the Citadella, was originally planned as a memorial to a son of Hungary's then-ruler, Miklós Horthy, whose warplane had crashed in the Ukraine in 1942. However, by the time of its comple-tion in 1947 (three years after Horthy was ousted), it had become a memorial to the Russian soldiers who fell in the 1944–45 siege of Buda-pest; and hence for decades was associated chiefly with this. From afar it looks light, airy, and even liberating. A sturdy young girl, her hair and robe swirling in the wind, holds a palm branch high above her head. Until recently, she was further embellished with sculptures of giants slaying dragons, Red Army soldiers, and peasants rejoicing at the free-dom that Soviet liberation promised (but failed) to bring to Hungary. Since 1992, her mood has lightened: In the Budapest city government's systematic purging of Communist symbols, the Red Combat in-fantrymen who had flanked the Liberation statue for decades were hacked off and carted away. A few are now on display among the other evicted statues in Szobor Park in the city's 22nd district (☞ Off the Beaten Path, *below*). ⊠ *Gellért-hegy.*

OFF THE
BEATEN PATH

SZOBOR PARK (Statue Park) – For a look at Budapest's too-recent Iron Curtain past, make the 30-minute drive out to this open-air exhibit, cleverly nicknamed "Tons of Socialism," where 42 of the Communist statues and memorials that once dominated the city's streets and squares have been put out to pasture since the political changes in 1989. Here you can wander among mammoth Lenin and Marx statues and buy socialist-nostalgia souvenirs while songs from the Hungarian and Russian workers' movements play bombastically in the background. ⊠ *XXII, Balatoni út, corner of Szabadkai út,* ☎ *1/227–7446.* ☞ *250 Ft.* ☉ *Mar.–mid-Nov., daily 8–dusk; mid-Nov.–Feb., weekends 10–dusk.*

Szarvas-ház (Stag House). This Louis XVI–style building is named for the former Szarvas Café or, more accurately, for its extant trade sign, with an emblem of a stag not quite at bay, which can be seen above the arched entryway. The structure houses the Aranyszarvas restaurant, which preserves some of the mood of the old Tabán. ⊠ *Szarvas tér 1.*

⓮ **Tabán plébánia-templom** (Tabán Parish Church). In 1736, this church was built on the site of a Turkish mosque and subsequently renovated and reconstructed several times. Its present form—mustard-color stone with a rotund, green clock tower—could be described as restrained Baroque. ⊠ *I, Attila u. 1.*

North Buda

Most of these sights are along Fő utca (Main Street), a long, straight thoroughfare that starts at the Chain Bridge and runs parallel to the Danube. It is lined on both sides with multistory late-18th-century houses—many darkened by soot and showing their age more than those you've seen in sparklingly restored areas such as Castle Hill. This northbound exploration can be done with the help of Bus 86, which covers the waterfront, or on foot, although distances are fairly great.

Numbers in the text correspond to numbers in the margin and on the Exploring Budapest map.

A Good Walk

Beginning at **Batthyány tér** ㉑, with its head-on view of Parliament across the Danube, continue north on Fő utca, passing (or stopping to bathe at) the famous Turkish **Király-fürdő** ㉒. From **Bem József tér** ㉓, one block north, turn left (away from the river) up Fekete Sas utca, crossing busy Margit körút and turning right, one block past, up Mecset utca. This will take you up the hill to **Gül Baba türbéje** ㉔.

TIMING

The tour can fit easily into a few hours, including a good 1½-hour soak at the baths; expect the walk from Bem József tér up the hill to Gül Baba türbéje to take about 25 minutes. Fő utca and Bem József tér can get congested during rush hours (from around 7:30 AM to 8:30 AM and 4:30 PM to 6 PM). Remember that museums are closed Monday and that the Király Baths are open to men and women on different days of the week.

SIGHTS TO SEE

㉑ **Batthyány tér.** This lovely square, open on its river side, affords a grand view of Parliament, directly across the Danube. The M2 subway, the HÉV electric railway from Szentendre, and various suburban and local buses converge on the square, as do peddlers hawking everything from freshly picked flowers to mismatched pairs of shoes. At No. 7 Batthyány tér is the beautiful, Baroque twin-tower **Szent Anna-templom** (Church of St. Anne), dating from 1740–1762, its oval cupola adorned with frescoes and statuary.

NEED A BREAK?

The **Angelika** café (✉ II, Batthyány tér 7, ☎ 1/212–3784), housed in the Church of St. Anne building, serves swirled meringues, chestnut-filled layer cakes, and a plethora of other heavenly pastries, all baked on the premises from family recipes. You can sit inside on small velvet chairs at marble-top tables or at one of the umbrella-shaded tables outdoors. It's open daily 10 AM–10 PM.

23 **Bem József tér.** This square near the river is not particularly picturesque and can get heavy with traffic, but it houses the statue of its important namesake, Polish general József Bem, who offered his services to the 1848 revolutionaries in Vienna and then Hungary. Reorganizing the rebel forces in Transylvania, he was the war's most successful general. It was at this statue on October 23, 1956, that a great student demonstration in sympathy with the Poles' striving for liberal reforms exploded into the brave and tragic Hungarian uprising suppressed by the Red Army.

19 **Corvin tér.** This small, shady square on Fő utca is the site of the turn-of-the-20th-century Folk Art Association administration building and the Budai Vigadó concert hall (☞ Nightlife and the Arts, *below*) at No. 8.

24 **Gül Baba türbéje** (Tomb of Gül Baba). Gül Baba, a 16th-century dervish and poet whose name means "father of roses" in Turkish, was buried in a tomb built of carved stone blocks with four oval windows. He fought in several wars waged by the Turks and fell during the siege of Buda in 1541. The tomb remains a place of pilgrimage; it is considered Europe's northernmost Muslim shrine and marks the spot where he was slain. Set at an elevation on Rózsadomb (Rose Hill), the tomb is near a good lookout for city views. ✉ *II, Mecset u. 14,* ☎ *1/355–8764.* *100 Ft.* ⏲ *May–Oct., Tues.–Sun. 10–4.*

Gyermek vasút (Children's Railway). The 12-km (7-mi) Children's Railway runs from Széchenyi-hegy to Hűvösvölgy. The sweeping views make the trip well worthwhile for children and adults alike. Departures are from Széchenyi-hegy; to get there, take a cog railway (public transport tickets valid) uphill to the last stop and walk a few hundred yards down a short, partly forested road to the left, in the direction most others will be going. ✉ *Cog railway station: intersection of Szillágyi Erzsébet fasor and Pasaréti út.* *Children's Railway: about 140 Ft. one-way.* ⏲ *Trains run (from Széchenyi-hegy) late Apr.–Oct., daily 8:45–5; Nov.–mid-Mar., Tues.–Fri. 10–4, weekends 10–5 (sometimes closed Tues.); mid-Mar.–late Apr., Tues.–Fri. 9:30–5, weekends 10–5.*

OFF THE BEATEN PATH

JÁNOSHEGY (Janos Hill) – A *libegő* (chairlift) will take you to Janos Hill—at 1,729 ft, the highest point in Budapest—where you can climb a lookout tower for the best view of the city. ✉ *Chairlift: Zugligeti út 97 (take Bus 158 from Moszkva tér to the last stop, Zugligeti út,* ☎ *1/394–3764.* *One-way 250 Ft., round-trip 450 Ft.* ⏲ *Mid-May–Aug., daily 9–6; Sept.–mid-May (depending on weather), daily 9:30–4; closed every other Mon.*

Kapucinus templom (Capuchin Church). This church was converted from a Turkish mosque at the end of the 17th century. Damaged during the revolution in 1849, it acquired its current romantic-style exterior when it was rebuilt a few years later. ✉ *II, Fő u. 32.*

22 **Király-fürdő** (King Baths). The royal gem of Turkish baths in Budapest was built in the 16th century by the Turkish pasha of Buda. Its stone cupola, crowned by a golden moon and crescent, arches over the steamy, dark pools indoors. It is open to men on Monday, Wednesday,

and Friday; to women on Tuesday, Thursday, and Saturday (☞ Outdoor Activities and Sports, *below*). These baths are very popular with the gay community. ⊠ *II, Fő u. 84,* ☎ *1/202–3688.* 🖃 *500 Ft.* ⊙ *Weekdays 6:30 AM–6 PM, Sat. 6:30–noon.*

㉔ **Szilágyi Dezső tér.** This is another of the charming little squares punctuating Fő utca; here you'll find the house where composer Béla Bartók lived, at No. 4.

Margit-sziget (Margaret Island)

More than 2½ km (1½ mi) long and covering nearly 200 acres, **Margit-sziget** ㉕ is ideal for strolling, jogging, sunbathing, or just loafing. In good weather, the island draws a multitudinous cross section of the city's population out to its gardens and sporting facilities. The outdoor pool complex of the Palatinus Baths (toward the Buda side), built in 1921, can attract tens of thousands of people on a summer day. Nearby are a tennis stadium, a youth athletic center, boathouses, sports grounds, and, most impressive of all, the Nemzeti Sportuszoda (National Sports Swimming Pool), designed by the architect Alfred Hajós (while still in his teens, Hajós won two gold medals in swimming at the first modern Olympic Games, held in Athens in 1896). In addition, walkers, joggers, bicyclists, and rollerbladers do laps around the island's perimeter and up and down the main road, closed to traffic except for Bus 26 (and a few official vehicles), which travels up and down the island and across the Margaret Bridge to and from Pest.

The island's natural curative hot springs have given rise to the Danubius Grand and Thermal hotels on the northern end of the island (☞ Lodging, *below*) and are piped in to two spa hotels on the mainland, the Aquincum on the Buda bank and the Hélia on the Pest side.

A Good Walk

Entering the island from its southern end at the **Margit híd,** stroll (or rent a bicycle and pedal) north along any of the several tree-shaded paths, including the **Muő vész sétány,** pausing for a picnic on an open lawn, and eventually ending up at the rock garden at the northern end. From here, you can wander back to the southern end or take Bus 26 on the island's only road.

TIMING

A leisurely walk simply from one end to the other would take about 40 minutes, but it's nice to spend extra time wandering. To experience Margaret Island's role in Budapest life fully, go on a Saturday or Sunday afternoon to join and/or watch people whiling away the day. Sunday is a particularly good choice for strategic sightseers, who can utilize the rest of the week to cover those city sights and areas that are closed on Sunday. On weekdays, you'll share the island only with joggers and children playing hooky from school.

Sights to See

Margit híd (Margaret Bridge). At the southern end of the island, the Margaret Bridge is the closer of the two entrances for those coming from downtown Buda or Pest. Just north of the Chain Bridge, the bridge walkway provides gorgeous midriver views of Castle Hill and Parliament. Toward the end of 1944, the bridge was blown up by the retreating Nazis while it was crowded with rush-hour traffic. It was rebuilt in the same unusual shape—forming an obtuse angle in midstream, with a short leg leading down to the island. The original bridge was built during the 1840s by French engineer Ernest Gouin in collaboration with Gustave Eiffel.

㉕ **Margit-sziget** (Margaret Island). The island was first mentioned almost 2,000 years ago as the summer residence of the commander of the Roman garrison at nearby Aquincum. Later known as Rabbit Island (Insula Leporum), it was a royal hunting ground during the Árpád dynasty. King Imre, who reigned from 1196 to 1204, held court here, and several convents and monasteries were built here during the Middle Ages. (During a walk round the island, you'll see the ruins of a few of these buildings.) It takes its current name from St. Margaret, the pious daughter of King Béla IV, who at the ripe old age of 10 retired to a Dominican nunnery here.

ⓒ **Margit-sziget Vadaspark** (Margaret Island Game Park). Just east of the rose garden is a small would-be petting zoo, if the animals were allowed to be petted. A fenced-in compound houses a menagerie of goats, rabbits, donkeys, assorted fowl and ducks, and gargantuan peacocks that sit heavily on straining tree branches. 🎟 *Free.*

Marosvásárhelyi zenélő kút (Marosvásárhely Musical Fountain). At the northern end of the island is a copy of the water-powered Marosvásárhely Musical Fountain, which plays songs and chimes. The original was designed more than 150 years ago by a Transylvanian named Péter Bodor. It stands near a serene, artificial **rock garden** with Japanese dwarf trees and lily ponds. The stream coursing through it never freezes, for it comes from a natural hot spring causing it instead to give off thick steam in winter that enshrouds the garden in a mystical cloud.

Muővész sétány (Artists' Promenade). Through the center of the island runs the Artists' Promenade, lined with busts of Hungarian visual artists, writers, and musicians. Shaded by giant plane trees, it's a perfect place to stroll. The promenade passes close to the **rose garden** (in the center of the island), a large grassy lawn surrounded by blooming flower beds planted with hundreds of kinds of flowers. It's a great spot to picnic or to watch a game of soccer or Ultimate Frisbee, both of which are regularly played here on weekend afternoons.

Downtown Pest and the Kis Körút (Little Ring Road)

Budapest's urban heart is full of bona fide sights plus innumerable tiny streets and grand avenues where you can wander for hours admiring the city's stately old buildings—some freshly sparkling after their first painting in decades, others silently but still gracefully crumbling.

Dominated by the Parliament building, the district surrounding Kossuth tér is the legislative, diplomatic, and administrative nexus of Budapest; most of the ministries are here, as are the National Bank and Courts of Justice. Downriver, the romantic Danube promenade, the Duna korzó, extends along the stretch of riverfront across from Castle Hill. With Vörösmarty tér and pedestrian shopping street Váci utca just inland, this area forms Pest's tourist core. Going south, the korzó ends at Március 15 tér. One block in from the river, Ferenciek tere marks the beginning of the university area, spreading south of Kossuth Lajos utca. Here, the streets are narrower and the sounds of your footsteps echo off the elegantly aging stone buildings.

Pest is laid out in broad circular *körúts* ("ring roads" or boulevards). Vámház körút is the first sector of the 2½-km (1½-mi) Kis körút (Little Ring Road), which traces the route of the Old Town wall from Szabadság híd (Liberty Bridge) to Deák tér. Construction of the inner körút began in 1872 and was completed in 1880. Changing names as it curves, after Kálvin tér it becomes Múzeum körút (passing by the National Museum), and then Károly körút for its final stretch ending at

Deák tér. Deák tér, the only place where all three subway lines converge, could be called the dead-center of downtown. East of Károly körút are the weathered streets of Budapest's former ghetto.

A Good Walk

Starting at Kossuth tér to see the **Országház** ㉖ and the **Néprajzi Múzeum** ㉗, it's worth walking a few blocks southeast to take in stately **Szabadság tér** ㉘ before heading back to the Danube and south to the foot of the **Széchenyi Lánchíd** at **Roosevelt tér** ㉙. As this tour involves quite a bit of walking, you may want to take Tram 2 from Kossuth tér a few stops downriver to Roosevelt tér to save your energy. While time and/or energy may not allow it just now, at some point during your visit, a walk across the Chain Bridge is a must. From Roosevelt tér go south, across the street, and join the **korzó** ㉚ along the river, strolling past the **Vigadó** ㉛ at Vigadó tér, all the way to the **Belvárosi plébánia templom** ㉜ at Március 15 tér, just under the Elizabeth Bridge. Double back up the korzó to Vigadó tér and walk in from the river on Vigadó utca to **Vörösmarty tér** ㉝.

Follow the crowds down pedestrian-only **Váci utca** ㉞, crossing busy Kossuth Lajos utca near Ferenciek tere and continuing along Váci utca's southern stretch to the **Vásárcsarnok** ㊱. Doubling back a few blocks on Váci utca, turn right onto Szerb utca and stroll past the **Szerb Ortodox templom** to the street's end at **Egyetem tér** ㊲. Here, you are going through the darker, narrower streets of this student-filled, increasingly trendy area. A detour into any of the other side streets will give you a good flavor of the area. Walking south on Kecskeméti utca, you will reach **Kálvin tér** ㊳. To save time and energy, you can also take Tram 47 or 49 from Fővám tér, in front of the Vásárcsarnok, one stop away from the Danube to Kálvin tér. Just north of Kálvin tér on Múzeum körút is the **Magyar Nemzeti Múzeum** ㊴. The **Nagy Zsinagóga** ㊵ is about ¾ km (⅓ mi) farther north along the Kis körút (Small Ring Road)—a longish walk or one short stop by tram. From here, more walking along the körút, or a tram ride to the last stop, brings you to Pest's main hub, Deák tér. The **Szent István Bazilika** ㊸ is an extra but rewarding 500-yard walk north on Bajcsy-Zsilinszky út.

TIMING

This is a particularly rich part of the city; the suggested walk will take the better part of a day, including time to visit the museums, stroll on the korzó, and browse on Vaci utca—not to mention time for lunch. Keep in mind that the museums are closed on Monday.

Sights to See

㉜ **Belvárosi plébánia templom** (Inner City Parish Church). Dating to the 12th century, this is the oldest ecclesiastical building in Pest. It's actually built on something even older—the remains of the Contra Aquincum, a 3rd-century Roman fortress and tower, parts of which are visible next to the church. There is hardly any architectural style that cannot be found in some part or another, starting with a single Romanesque arch in its south tower. The single nave still has its original Gothic chancel and some 15th-century Gothic frescoes. Two side chapels contain beautifully carved Renaissance altarpieces and tabernacles of red marble from the early 16th century. During Budapest's years of Turkish occupation, the church served as a mosque—a *mihrab,* a Muslim prayer niche, is a reminder of this. During the 18th century, the church was given two Baroque towers and its present facade. In 1808 it was enriched with a rococo pulpit, and still later a superb winged triptych was added to the main altar. From 1867 to 1875, Franz Liszt lived only a few steps away from the church, in a town house where he held regular "musical Sundays" at which Richard and Cosima Wagner were frequent guests and participants. Liszt's own musical Sunday mornings often began in this church. An admirer of its acoustics and organ, he conducted many masses here, including the first Budapest performance of his *Missa Choralis,* in 1872. ⊠ *V, Március 15 tér 2,* ☎ *1/318–3108.*

㊲ Egyetem tér (University Square). Budapest's University of Law sits here in the heart of the city's university neighborhood. On one corner is the cool gray-and-green marble **Egyetemi Templom** (University Church), one of Hungary's most beautiful Baroque buildings. Built between 1725 and 1742, it has an especially splendid pulpit.

㊷ Evangélikus Templom and Evangélikus Múzeum (Lutheran Church and Lutheran Museum). The neoclassical Lutheran Church sits in the center of it all on busy Deák tér. Classical concerts are regularly held here. The church's interior designer, János Krausz, flouted then-traditional church architecture by placing a single large interior beneath the huge vaulted roof structure. The adjoining school is now the Lutheran Museum, which traces the role of Protestantism in Hungarian history and contains Martin Luther's original will. ⊠ *V, Deák Ferenc tér 4,* ☎ *1/317–4173.* ▦ *Museum 300 Ft. (includes tour of church).* ☯ *Museum: Mar.–Dec., Tues.–Sun. 10–6; Jan.–Feb. until 5. Church: open only in conjunction with museum visit and during services (Sun. 9, 11, and 6).*

㉟ Ferenciek Templom (Franciscan church). This pale-yellow church was built in 1743. On the wall facing Kossuth Lajos utca is a bronze relief showing a scene from the devastating flood of 1838; the detail is so vivid that it almost makes you seasick. A faded arrow below the relief indicates the high-water mark of almost 4 ft. Next to it is the **Nereids Fountain,** a popular meeting place for students from the nearby Eötvös Loránd University. ⊠ *V, Ferenciek tere.*

NEED A
BREAK?

Budapest's newest, most touted café, the **Centrál** (⊠ V, Károlyi Mihály u. 9, ☎ 1/266–4572), is really nothing new: From 1887, famous writers scribbled away here every day. This, not to mention libraries-worth of thoughtful conversation, kept up until the Communists, who disapproved of such gathering places, shut it down in 1949. At the turn of the new millennium it reopened (after a stint as a video arcade) with a bang. Elegant, smoky, and crowded, the Centrál offers time-honored sweets and both traditional and lighter meals.

Görög Ortodox templom (Greek Orthodox Church). Built at the end of the 18th century in late-Baroque style, the Greek Orthodox Church was remodeled a century later by Miklós Ybl, who designed the Opera House and many other important Budapest landmarks. The church retains some fine wood carvings and a dazzling array of icons by a late-18th-century Serbian master Miklós Jankovich. ⊠ *V, Petőfi tér 2/b.*

㊳ Kálvin tér (Calvin Square). Calvin Square takes its name from the neoclassical Protestant church that tries to dominate this busy traffic hub; more glaringly noticeable, however, is a Pepsi billboard as tall and wide as the bottom half of the church. The Kecskeméti Kapu, a main gate of Pest, once stood here, as well as a cattle market that was a notorious den of thieves. At the beginning of the 19th century, this was where Pest ended and the prairie began.

★ **Korzó** (Promenade). The neighborhood to the south of Roosevelt tér has regained much of its past elegance—if not its architectural grandeur—with the erection of the Atrium Hyatt, Inter-Continental, and Budapest Marriott luxury hotels. Traversing all three and continuing well beyond them is the riverside korzó, a pedestrian promenade lined with park benches and appealing outdoor cafés from which one can enjoy postcard-perfect views of Gellért Hill and Castle Hill directly across the Danube. Try to take a stroll in the evening, when the views are lit up in shimmering gold. ⊠ *From Eötvös tér to Március 15 ter.*

Közgazdagsági Egyetem (University of Economics). Just below the Liberty Bridge on the waterfront, the monumental neo-Renaissance building was once the Customs House. Built in 1871–1874 by Miklós Ybl, it is now also known as *közgáz* ("econ."), following a stint during the Communist era as Karl Marx University. ⊠ *V, Fővám tér.*

㊴ Magyar Nemzeti Múzeum (Hungarian National Museum). Built between 1837 and 1847, the museum is a fine example of 19th-century classicism—simple, well proportioned, and surrounded by a large garden. In front of this building on March 15, 1848, Sándor Petőfi recited his revolutionary poem, the "National Song" ("Nemzeti dal"), and the "12 Points," a list of political demands by young Hungarians calling on the people to rise up against the Hapsburgs. Celebrations of the national holiday commemorating the failed revolution are held on these steps every year on March 15.

What used to be the museum's biggest attraction, the **Szent Korona** (Holy Crown), was moved to the Parliament building in early 2000 to mark the millenary of the coronation of Hungary's first king, St. Stephen (☞ *Országház, below*). The museum still has worthwhile rarities, however, including a completely furnished Turkish tent; masterworks of cabinetmaking and woodcarving, including pews from churches in Nyírbátor and Transylvania; a piano that belonged to both Beethoven and Liszt; and, in the treasury, masterpieces of goldsmithing, among them the 11th-century Constantions Monomachos crown from Byzantium and the richly pictorial 16th-century chalice of Miklós Pálffy. Looking at it is like reading the "Prince Valiant" comic strip in gold. The epic Hungarian history exhibit chronicles, among other things, the end of Communism and the much-celebrated exodus of the Russian troops. ⊠ *IX, Múzeum krt. 14–16,* ☎ *1/327–7773.* ▩ *400 Ft.* ☉ *Mid-Mar.–mid-Oct., Tues.–Sun. 10–6; mid-Oct.–mid-Mar., Tues.–Sun. 10–5.*

★ ㊵ Nagy Zsinagóga (Great Synagogue). Seating 3,000, Europe's largest synagogue was designed by Ludwig Förs and built between 1844 and 1859 in a Byzantine-Moorish style described as "consciously archaic Romantic-Eastern." Desecrated by German and Hungarian Nazis, it was painstakingly reconstructed with donations from all over the world; its doors reopened in fall 1996. While it is used for regular services during much of the year, it is generally not used in midwinter as the space is too large to heat; between December and February, visiting hours are erratic. In the courtyard behind the synagogue, a weeping willow made of metal honors the victims of the Holocaust. Liszt and Saint-Saëns are among the great musicians who have played the synagogue's grand organ. ⊠ *VII, Dohány u. 2–8,* ☎ *1/342–1335.* ▩ *Free.* ☉ *Weekdays 10–3, Sun. 10–3. Closed Jewish holidays and Dec.*

★ ㉗ Néprajzi Múzeum (Museum of Ethnography). The 1890s neoclassical temple formerly housed the Supreme Court. Now an impressive permanent exhibition, "The Folk Culture of the Hungarian People," explains all aspects of peasant life from the end of the 18th century until World War I; explanatory texts are provided in both English and Hungarian. Besides embroideries, pottery, and carvings—the authentic pieces you can't see at touristy folk shops—there are farming tools, furniture, and traditional costumes. The central room of the building alone is worth the entrance fee: a majestic hall with ornate marble staircases and pillars, and towering stained-glass windows. ⊠ V, Kossuth tér 12, ☎ 1/332–6340. 🎫 300 Ft. ⊙ Mar.–mid-Oct., Tues.–Sun. 10–5:30; mid-Oct.–Feb., Tues.–Sun. 10–4:30. Hours may vary during special exhibits. ✍

★ ㉖ **Országház** (Parliament). The most visible symbol of Budapest's left bank is the huge neo-Gothic Parliament. Mirrored in the Danube much the way Britain's Parliament is reflected by the Thames, it lies midway between the Margaret and Chain bridges and can be reached by the M2 subway (Kossuth tér station) and waterfront Tram 2. A fine example of historicizing, eclectic fin-de-siècle architecture, it was designed by the Hungarian architect Ímre Steindl and built by a thousand workers between 1885 and 1902. The grace and dignity of its long facade and 24 slender towers, with spacious arcades and high windows balancing its vast central dome, lend this living landmark a refreshingly Baroque spatial effect. The exterior is lined with 90 statues of great figures in Hungarian history; the corbels are ornamented by 242 allegorical statues. Inside are 691 rooms, 10 courtyards, and 29 staircases; some 88 pounds of gold were used for the staircases and halls. These halls are also a gallery of late-19th-century Hungarian art, with frescoes and canvases depicting Hungarian history, starting with Mihály Munkácsy's large painting of the Magyar Conquest of 896.

Since early 2000 Parliament's most sacred treasure has not been the Hungarian legislature but the newly exhibited **Szent Korona** (Holy Crown), which reposes with other royal relics under the cupola. The crown sits like a golden soufflé above a Byzantine band of holy scenes in enamel and pearls and other gems. It seems to date from the 12th century, so it could not be the crown that Pope Sylvester II presented to St. Stephen in the year 1000, when he was crowned the first king of Hungary. Nevertheless, it is known as the Crown of St. Stephen and has been regarded—even by Communist governments—as the legal symbol of Hungarian sovereignty and unbroken statehood. In 1945 the fleeing Hungarian army handed over the crown and its accompanying regalia to the Americans rather than have them fall into Soviet hands. They were restored to Hungary in 1978. Through at least August 20, 2001 the crown can be seen in the scope of daily tours of the Parliament building, except during ceremonial events and when the legislature is in session (usually Monday and Tuesday from late summer to spring); its permanent home beyond that date has yet to be decided. Lines may be long, so it's best to call in advance. The building can also be visited on group tours organized by IBUSZ Travel (☞ Visitor Information, below). ⊠ V, Kossuth tér, ☎ 1/441–4904 or 1/441–4415. 🎫 1,100 Ft.. ⊙ Daily tours in English at 10 and 2, starting from Gate No. 10, just right of the main stairs. ✍

㉙ **Roosevelt tér** (Roosevelt Square). This square opening onto the Danube is less closely connected with the U.S. president than with the progressive Hungarian statesman Count István Széchenyi, dubbed "the greatest Hungarian" even by his adversary, Kossuth. The neo-Renaissance palace of the **Magyar Tudományos Akadémia** (Academy of Sciences) on the north side was built between 1862 and 1864, after Széchenyi's suicide. It is a fitting memorial, for in 1825, the statesman donated a year's income from all his estates to establish the academy. Another Széchenyi project, the Széchenyi Lánchíd (☞ below), leads into the square; there stands a statue of Széchenyi near one of another statesman, Ferenc Deák, whose negotiations led to the establishment of the dual monarchy after Kossuth's 1848–1849 revolution failed. Both men lived on this square.

★ ㉘ **Szabadság tér** (Liberty Square). This sprawling square is dominated by the longtime headquarters of **Magyar Televizió** (Hungarian Television), a former stock exchange with what look like four temples and two castles on its roof. (At press time the building was due to be auctioned off as the broadcasters move elsewhere.) Across from it is a solemn-looking neoclassical shrine, the **Nemzeti Bank** (National Bank). The bank's Postal Savings Bank branch, adjacent to the main building but visible from behind Szabadság tér on Hold utca, is another exuberant Art Nouveau masterpiece of architect Ödön Lechner, built in 1901 with colorful majolica mosaics, characteristically curvaceous windows, and pointed towers ending in swirling gold flourishes. In the square's center remains one of the few monuments to the Russian "liberation" that were spared the cleansing of symbols of one-party rule. The decision to retain this obelisk—primarily because it marks a gravesite of fallen Soviet troops—caused outrage among some groups. With the Stars and Stripes flying out in front, the **American Embassy** is at Szabadság tér 12.

Széchenyi Lánchíd (Chain Bridge). This is the oldest and most beautiful of the seven road bridges that span the Danube in Budapest. Before it was built, the river could be crossed only by ferry or by a pontoon bridge that had to be removed when ice blocks began floating downstream in winter. It was constructed at the initiative of the great Hungarian reformer and philanthropist Count István Széchenyi, using an 1839 design by the French civil engineer William Tierney Clark. This classical, almost poetically graceful and symmetrical suspension bridge was finished by his Scottish namesake, Adam Clark, who also built the 383-yard tunnel under Castle Hill, thus connecting the Danube quay with the rest of Buda. After it was destroyed by the Nazis, the bridge was rebuilt in its original form (though slightly widened for traffic) and was reopened in 1949, on the centenary of its inauguration. At the Buda end of the bridge is **Clark Ádám tér** (Adam Clark Square), where you can zip up to Castle Hill on the sometimes crowded Sikló funicular. 🚠 *250 Ft.* ☉ *Funicular daily 7:30 AM–10 PM; closed every other Mon.*

★ ㊸ **Szent István Bazilika** (St. Stephen's Basilica). Handsome and massive, this is one of the chief landmarks of Pest and the city's largest church— it can hold 8,500 people. Its very Holy Roman front porch greets you with a tympanum bustling with statuary. The basilica's dome and the dome of Parliament are by far the most visible in the Pest skyline, and this is no accident: With the Magyar Millennium of 1896 in mind (the lavishly celebrated thousandth anniversary of the settling of the Carpathian Basin in 896), both domes were planned to be 315 ft high.

The millennium was not yet in sight when architect József Hild began building the basilica in neoclassical style in 1851, two years after the revolution was suppressed. After Hild's death, the project was taken over in 1867 by Miklós Ybl, the architect who did the most to transform modern Pest into a monumental metropolis. Wherever he could, Ybl shifted Hild's motifs toward the neo-Renaissance mode that Ybl favored. When the dome collapsed, partly damaging the walls, he made even more drastic changes. Ybl died in 1891, five years before the 1,000-year celebration, and the basilica was completed in neo-Renaissance style by József Kauser—but not until 1905.

Below the cupola is a rich collection of late-19th-century Hungarian art: mosaics, altarpieces, and statuary (what heady days the Magyar Millennium must have meant for local talents!). There are 150 kinds of marble, all from Hungary except for the Carrara in the sanctuary's centerpiece: a white statue of King (St.) Stephen I, Hungary's first king and patron saint. Stephen's mummified right hand is preserved as a relic in the **Szent Jobb Kápolna** (Holy Right Chapel); press a button and it will be illuminated for two minutes. Visitors can also climb the

364 stairs (or take the elevator) to the top of the cupola for a spectacular view of the city. Extensive restorations have been under way at the aging basilica for years and should wrap up within this decade. ⊠ *V, Szt. István tér,* ☎ *1/311–0839.* 🎦 *Church free, Szt. Jobb chapel 100 Ft., cupola 400 Ft.* ☉ *Church Mon.–Sat. 9–7, Sun. 1–5; Szt. Jobb Chapel Apr.– Sept., Mon.–Sat. 9–5, Sun. 1–5; Oct.–Mar., Mon.–Sat. 10–4, Sun. 1–4; Cupola Apr. and Sept.–Oct., daily 10–5; May–Aug., daily 9–6.*

Szerb Ortodox templom (Serbian Orthodox Church). Built in 1688, this lovely burnt-orange church, one of Budapest's oldest buildings, sits in a shaded garden surrounded by thick stone walls of the same color detailed with large-tile mosaics and wrought-iron gates. ⊠ *V, Szerb u.*

③④ **Váci utca.** Immediately north of Elizabeth Bridge is Budapest's best-known shopping street and most unabashed tourist zone, Váci utca, a pedestrian precinct with electrified 19th-century lampposts and smart shops with credit-card emblems on ornate doorways. No bargain basement, Váci utca gets its special flavor from the mix of native furriers, tailors, designers, shoemakers, and folk artists, as well as an increasing number of internationally known boutiques. There are also bookstores and china and crystal shops, as well as gourmet food stores redolent of paprika. Váci utca's second half, south of Kossuth Lajos utca, was transformed into another pedestrian-only zone a few years ago: This somewhat broader stretch of road, while coming to resemble the northern side, still retains a flavorful, more soothing ambiance of its own. On both halves of Váci utca, watch your purses and wallets—against inflated prices *and* active pickpockets. ⊠ *V, from Vörösmarty tér to Fővám tér.*

④① **Városház** (City Hall). The monumental former city council building, which used to be a hospital for wounded soldiers and then a resort for the elderly ("home" would be too cozy for so vast a hulk), is now Budapest's city hall. It's enormous enough to loom over the row of shops and businesses lining Károly körút in front of it but can only be entered through courtyards or side streets (it is most accessible from Gerlóczy utca). The Tuscan columns at the main entrance and the allegorical statuary of *Atlas, War,* and *Peace* are especially splendid. There was once a chapel in the center of the main facade, but now only its spire remains. ⊠ *V, Városház u. 9–11,* ☎ *1/327–1000.*

③⑥ **Vásárcsarnok** (Central Market Hall). The magnificent hall, a 19th-century iron-frame construction, was reopened in late 1994 after years of renovation (and disputes over who would foot the bill). Even during the leanest years of Communist shortages, the abundance of food came as a revelation to shoppers from East and West. Today, the cavernous, three-story market once again teems with people browsing among stalls packed with salamis and red-paprika chains. Upstairs you can buy folk embroideries and souvenirs. ⊠ *IX, Vámház krt. 1–3.* ☉ *Mon. 6–5, Tues.–Fri. 6 AM–6 PM, Sat. 6–2.*

③① **Vigadó** (Concert Hall). Designed in a striking romantic style by Frigyes Feszl and inaugurated in 1865 with Franz Liszt conducting his own *St. Elizabeth Oratorio,* the concert hall is a curious mixture of Byzantine, Moorish, Romanesque, and Hungarian motifs, punctuated by dancing statues and sturdy pillars. Brahms, Debussy, and Casals are among the other phenomenal musicians who have graced its stage. Mahler's *Symphony No. 1* and many works by Bartók were first performed here. While you can go into the lobby on your own, the hall is open only for concerts. ⊠ *V, Vigadó tér 2.*

★ ③③ **Vörösmarty tér** (Vörösmarty Square). This large, handsome square at the northern end of Váci utca is the heart of Pest's tourist life. Street musicians and sidewalk cafés make it one of the liveliest places in Budapest and a good spot to sit and relax—if you can ward off the aggressive caricature sketchers. Grouped around a white-marble statue of the 19th-century poet and dramatist Mihály Vörösmarty are luxury shops, an airline office, and an elegant former pissoir. Now a lovely kiosk, it displays gold-painted historic scenes of the square's golden days. ⊠ *V, at northern end of Váci u.*

<table>
<tr><td>NEED A
BREAK?</td><td>The best-known, tastiest, and most tasteful address on Vörösmarty Square belongs to the **Gerbeaud** pastry shop (⊠ V, Vörösmarty tér 7, ☎ 1/429–9000), founded in 1858 by a French confectioner and later taken over by the Swiss family Gerbeaud. Filling most of a square block, it offers dozens of sweets (as well as sandwiches, coffee, and other not so sugary snacks), served in a salon with green-marble tables and Regency-style marble fireplaces or at tables outside in summer. A mildly hostile staff is an integral part of the Gerbeaud tradition.</td></tr>
</table>

Zsidó Múzeum (Jewish Museum). The four-room museum, around the corner from the Great Synagogue (☞ *above*) has displays explaining the effect of the Holocaust on Hungarian and Transylvanian Jews. (There are labels in English.) In late 1993, burglars ransacked the museum and got away with approximately 80% of its priceless collection; several months later, the stolen objects were found in Romania and returned to their home. ⊠ *Dohány u. 2*, ☎ *1/342–8949.* ☞ *600 Ft.* ⊙ *Mid-Mar.–mid-Oct., Mon.–Thurs. 10–5, Fri. and Sun. 10–3; mid-Oct.–mid-Mar., weekdays 10–3, Sun. 10–1.*

Andrássy Út

Behind St. Stephen's Basilica, at the crossroad along Bajcsy-Zsilinszky út, begins Budapest's grandest avenue, **Andrássy út.** For too many years, this broad boulevard bore the tongue-twisting name of Népköztársaság útja (Avenue of the People's Republic) and, for a while before that, Stalin Avenue. In 1990, however, it reverted to its old name honoring Count Gyula Andrássy, a statesman who in 1867 became the first constitutional premier of Hungary. The boulevard that would eventually bear his name was begun in 1872, as Buda and Pest (and Óbuda) were about to be unified. Most of the mansions that line it were completed by 1884. It took another dozen years before the first **underground railway** on the Continent was completed for—you guessed it—the Magyar Millennium in 1896. Though preceded by London's Underground (1863), Budapest's was the world's first electrified subway. Only slightly modernized but refurbished for the 1996 millecentenary, this "Little Metro" is still running a 4-km (2½-mi) stretch from Vörösmarty tér to the far end of City Park. Using tiny yellow trains with tanklike treads, and stopping at antique stations marked FÖLDALATTI (Underground) on their wrought-iron entranceways, Line 1 is a tourist attraction in itself. Six of its 10 stations are along Andrássy út.

A Good Walk

A walking tour of Andrássy út's sights is straightforward: Begin at its downtown end, near Deák tér, and stroll its length (about 2 km [1¼ mi]) all the way to Hősök tere. The first third of the avenue, from Bajcsy-Zsilinszky út to the eight-sided intersection called Oktogon, boasts a row of eclectic city palaces with balconies held up by stone giants. Pause at the **Magyar Állami Operaház** ㊹ and other points along the way. One block past the Operaház, Andrássy út intersects Budapest's Broadway: Nagymező utca contains several theaters, cabarets, and nightclubs. Andrássy út alters when it crosses the Nagy körút (Outer Ring Road), at the Oktogon crossing. Four rows of trees and scores of flower beds make the thoroughfare look more like a garden promenade, but its cultural character lingers. Farther up, past **Kodály körönd,** the rest of Andrássy út is dominated by widely spaced mansions surrounded by private gardens. At **Hősök tere** ㊽, browse through the **Műcsarnok** ㊾ and/or the **Szépművészeti Múzeum** ㊿, and finish off with a stroll into the Városliget (City Park; ☞ *below*). You can return to Deák tér on the subway, the Millenniumi Földalatti (Millennial Underground).

TIMING
As most museums are closed Monday, it's best to explore Andrássy út on other days, preferably weekdays or early Saturday, when stores are also open for browsing. During opera season, you can time your exploration to land you at the Operaház stairs just before 7 PM to watch the spectacle of operagoers flowing in for the evening's performance.

Sights to See

Ⓒ **Budapest Bábszínház** (Budapest Puppet Theater). In this templelike, eclectic building, you'll find colorful shows that both children and adults enjoy even if they don't understand Hungarian. Watch for showings of *Cinderella* (*Hamupipőke*) and *Snow White and the Seven Dwarfs* (*Hófehérke*), part of the theater's regular repertoire. ⊠ *VI, Andrássy út 69,* ☏ *1/321–5200.*

Drechsler Kastély (Drechsler Palace). Across the street from the Operaház is the French Renaissance–style Drechsler Palace. An early work by Ödön Lechner, Hungary's master of Art Nouveau, it is now the home of the National Ballet School and is generally not open to tourists. ⊠ *VI, Andrássy út 25.*

The **Ráth György Múzeum** (György Ráth Museum), just off Andrássy út, houses a rich collection of exotica from the Indian subcontinent and Chinese ceramics. A few blocks away, back on Andrássy út, the affiliated **Hopp Ferenc Kelet-Ázsiai Művészeti Múzeum** (Ferenc Hopp Museum of Eastern Asiatic Arts; VI, Andrássy út 103, ☏ 1/322–8476) hosts changing exhibits. ⊠ *VI, Városligeti fasor 12,* ☏ *1/342–3916.* 🎫 *Both museums 160 Ft.* ⊙ *Both museums: Oct.–mid-Apr., Tues.–Sun. 10–4; mid-Apr.–Sept., Tues.–Sun. 10–6).*

★ ㊽ **Hősök tere** (Heroes' Square). Andrássy út ends in grandeur at Heroes' Square, with Budapest's answer to Berlin's Brandenburg Gate. Cleaned and refurbished in 1996 for the millecentenary, the **Millenniumi Emlékmű** (Millennial Monument) is a semicircular twin colonnade with statues of Hungary's kings and leaders between its pillars. Set back in its open center, a 118-ft stone column is crowned by a dynamic statue of the archangel Gabriel, his outstretched arms bearing the ancient emblems of Hungary. At its base ride seven bronze horsemen: the Magyar chieftains, led by Árpád, whose tribes conquered the land in 896. Before the column lies a simple marble slab, the **Nemzeti Háborús Emlék Tábla** (National War Memorial), the nation's altar, at which every visiting foreign dignitary lays a ceremonial wreath. England's Queen Elizabeth upheld the tradition during her royal visit in May of 1992. In 1991 Pope John Paul II conducted a mass here. Just a few months earlier, half a million Hungarians had convened to recall the memory of Imre Nagy, the reform-minded Communist prime minister who partially inspired the 1956 revolution. Little would anyone have guessed then that in 1995, palm trees, and Madonna, would spring up on this very square in a scene from the film *Evita* (set in Argentina, not Hungary); nor that Michael Jackson would do his part to consecrate the square with a music video. Heroes' Square is flanked by the **Műcsarnok** and the **Szépművészeti Múzeum** (☞ *below*).

Kodály körönd. A handsome traffic circle with imposing statues of three Hungarian warriors—leavened by a fourth one of a poet—Kodály körönd is surrounded by plane and chestnut trees. Look carefully at the towered mansions on the north side of the circle—behind the soot you'll see the fading colors of ornate frescoes peeking through. The circle takes its name from the composer Zoltán Kodály, who lived just beyond it at Andrássy út 89. ⊠ *VI, Andrássy út at Szinyei Merse u.*

㊼ Liszt Ferenc Emlékmúzeum (Franz Liszt Memorial Museum). Andrássy út No. 67 was the original location of the old Academy of Music and Franz Liszt's last home; entered around the corner, it now houses a museum. Several rooms display the original furniture and instruments from Liszt's time there; another room shows temporary exhibits. The museum hosts excellent, free classical concerts year-round, except in August. ⊠ *VI, Vörösmarty u. 35,* ☎ *1/342–7320.* ⧉ *200 Ft.* ☉ *Weekdays 10–6, Sat. 9–5. Classical concerts (free with admission) Sept.–July, Sat. 11 AM. Closed Aug. 1–20.*

㊻ Liszt Ferenc Zeneakadémia (Franz Liszt Academy of Music). Along with the **Vigadó** (☞ Downtown Pest and the Kis körút [Little Ring Road], *above*), this is one of the city's main concert halls. The academy in fact has two auditoriums: a green-and-gold 1,200-seat main hall and a smaller hall for chamber music and solo recitals. Outside this exuberant Art Nouveau building, a statue of Liszt oversees the square. The academy has been operating as a highly revered teaching institute since 1907; Liszt was its first chairman and the composer Ferenc Erkel its first director. The pianist Ernő (formerly Ernst) Dohnányi and composers Béla Bartók and Zoltán Kodály were teachers here. ⊠ *VI, Liszt Ferenc tér 8,* ☎ *1/342–0179.*

★ **㊹ Magyar Állami Operaház** (Hungarian State Opera House). Miklós Ybl's crowning achievement is the neo-Renaissance Opera House, built between 1875 and 1884. Badly damaged during the siege of 1944–1945, it was restored for its 1984 centenary. Two buxom marble sphinxes guard the driveway; the main entrance is flanked by Alajos Strobl's "romantic-realist" limestone statues of Liszt and of another 19th-century Hungarian composer, Ferenc Erkel, the father of Hungarian opera (his patriotic opera *Bánk bán* is still performed for national celebrations).

Inside, the spectacle begins even before the performance does. You glide up grand staircases and through wood-paneled corridors and gilt lime-green salons into a glittering jewel box of an auditorium. Its four tiers of boxes are held up by helmeted sphinxes beneath a frescoed ceiling by Károly Lotz. Lower down there are frescoes everywhere, with intertwined motifs of Apollo and Dionysus. In its early years, the Budapest Opera was conducted by Gustav Mahler (from 1888 to 1891) and, after World War II, by Otto Klemperer.

The best way to experience the Opera House's interior is to see a ballet or opera; and while performance quality varies, tickets are relatively cheap and easy to come by, at least by tourist standards. And descending from *La Bohème* into the Földalatti station beneath the Opera House was described by travel writer Stephen Brook in *The Double Eagle* as stepping "out of one period piece and into another." There are no performances in summer, except for the week-long BudaFest international opera and ballet festival in mid-August. You cannot view the interior on your own, but forty-five-minute tours in English are usually conducted daily at 3 PM and 4 PM; buy tickets in the Opera Shop, by the sphinx at the Hajós utca entrance. (Large groups should call in advance.) ✉ *VI, Andrássy út 22,* ☎ *1/331–2550 (ext. 156 for tours).* 🎞 *Tours 1,000 Ft.*

45 **Magyar Fotográfusok Háza (Mai Manó Ház)** (Hungarian Photographers' House). This ornate turn-of-the-20th-century building was built as a photography studio, where the wealthy bourgeoisie would come to be photographed by imperial and royal court photographer Manó Mai. Inside, ironwork and frescoes ornament the curving staircase leading up to the recently expanded facility, the largest of Budapest's three photo galleries. ✉ *V, Nagymező u. 20,* ☎ *1/302–4398.* 🎞 *200 Ft.* ☾ *Weekdays 2–6.*

NEED A
BREAK?

The **Lukács** café (✉ VI, Andrássy út 70, ☎ 1/302–8747) shares its entrance with an international bank, but its upstairs salon is steeped in classic café elegance. The room is anchored at one end by an ornate fireplace; you can recharge with an espresso at one of the marble-top tables clustered under a sparkling chandelier. The Lukács was built in 1912, during Budapest's café-culture glory days, but in the repressive 1950s it was taken over by the secret police to serve as a meeting spot. To many locals, it still evokes those dark times.

49 **Műcsarnok** (Palace of Exhibitions). The city's largest hall for special exhibitions is a striking 1895 temple of culture with a colorful tympanum. Its program of events includes exhibitions of contemporary Hungarian and international art and a rich series of films, plays, and concerts. ✉ *XIV, Hősök tere,* ☎ *1/343–7401.* 🎞 *300 Ft., Tues. free.* ☾ *Tues.–Sun. 10–6.*

Postamúzeum (Postal Museum). The best of Andrássy út's many marvelous stone mansions is luckily visitable, for the Postal Museum occupies an apartment with frescoes by Károly Lotz (whose work adorns St. Stephen's Basilica and the Opera House). Among the displays is an exhibition on the history of Hungarian mail, radio, and telecommunications. English-language pamphlets are available. Even if the exhibits don't thrill you, the venue, being restored at press time and expected to reopen by 2001, is worth the visit. ✉ *VI, Andrássy út 3,* ☎ *1/269–6838.* 🎞 *70 Ft.* ☾ *Apr.–Oct., Tues.–Sun. 10–6; Nov.–Mar., Tues.–Sun. 10–4.*

★ **50** **Szépművészeti Múzeum** (Museum of Fine Arts). Across Heroes' Square from the Palace of Exhibitions and built by the same team of Albert Schickedanz and Fülöp Herzog, the Museum of Fine Arts houses Hungary's finest collection, rich in Flemish and Dutch old masters. With seven fine El Grecos and five beautiful Goyas as well as paintings by Velázquez and Murillo, the collection of Spanish old masters is one of the best outside Spain. The Italian school is represented by Giorgione, Bellini, Correggio, Tintoretto, and Titian masterpieces and, above all, two superb Raphael paintings: *Eszterházy Madonna* and his immortal *Portrait of a Youth,* rescued after a world-famous art heist. Nineteenth-century French art includes works by Delacroix, Pissarro, Cézanne, Toulouse-Lautrec, Gauguin, Renoir, and Monet. There are also more than 100,000 drawings (including five by Rembrandt and three studies by Leonardo), Egyptian and Greco-Roman exhibitions, late-Gothic winged altars from northern Hungary and Transylvania, and works by all the leading figures of Hungarian art up to the present. A 20th-century collection was added to the museum's permanent exhibits in 1994, comprising an interesting series of statues, paintings, and drawings by Chagall, Le Corbusier, and others. Labels are in both Hungarian and English; there's also an English-language booklet for sale about the permanent collection. ⊠ *XIV, Hősök tere,* ☎ *1/343–9759.* ☜ *500 Ft.* ⊙ *Tues.–Sun. 10–5:30.*

Városliget (City Park)

A Good Walk

Heroes' Square is the gateway to the **Városliget** (City Park): a square km (almost ½ square mi) of recreation, entertainment, beauty, and culture. A bridge behind the Millennial Monument leads across a boating basin that becomes an artificial ice-skating rink in winter; to the south of this lake stands a statue of George Washington, erected in 1906 with donations by Hungarian emigrants to the United States. Next to the lake stands **Vajdahunyad Vár,** built in myriad architectural styles. Visitors can soak or swim at the turn-of-the-20th-century Széchenyi Fürdő, jog along the park paths, or careen on Vidám Park's roller coaster. There's also the Petőfi Csarnok, a leisure-time youth center and major concert hall on the site of an old industrial exhibition.

TIMING

Fair-weather weekends, when the children's attractions are teeming with youngsters and parents and the Széchenyi Fürdő brimming with bathers, are the best time for people-watchers to visit City Park; if you go on a weekday, the main sights are rarely crowded.

Sights to See

© **Budapesti Állatkert** (Budapest Zoo). The renovation that began in this once depressing urban zoo in the late 1990s is expected to take until 2004, but the place is already cheerier, at least for humans—petting opportunities aplenty, and a new monkey-house where endearing, seemingly clawless little simians climb all over you (beware of pickpockets!). Don't miss the elephant pavilion, decorated with Zsolnay majolica and glazed ceramic animals. ⊠ *XIV, Állatkerti krt. 6–12,* ☎ *1/343–6075.* ☜ *650 Ft.* ⊙ *Mar. and Oct., daily 9–5; Apr. and Sept., daily 9–6; May, daily 9–6:30; June–Aug., daily 9–7; Nov.–Feb., daily 9–4 (last tickets sold 1 hr before closing).*

© **Fővárosi Nagycirkusz** (Municipal Grand Circus). Colorful performances by local acrobats, clowns, and animal trainers, as well as by international guests, are staged here in a small ring. ⊠ *XIV, Állatkerti krt. 7,* ☎ *1/343–9630.* ☜ *Weekdays 500–900 Ft., weekends 550–950 Ft.* ⊙ *July–Aug., Wed.–Fri. 3 and 7, Thu. 3, Sat. 10, 3, and 7, Sun. 10 and 3; Nov.–June, schedule varies.*

Széchenyi Fürdő (Széchenyi Baths). Dating from 1876, these vast baths are in a beautiful neo-Baroque building in the middle of City Park; they comprise one of the biggest spas in Europe. There are several thermal pools indoors as well as two outdoors, which remain open even in winter, when dense steam hangs thick over the hot water's surface—you can just barely make out the figures of elderly men, submerged shoulder deep, crowded around waterproof chessboards (☞ Outdoor Activities and Sports, *below*). ⊠ *XIV, Állatkerti krt. 11,* ☎ *1/321–0310.* ☜ *400 Ft. (changing room), 700 Ft. (cabin).* ⊙ *Weekdays 6 AM–6 PM, weekends 6–5.*

★ **Vajdahunyad Vár** (Vajdahunyad Castle). Beside the City Park's lake stands this castle, an art historian's Disneyland, this fantastic medley borrows from all of Hungary's historic and architectural past, starting with the Romanesque gateway of the cloister of Jak in western Hungary. A Gothic castle, Transylvanian turrets, Renaissance loggia, Baroque portico, and Byzantine decoration are all guarded by a spooky modern (1903) bronze statue of the anonymous medieval chronicler who was the first recorder of Hungarian history. Designed for the millennial celebration in 1896 but not completed until 1908, this hodge-podge houses the surprisingly interesting **Mezőgazdasági Múzeum** (Agricultural Museum), with intriguingly arranged sections on animal husbandry, forestry, horticulture, hunting, and fishing. ☒ *XIV, Városliget, Széchenyi Island,* ☏ *1/343–3198.* ▦ *Museum 200 Ft.* ☉ *Mid-Feb.–mid-Nov., Tues.–Fri. and Sun. 10–5, Sat. 10–6; mid-Nov.–mid-Feb., Tues.–Fri. 10–4, weekends 10–5.*

🐾 **Vidám Park.** Budapest's somewhat weary amusement park is next to the zoo and is crawling with happy children with their parents or grandparents in tow. Rides cost around $1 (some are for preschoolers). There are also game rooms and a scenic railway. Next to the main park is a separate, smaller section for toddlers. In winter, only a few rides operate. ☒ *XIV, Városliget, Állatkerti krt. 14–16,* ☏ *1/343–0996.* ▦ *100 Ft.* ☉ *Apr.–Oct., daily 10–about 8 (varies); Nov.–Mar., daily 10–late afternoon.*

Eastern Pest and the Nagy Körút (Great Ring Road)

This section covers primarily Kossuth Lajos–Rákóczi út and the Nagy körút (Great Ring Road)—busy, less-touristy urban thoroughfares full of people, cars, shops, and Budapest's unique urban flavor.

Beginning a few blocks from the Elizabeth Bridge, Kossuth Lajos utca is Budapest's busiest shopping street. Try to look above and beyond the store windows to the architecture and activity along Kossuth Lajos utca and its continuation, Rákóczi út, which begins when it crosses the Kis körút (Little Ring Road) at the busy intersection called Astoria. Most of Rákóczi út is lined with hotels, shops, and department stores and it ends at the grandiose Keleti (East) Railway Station, on Baross tér.

Pest's Great Ring Road, the Nagy körút, was laid out at the end of the 19th century in a wide semicircle anchored to the Danube at both ends; an arm of the river was covered over to create this 114-ft-wide thoroughfare. The large apartment buildings on both sides also date from this era. Along with theaters, stores, and cafés, they form a boulevard unique in Europe for its "unified eclecticism," which blends a variety of historic styles into a harmonious whole. Its entire length of almost 4½ km (2¾ mi) from Margaret Bridge to Petőfi Bridge is traversed by Trams 4 and 6, but strolling it in stretches is also a good way to experience the hustle and bustle of downtown Budapest.

Like its smaller counterpart, the Kis körút (Small Ring Road), the Great Ring Road comprises sectors of various names. Beginning with Ferenc körút at the Petőfi Bridge, it changes to József körút at the intersection marked by the Museum of Applied Arts, then to Erzsébet körút at Blaha Lujza Square. Teréz körút begins at the busy Oktogon crossing with Andrássy út and ends at the Nyugati (West) Railway Station, where Szent István takes over for the final stretch to the Margaret Bridge.

A Good Walk

Beginning with a visit to the **Iparművészeti Múzeum** ㊾, near the southern end of the boulevard, walk or take Tram 4 or 6 north (away from the Petőfi Bridge) to the New York Kávéház on Erzsébet körút, just past Blaha Lujza tér—all in all about 1¾ km (1 mi) from the museum. The neo-Renaissance **Keleti pályaudvar** is a one-metro-stop detour away from Blaha Lujza tér. Continuing in the same direction on the körút, go several stops on the tram to **Nyugati pályaudvar** and walk the remaining sector, Szent István körút, past the **Vígszínház** ㊽ to Margaret Bridge. From the bridge, views of Margaret Island, to the north, and Parliament, Castle Hill, the Chain Bridge, and Gellért Hill, to the south, are gorgeous.

TIMING

As this area is packed with stores, it's best to explore during business hours—weekdays until around 5 PM and Saturday until 1 PM; Saturday will be most crowded. Keep in mind that the Iparművészeti Múzeum is closed Monday.

Sights to See

★ ❺ **Iparművészeti Múzeum** (Museum of Applied and Decorative Arts). The templelike structure housing this museum is indeed a shrine to Hungarian Art Nouveau, and in front of it, drawing pen in hand, sits a statue of its creator, Hungarian architect Ödön Lechner. Opened in the Magyar Millennial year of 1896, it was only the third museum of its kind in Europe. Its dome of tiles is crowned by a majolica lantern from the same source: the Zsolnay ceramic works in Pécs. Inside its central hall are playfully swirling whitewashed, double-decker, Moorish-style galleries and arcades. The museum, which collects and studies objects of interior decoration and use, has five departments: furniture, textiles, goldsmithing, ceramics, and everyday objects. ⊠ *Üllői út 33–37,* ☎ *1/217–5222.* ☜ *300 Ft.* ⏱ *Mid-Mar.–Oct., Tues.–Sun. 10–6; Nov.– mid-Mar., Tues.–Sun. 10–4.* ✎

Kapel Szent Roch (St. Roch Chapel). The impact of this cheerful, yellow, 18th-century chapel is rendered even more colorful by peasant women peddling lace and embroidery on its small square. The chapel is the oldest remnant of Pest's former outer district. It was built beside a hospice where doomed victims of the great plague of 1711 were sent to die as far away as possible from residential areas. ⊠ *Corner of Rákóczi út and Gyulai Pál u.*

NEED A BREAK?

Once the haunt of famous writers and intellectuals, whose caricatures decorate the walls, now mostly that of tourists—those who manage to find the entrance under the seemingly permanent scaffolding—the **New York Kávéház** (⊠ VII, Erzsébet krt. 9–11, ☎ 1/322–1648) is an eclectic, neo-Baroque café and restaurant in the ornate 1894 New York Palace building.

Keleti pályaudvar (East Railway Station). The grandiose, imperial-looking East Railway Station was built in 1884 and considered Europe's most modern until well into the 20th century. Its neo-Renaissance facade, which resembles a gateway, is flanked by statues of two British inventors and railway pioneers, James Watt and George Stephenson. ⊠ *VIII, Baross tér.*

Klotild and Matild buildings. Braced on either side of heavily trafficked Kossuth Lajos utca, the imposing Klotild and Matild buildings, with their distinctive twin towers, were built in an interesting combination of Art Nouveau and eclectic styles. They house the headquarters of the IBUSZ travel agency, among other tenants.

❺ **Köztársaság tér** (Square of the Republic). Surrounded by faceless concrete buildings, this square is not particularly alluring aesthetically but is significant because it was where the Communist Party of Budapest had its headquarters, and it was also the scene of heavy fighting in 1956. Here also is the city's second opera house, and Budapest's largest, the **Erkel Ferenc színház** (Ferenc Erkel Theater).

Nyugati pályaudvar (West Railway Station). The iron-laced glass hall of the West Railway Station is in complete contrast to—and much more modern than—the newer East Railway Station. Built in the 1870s, it was designed by a team of architects from Gustav Eiffel's office in Paris. ⊠ *VI, Teréz krt.*

Párizsi Udvar (Paris Court). This glass-roof arcade was built in 1914 in richly ornamental neo-Gothic and eclectic styles. Nowadays it's filled with touristy boutiques. ⊠ *VI, Corner of Petőfi Sándor u. and Kossuth Lajos u.*

NEED A BREAK?	Hands down the best café in this part of town, the **Európa kávéház** (⊠ V, Szent István krt. 7–9, ☎ 1/312–2362) has marble-top tables; top-notch elegance; and, yes, delectable sweets. While it seems (in the best sense) a century old, it's in fact only about two years. Here you can sample some Eszterházy torta (a rich, buttery cake with walnut batter and, here at least, a walnut on top) or, say, a Tyrolean strudel with poppy-seed filling.

★ ⑤ **Vígszínház** (Comedy Theater). This neo-Baroque, late-19th-century, gem-like theater twinkles with just a tiny, playful anticipation of Art Nouveau and sparkles inside and out since its 1994 refurbishment. The theater hosts primarily musicals, such as Hungarian adaptations of *Cats*, as well as dance performances and classical concerts. ⊠ *XIII, Pannónia u. 1,* ☎ *1/329–2340.* 🐾

Óbuda

Until its unification with Buda and Pest in 1872 to form the city of Budapest, Óbuda (meaning Old Buda) was a separate town that used to be the main settlement; now it is usually thought of as a suburb. Although the vast new apartment blocks of Budapest's biggest housing project and busy roadways are what first strike the eye, the historic core of Óbuda has been preserved in its entirety.

A Good Walk

Óbuda is easily reached by car, bus, or streetcar via the Árpád Bridge from Pest or by the HÉV suburban railway from Batthyány tér to the Árpád Bridge. Once you're there, covering all the sights on foot involves large but manageable distances along major exhaust-permeated roadways. One way to tackle it is to take Tram 17 from its southern terminus at the Buda side of the Margaret Bridge to Kiscelli utca and walk uphill to the **Kiscelli Múzeum.** Then walk back down the same street all the way past **Flórián tér,** continuing toward the Danube and making a left onto Hídfő utca or Szentlélek tér to enter **Fő tér.** After exploring the square, walk a block or two southeast to the HÉV suburban railway stop and take the train just north to the museum complex at **Aquincum.**

TIMING

It's best to begin touring Óbuda during the cooler, early hours of the day, as the heat on the area's busy roads can get overbearing. Avoid Monday, when museums are closed.

Sights to See

Aquincum. This complex comprises the reconstructed remains of a Roman settlement dating from the 1st century AD and the capital of the Roman province of Pannonia. Careful excavations have unearthed a varied selection of artifacts and mosaics, giving a tantalizing inkling of what life was like in the provinces of the Roman Empire. A gymnasium and a central heating system have been unearthed, along with the ruins of two baths and a shrine to Mithras, the Persian god of light, truth, and the sun. The **Aquincum múzeum** (Aquincum Museum) displays the dig's most notable finds: ceramics; a red-marble sarcophagus showing a triton and flying Eros on one side and on the other, Telesphorus, the angel of death, depicted as a hooded dwarf; and jewelry from a Roman lady's tomb. ⊠ *III, Szentendrei út 139,* ☎ *1/250–1650.* 🎟 *400 Ft.* ⊙ *Mid-Apr.–Apr. 30 and Oct., Tues.–Sun. 10–5; May–Sept., Tues.–Sun. 10–6. Grounds open at 9.*

Flórián tér (Flórián Square). The center of today's Óbuda is Flórián tér, where Roman ruins were first discovered when the foundations of a house were dug in 1778. Two centuries later, careful excavations were carried out during the reconstruction of the square, and today the restored ancient ruins lie in the center of the square in boggling contrast to the racing traffic and cement-block housing projects. ⊠ *III, Vörösvári út at Pacsirtamező u.*

Fő tér (Main Square). Óbuda's old main square is its most picturesque part. The square has been spruced up in recent years, and there are now several good restaurants and interesting museums in and around the Baroque **Zichy Kúria** (Zichy Mansion), which has become a neighborhood cultural center. Among the most popular offerings are the summer concerts in the courtyard and the evening jazz concerts. ⊠ *III, Kórház u. at Hídfő u.*

Hercules Villa. A fine 3rd-century Roman dwelling, it takes its name from the myth depicted on its beautiful mosaic floor. The ruin was unearthed between 1958 and 1967 and is now only open by request (inquire at Aquincum). ⊠ *III, Meggyfa u. 19–21.*

Kiscelli Múzeum (Kiscelli Museum). A strenuous climb up the steep, dilapidated sidewalks of Remetehegy (Hermit's Hill) will deposit you at this elegant, mustard-yellow Baroque mansion. Built between 1744 and 1760 as a Trinitarian monastery, today it holds an eclectic mix of paintings, sculptures, engravings, and sundry items related to the history of Budapest. Included here is the printing press on which poet and revolutionary Sándor Petőfi printed his famous "Nemzeti Dal" ("National Song"), in 1848, inciting the Hungarian people to rise up against the Hapsburgs. ⊠ *III, Kiscelli u. 108,* ☎ *1/250–0304.* 🎟 *200 Ft.* ⊙ *Nov.–Mar., Tues.–Sun. 10–4; Apr.–Oct., Tues.–Sun. 10–6.*

Római amfiteátrum (Roman Amphitheater). Probably dating back to the 2nd century, Óbuda's Roman military amphitheater once held some 16,000 people and, at 144 yards in diameter, was one of Europe's largest. A block of dwellings called the Round House was later built by the Romans above the amphitheater; massive stone walls found in the Round House's cellar were actually parts of the amphitheater. Below the amphitheater are the cells where prisoners and lions were held while awaiting confrontation. ⊠ *III, Pacsirtamező u. at Nagyszombat u.*

Zichy Kúria (Zichy Mansion). One wing of the Zichy Mansion is taken up by the **Óbudai Helytörténeti Gyűjtemény** (Óbuda Local History Collection; ☎ 1/250–1020, 🎟 120 Ft.; ⊙ mid-Mar.–mid-Oct., Tues.–Fri. 2–6, weekends 10–6; mid-Oct.–mid-Mar. Tues.–Fri. 2–5, weekends 10–5); permanent exhibitions here include traditional rooms from typical homes in the district of Békásmegyer and a popular exhibit covering the history of toys from 1860 to 1960. Another wing houses the **Kassák Múzeum** (☎ 1/368–7021, 🎟 100 Ft., ⊙ Oct.–Feb., Tues.–Sun. 10–4; Mar.–Sept., Tues.–Sun. 10–6), which honors the literary and artistic works of a pioneer of the Hungarian avant-garde, Lajos Kassák. ⊠ *III, Fő tér 1.*

DINING

Updated by
Betsy Maury

In Budapest, numerous new ethnic restaurants—from Chinese to Mexican to Hare Krishna Indian—are springing up all the time. The pulse of the city's increasingly vibrant restaurant scene is in downtown Pest; restaurants on Castle Hill tend to be more touristy and expensive. Our choice of restaurants is primarily Hungarian and Continental, but if you get a craving for sushi or tortellini, consult the restaurant listings in the English-language publications for the latest information on what's cooking where. Remember that some restaurants, particularly the tourist-oriented ones, occasionally fall into the international practice of embellishing tourists' bills. Authorities in Budapest, however, have been cracking down on establishments reported for overcharging. Don't order from menus without prices, and don't accept dining or drinking invitations from women hired to lure people into shady situations.

For price range information, *see* Dining *in* Pleasures and Pastimes, *above.*

Downtown Pest and the Small Ring Road

$$$–$$$$ ✗ **Múzeum.** The gustatory anticipation sparked by this elegant, candlelit salon with mirrors, mosaics, and swift-moving waiters is matched by wholly satisfying, wonderful food. The salads are generous, the Hungarian wines excellent, and the chef dares to be creative. ⊠ *VIII, Múzeum krt. 11,* ☎ *1/267–0375. Jacket and tie. AE. Closed Sun.*

$$$ ✗ **Lou Lou.** This glowing bistro tucked onto a side street near the
★ Danube has been one of the hottest restaurants in Budapest for years. Blending local and Continental cuisines, the menu includes a succulent fresh salmon with lemongrass; the venison fillet with wild berry sauce is another mouthwatering choice. Although recently expanded, Lou Lou retains its intimate charm. ⊠ *V, Vigyázó Ferenc u. 4,* ☎ *1/ 312–4505. Reservations essential. AE. No lunch Sat. Closed daily 3– 7 and Sun.*

$$$ ✗ **Müvészinas.** Walls hung with framed vintage prints and photos, an-
★ tique vitrines filled with old books, and tall, slender candles on the tables create a romantic haze here. Dozens of Hungarian specialties fill the long menu, from sirloin "Budapest style" (smothered in a gooseliver, mushrooms, and sweet-pepper ragout) to spinach-stuffed turkey breast in garlic sauce. Poppy-seed palacsinta with plum sauce are a sublime dessert. ⊠ *VI, Bajcsy-Zsilinszky út 9,* ☎ *1/268–1439. Reservations essential. AE, MC, V.*

$$ ✗ **Amstel River Café.** Just steps from the tourist-filled Vái utca, you'll find this welcoming, low-key Dutch café. The menu has something for everyone—from rabbit to Caesar salad to grilled chicken, served on tables outside in the summer. Besides the Amstel beers (of course), there's a weekly changing wine list. A guitarist serenades with Spanish music on Sundays. ⊠ *V, Párizsi u. 6,* ☎ *1/266–4334. No credit cards.*

$$ ✗ **Café Kör.** The wrought-iron tables, vault ceilings and crisp white table-
★ cloths give this chic bistro a decidedly downtown feel. In the heart of the busy fifth district, Café Kör is ideal for lunch or dinner when touring nearby Andrássy út or St. Stephen's Basilica. The Café Kör specialty plate is a feast of rich goose liver paté, grilled meats, and cheeses, to be savored with a glass of Hungarian *pezsgő* (sparkling wine). True to its bistro aspirations, the daily specials are scribbled on the wall, in both Hungarian and English. ⊠ *V, Sas u. 17,* ☎ *1/311–0053. Reservations essential. MC, V. Closed Sun.*

$$ ✗ **Cyrano.** This smooth young bistro just off Vörösmarty tér has an
★ arty, contemporary bent, with wrought-iron chairs, green-marble floors, and long-stem azure glasses. The creative kitchen sends out el-

122

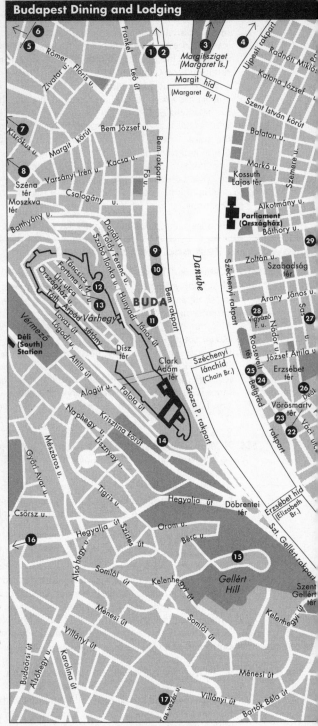
Budapest Dining and Lodging

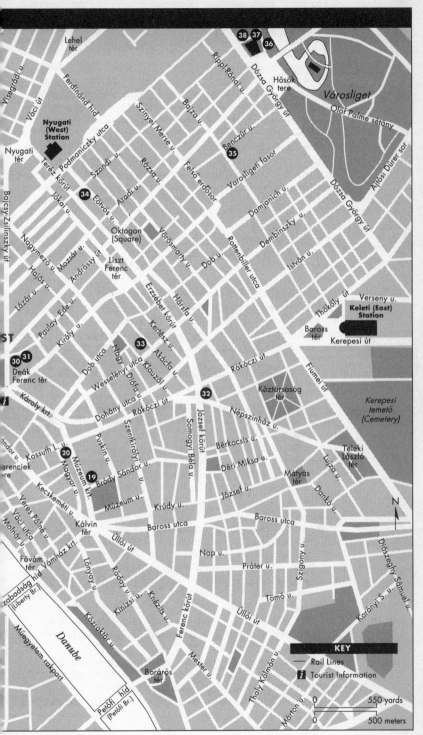

egantly presented Hungarian and Continental dishes, from standards such as goulash and chicken paprikás to more eclectic tastes such as tender fried Camembert cheese with blueberry jam. ☒ *V, Kristóf tér 7–8,* ☎ *1/266–3096. Reservations essential. AE, DC, MC.*

$$ ✗ **Kispipa.** This tiny, well-known restaurant with arched yellow-glass windows and piano bar is a favorite for both Budapest residents and passers-through. The kitchen delivers an expansive menu of first-rate Hungarian food; the venison ragout soup with tarragon is excellent. ☒ *VII, Akácfa u. 38,* ☎ *1/342–2587. Reservations essential. AE, MC. Closed Sun. and July–Aug.*

$ ✗ **Tüköry Söröző.** Hearty, decidedly nonvegetarian Hungarian fare comes in big portions at this popular spot close to Parliament. Best bets include pork cutlets stuffed with savory liver or apples and cheese, paired with a big mug of inexpensive beer. Courageous carnivores can sample the beefsteak tartare, topped with a raw egg. ☒ *V, Hold u. 15,* ☎ *1/269–5027. MC, V. Closed weekends.*

$ ✗ **Vista Travel Café.** Opened in 1999 in a contemporary building just
★   off Deák tér, this popular spot is an extension of the successful Vista travel agency complex down the street (☞ Contacts and Resources, *below*). Local regulars and visitors alike flock here for the affordable daily lunch menu and quiche specials. The menu is international, but Hungarian flags appear next to the local specialties—so you can try traditional *hortobágyi* (meat-filled) palacsinta and still get a chef salad. After you fill out your paper place mat rating the service and food, you can walk upstairs and check your e-mail at the Internet café. Note that there is a 3,000 Ft. minimum for credit card use. ☒ *VII, Paulay Ede u. 7,* ☎ *1/268 0888. AE, MC, V.*

North Buda

$$$$ ✗ **Vadrózsa.** The "Wild Rose" always has fresh ones on the table; the restaurant is in a romantic old villa perched on a hilltop in the exclusive Rózsadomb district of Buda. It's elegant to the last detail, with white-glove service and piano music, and the garden is delightful in summer. Try the venison or grilled fish; the house specialty, grilled goose liver, is succulent perfection. ☒ *II, Pentelei Molnár u. 15,* ☎ *1/326–5817. Reservations essential. AE, DC, MC, V. Closed daily 4–7.*

$$$–$$$$ ✗ **Udvarház.** The views from this Buda hilltop restaurant are unsurpassed. As you dine indoors at tables set with white linens or outdoors on the open terrace, your meals are accompanied by vistas of the Danube bridges and Parliament far below. Excellent fresh fish is prepared tableside; you could also try veal and goose liver in paprika sauce, served with salty cottage cheese dumplings. Catering to the predominantly tourist crowd, folklore shows and live Gypsy music frequently enliven the scene. The buses up here are infrequent; it's easier to take a car or taxi. ☒ *III, Hármashatárhegyi út 2,* ☎ *1/388–6921. AE, DC, MC, V. Closed Mon. Nov.–Mar. No lunch weekdays Nov.–Mar.*

$$ ✗ **Náncsi Néni.** Aunt Nancy's restaurant is a perennial favorite, de-
★   spite its out-of-the-way location. Irresistibly cozy, the dining room feels like Grandma's country kitchen: Chains of paprika and garlic dangle from the low wooden ceiling above tables set with red-and-white gingham tablecloths and fresh bread tucked into tiny baskets. Shelves along the walls are crammed with jars of home-pickled vegetables, which you can purchase to take home. On the home-style Hungarian menu (large portions!) turkey dishes manifest a creative flair, such as breast fillets stuffed with apples, peaches, mushrooms, cheese, and sour cream. Special touches include a popular outdoor garden in summer and free champagne for all couples in love. ☒ *II, Ördögárok út 80,* ☎ *1/397–2742. Reservations essential July–Aug. AE, MC, V.*

$ ✕ **Marxim.** Two years after the death of socialism in Hungary, this simple pizza-and-pasta restaurant opened up to mock the old regime—and milk it for all it's worth. From the flashing red star above the door outside to the clever puns on the menus and photos of decorated hardliners on the walls, the theme is "Communist nostalgia." Crowds of teenagers and blaring rock music make Marxim best suited for a lunch or snack. ✉ *II, Kisrókus u. 23,* ☎ *1/212–4183. AE, DC, MC, V. No lunch Sun.*

Óbuda

$$$ ✕ **Kéhli.** This pricey but laid-back, sepia-tone neighborhood tavern is on a hard-to-find street near the Óbuda end of the Árpád Bridge. The food is hearty and heavy, just the way legendary Hungarian writer and voracious eater Gyula Krúdy (to whom the restaurant is dedicated) liked it when he lived in the neighborhood. Select from appetizers, such as hot bone marrow with garlic toast, before moving on to fried goose livers with mashed potatoes or turkey breast stuffed with cheese and goose liver. ✉ *III, Mókus u. 22,* ☎ *1/250–4241 or 1/368–0613. AE, MC, V. No lunch weekdays.*

$$$ ✕ **Kisbuda Gyöngye.** Considered one of the city's finest restaurants,
★ this intimate Óbuda restaurant is filled with antique furniture, and its walls are creatively decorated with an eclectic but elegant patchwork of carved wooden cupboard doors and panels. A violin-piano duo sets a romantic mood, and in warm weather you can dine outdoors in the cozy back garden. Try the venison with Transylvanian mushrooms or the popular *liba lakodalmas* (goose wedding feast), a roast goose leg, goose liver, and goose cracklings. ✉ *III, Kenyeres u. 34,* ☎ *1/368–6402 or 1/368–9246. Reservations essential. AE, DC, MC, V. Closed Sun.*

Tabán and Gellért Hill

$$ ✕ **Tabáni Kakas.** This popular restaurant just below Castle Hill has a distinctly friendly atmosphere and specializes in large helpings of poultry dishes, particularly goose. Try the catfish paprikás or the roast duck with steamed cabbage. ✉ *I, Attila út 27,* ☎ *1/375–7165. AE, MC, V.*

City Park

$$$$ ✕ **Gundel.** George Lang, Hungary's best-known restaurateur, show-
★ cases his native country's cuisine at this turn-of-the-20th-century palazzo. Dark-wood paneling, a dozen oil paintings by exemplary Hungarian artists, and tables set with Zsolnay porcelain make this the city's plushest, most handsome dining room. Violinist György Lakatos, of the legendary Lakatos Gypsy musician dynasty, strolls from table to table playing folk music, as waiters in black tie serve traditional favorites such as tender veal in a paprika-and-sour-cream sauce and carp *Dorozsma* (panfried with mushrooms). There's a large garden area where Sunday brunch is served in warm weather. ✉ *XIV, Állatkerti út 2,* ☎ *1/321–3550. Reservations essential. Jacket and tie. AE, DC, MC, V. Closed daily 4–6.*

$$$$ ✕ **Robinson Restaurant.** At this intimate dining room on the park's small lake, service is doting and the menu creative, with dishes such as crisp roast suckling pig with champagne-drenched cabbage or fresh fogas stuffed with spinach. Finish it off with a flaming cup of coffee *Diablo*, fueled with Grand Marnier. Padded pastel decor and low lighting wash the room in pleasant, if not Hungarian, elegance. ✉ *XIV, Városliget,* ☎ *1/343–0955. Reservations essential. Jacket and tie. AE, DC, MC, V. Closed daily 4–6.*

$$ ✕ **Bagolyvár.** George Lang opened this restaurant next door to his gastronomic palace, Gundel (☞ *above*), in 1993. The informal yet polished dining room has a soaring wooden-beam ceiling, and the kitchen produces first-rate daily menus of home-style Hungarian specialties. Soups, served in shiny silver tureens, are particularly good. Musicians entertain with *cimbalom* (hammered dulcimer) music nightly from 7. In warm weather there is outdoor dining in a lovely back garden. ⊠ *XIV, Állatkerti út 2,* ☏ *1/343–0217. AE, DC, MC, V.*

LODGING

Updated by
Betsy Maury

Budapest is well equipped with hotels and hostels, but the increase in tourism since 1989 has put a strain on the city's often crowded lodgings. Advance reservations are strongly advised, especially at the lower-price hotels. Many of the major luxury and business-class hotel chains are represented in Budapest; however, all of them are Hungarian-run franchise operations with native touches that you won't find in any other Hilton or Marriott.

In winter it's not difficult to find a hotel room, even at the last minute, and prices are usually reduced by 20%–30%. By far the cheapest and most accessible beds in the city are rooms ($20–$25 for a double room) in private homes. Although most tourist offices book private rooms, the supply is limited, so try to arrive in Budapest early in the morning.

Addresses below are preceded by the district number (in Roman numerals) and include the Hungarian postal code. Districts V, VI, and VII are in downtown Pest; I includes Castle Hill, the main tourist district of Buda. For price range information, *see* Lodging *in* Pleasures and Pastimes, *above.*

$$$$ 🏨 **art'otel.** A short walk up the Danube from the Chain Bridge, this hip new boutique hotel is the first of its kind in Budapest. Like its sibling properties in Berlin and Dresden, the hotel-cum-gallery is completely dedicated to the work of a single artist—in this case, American Donald Sultan. From the carpets to the paintings, the china to the water fountains, the entire hotel is decorated with Sultan's designs, amounting to a multimillion-dollar collection of his art. Interconnecting a new building and four 18th-century Baroque houses on the Buda riverfront, the art'otel adroitly blends old and new. Spiffy, chic contemporary furniture contrasts elegantly with restored original moldings and doorframes in the older buildings' rooms. ⊠ *I, Bem rakpart 16–19, H-1011,* ☏ *1/487–9487,* 🖷 *1/487–9488. 156 rooms, 9 suites. Restaurant, café, air-conditioning, in-room data ports, no-smoking rooms, beauty salon, sauna, meeting rooms, parking (fee). AE, DC, MC, V.* 🐾

$$$$ 🏨 **Budapest Hilton.** Built in 1977 around a 13th-century monastery adjacent to the Matthias Church, this perfectly integrated architectural wonder overlooks the Danube from the choicest site on Castle Hill. Every contemporary room has a remarkable view; Danube vistas cost more. Complete renovations during 2000 promised a welcome update in room decor. Children, regardless of age, get free accommodation when sharing a room with their parents. Note: Breakfast is not included in room rates. ⊠ *I, Hess András tér 1–3, H-1014,* ☏ *1/488–6600; 800/ 445–8667 in the U.S. and Canada;* 🖷 *1/488–6644. 295 rooms, 26 suites. 3 restaurants, 2 bars, café, air-conditioning, in-room data ports, beauty salon, sauna, exercise room, dry cleaning, laundry service, business services, meeting rooms, travel services, parking (free and fee). AE, DC, MC, V.* 🐾

$$$$ 🏨 **Budapest Marriott.** In this sophisticated yet friendly hotel on the Danube in downtown Pest, attention to detail is evident, from the impeccable buffet of colorfully glazed pastries served daily in the lobby to the feather-light ring of the front-desk bell. Guest rooms have lushly patterned carpets, floral bedspreads, and etched glass. The layout takes full advantage of the hotel's prime Danube location, offering breathtaking views of Gellért Hill, the Chain and Elizabeth bridges, and Castle Hill from the lobby, ballroom, every guest room, and even the impressive health club—which is unquestionably the best hotel fitness center in the city. ⊠ *V, Apáczai Csere János u. 4, H-1052,* ☎ *1/266–7000; 800/831–4004 in the U.S. and Canada;* 📠 *1/266–5000. 362 rooms, 11 suites. 3 restaurants, bar, air-conditioning, in-room data ports, no-smoking rooms, health club, squash, shops, baby-sitting, dry cleaning, laundry service, business services, meeting rooms, travel services, parking (fee). AE, DC, MC, V.* 🕸

$$$$ 🏨 **Danubius Hotel Gellért.** The double-deck rotunda of this grand
★ Hungarian spa hotel leads you to expect a string orchestra playing "The Emperor Waltz." Built in 1918, the Jugendstil Gellért was favored by Otto von Hapsburg, son of the last emperor. Rooms come in all shapes and sizes—from palatial suites to awkward, tiny spaces. Now part of the Danubius hotel chain, the Gellért has begun an ambitious overhaul, refurnishing all rooms in the mood of the original Jugendstil style. Inquire about completed rooms when you reserve. The best views—across the Danube or up Gellért Hill—are more expensive; avoid those that face the building's inner core. If you're planning a weekend trip well in advance, inquire about special packages; the prices can be more friendly. Though the hotel's service can be a bit inconsistent, its famous pièce de résistance will make up for it: the monumental, ornate thermal baths. Admission to the spa is free to hotel guests (medical treatments cost extra); corridors and an elevator lead directly to the baths from the second, third, and fourth floors. ⊠ *XI, Gellért tér 1, H-1111,* ☎ *1/385–2200,* 📠 *1/466–6631. 220 rooms, 13 suites. Restaurant, bar, brasserie, café, no-smoking rooms, indoor pool, beauty salon, spa, mineral baths, baby-sitting, business services, meeting rooms, parking (fee). AE, DC, MC, V.* 🕸

$$$$ 🏨 **Hotel Inter-Continental Budapest.** Formerly the Fórum Hotel, this boxy, modern, riverside hotel consistently wins applause for its gracious appointments, excellent service, and gorgeous views across the Danube to Castle Hill. Sixty percent of the rooms have river views (these are more expensive); rooms on higher floors ensure the least noise. The hotel café, Corso Bar, is locally known for its pastries. The central location and efficient business services makes the Inter-continental popular with businesspeople. Note: breakfast is not included in the room rates. ⊠ *V, Apáczai Csere János u. 12–14, Box 231, H-1368,* ☎ *1/327–6333,* 📠 *1/327–6357. 398 rooms, 16 suites. 2 restaurants, bar, café, air-conditioning, in-room data ports, no-smoking floors, pool, health club, business services, meeting rooms, car rental, parking (fee). AE, DC, MC, V.* 🕸

$$$$ 🏨 **Hyatt Regency Budapest.** The spectacular 10-story interior—a mix
★ of glass capsule elevators, cascading tropical greenery, an open bar, and café—is surpassed only by the views across the Danube to Castle Hill (rooms with a river view cost substantially more). Rooms have been tastefully redesigned with classy, unobtrusive decor in muted blues and light woods, and sparkling bathrooms. ⊠ *V, Roosevelt tér 2, H-1051,* ☎ *1/266–1234,* 📠 *1/266–9101. 330 rooms, 23 suites. 3 restaurants, 2 bars, air-conditioning, in-room data ports, no-smoking rooms, indoor pool, beauty salon, sauna, exercise room, casino, solarium, business services, meeting rooms, travel services, parking (fee). AE, DC, MC, V.* 🕸

$$$$ 🏨 **Kempinski Hotel Corvinus Budapest.** This sleek luxury hotel is the
★   favored lodging of visiting VIPs—from rock superstars to business
moguls. From overnight shoe-shine service to afternoon chamber music
in the lobby, the Kempinski exudes solicitousness. Unlike those of
other nearby hotels, rooms are spacious, with blond and black Swedish
geometric inlaid woods and an emphasis on functional touches, such
as three phones in every room. Large, sparkling bathrooms, most with
tubs and separate shower stalls and stocked with every toiletry, are the
best in Budapest. The hotel's business services also stand out as the
city's best. An automatic current in the smallish pool allows you to
swim long distances without getting anywhere. Breakfast is not included
in the room rates. ⊠ *V, Erzsébet tér 7–8, H-1051,* ☎ *1/429–3777; 800/
426–3135 in the U.S. and Canada;* 𝔽𝔸𝕏 *1/429–4777. 342 rooms, 27 suites.
2 restaurants, bar, lobby lounge, pub, shopping arcade, air-conditioning, in-room data ports, no-smoking rooms, indoor pool, barbershop,
beauty salon, massage, health club, shops, dry cleaning, laundry service, business services, meeting rooms, travel services, parking (fee).
AE, DC, MC, V.* 🐾

$$$ 🏨 **Danubius Grand Hotel Margitsziget.** Built in 1873 and long in dis-
repair, this venerable hotel reopened in 1987 as a Ramada Inn and was
recently taken over by the Danubius hotel chain. Room rates may have
increased since the 1870s, but the high ceilings haven't been lowered.
Nor have the old-fashioned room trimmings—down comforters, ornate
chandeliers—been lost in the streamlining. Choose between views across
the Danube onto an industrial section of Pest or out onto the verdant lawns
and trees of a tranquil park. Because it's connected to a bubbling thermal
spa next door and is located on car-free Margaret Island in the Danube
right between Buda and Pest, the Danubius Grand feels removed from the
city but is still only a short taxi or bus ride away. ⊠ *XIII, Margit-sziget,
H-1138,* ☎ *1/329–2300; 1/349–2769 (reservations);* 𝔽𝔸𝕏 *1/329–3923
(reservations), 1/329–2429 (reception). 164 rooms, 10 suites. 2 restaurants,
no-smoking rooms, indoor pool, beauty salon, massage, sauna, spa,
mineral baths, exercise room, bicycles, meeting rooms, travel services,
free parking. AE, DC, MC, V.* 🐾

$$$ 🏨 **Danubius Thermal Hotel Helia.** A sleek Scandinavian design and less
hectic location upriver from downtown make this spa hotel on the
Danube a change of pace from its Pest peers. Its neighborhood is non-
descript, but guests can be in town in minutes or take advantage of
the thermal baths and special health packages—including everything
from Turkish baths to electrotherapy and fitness tests. The staff is friendly
and helpful, and most of the comfortable rooms have Danube views.
⊠ *XIII, Kárpát u. 62–64, H-1133,* ☎ *1/452–5800,* 𝔽𝔸𝕏 *1/452–5801.
254 rooms, 8 suites. Restaurant, bar, café, indoor pool, beauty salon,
hot tub, massage, sauna, spa, steam room, mineral baths, tennis courts,
exercise room, business services, meeting rooms, free parking. AE, DC,
MC, V.*

$$$ 🏨 **Radisson SAS Béke.** The well-situated Béke (on a main boulevard
near the Nyugati railroad station) is a budget family inn turned lux-
ury hotel—it now has a glittering turn-of-the-20th-century facade, a
lobby lined with mosaics and statuary, and bellmen bowing before the
grand marble staircase. Guest rooms resemble solidly modern living
rooms, with two-tone wood furnishings and pastel decor. ⊠ *VI, Teréz
krt. 43, H-1067,* ☎ *1/301–1600,* 𝔽𝔸𝕏 *1/301–1615. 238 rooms, 8 suites.
2 restaurants, 2 bars, café, air-conditioning, in-room data ports, no-
smoking rooms, pool, beauty salon, sauna, solarium, business ser-
vices, meeting rooms, travel services, parking (fee). AE, DC, MC, V.*

$$ 🏨 **Astoria.** At a busy intersection in downtown Pest stands a revital-
ized turn-of-the-20th-century hotel that remains an oasis of quiet in
hectic surroundings. Staff members are always—but unobtrusively—

on hand. Rooms are genteel, spacious, and comfortable, and renovations have remained faithful to the original decor: rather like Grandma's sitting room, in Empire style with an occasional antique. The Astoria's vintage Café Mirror is a wonderful place to relive the Hungarian coffeehouse tradition. ⊠ *V, Kossuth Lajos u. 19–21, H-1053,* ☎ *1/317–3411,* ℻ *1/318–6798. 125 rooms, 5 suites. Restaurant, bar, café, no-smoking rooms, nightclub, business services, meeting rooms, free parking. AE, DC, MC, V.*

$$ 🏨 **Carlton Hotel.** Tucked behind an alleyway at the foot of Castle Hill, this modern property (formerly named the Alba Hotel) is a short walk via the Chain Bridge from lively business and shopping districts. Rooms are clean and quiet, with white-and-pale-gray contemporary decor and typical Budapest views over a kaleidoscope of rooftops and chimneys. Half have bathtubs. ⊠ *I, Apor Péter u. 3, H-1011,* ☎ *1/224–0999 or 1/375–8658,* ℻ *1/224–0990. 95 rooms. Bar, breakfast room, air-conditioning, no-smoking rooms, meeting room, parking (fee). AE, DC, MC, V.* 🐾

$$ 🏨 **Flamenco.** Classy though sometimes overlooked, this hotel in the Buda foothills is a welcome addition to this side of the river. A wall of windows in the low-ceiling lobby opens out onto views of a park. Service is professional, and the well-kept contemporary rooms are above average in this price category. ⊠ *XI, Tas Vezér u. 7, H-1113,* ☎ *1/372–2165 or 1/372–2000,* ℻ *1/372–2100. 352 rooms, 8 suites. 2 restaurants, indoor pool, beauty salon, sauna, solarium, business services, meeting rooms, travel services, parking (fee). AE, DC, MC, V.*

$$ 🏨 **Hotel Benczúr.** Escape to this quiet hotel in the leafy embassy district off Andrássy út via the city's antique underground, the *Földalatti.* Majestic Heroes' Square is a short walk away. Rooms here are well-equipped, with minibars, modern phones, and larger than usual bathrooms, though the furnishings are quite plain. The refreshingly green neighborhood and proximity to outdoor restaurants and bars make this hotel an attractive option, especially in summer months. The Benczúr shares the building with Hotel Pedagógus. ⊠ *VI, Benczúr u. 35, H-1068,* ☎ *1/342–7970,* ℻ *1/342–1558. 93 rooms. Restaurant, no-smoking rooms, meeting room, free parking. MC, V.*

$$ 🏨 **Mercure Hotel Budapest Nemzeti.** With a lovely, baby-blue Baroque facade, the Nemzeti reflects the grand mood of the turn of the 20th century. The high-ceiling lobby and public areas—with pillars, arches, and wrought-iron railings—are elaborately elegant. Many of the once unexceptional rooms have been revamped with pretty, new furnishings and air-conditioning; be sure to ask for one of these rooms ($10 extra) for optimal comfort. The hotel is located at bustling Blaha Lujza tér in the center of Pest, which tends toward the seedy after dark; although windows are double-paned, to ensure a quiet night, ask for a room facing the inner courtyard. ⊠ *VIII, József krt. 4, H-1088,* ☎ *1/303–9310,* ℻ *1/314–0019,* ☎ ℻ *1/303–9162. 75 rooms, 1 suite. Restaurant, piano bar, air-conditioning, meeting room, travel services. AE, DC, MC, V.* 🐾

$$ 🏨 **Molnár Panzió.** Fresh air and peace and quiet could lure you to this immaculate guest house nestled high above Buda on Széchenyi Hill. Rooms in the octagonal main house are polyhedric, clean, and bright, with pleasant wood paneling and pastel-color modern furnishings; most have distant views of Castle Hill and Gellért Hill, and some have balconies. Eight rooms in a newer addition next door are more private and have superior bathrooms. Breakfast here is more appealing than usual—with scrambled eggs in addition to the standard breads and jams. ⊠ *XII, Fodor u. 143, H-1124,* ☎ *1/395–1873,* ☎ ℻ *1/395–1872. 23 rooms. Restaurant, bar, sauna, exercise room, playground, travel services, free parking. AE, DC, MC, V.* 🐾

$$ **Victoria.** The Parliament building and city lights twinkling over the
★   river can be seen from the picture windows of every room at this young
establishment right on the Danube. The tiny hotel mixes the charm of a
small inn with the modern comforts and efficiency of a business hotel. The
location—an easy walk from Castle Hill sights and downtown Pest—could-
n't be better. ⊠ *I, Bem rakpart 11, H-1011,* ☎ *1/457–8080,* FAX *1/457–
8088. 27 rooms, 1 suite. Bar, air-conditioning, sauna, meeting room,
travel services, parking (fee). AE, DC, MC, V.*❧

$ **Citadella.** Comparatively basic, the Citadella is nevertheless very pop-
ular for its price and for its stunning location—right inside the fortress.
Half of the rooms compose a youth hostel, giving the hotel a lively com-
munal atmosphere. None of the rooms have bathrooms, but half have
showers. Breakfast is not included in the rates. ⊠ *XI, Citadella sétány,
Gellérthegy, H–1118,* ☎ *1/466–5794,* FAX *1/386–0505. 20 rooms, none
with bath. Breakfast room. No credit cards.*

$ **Kulturinov.** One wing of a magnificent 1902 neo-Baroque castle now
★   houses basic budget accommodations. Rooms come with two or three
beds and are clean and delightfully peaceful; they have showers but
no tubs. The neighborhood—one of Budapest's most famous squares
in the luxurious castle district—is magical. ⊠ *I, Szentháromság tér 6,
H-1014,* ☎ *1/355–0122 or 1/375–1651,* FAX *1/375–1886. 16 rooms.
Snack bar, library, meeting rooms. AE, DC, MC, V.*

NIGHTLIFE AND THE ARTS

Nightlife

Budapest's nightlife is vibrant and diverse. For basic beer and wine drink-
ing, sörözős and *borozós* (wine bars) abound, although the latter tend
to serve the early-morning-spritzer-before-work types rather than
nighttime revelers. For quiet conversation there are *drink-bárs* in most
hotels and all over town, but beware of the inflated prices and steep
cover charges. Cafés are preferable for unescorted women.

Most nightspots and clubs have bars, pool tables, and dance floors.
Although some places do accept credit cards, it's best to expect to pay
cash for your night on the town. As is the case in most other cities, the
life of a club or disco in Budapest can be somewhat ephemeral. Those
listed below are quite popular and seem to be here to stay. But for the
very latest on the more transient "in" spots, consult the nightlife sec-
tions of the weekly *Budapest Sun* or *Budapest in Your Pocket*, pub-
lished five times a year.

Budapest also has its share of seedy go-go clubs and so-called "cabarets,"
some of which are known for scandalously excessive billing and phys-
ical intimidation. Be wary if you are "invited" in by women lingering
nearby, and don't order anything without first seeing the price. What's
more, in some pulsing nightspots it is not uncommon to find men weav-
ing through the crowd selling drugs or themselves; the penalties for pos-
sessing even small amounts of illegal drugs are stiff.

A word of warning to the smoke-sensitive: Although a 1999 law re-
quiring smoke-free areas in many public establishments has already had
a discernible impact in restaurants, the bar scene is a firm reminder
that Budapest remains a city of smokers. No matter where you spend
your night out, chances are you'll come home smelling of cigarette smoke.

Bars and Clubs

Angel Bar and Disco (⊠ VII, Szövetség u. 33, ☎ 1/351–6490) is one
of Budapest's enduring and most popular gay bars (though all persuasions

Pack an easy way to reach the world.

Wherever you travel, the MCI WorldCom Card℠ is the easiest way to stay in touch. You can use it to call to and from more than 125 countries worldwide. And you can earn bonus miles every time you use your card. So go ahead, travel the world. MCI WorldCom℠ makes it even more rewarding. For additional access codes, visit www.wcom.com/worldphone.

MCI WORLDCOM.

EASY TO CALL WORLDWIDE

1. Just dial the WorldPhone® access number of the country you're calling from.

2. Dial or give the operator your MCI WorldCom Card number.

3. Dial or give the number you're calling.

Austria ◆	0800-200-235
Belgium ◆	0800-10012
Czech Republic ◆	00-42-000112
Denmark ◆	8001-0022
Estonia ★	800-800-1122
Finland ◆	08001-102-80
France ◆	0-800-99-0019
Germany	0800-888-8000
Greece ◆	00-800-1211
Hungary ◆	06▼-800-01411
Ireland	1-800-55-1001
Italy ◆	172-1022
Luxembourg	8002-0112
Netherlands ◆	0800-022-91-22
Norway ◆	800-19912
Poland ·❖·	800-111-21-22
Portugal ·❖·	800-800-123
Romania ·❖·	01-800-1800
Russia ◆ ·❖·	747-3322
Spain	900-99-0014
Sweden ◆	020-795-922
Switzerland ◆	0800-89-0222
Ukraine ·❖·	8▼10-013
United Kingdom	0800-89-0222
Vatican City	172-1022

◆ Public phones may require deposit of coin or phone card for dial tone.   ★ Not available from public pay phones.
▼ Wait for second dial tone.   ·❖· Limited availability.

EARN FREQUENT FLIER MILES

American Airlines
A'Advantage®

China Airlines

▲ Delta Air Lines
SkyMiles·

TWA

✈ UNITED
Mileage Plus®

≡ US AIRWAYS
DIVIDEND MILES

Bureau de change

Cambio

外国為替

In this city, you can find money on almost any street.

NO-FEE FOREIGN EXCHANGE

The Chase Manhattan Bank has over 80 convenient
locations near New York City destinations such as:

      Times Square
      Rockefeller Center
      Empire State Building
      2 World Trade Center
      United Nations Plaza

Exchange any of 75 foreign currencies

◯ CHASE

THE RIGHT RELATIONSHIP IS EVERYTHING.®

are welcome), with a rollicking dance floor. It's closed Monday–Wednesday.

Bahnhof (⊠ VI, Váci út 1, at Nyugati pu.) is, appropriately, in the Nyugati (West) train station and attracts swarms of young people to its large, crowded dance floor to live bands and DJ'd music. It's closed Sunday–Tuesday.

The most popular of Budapest's Irish pubs and a favorite expat watering hole is **Becketts** (⊠ V, Bajcsy-Zsilinszky út 72, ☎ 1/311–1035), where Guinness flows freely and excellent Irish fare is served amid the gleams of polished wood and brass.

One of the city's hottest spots is **Café Capella** (⊠ V, Belgrád rakpart 23, ☎ 1/318–6231), where a welcoming, gay-friendly crowd flocks to the glittery drag shows (held a few times a week) and revels to DJ'd club music until dawn.

A hip, mellow crowd mingles at the stylish **Cafe Incognito** (⊠ VI, Liszt Ferenc tér 3, ☎ 1/351–9428), with low lighting and funky music kept at a conversation-friendly volume. Couches and armchairs in the back are comfy and private. It closes relatively early—at midnight.

Café Pierrot (⊠ I, Fortuna u. 14, ☎ 1/375–6971), an elegant café and piano bar on a small street on Castle Hill, is well suited to a secret rendezvous.

With its abundance of soft chairs and changing exhibits of chic, abstract paintings, **Cafe Vian** (⊠ VI, Liszt Ferenc tér 9, ☎ 1/342–8991) is *the* place to lounge about sipping cappuccino, beer, or a cocktail (nonalcoholic varieties available) while chatting, not to mention seeing and being seen. It closes at midnight.

Established Hungarian jazz headliners and young up-and-comers play Sunday–Tuesday in the popular if small, stylishly brick-walled **Fat Mo's** (⊠ VII, Nyári Pál u. 11, ☎ 1/267–3199), which is open daily.

If crowds, low newspaper-mosaicked ceilings, and smoke-permeated air aren't your thing, avoid the **Old Man's Music Pub** (⊠ VII, Akácfa u. 13, ☎ 1/322–7645). If hard-core live blues and friendly chaos *are,* don't miss out on the fun—complemented by a small dance floor.

Cool (and trendily dark) **Underground** (⊠ VI, Teréz krt. 30, ☎ 1/311–1481) is below the artsy Művész movie theater. Exposed metal beams and girders and wackily shaped scrap-metal chairs and tables give this bar the requisite industrial look; the DJ spins progressive popular music. Weekends are packed with younger, sometimes rowdy, hipsters.

Casinos

Most of Budapest's 10 or so major casinos are open daily from 2 PM until 4 or 5 AM and offer gambling in hard currency—usually dollars—only.

The centrally located and popular **Las Vegas Casino** (⊠ V, Roosevelt tér 2, ☎ 1/317–6022) is in the Hyatt Regency Hotel. In an 1879 building designed by prolific architect Miklós Ybl, who also designed the State Opera House, the **Várkert Casino** (⊠ I, Miklós Ybl tér 9, ☎ 1/202–4244) is the most visually striking of the city's casinos.

The Arts

For the latest on arts events, consult the entertainment listings of the English-language press (☞ Contacts and Resources, *below*). Their entertainment calendars map out all that's happening in Budapest's arts and culture world—from thrash bands in wild clubs to performances at the Opera House. Another option is to stop in at the **National Philharmonic ticket office** (⊠ V, Mérleg u. 10, ☎ 1/318–0281) and browse through the scores of free programs and fliers and scan the walls coated with upcoming concert posters. Hotels and tourist offices will provide you with a copy of the monthly publication *Programme,* which contains details of all cultural events.

Tickets can be bought at the venues themselves, but many ticket offices sell them without extra charge. Prices are still very low, so markups of even 30% shouldn't dent your wallet if you book through your hotel. Inquire at Tourinform (☞ Visitor Information, *below*) if you're not sure where to go. Ticket availability depends on the performance and season—it's usually possible to get tickets a few days before a show, but performances by major international artists sell out early. Tickets to Budapest Festival Orchestra concerts and festival events also go particularly quickly.

Theater and opera tickets are sold at the **Central Theater Booking Office** (⊠ VI, Andrássy út 18, ☎ 1/312–0000). For classical concert, ballet, and opera tickets, as well as tickets for major pop and rock shows, go to the **National Philharmonic Ticket Office** (☞ *above*). **Music Mix Ticket Service** (⊠ V, Váci utca 33, ☎ 1/317–7736) specializes in popular music but handles other genres as well.

Classical Music and Opera

The tiny recital room of the **Bartók Béla Emlékház** (Béla Bartók Memorial House; ⊠ II, Csalán út 29, ☎ 1/394–4472) hosts intimate Friday evening chamber music recitals by well-known ensembles from mid-March to June and September to mid-December.

The **Budapest Kongresszusi Központ** (Budapest Convention Center; ⊠ XII, Jagelló út 1–3, ☎ 1/209–1990) is the city's largest-capacity (but least atmospheric) classical concert venue and usually hosts the largest-selling events of the Spring Festival.

The homely little sister of the Opera House, the **Erkel Színház** (Erkel Theater; ⊠ VII, Köztársaság tér 30, ☎ 1/333–0540) is Budapest's other main opera and ballet venue. There are no regular performances in the summer.

Liszt Ferenc Zeneakadémia (Franz Liszt Academy of Music; ⊠ VI, Liszt Ferenc tér 8, ☎ 1/342–0179), usually referred to as the Music Academy, is Budapest's premier classical concert venue, hosting orchestra and chamber music concerts in its splendid main hall. It's sometimes possible to grab a standing-room ticket just before a performance here.

The glittering **Magyar Állami Operaház** (Hungarian State Opera House; ⊠ VI, Andrássy út 22, ☎ 1/331–2550), Budapest's main venue for operas and classical ballet, presents an international repertoire of classical and modern works as well as such Hungarian favorites as Kodály's *Háry János.* Except during the one-week BudaFest international opera and ballet festival in mid-August, the Opera House is closed during the summer.

Colorful operettas such as those by Lehár and Kálmán are staged at their main Budapest venue, the **Operetta Theater** (⊠ VI, Nagymező u. 19, ☎ 1/353–2172); also look for modern dance productions and Hungarian renditions of popular Broadway classics.

Classical concerts are held regularly at the **Pesti Vigadó** (Pest Concert Hall; ⊠ V, Vigadó tér 2, ☎ 1/318–9167).

English-Language Movies

Many of the English-language movies that come to Budapest are subtitled in Hungarian rather than dubbed; this applies less so, however, to independent and art films. There are more than 30 cinemas that regularly show films in English, and tickets are very inexpensive by Western standards (400–700 Ft.). Consult the movie matrix in the *Budapest Sun* for a weekly list of what's showing.

Folk Dancing

Many of Budapest's district cultural centers regularly hold traditional regional folk-dancing evenings, or dance houses (*táncház*), often with general instruction at the beginning. These sessions provide a less touristy way to taste Hungarian culture.

Almássy téri Szabadidő központ (Almássy Square Recreation Center; ⊠ VII, Almássy tér 6, ☎ 1/352–1572) holds numerous folk-dancing evenings, representing Hungarian as well as Greek and other ethnic cultures. Traditionally the wildest táncház is held Saturday night at the **Belvárosi Ifjúsági ház** (City Youth Center; ⊠ V, Molnár u. 9, ☎ 1/317–5928), where the stomping and whirling go on way into the night; the center, like many such venues, closes from mid-July to mid-August. A well-known Transylvanian folk ensemble, Tatros, hosts a weekly dance house at the **Marczibányi téri Művelődési ház** (Marczibányi tér Cultural Center; ⊠ II, Marczibányi tér 5/a, ☎ 1/212–5789), usually on Wednesday night.

Folklore Performances

The Hungarian State Folk Ensemble performs regularly at the **Budai Vigadó** (⊠ I, Corvin tér 8, ☎ 1/201–3766); shows incorporate instrumental music, dancing, and singing.

The **Folklór Centrum** (⊠ XI, Fehérvári út 47, ☎ 1/203–3868) has been a major venue for folklore performances for more than 30 years. It hosts regular traditional folk concerts and dance performances from spring through fall.

Theaters

The **Madách Theater** (⊠ VII, Erzsébet krt. 31–33, ☎ 1/478–2041) produces colorful musicals in Hungarian, including a popular adaptation of *Cats*. For English-language dramas check out the **Merlin Theater** (⊠ V, Gerlóczy u. 4, ☎ 1/317–9338). Another musical theater is the **Thália Theater** (⊠ VI, Nagymező u. 22–24, ☎ 1/331–0500). The sparkling **Vígszínház** (Comedy Theater; ⊠ XIII, Pannónia u. 1, ☎ 1/329–2340) hosts classical concerts and dance performances but is primarily a venue for musicals, such as the Hungarian adaptation of *West Side Story.*

OUTDOOR ACTIVITIES AND SPORTS

Bicycling

Because of constant thefts, bicycle rentals are difficult to find in Hungary. **Bringóhintó,** a rental outfit on Margaret Island (⊠ Hajós Alfréd sétány 1, across from Thermal Hotel, ☎ 1/329–2072), offers popular four-wheel pedaled contraptions called *Bringóhintók,* as well as traditional two-wheelers; standard bikes cost about 800 Ft. per hour or 1,500 Ft. until 8 AM the next day, with a 10,000 Ft. deposit. For more information about renting in Budapest, contact **Tourinform** (⊠ V, Sütő u. 2, ☎ 1/317–9800). For brochures and general information on bicycling conditions and suggested routes, try Tourinform or contact the **Magyar Kerékpáros Túrázók Szövetsége** (Bicycle Touring Association of Hungary; ⊠ V, Bajcsy-Zsilinszky út 31, 2nd floor, Apt. 3, ☎ 1/332–7177).

Golf

Golf is still a new sport in Hungary, one that few Hungarians can afford. The closest place to putt is 35 km (22 mi) north of the city at the **Budapest Golfpark** (☎ 1/317–6025, 1/317–2749, or 06–26/392–463) in Kisoroszi. The park has an 18-hole, 72-par course and a driving range. Greens fees range from 7,000 Ft. to 8,000 Ft. Carts and equipment can be rented. The park is closed from about mid-November–mid-March.

Health and Fitness Clubs

Andi Stúdió (✉ V, Hold u. 29, ☎ 1/311–0740) is a trendy fitness club with adequate but sometimes overcrowded facilities. For about 650 Ft. you can work out on the weight machines (no real cardiovascular equipment to speak of) and sit in the sauna, or take an aerobics class, held every hour. **Gold's Gym** (✉ VIII, Szentkirályi u. 26, ☎ 1/267–4334) stands out as being the least cramped gym, with good weight-training and cardiovascular equipment and hourly aerobics classes in larger-than-usual spaces. A one-visit pass costs around 650 Ft.

Horseback Riding

Experienced riders can ride at the **Budapesti Lovas Klub** (Budapest Equestrian Club; ✉ VIII, Kerepesi út 7, ☎ ⒻⒶⓍ 1/313–5210) for about 1,500 Ft. per hour. Call about two weeks ahead to assure yourself a horse. In the verdant outskirts of Buda, the **Petneházy Lovas Centrum** (Petneházy Equestrian Center; ✉ 1029 Feketefej út 2, Adyliget, ☎ 1/397–5048) offers horseback-riding lessons and trail rides for 1,800 Ft.–2,500 Ft. per hour. Note that English saddle, not Western, is the standard in Hungary.

Jogging

The path around the perimeter of **Margaret Island,** as well as the numerous pathways in the center, is level and inviting for a good run. **Városliget** (City Park) in flat Pest has paths good for jogging.

Spas and Thermal Baths

In addition to those listed below, newer, modern baths are open to the public at hotels, such as the **Danubius Grand Hotel Margitsziget** and the **Danubius Thermal Hotel Helia** (☞ Lodging, *above*). They lack the charm of their older peers but provide the latest treatments.

Gellért Thermal Baths (☞ Tabán and Gellért Hill, *above*); **Király Baths** (☞ North Buda, *above*); **Rác Baths** (☞ Tabán and Gellért Hill, *above*); **Rudas Baths** (☞ Tabán and Gellért Hill, *above*); **Széchenyi Baths** (☞ Városliget, *above*).

The **Lukács Baths** (✉ II, Frankel Leó u. 25–29, ☎ 1/326–1695) were built in the 19th century but modeled on the Turkish originals and fed with waters from a source dating from the Bronze Age and Roman times. The complex is open Monday–Saturday 6–7, Sunday 6–5; the facilities are coed. Admission to the baths costs 450 Ft.

Tennis and Squash

On Margaret Island, **Euro-Gym Fitness Club** (✉ XIII, Europa House, Margitsziget, ☎ 1/339–8672) charges 700 Ft.–900 Ft. per hour to play on one of its eight clay courts; it's open from mid-April to mid-October, and you'll need to reserve a day or two in advance. **On-line Squash Club** (✉ Budaörs, Forrás u. 8, ☎ 23/501–2620), on the near outskirts of town, is a trendy full-facility fitness club with five squash courts.

Hourly rates run 2,000 Ft.–2,800 Ft., depending on when you play. The club rents equipment and stays open until 11 PM on weekdays, 9 PM on weekends. **Városmajor Tennis Academy** (⊠ XII, Városmajor u. 63–69, ☎ 1/202–5337) has five outdoor courts (clay and hexapet) available daily 7 AM–10 PM. They are lit for night play and covered by a tent in winter. Court fees run around 1,400 Ft. per hour in summer, 1,800 Ft.–3,000 Ft. in winter. Racket rentals and lessons are also offered. The Marriott Hotel's **World Class Fitness Center** (⊠ V, Apáczai Csere János u. 4, ☎ 1/266–4290) has one excellent squash court available for 2,500 Ft.–4,500 Ft. an hour, depending on when you play; be sure to reserve it a day or two in advance.

SHOPPING

Shopping Districts

You'll find plenty of expensive boutiques, folk-art and souvenir shops, foreign-language bookstores, and classical-record shops on or around touristy **Váci utca,** Budapest's famous, upscale pedestrian-only promenade. While a stroll along Váci utca is integral to a Budapest visit, browsing among some of the smaller, less touristy, more typically Hungarian shops in Pest—on the **Kis körút** (Small Ring Road) and **Nagy körút** (Great Ring Road)—may prove more interesting and less pricey. Lots of arty boutiques are springing up in the section of District V **south of Ferenciek tere and toward the Danube,** and around **Kálvin tér. Falk Miksa utca,** also in the fifth district, running south from Szent István körút, is one of the city's best antiques districts, lined on both sides with atmospheric little shops and galleries.

Department Stores and Malls

Skála Metro (⊠ VI, Nyugati tér 1–2, ☎ 1/353–2222), opposite the Nyugati (West) Railroad Station, is one of the largest and best-known department stores, selling a little bit of not entirely everything. **Fontana** (⊠ Váci u. 16), has several floors of cosmetics, clothing, and other goods, all with price tags reflecting the store's expensive address. Pest's huge **Westend City Center** (⊠ VI, Váci út 1–3 [next to the Nyugati railroad station], ☎ 1/238–7777) and Buda's **Mammut** (⊠ II, Széna tér, ☎ 1/345–8020) are just two of the many American-style malls that have sprung up in Hungary in recent years. They offer everything—except a genuine Hungarian atmosphere.

Markets

For true bargains and possibly an adventure, make an early morning trip to the vast **Ecseri Piac** (⊠ IX, Nagykőrösi út 156; take Bus 54 from Boráros tér), on the outskirts of the city. A colorful, chaotic market that shoppers have flocked to for decades, it is an arsenal of second-hand goods, where you can find everything from frayed Russian army fatigues to Herend and Zsolnay porcelain vases to antique silver chalices. Goods are sold at permanent tables set up in rows, from trunks of cars parked on the perimeter, and by lone, shady characters clutching just one or two items. As a foreigner, you may be overcharged, so prepare to haggle—it's part of the flea-market experience. Also, watch out for pickpockets. Ecseri is open weekdays 8–4, Saturday 8–3, but the best selection is on Saturday morning.

A colorful outdoor flea market is held weekend mornings from 7 to 2 at **Petőfi Csarnok** (⊠ XIV, Városliget, Zichy Mihály út 14, ☎ 1/251–7266), in City Park. The quantity and selection are smaller than at Ecseri Piac, but it offers a fun flea-market experience closer to the city center. Many visitors buy red-star medals, Russian military watches, and other memorabilia from Communist days here. One other option is the **Vásárcsarnok** (☞ Downtown Pest and the Kis körút [Little Ring Road], *above*).

Specialty Stores

Antiques

Falk Miksa utca (☞ Shopping Districts, *above*), lined with antiques stores, is a delightful street for multiple-shop browsing.

The shelves and tables at tiny **Anna Antikvitás** (☒ V, Falk Miksa u. 18–20, ☎ 1/302–5461) are stacked with exquisite antique textiles—from heavily embroidered wall hangings to dainty lace gloves. Exquisite cloth and lace parasols line the ceiling, but these, unfortunately, are not for sale; similar ones are, however, sometimes available. The store also carries assorted antique objets d'art. **BÁV Műtárgy** (☒ V, Ferenciek tere 12, ☎ 1/318–3381; ☒ V, Kossuth Lajos u. 1–3, ☎ 1/318–6934; ☒ V, Szent István krt. 3, ☎ 1/331–4534), the State Commission Trading House, has antiques of all shapes, sizes, kinds, and prices at its several branches around the city. While they all have a variety of objects, porcelain is the specialty at the branch on Kossuth Lajos utca, and paintings at the Szent István körút store. **Polgár Galéria és Aukciósház** (☒ V, Kossuth Lajos u. 3, ☎ 1/318–6954) sells everything from jewelry to furniture and also holds several auctions a year. **Qualitás** (☒ V, Falk Miksa u. 32; ☒ V, Kígyó u. 5; ☒ VII, Dohány u. 1) sells paintings, furniture, and decorative objects at its branches around town.

Art Galleries

Budapest has dozens of art galleries showing and selling old works as well as the very latest. **Dovin Gallery** (☒ V, Galamb u. 6, ☎ 1/318–3673) specializes in Hungarian contemporary paintings. New York celebrity Yoko Ono opened **Gallery 56** (☒ V, Falk Miksa u. 7, ☎ 1/269–2529) to show art by internationally famed artists, such as Keith Haring, as well as works by up-and-coming Hungarian artists. You can also visit **Magyar Fotógráfusok Háza** (☞ Andrássy út, *above*) for photography exhibits.

Books

You'll encounter bookselling stands throughout the streets and metro stations of the city, many of which sell English-language souvenir picturebooks at discount prices. **Váci utca** is lined with bookstores that sell glossy coffee-table books about Budapest and Hungary.

Atlantisz (☒ V, Váci u. 31–33) has a selection of English classics, as well as academic texts. **Bestsellers** (☒ V, Október 6 u. 11, ☎ 1/312–1295) sells exclusively English-language books and publications, including best-selling paperbacks and a variety of travel guides about Hungary and beyond. The **Central European University Bookshop** (☒ V, Nádor u. 9, ☎ 1/327–3096), in the Central European University, is a more academically focused branch of Bestsellers bookstore. If you're interested in reading up on this part of the world, this is the store for you. You'll also find a good selection of books in English at **Idegennyelvű Könyvesbolt** (☒ V, Petőfi Sándor u. 2 [in Párizsi udvar]), which specializes in foreign-language books. **Írók boltja** (Writers' Bookshop; ☒ VI, Andrássy út 45, ☎ 1/322–1645), one of Budapest's main literary bookstores, has a small but choice selection of Hungarian fiction and poetry translated into English. The hushed, literary atmosphere is tangible, and small tables are set out for reading and enjoying a cup of self-serve tea and coffee.

China, Crystal, and Porcelain

Hungary is famous for its age-old Herend porcelain, which is hand-painted in the village of Herend near Lake Balaton. For the Herend name and quality without the steep price tag, visit **Herend Village Pottery** (⊠ II, Bem rakpart 37, ☎ 1/356–7899), where you can choose from Herend's practical line of durable ceramic cups, dishes, and table settings. The brand's largest Budapest store, **Herendi Porcelán Márkabolt** (⊠ V, József Nádor tér 11, ☎ 1/317–2622), sells a variety of the delicate (and pricey) pieces, from figurines to dinner sets. Hungary's exquisite Zsolnay porcelain, created and hand-painted in Pécs, is sold at the **Zsolnay Márkabolt** (⊠ V, Kígyó u. 4, ☎ 1/318–3712) and a few other locations.

Hungarian and Czech crystal is considerably less expensive here than in the United States. **Goda Kristály** (⊠ V, Váci u. 9, ☎ 1/318–4630) has beautiful colored and clear pieces. **Haas & Czjzek** (⊠ VI, Bajcsy-Zsilinszky út 23, ☎ 1/311–4094) has been in the business for more than 100 years, selling a variety of porcelain, glass, and ceramic pieces in traditional and contemporary styles. Crystal and porcelain dealers also sell their wares at the Ecseri Piac flea market (☞ Markets, *above*), often at discount prices, but those looking for authentic Herend and Zsolnay should beware of imitations.

Clothing

El Cabito (⊠ V, Múzeum krt. 35, ☎ 318–8963), a tiny boutique across from the National Museum, offers cotton dresses of Hungarian and Far Eastern design—for reasonable prices. The **Hugo Boss Shop** (⊠ V, Aranykéz u. 2, ☎ 318–3016) has a good selection of men's suits. High-fashion women's outfits by top Hungarian designers are for sale at **Monarchia** (⊠ V, Szabadsajtó út 6, ☎ 1/318–3146), whose rich burgundy velvet draperies and ceilings are higher than its floor space. **Manier** (⊠ V, Váci u. 48 [entrance at Nyári Pál u. 4], ☎ 1/318–1812) is a popular haute couture salon run by talented Hungarian designer Anikó Németh offering women's pieces ranging from quirky to totally outrageous. The store's second branch is across the street at Váci utca 53.

Folk Art

Handmade articles, such as embroidered tablecloths and painted plates, are sold all over the city by Transylvanian women wearing traditional scarves and colorful skirts. You can usually find them standing at **Moszkva tér, Jászai Mari tér,** outside the **Kossuth tér** metro, around **Váci utca,** and in the larger metro stations.

All types of folk art—pottery, blouses, jewelry boxes, wood carvings, embroidery—can be purchased at one of the many branches of Népművészet Háziipar, also called **Folkart Centrum** (⊠ V, Váci u. 14, ☎ 1/318–5840), a large cooperative chain. Prices are reasonable, and selection and quality are good. **Holló Műhely** (⊠ V, Vitkovics Mihály u. 12, ☎ 1/317–8103) sells the work of László Holló, a master wood craftsman who has resurrected traditional motifs and styles of earlier centuries. There are lovely hope chests, chairs, jewelry boxes, candlesticks, and more, all hand-carved and hand-painted with cheery folk motifs—a predominance of birds and flowers in reds, blues, and greens.

Home Decor and Gifts

Impresszió (⊠ V, Károly krt. 10, ☎ 1/337–2772) is a little boutique packed with home-furnishings, baskets, picture frames, and decorative packaging, all made of natural materials and reasonably priced. The courtyard it calls home includes similar shops and a pleasant café. A few blocks away, just down the street from the Holló Műhely (☞ *above*), lies the **Interieur Stúdió** (⊠ V, Vitkovics Mihály u. 6, ☎ 1/266–

1666), offering wooden brushes, bookmarks, and even a birdcage; candles of all shapes and sizes; and sundry other objects for the home.

Music

Recordings of Hungarian folk music or of pieces played by Hungarian artists are widely available on compact discs, though cassettes and records are much cheaper and are sold throughout the city. CDs are normally quite expensive—about 4,000 Ft.

MCD Amadeus (⊠ V, Szende Pál u. 1, ☎ 1/318–6691), just off the Duna korzó, has an extensive selection of classical CDs. **FOTEX Records** (⊠ V, Szervita tér 2, ☎ 1/318–3395; ⊠ V, Váci u. 13, ☎ 1/318–3128; ⊠ VI, Teréz krt. 27, ☎ 1/332–7175; ⊠ XII, Alkotás út 11, ☎ 1/355–6886) is a flashy, Western-style music store with a cross section of musical types but focused on contemporary pop. **MCD Zeneszalon** (⊠ V, Vörösmarty tér 1, ☎ no phone) has a large selection of all types of music and is centrally located. Its separate, extensive section on Hungarian artists is great for gift- or souvenir-browsing. The **Rózsavölgyi Zenebolt** (⊠ V, Szervita tér 5, ☎ 1/318–3500) is an old, established music store crowded with sheet music and largely classical recordings, but with other selections as well.

Toys

For a step back into the world before Pokemon cards and action figures, stop in at the tiny **Játékszerek Anno** (Toys Anno; ⊠ VI, Teréz krt. 54, ☎ 1/302–6234) store, where fabulous repros of antique European toys are sold. From simple paper puzzles to lovely stone building blocks to the 1940s wind-up metal monkeys on bicycles, these "nostalgia toys" are beautifully simple and exceptionally clever. Even if you're not a collector, it's worth a stop just to browse.

Wine

Stores specializing in Hungarian wines have become a trend in Budapest over the past few years. The best of them is the store run by the **Budapest Bortársaság** (Budapest Wine Society; ⊠ I, Batthyány u. 59, ☎ 1/212–2569 or 1/212–0262, FAX 1/212–5285). The cellar shop at the base of Castle Hill always has an excellent selection of Hungary's finest wines, chosen by the wine society's discerning staff, who will happily help you with your purchases. Tastings are held Saturday from 2 to 6.

SIDE TRIP TO LAKE BALATON

Lake Balaton, the largest lake in Central Europe, stretches 80 km (50 mi) across Hungary. Its vast surface area is drastically contrasted with its modest depths—only 9.8 ft at the center and just 52.5 ft at its deepest point, at the Tihany Peninsula. The Balaton—the most popular playground of this landlocked nation—is just 90 km (56 mi) to the southwest of Budapest, so it is within easy reach of the capital by car, train, bus, and even bicycle. On a hot day in July or August, it seems the entire country and half of Germany are packed towel to towel on the lake's grassy public beaches, paddling about in the warm water and consuming fried meats and beer at the omnipresent snack bars.

On the lake's hilly northern shore, ideal for growing grapes, is Balatonfüred, Hungary's oldest spa town, famed for natural springs that bubble out curative waters. The national park on the Tihany Peninsula is just to the south, and regular boat service links Tihany and Balatonfüred with Siófok on the southern shore. Flatter and more crowded with resorts, cottages, and trade-union rest houses, the southern shore (beginning with Balatonszentgyörgy) is not as attractive as the northern one (north-shore locals say the only redeeming quality of the south-

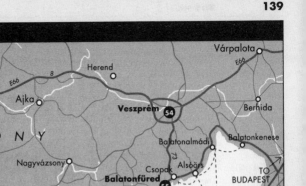

Lake Balaton

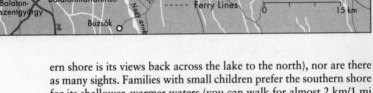

ern shore is its views back across the lake to the north), nor are there as many sights. Families with small children prefer the southern shore for its shallower, warmer waters (you can walk for almost 2 km/1 mi before it deepens). The water warms up to 25°C (77°F) in summer.

Every town along both shores has at least one *strand* (beach). The typical Balaton strand is a complex of blocky wooden changing cabanas and snack bars, fronted by a grassy flat stretch along the water for sitting and sunbathing. Most have paddleboat and other simple boat rentals. A small entrance fee is usually charged.

Those interested in exploring beyond the beach can set out by car, bicycle, or foot, on beautiful village-to-village tours—stopping to view lovely old Baroque churches, photograph a stork family perched high in its chimney-top nest, or climb a vineyard-covered hill for sweeping vistas. Since most vacationers keep close to the shore, a small amount of exploring into the roads and countryside heading away from the lake will reward you with a break from the summer crowds.

Numbers in the margin correspond to numbers on the Lake Balaton and Transdanubia map.

Veszprém

54 *116 km (72 mi) southwest of Budapest, 18 km (11 mi) north of Balatonfüred.*

Hilly Veszprém is the center of cultural life in the Balaton region. ★**Várhegy** (Castle Hill) is the most picturesque part of town, north of Szabadság tér. **Hősök kapuja** (Heroes' Gate), at the entrance to the castle, houses a small exhibit on Hungary's history. Just past the gate and down a little alley to the left is the **Tűztorony** (Fire Tower); note that the lower level is medieval, while the upper stories are Baroque. There is a good view of the town and surrounding area from the balcony. *Tower:* ☎ *88/425–204.* ⊙ *Apr.–mid-Oct., daily 10–6.*

Vár utca, the only street in the castle area, leads to a small square in front of the **Bishop's Palace** and the **cathedral**; outdoor concerts are held here in the summer. Vár utca continues past the square up to a terrace erected on the north staircase of the castle. Stand beside the modern statues of St. Stephen and his queen, Gizella, for a far-reaching view of the old quarter of town.

<table>
<tr><td>OFF THE
BEATEN PATH</td><td>**HEREND** – Sixteen kilometers (10 mi) northwest of Veszprém on Road 8, Herend is the home of Hungary's renowned hand-painted porcelain. The factory, founded in 1839, displays many valuable pieces in its **Herend Porcelán Művészeti Múzeum** (Herend Museum of Porcelain Arts). ⊠ *Kossuth Lajos u. 144,* ☎ *88/261–144.* ☞ *300 Ft., 2,000 Ft. for group tours in English.* ⊙ *Apr.–Oct., Tues.–Sun. 9–6; Nov.–Mar., weekdays 10–3. Hours may change so call first.*</td></tr>
</table>

Dining

$ ✕ **Szürkebarát Borozó.** The plain off-white walls of the Gray-Monk Tavern may be less than inspiring, but the hearty Hungarian fare at this cellar restaurant in the city center more than compensates. For an unusual (but very Hungarian) appetizer, try the paprika-spiced *velős pirítós* (marrow on toast; missing from the English menu and sometimes unavailable); or for a main course, gnaw away at "Ms. Baker's Pork Hoofs." ⊠ *Szabadság tér 12,* ☎ *88/327–684. No credit cards.*

$$ ⊡ **Éllő Panzió.** In this 18-room pension just southwest of the town center, you'll find ubiquitous golden lamp shades coupled with no lack of red—on the carpeting, the velvety chairs, and the curtains. Rooms in the newer annex building are more spacious than those in the chalet-like main house. Service is friendly. ⊠ *József Attila u. 25, H-8200,* ☎ *88/420–097 or 88/424–118,* 𝐅𝐀𝐗 *88/329–711. 18 rooms. Breakfast room. MC, V.* ☙

Balatonfüred

⑤⑤ *115 km (71 mi) southwest of Budapest.*

Fed by 11 medicinal springs, Balatonfüred first gained popularity as a health resort (the lake's oldest) where ailing people with heart conditions and fatigue would come to take or, more accurately, to drink a cure. The waters, said to have stimulating and beneficial effects on the heart and nerves, are still an integral part of the town's identity and consumed voraciously, but only the internationally renowned cardiac hospital has actual bathing facilities. Today Balatonfüred, also known simply as Füred, is probably the Balaton's most popular destination, with every amenity to match. Above its busy boat landing, beaches, and promenade lined with great plane and poplar trees, the twisting streets of the Old Town climb hillsides thickly planted with vines. The climate and landscape also make this one of the best wine-growing districts in Hungary. Every year in July, the most elaborate of Lake Balaton's debutante cotillions, the Anna Ball, is held here.

The center of town is **Gyógy tér** (Spa Square), where the bubbling waters from five volcanic springs rise beneath a slim, colonnaded pavilion. In the square's centerpiece, the neoclassical **Well House** of the Kossuth Spring, you can sample the water, which has a pleasant, surprisingly refreshing taste despite the sulfurous aroma; for those who can't get enough, a 30-liter-per-person limit is posted. All the buildings on the square are pillared like Greek temples. At No. 3 is the **Horváth Ház** (Horváth House), where the Szentgyörgyi-Horváth family arranged the first of what was to become the Anna Ball in 1825 in honor of their daughter Anna.

The Anna Ball is now held every July in another colonnaded building on the square, the **former Trade Unions' Sanatorium** (1802); at press time, renovations here had been completed and it was due to reopen as a hotel. Under its arcades is the **Balatoni Pantheon** (Balaton Pantheon): aesthetically interesting tablets and reliefs honoring Hungarian and foreign notables who either worked for Lake Balaton or spread the word about it. Among them is Jaroslav Hašek, the Czech author of the *Good Soldier Schweik,* who also wrote tales about Balaton. On the eastern side of the square is the **Állami Kórház** (State Hospital), where hundreds of patients from all over the world are treated. Here, too, Rabindranath Tagore, the Indian author and Nobel Prize winner, recovered from a heart attack in 1926. The tree that he planted to commemorate his stay stands in a little grove at the western end of the paths leading from the square down to the lakeside. Tagore also wrote a poem for the planting, which is memorialized beneath the tree on a strikingly animated bust of Tagore: WHEN I AM NO LONGER ON EARTH, MY TREE,/LET THE EVER-RENEWED LEAVES OF THY SPRING/MURMUR TO THE WAYFARER:/THE POET DID LOVE WHILE HE LIVED. In the same grove are trees honoring visits by another Nobel laureate, the Italian poet Salvatore Quasimodo, in 1961; and Indian prime minister Indira Gandhi, in 1972. An adjoining grove honors Soviet cosmonauts and their Hungarian partner-in-space, Bertalan Farkas.

Beginning near the boat landing, the **Tagore sétány** (Tagore Promenade) runs for nearly a kilometer (almost ½ mi) and is lined by trees, restaurants, and shops.

A stroll up **Blaha Lujza utca** from Gyógy tér will take you past several landmarks, such as the **Blaha Lujza Ház** (Lujza Blaha House), a neoclassical villa built in 1867 and, later, the summer home of this famous turn-of-the-20th-century actress, humanist, and singer (today it's a hotel); and the sweet little **Kerek templom** (Round Church), consecrated in 1846, built in a classical style and with a truly rounded interior.

NEED A BREAK?
The plush **Kedves Café** (✉ Blaha Lujza u. 7, ☎ 87/343–229), built in 1795, was once the favorite summer haunt of well-known Hungarian writers and artists. Now more touristy than literary, it is still one of Lake Balaton's most popular and famous pastry shops.

Dining and Lodging

$$ ✗ **Baricska Csárda.** Perched on a hill overlooking wine and water—
★ its own vineyard and Lake Balaton—this rambling, reed-thatched inn is complete with wood-beamed rooms, vaulted cellars, and terraces. The food is hearty yet ambitious: roasted trout, fish paprikás with gnocchi to soak up the creamy sauce, and delicious desserts mixing pumpkin and poppy seed. In summer, Gypsy wedding shows are held nightly under the grape arbors. ✉ *Baricska dülő off Rte. 71 (Széchenyi út) behind Shell station,* ☎ *87/343–105. Reservations essential. AE, V. Closed mid-Nov.–mid-Mar.*

$$ ✗ **Tölgyfa Csárda.** Perched high on a hilltop, the Oak Tree Tavern has breathtaking views over the steeples and rooftops of Balatonfüred and the Tihany Peninsula. Its decor and menu are worthy of a first-class Budapest restaurant, and nightly live Gypsy music keeps the atmosphere

festive. ⊠ *Meleghegy (up the hill at the end of Csárda u.)*, ☎ *87/343–036. No credit cards. Closed late Oct.–mid-Apr.*

$$$$ ⬛ **Annabella.** The cool, spacious guest quarters in this large, Miami-
★   style high-rise are especially pleasant in summer heat. Overlooking the
lake and Tagore Promenade, it has access to excellent swimming and
water-sports facilities. All rooms have balconies; for best vistas, request
a room on a high floor with a view of the Tihany peninsula. ⊠ *Deák
Ferenc u. 25, H-8231,* ☎ *87/342–222,* 𝔽𝔸𝕏 *87/483–029. 383 rooms, 5
suites. Restaurant, bar, brasserie, café, indoor pool, pool, barbershop,
massage, sauna, bicycles, nightclub, solarium, baby-sitting, laundry service, travel services. AE, DC, MC, V. Closed mid-Oct.–mid-Apr.* 🐾

$$$$ ⬛ **Marina.** The Marina's central beachfront location is its main draw.
Built in the mid-'80s, it is undergoing a major overhaul, which should
cheer up its dated feel. Rooms in the homely 12-story "Marina" building range from snug to small; suites have balconies but suffer from tiny
bathrooms and extremely dark bedrooms. Your safest bet is to get a
newly renovated, high-floor "Superior" room with a lake view. Or better, stay in the "Lido" wing, which opens directly onto the water and
where rooms (suites only) get plenty of sun. ⊠ *Széchenyi út 26, H-
8230,* ☎ *87/343–644,* 𝔽𝔸𝕏 *87/343–052. 291 rooms, 58 suites. Restaurant, bar, pub, indoor pool, beauty salon, massage, sauna, bowling,
beach, boating, nightclub, solarium, laundry service, travel services.
AE, DC, MC, V. Closed Oct.–late Apr.* 🐾

$$$ ⬛ **Park.** Hidden on a side street in town but close to the lakeshore,
the Park is noticeably calmer than Füred's bustling main hotels. Rooms
are large and bright, with high ceilings and tall windows. Suites have
large, breezy balconies but small bathrooms. While at press time the
decor was uninspired—Eastern Bloc–style, with low, narrow beds and
plain green and brown upholstery—extensive renovations were being
planned to freshen things up. ⊠ *Jókai u. 24, H-8230,* ☎ 𝔽𝔸𝕏 *87/343–
203 or 87/342–005. 38 rooms, 3 suites. Restaurant, bar, exercise
room, sauna, solarium, meeting room, free parking. No credit cards.*

Outdoor Activities and Sports

Most hotels have their own private beaches, with water-sports facili-
ties and equipment or special access to these nearby. Besides these, Bal-
atonfüred has three public beaches, where you can rent sailboards,
paddleboats, and other water toys; these are also available at Hungary's
largest campground, **Füred Camping** (⊠ Széchenyi u. 24, next to the
Hotel Marina, ☎ 87/343–823). Although motorboats are banned
from the lake, those desperate to water-ski can try the campground's
electric water-ski machine, which tows enthusiasts around a 1-km (½-
mi) circle. A two-tow ticket runs around 900 Ft.

In season you can rent **bicycles** from temporary, private outfits set up
in central locations around town and near the beaches; one is usually
working at the entrance to Füred Camping. Inquire at the tourist of-
fice for other current locations. Average prices for mountain-bike
rentals are 1,000 Ft. per hour or 3,500 Ft. per day. You can also usu-
ally rent **mopeds** in front of the Halászkert restaurant (⊠ Széchenyi
út 2) for around 1,300 Ft. per hour and 5,000 Ft. per day.

Trail rides and horseback-riding lessons are available from mid-May
to the end of September for about 2,500 Ft. an hour at the **Diana Lo-
vasudvar** (Diana Riding Center; ⊠ Rte. 71 just southwest of the town
center; turn right at the sign about 100 yards beyond the giant camp-
ground on the lake, ☎ 87/481–894).

Tihany and the Tihany Félsziget (Tihany Peninsula)

⑤⑥ *11 km (7 mi) southwest of Balatonfüred.*

The famed town of Tihany, with its twisting, narrow cobblestone streets and hilltop abbey, is on the Tihany Félsziget (Tihany Peninsula), joined to the mainland by a narrow neck and jutting 5 km (3 mi) into the lake. Only 12 square km (less than 5 square mi), the peninsula is not only a major tourist resort but perhaps the most historic part of the Balaton area. In 1952 the entire peninsula was declared a national park, and because of its geological rarities, it became Hungary's first nature-conservation zone. On it are more than 110 geyser craters, remains of former hot springs, reminiscent of those found in Iceland, Siberia, and Wyoming's Yellowstone Park.

The smooth Belső Tó (Inner Lake), 82 ft higher than Lake Balaton, is one of the peninsula's own two lakes; around it are barren yellowish-white rocks and volcanic cones rising against the sky. Though the hills surrounding the lake are known for their white wines, this area produces a notable Hungarian red, Tihany cabernet.

Tihany's crowning glory is the ★**Bencés Apátság** (Benedictine Abbey; ✎), with foundations laid by King András I in 1055. The abbey's charter—containing some 100 Hungarian words in its Latin text, thus making it the oldest written source of the Hungarian language—is kept in Pannonhalma. Rebuilt in Baroque style between 1719 and 1784, the abbey's church towers above the village. Its gilt-silver high altar, abbot's throne, pulpit, organ case, choir parapet, and swirling crowd of saintly and angelic faces are all the work (between 1753 and 1765) of Sebestyén Stuhlhoff. A joiner from Augsburg, Stulhoff lived and worked in the monastery as a lay brother for 25 years after the death of his Hungarian sweetheart. Local tradition says he immortalized her features as the angel who is kneeling on the right-hand side of the altar to the Virgin Mary. The magnificent Baroque organ, adorned by stucco cherubs, can be heard during evening concerts in summer.

In a Baroque house adjoining and entered through the abbey is the **Bencés Apátsági Múzeum** (Benedictine Abbey Museum). The best exhibits are in the basement lapidarium: relics from Roman colonization, including mosaic floors; a relief of David from the 2nd or 3rd century; and 1,200-year-old carved stones—all labeled in English as well as Hungarian. Three of the upstairs rooms were lived in for five days in 1921 by the last emperor of the dissolved Austro-Hungarian monarchy, Karl IV, in a futile foray to regain the throne of Hungary. Banished to Madeira, he died of pneumonia there a year later. The rooms are preserved with nostalgic relish for Franz Joseph's doomed successor. ⊠ *Első András tér 1,* ☎ *87/448–405 abbey; 87/448–650 museum.* ⌷ *200 Ft.* ☉ *May–Sept., Mon.–Sat. 9–5:30, Sun. 11–5:30; Apr. and Oct., Mon.–Sat. 10–4:30, Sun. 11–4:30; Nov.–Mar. (only church and lapidarium), Mon.–Sat. 10–3:30.*

The **Szabadtéri Múzeum** (Open-air Museum), Tihany's outdoor museum of ethnography, assembles a group of old structures, including a potter's shed (with a local artist-in-residence) and the former house of the Fishermen's Guild, with an ancient boat (used until 1934) parked inside. ⊠ *Along Batthyány u. and neighboring streets,* ☎ *no phone.* ☉ *May–Sept., Tues.–Sun. 10–6.*

Visszhang domb (Echo Hill), at the end of Piski István sétány, is where as many as 16 syllables can be bounced off the abbey wall. Nowadays, with the inroads of traffic and construction, you'll have to settle for a two-second echo.

NEED A
BREAK?

You can practice projecting from the terraces of the **Echo Restaurant** (⊠ Visszhang út 23, ☎ 87/448–460), an inn atop Echo Hill. While you're at it, try some fogas, carp, and catfish specialties.

Dining and Lodging

$$ ✕ **Pál Csárda.** Two thatch cottages house this simple restaurant, where cold fruit soup and fish stew are the specialties. You can eat in the garden, which is decorated with gourds and strands of dried peppers. ⊠ *Visszhang u. 19,* ☎ *87/448–605. Reservations not accepted. AE, MC, V. Closed Oct.–Apr.*

$ ✕ **Halásztanya.** The relaxed atmosphere and local fish specialties—such as fogas fillets with garlic—contribute to this restaurant's popularity. ⊠ *Visszhang u. 11,* ☎ *87/448–771. Reservations not accepted. AE, MC, V. Closed Nov.–Easter.*

$$$$ ▥ **Kastély Hotel.** Lush landscaped lawns surround this stately neo-
★   Baroque mansion on the water's edge, built in the 1920s for József Hapsburg and taken over by the Communist state in the '40s (it is still owned by the government). Inside, it's all understated elegance; rooms have soaring ceilings and crisp sheets. Rooms with lake-facing windows and/or balconies (slightly more expensive) are the best. Next door, a newer, uninviting concrete building houses the Kastély's sister, the Park Hotel, with 44 less expensive, though dated, rooms. ⊠ *Fürdő telepi út 1, H-8237,* ☎ *87/448–611,* ☎ *87/448–409. 25 rooms, 1 suite. Restaurant, bar, café, sauna, miniature golf, 2 tennis courts, beach. AE, DC, MC, V. Closed mid-Oct.–mid-Apr.* ✇

$$$–$$$$ ▥ **Club Tihany.** This 32-acre holiday village is essentially a year-round resort of almost Club Med proportions at the tip of the Tihany Peninsula. The list of activities is formidable—from fishing to thermal bathing at the full-service spa. The best and largest rooms in the resort's six-floor main building, the Hotel Tihany, are in its newer wing. Less fancy but more convenient for families are the 160 bungalows in various architectural styles—suburban A-frame, modern atrium, or mini-farmhouse—but all with kitchen facilities. Note: Hotel building prices include mandatory breakfast and dinner. ⊠ *Rév u. 3, H-8237,* ☎ *87/448–088 or 87/538–500,* ☎ *87/448–083. 330 rooms, 161 bungalows. 3 restaurants, 2 bars, wine bar, pool, mineral baths, beauty salon, spa, tennis, exercise room, beach, meeting rooms. AE, DC, MC, V.* ✇

$$ ▥ **Kolostor.** Cozy, wood-paneled rooms are built into an attic above a popular restaurant and brewery in the heart of Tihany village. Rates include breakfast. ⊠ *Kossuth u. 14, H-8237,* ☎ ☎ *87/448–408. 5 rooms. Restaurant. MC, V. Closed Nov.–Mar.*

Nightlife and the Arts

The **Benedictine Abbey**'s popular summer organ-concert series runs from July to August 20 and features well-known musicians performing on the abbey's magnificent organ. Concerts are generally held weekends at 8:30 PM. Contact the abbey (☞ *above*) for information and tickets.

Outdoor Activities and Sports

BICYCLING

Bicycle rentals are available from **Tihany Tourist** (☞ Visitor Information, *below*); a mountain bike costs about 700 Ft. per hour.

FISHING

Belső-tó (Inner Lake) is a popular angling spot in which you can try your luck at hooking ponty, catfish, and other local fish. Fishing permits can be bought on site at the fishing warden's office (☎ 87/448–082), on the premises of the Horgásztanya restaurant, on the southwest side of the lake.

HIKING

Footpaths crisscross the entire peninsula, allowing visitors to climb the small hills on its west side for splendid views of the area or hike down Belső-tó (Inner Lake). If in midsummer you climb its highest hill, the **Csúcshegy** (761 ft—approximately a two-hour hike), you will find the land below carpeted with purple lavender. Introduced from France into Hungary, lavender thrives on the lime-rich soil and strong sunshine of Tihany. (The State Lavender and Medicinal Herb Farm here supplies the Hungarian pharmaceutical and cosmetics industries.)

En Route   The miniature town of Örvényes, about 7 km (4½ mi) west of Tihany, has the only working **vízi malom** (water mill; Szent Imre u. 1, ☎ 87/ 449–360; 🎫 100 Ft.; ⊙ May–Sept., Tues.–Sun. 9–4) in the Balaton region. Built in the 18th century, it still grinds grain into flour while also serving as a tiny museum. In the miller's room is a collection of folk art, wood carvings, pottery, furniture, and pipes. On a nearby hill are the ruins of a **Romanesque church**; only its chancel has survived. On Templom utca, a few steps from the bridge, is the Baroque **St. Imre templom** (St. Imre Church), built in the late 18th century.

Another kilometer (½ mi) west of Örvényes, **Balatonudvari** is a pleasant beach resort famous for its cemetery, which was declared a national shrine because of its beautiful, unique heart-shape tombstones carved from white limestone at the turn of the 18th century. The cemetery is essentially on the highway, at the eastern end of town; it is easily visible from the road. Balatonudvari's beach itself is at **Kiliántelep**, 2 km (1 mi) to the west.

Badacsony

★ ⑤⑦   *20 km (12 mi) southwest of Zánka.*

One of the northern shore's most treasured images is the slopes of Mt. Badacsony (1,437 ft high), simply called the Badacsony, rising from the lake. The mysterious, coffinlike basalt peak of the Balaton Highlands is actually an extinct volcano flanked by smaller cone-shape hills. The masses of lava that coagulated here created bizarre and beautiful rock formations. At the upper edge, salt columns tower 180– 200 ft like organ pipes in a huge semicircle. In 1965 Hungarian conservationists won a major victory that ended the quarrying of basalt from Mt. Badacsony, which is now a protected nature-preservation area.

The land below has been tilled painfully and lovingly for centuries. There are vineyards everywhere and splendid wine in every inn and tavern. In descending order of dryness, the best-loved Badacsony white wines are Rizlingszilváni, Kéknyelű, and Szürkebarát. Their proud producers claim that "no vine will produce good wine unless it can see its own reflection in the Balaton." They believe it is not enough for the sun simply to shine on a vine; the undersides of the leaves also need light, which is reflected from the lake's mirrorlike surface. Others claim the wine draws its strength from the fire of old volcanoes.

Badacsony is really an administrative name for the entire area and includes not just the mountain but also five settlements at its foot.

A good starting point for Badacsony sightseeing is the **Egry József Múzeum** (József Egry Museum), formerly the home and studio of a famous painter of Balaton landscapes. His evocative paintings depict the lake's constantly changing hues, from its angry bright green during storms to its tranquil deep blues. ✉ *Egry sétány 12,* ☎ *87/431–044.* 🎫 *120 Ft.* ⊙ *May–Sept., Tues.–Sun. 10–6.*

Szegedy Róza út, the steep main street climbing the mountain, is flanked by vineyards and villas. This is the place to get acquainted with the writer Sándor Kisfaludy and his beloved bride from Badacsony, Róza Szegedy, to whom he dedicated his love poems. At the summit of her street is **Szegedy Róza Ház** (Róza Szegedy House), a Baroque winepress house built in 1790 on a grand scale—with thatch roof, gabled wall, six semicircular arcades, and an arched and pillared balcony running the length of the four raftered upstairs rooms (it was here that the hometown girl met the visiting bard from Budapest). The house is now a memorial museum to both of them, furnished much the way it was when he was doing his best work immortalizing his two true loves, the Badacsony and his wife. ⊠ *Szegedy Róza út 87,* ☎ *87/430–906.* 🎫 *120 Ft.* ⊙ *Apr.–Sept., Tues.–Sun. 10–6.*

The steep climb to the **Kisfaludy kilátó** (Kisfaludy Lookout Tower) on Mt. Badacsony's summit is an integral part of the Badacsony experience and a rewarding bit of exercise. Serious summitry begins behind the Kisfaludy House at the **Rózsakő** (Rose Stone), a flat, smooth basalt slab with many carved inscriptions. Local legend has it that if a boy and a girl sit on it with their backs to Lake Balaton, they will marry within a year. From here, a trail marked in yellow leads up to the foot of the columns that stretch to the top. Steep flights of stone steps take you through a narrow gap between rocks and basalt walls until you reach a tree-lined plateau. You are now at the 1,391-ft level. Follow the blue triangular markings along a path to the lookout tower. Even with time out for rests and views, the ascent from Rózsakő should take less than an hour.

Wine-tasting opportunities abound in Badacsony. Many restaurants and inns have their own tastings, as do the numerous smaller, private cellars dotting the hill. Look for signs saying *bor* or *Wein* (wine, in Hungarian and German, respectively) to point the way. Most places are open mid-May to mid-September daily from around noon until 9 or 10. Just outside of town, **Rizapuszta** (⊠ Badacsonytomaj, Rizapuszta, ☎ 87/471–243) is a cellar and restaurant with regular tastings.

Dining and Lodging

$$ ✕ **Halászkert.** The festive Fish Garden has won numerous international awards for its tasty Hungarian cuisine. Inside are wooden rafters and tables draped with cheerful traditional blue-and-white *kékfestő* tablecloths; outside is a large terrace with umbrella-shaded tables. The extensive menu has such fresh-from-the-lake dishes as the house halászlé, and *párolt* (steamed) harcsa drenched with a paprika-caper sauce. ⊠ *Park u. 5,* ☎ *87/431–054 or 87/431–113. AE, DC, MC, V. Closed Nov.–Apr.*

$$ ✕ **Kisfaludy-ház.** Perched above the Szegedy Róza House is this Badacsony institution, once a winepress house owned by the poet's family. Its wine cellar lies directly over a spring, but the main draw is a vast two-tier terrace that affords a breathtaking panoramic view of virtually the entire lake. Naturally, the wines are excellent and are incorporated into some of the cooking, such as creamy wine soup. ⊠ *Szegedy Róza u. 87,* ☎ *87/431–016. MC, V. Closed Nov.–Apr.*

$$–$$$ 🏨 **Club Hotel Badacsony.** On the shore of Lake Balaton in the Badacsonytomaj neighborhood, this is the largest hotel in the area. Recently renovated, rooms are bright and clean. The hotel's private beach is just a step away. ⊠ *Balatoni út 14, H-8258 Badacsonytomaj,* ☎ *87/471–040,* 📠 *87/471–059. 52 rooms, 4 suites. Restaurant, café, sauna, tennis court, bowling, beach. MC, V. Closed mid-Oct.–Apr.* 🐾

$$–$$$ 🖭 **Hotel Volán.** This bright yellow, restored 19th-century mansion is a cheerful, family-oriented inn with a manicured yard for sunning and relaxing. Well-kept rooms are in the main house and in four modern additions behind it. ⊠ *Római út 168, H-8261 Badacsony,* ☎ ℻ *87/ 431–013. 23 rooms. Restaurant, bar, pool. No credit cards.* ✑

Outdoor Activities and Sports

The upper paths and roads along the slopes of Mt. Badacsony are excellent for scenic walking. Well-marked trails lead up to the summit of Mt. Badacsony.

For beach activities, you can go to one of Badacsony's several beaches or head 6 km (4 mi) northeast, to those at Balatonrendes and Ábrahámhegy, combined communities forming quiet resorts.

Keszthely

58   *18 km (10 mi) west of Szigliget.*

Keszthely, the largest town on the northern shore, lies at the westernmost end of Lake Balaton. With a beautifully preserved pedestrian avenue (Kossuth Lajos utca) in the historic center of town, the spectacular Baroque Festetics Kastély, and a relative absence of honky-tonk, Keszthely is far more classically attractive and sophisticated than other large Balaton towns. Continuing the cultural and arts tradition begun by Count György Festetics two centuries ago, Keszthely hosts numerous cultural events, including an annual summer arts festival. Just south of town is the vast swamp called Kis-Balaton (Little Balaton), formerly part of Lake Balaton and now a nature preserve filled with birds. Water flowing into Lake Balaton from its little sibling frequently churns up sediment, making the water around Keszthely's beaches disconcertingly cloudy.

The **Pethő Ház,** a striking town house of medieval origin, was rebuilt in Baroque style with a handsome arcaded gallery above its courtyard. Hidden deep inside its courtyard you'll find the restored 18th-century **synagogue,** in front of which stands a small memorial honoring the 829 Jewish people from the neighborhood, turned into a ghetto in 1944, who were killed during the Holocaust. ⊠ *Kossuth Lajos u. 22.*

★   Keszthely's magnificent **Festetics Kastély** (Festetics Palace) is one of the finest Baroque complexes in Hungary. Begun around 1745, it was the seat of the enlightened and philanthropic Festetics dynasty, which had acquired Keszthely six years earlier. The palace's distinctive churchlike tower and more than 100 rooms were added between 1883 and 1887; the interior is exceedingly lush. The **Helikon Könyvtár** (Helikon Library) in the south wing contains some 52,000 volumes, with precious codices and documents of Festetics family history. Chamber and orchestral concerts are held in the **Mirror Gallery** ballroom or, in summer, in the courtyard. The palace opens onto a splendid park lined with rare plants and fine sculptures. ⊠ *Kastély u. 1,* ☎ *83/312–191.* 🎟 *1,100 Ft. (1,200 Ft. extra for videotaping, 500 Ft. for no-flash photos).* ☉ *June, Tues.–Sun. 9–5; July–Aug., daily 9–6; Sept.–May, Tues.–Sun. 10–5.*

Keszthely's newest cultural attraction, the **Babamúzeum** (Doll Museum), opened in 1999. Supposedly the largest of its kind in Central Europe, the museum exhibits some 450 porcelain figurines dressed in 240 types of colorful folk dress. The building's pastoral ambience is created not only by the figurines—which convey the multifarious beauty of village garb—but in the ceiling's huge, handcrafted wooden beams. On the two upper floors you'll also find wooden models of typical homes, churches, and ornate wooden gates likewise representative of all regions in and near present-day Hungary that Magyars have inhabited since conquering the Carpathian basin in 896. What is perhaps the museum's *pièce de resistance* is the lifework of an elderly peasant woman from northern Hungary: a 9-yard-long model of Budapest's Parliament building, patched together over 14 years from almost 4 million snail shells (which are 28 million years old, no less) originating from the Pannon Sea, which once covered much of Hungary. ✉ *Kossuth u. 11,* ☎ *83/318–855.* ☷ *Doll Museum, 250 Ft.; model of Parliament, 200 Ft.* ☉ *May–Sept., daily 10–5; Oct.–Apr., daily 9–5.*

Dining and Lodging

$–$$ ✕ **Hungária Gösser Söröző.** This beer garden keeps long hours and plenty of beer on tap. The food is better than you might guess judging just from the touristy atmosphere. Aside from barroom snacks, the huge menu includes *ropogós libacomb hagymás törtburgonyával* (crunchy goose-drumstick with mashed potatoes and onions) and *töltött paprika* (stuffed peppers). ✉ *Kossuth Lajos u. 35, just north of Fő tér,* ☎ *83/312–265. AE, MC, V.*

$$$$ ▦ **Danubius Hotel Helikon.** This large lakeside hotel has plenty of sports facilities, such as an indoor swimming pool, indoor tennis courts, sailing, surfing, rowing, fishing, and, in winter, skating. The comfortable, modern rooms are on the small side, but they have soothing, cream-and-blue bedspreads and curtains. ✉ *Balaton part 5, H-8360,* ☎ *83/311–330,* FAX *83/315–403. 224 rooms, 8 suites. Restaurant, bar, indoor pool, beauty salon, sauna, 2 indoor tennis courts, bowling, health club, beach. AE, DC, MC, V.* ✍

$$$ ▦ **Béta Hotel Hullám.** This turn-of-the-20th-century mansion with an elegant twin tower sits right on the Balaton shore. Rooms are clean and simply furnished with functional brown furniture; they have TVs and minibars but no telephones. Guests can use the pool and other recreational facilities at the nearby Danubius Hotel Helikon (☞ *above*). ✉ *Balatonpart 1, H-8360,* ☎ *83/312–644,* FAX *83/315–338. 28 rooms, 6 suites. Restaurant, bar, beach. AE, DC, MC, V. Closed Oct.–Apr.* ✍

Nightlife and the Arts

The **Balaton Festival,** held annually in May, features high-caliber classical concerts and other festivities in venues around town and outdoors on Kossuth Lajos utca. In summer, classical concerts and master classes are held almost daily in the Festetics Palace's (☞ *above*) Mirror Hall.

Outdoor Activities and Sports

BALLOONING

Hot-air balloon rides in the Keszthely region have become popular with those tourists who can afford it (about 20,000 Ft. per person). Dr. Bóka György (a practicing M.D. and balloon pilot) and his friendly team will take you up in his blue-and-yellow balloon for an hour-long tour—the trip includes a post-landing champagne ritual. Flights depend strongly on wind and air-pressure conditions; in summer, they can usually fly only in early morning and early evening. Transportation to and from the site is included. Contact **Med-Aer** (✉ *Móricz Zsigmond u. 7,* ☎ *83/312–421 or 06/309–576–321*) at least one week in advance to reserve your spot.

HORSEBACK RIDING

János Lovarda (János Stable; ✉ *Sömögyedüllő,* ☎ *83/314–855*) offers lessons, rides in the ring, and carriage rides.

WATER SPORTS

You can rent paddleboats and other water toys at the public beach next to the Béta Hotel Hullám) or from the Danubius Hotel Helikon (☞ Dining and Lodging, *above*).

Lake Balaton A to Z

Arriving and Departing

BY BUS

Buses headed for the Lake Balaton region depart from Budapest's Erzsébét tér station daily; contact **Volánbusz** (☎ 1/317–2318) for current schedules.

BY CAR

Expressway E71/M7 is the main artery between Budapest and Lake Balaton. At press time still under construction, it had gotten as far as the lake's northeastern point and will eventually reach southwestern Hungary. From here Route 7 from Budapest joins the E71 and continues along the lake's southern shore to Siófok and towns farther west. Route 71 goes along the northern shore to Balatonfüred and lakeside towns southwest. The drive from Budapest to Siófok takes about 1½ hours, except on weekends, when traffic can be severe. From Budapest to Balatonfüred is about the same.

BY TRAIN

Daily express trains run from Budapest's Déli (South) Station to Siófok and Balatonfüred. The roughly two-hour trip costs about 900 Ft. each way.

Getting Around

BY BOAT

The slowest but most scenic way to travel between Lake Balaton's major resorts is by ferry. Schedules for **MAHART Tours** (☎ 1/318–1704 in Budapest), the national ferry company, are available from most of the tourist offices listed below.

BY BUS

Buses frequently link Lake Balaton's major resorts. Arrive at the bus station early. Tickets with seat reservations can be bought in the stations up to 20 minutes prior to departure, otherwise from the driver; reservations cannot be made by phone. Contact the tourist offices or **Volánbusz** (☎ 1/317–2318 in Budapest) for schedule and fare information.

BY CAR

Route 71 runs along the northern shore; Route E71 (here merged with Route 7) covers the southern shore. Driving is the most convenient way to explore the area, but remember that traffic can be heavy during summer weekends.

BY TRAIN

Trains from Budapest serve the resorts on the northern shore; a separate line links resorts on the southern shore. The **Siófok** station (⊠ Millenium tér, ☎ 84/310–061) is in the center of town; the **Balatonfüred** station (⊠ Castricum tér, ☎ 87/343–652) is very close to town center. **Veszprém**'s train station (⊠ Jutasi út 34, ☎ 88/329–999) is about 2 km (1 mi) outside town. There is no train service to Tihany. While most towns are on a rail line, it's inconvenient to decipher the train schedules; trains don't run very frequently, so planning connections can be tricky. Since many towns are just a few kilometers apart, getting stuck on a local train can feel like an endless stop-start cycle. Also bear in mind that, excepting some trains between Budapest and Veszprém, you cannot reserve seats on the Balaton trains—it's first come, first seated.

Contacts and Resources

EMERGENCIES

Ambulance (☎ 104). **Fire** (☎ 105). **Police** (☎ 107).

GUIDED TOURS

IBUSZ Travel has several tours to Balaton from Budapest; inquire at the office in Budapest (⊠ V, Ferenciek tere 10, ☎ 1/485–2762 or 1/317–7767). You can also arrange tours directly with the hotels in the Balaton area and with the help of Tourinform offices (see Visitor Information, *below*); these can include boat trips to vineyards, folk-music evenings, and overnight trips to local inns.

Cityrama (in Budapest, ☎ 1/302–4382) takes groups twice a week from April to October from Budapest to Balatonfüred for a walk along the promenade and then over to Tihany for a tour of the abbey. After lunch, you'll take a ferry across the Balaton, and then head back to Budapest, with a wine-tasting stop on the way.

MAHART (☎ 84/310–050) offers several sailing excursions on Lake Balaton. From Balatonfüred, the *Csongor* sets out several times daily in July and August for an hour-long jaunt around the Tihany peninsula. Most other tours depart from Siófok also in the same period, including the "Tihany Tour", on Saturday at 10 AM, with stops for guided sightseeing in Balatonfüred and Tihany; and the "Sunset Tour", a 1½-hour cruise at 7:30 PM daily during which guests can sip a glass of champagne while watching the sun sink. The "Badacsony Tour" departs from Keszthely and goes to Badacsony at 10:30 AM Thursday.

VISITOR INFORMATION

Badacsony: Tourinform (⊠ Park u. 6, Badacsony, ☎ FAX 87/431–046). **Balatonfüred: Tourinform** (⊠ Petőfi u. 8, ☎ 87/342–237); **Balatontourist** (⊠ Tagore sétány 1, ☎ 87/342–822 or 87/343–471). **Hévíz: Hévíz Tourist** (⊠ Rákóczi u. 4, ☎ 83/341–348). **Keszthely: Tourinform** (⊠ Kossuth u. 28, ☎ FAX 83/314–144). **Siófok: Tourinform** (⊠ Víztorony, ☎ FAX 84/310–117); **IBUSZ** (⊠ Fő u. 174, ☎ 84/311–066). **Tihany: Tourinform** (⊠ Kossuth u. 20, ☎ FAX 87/448–804); **Tihany Tourist** (⊠ Kossuth u. 11, ☎ FAX 87/448–481). **Veszprém: Tourinform** (⊠ Vár u. 4, ☎ FAX 88/404–548).

BUDAPEST A TO Z

Arriving and Departing

By Boat

From late July through early September, two swift hydrofoils leave Vienna daily at 8 AM and 1 PM (once-a-day trips are scheduled mid-April–late July and September–late October). After a 5½-hour journey downriver, with a stop in the Slovak capital, Bratislava, and views of Hungary's largest church, the cathedral in Esztergom, the boats head into Budapest via its main artery, the Danube. The upriver journey takes about an hour longer. For reservations and information in Budapest, call **MAHART Tours** (☎ 1/484–4025; 1/484–4010; 43–1/729–2161; 43–1/729–2162 in Vienna). The cost is 780 AS one-way.

By Car

The main routes into Budapest are the M1 from Vienna (via Győr), the M3 from near Gyöngyös, the M5 from Kecskemét, and the M7 from the Balaton; the M3 and M5 are being upgraded over the next few years and extended to Hungary's borders with Slovakia and Yugoslavia, respectively.

By Plane

Ferihegy Repülőtér (☎ 1/296–9696), Hungary's only commercial airport with regularly scheduled service, is 24 km (15 mi) southeast of downtown Budapest. All non-Hungarian airlines operate from Terminal

2B; those of Malév, from Terminal 2A. (A note of clarification should you run into some confusion: The older part of the airport, Terminal 1, no longer serves commercial flights; and so the main airport is now often referred to as "Ferihegy 2," and the terminals as simply "A" and "B.") For same-day **flight information,** call ☎ 1/296–8000 (arrivals) or 1/296–7000 (departures); operators theoretically speak some English.

The most convenient way to fly between Hungary and the United States is with **Malév Hungarian Airlines** (☎ 06/40–212–121 toll free; 1/235–3804 [ticketing]; 1/296–9696 [after-hours flight information]) nonstop direct service between JFK International Airport in New York and Budapest's Ferihegy Airport—the only nonstop flight that exists. All are on roomy Boeing 767-200s and take approximately nine hours. The service runs daily most of the year.

Malév and other national airlines fly nonstop from most European capitals. **British Airways** (☎ 1/318–3299 or 1/266–6699) and Malév offer daily nonstop service between Budapest and London.

Between the Airport and Downtown: Many hotels offer their guests car or minibus transportation to and from Ferihegy, but all of them charge for the service. You should arrange for a pickup in advance. If you're taking a taxi, allow 40 minutes during nonpeak hours and at least an hour during rush hours (7 AM–9 AM from the airport, 4 PM–6 PM from the city). Official **Airport Taxis** (☎ 1/282–2222) are queued at the exit and overseen by a taxi monitor; rates are fixed according to the zone of your final destination. A taxi ride to the center of Budapest will cost around 4,500 Ft. Trips to the airport are about 3,500 Ft. from Pest, 4,000 Ft. from Buda. Avoid taxi drivers who approach you before you are out of the arrivals lounge.

LRI Centrum Bus (☎ 1/296–8555 or 1/296–6283) minibuses run every half hour from 5:30 AM to 9:30 PM to and from the Hotel Kempinski on Erzsébet tér (near the main bus station and the Deák tér metro hub) in downtown Budapest. It takes almost the same time as taxis but costs only about 700 Ft. The **LRI Airport Shuttle** provides convenient door-to-door service between the airport and any address in the city. To get to the airport, call to arrange a pickup (☎ 1/296–8555 or 1/296–6283); to get to the city, make arrangements at LRI's airport desk. Service to or from either terminal costs around 1,500 Ft. per person; since it normally shuttles several people at once, remember to allow time for a few other pickups or dropoffs.

By Train

There are three main *pályaudvar* (train stations) in Budapest: **Keleti** (East; ✉ VIII, Baross tér); **Nyugati** (West; ✉ V, Nyugati tér); and **Déli** (South; ✉ XII, Alkotás u.). The most reliable, 24-hour phone numbers for information on trains in and out of any station are 1/461–5500 (international) and 1/461–5400 (domestic). Trains to and from Vienna usually operate from the Keleti Station, while those to the Lake Balaton region depart from the Déli.

Getting Around

By Bus and Tram

Trams (*villamos*) and buses (*autóbusz*) are abundant and convenient. One fare ticket (95 Ft.; valid on all forms of public transportation) is valid for only one ride in one direction. Tickets cannot be bought on board; they are widely available in metro stations and newsstands and must be validated on board by inserting them downward facing you into the little devices provided for that purpose, then pulling the knob.

Alternatively, you can purchase a *napijegy* (day ticket, 740 Ft.; a three-day "tourist ticket" costs 1,500 Ft.), which allows unlimited travel on all services within the city limits. Hold on to whatever ticket you have; spot-checks by aggressive undercover checkers (look for the red armbands) are numerous and often targeted at tourists. Trolley-bus stops are marked with red, rectangular signs that list the route stops; regular bus stops are marked with similar light blue signs. (The trolley-buses and regular buses themselves are red and blue, respectively.) Tram stops are marked by light blue or yellow signs. Most lines run from 5 AM and stop operating at 11 PM, but there is all-night service on certain key routes. Consult the separate night-bus map posted in most metro stations for all-night service.

By Car

Budapest, like any Western city, is plagued by traffic jams during the day, but motorists should have no problem later in the evening. Parking, however, is a problem—prepare to learn new parking techniques such as curb balancing and sidewalk straddling. Free parking is a thing of the past on most central city streets; hourly fees are paid either to automats or attendants. Motorists not accustomed to sharing the city streets with trams should pay extra attention. You should be prepared to be flagged down numerous times by police conducting routine checks for drunk driving and stolen cars. Be sure all of your papers are in order and readily accessible; unfortunately, the police have been known to give foreigners a hard time.

Speed traps are numerous, so it's best to keep at the speed limit; fines start from the equivalent of roughly $40, but they can easily reach $230! Using—even holding—a cell phone while driving is an offense. In an effort to forestall bribe-taking, the time-honored practice of on-the-spot payment for violations was abolished in early 2000, so police must now give accused speedsters an invoice payable at post offices. (Remember this should you feel innocent and an officer suggests an on-the-spot "discount.") Spot checks are frequent as well, and police occasionally try to take advantage of foreigners, so always have your papers at hand.

Gas stations are plentiful in Hungary, and many on the main highways stay open all night, even on holidays. Major chains, such as MOL, Shell, and OMV, now have Western-style full-facility stations with rest rooms, brightly lit convenience stores, and 24-hour service. Lines are rarely long, and supplies are essentially stable. Unleaded gasoline (*bleifrei* or *ólommentes*) is generally available at most stations and is usually the 95-octane-level choice. If your car requires unleaded gasoline, be sure to double-check that you're not reaching for the leaded before you pump.

To drive in Hungary, U.S. and Canadian visitors need an International Driver's License—although their domestic licenses are usually accepted anyway. A caveat: It can get messy and expensive if you are stopped by a police officer who insists you need an International Driver's License (which, legally, you do). U.K. visitors may use their own domestic licenses.

PARKING

Gone are the "anything goes" days of parking in Budapest, when cars parked for free practically anywhere in the city, straddling curbs or angled in the middle of sidewalks. Now most streets in Budapest's main districts have restricted, fee parking; there are either parking meters that accept coins (usually for a maximum of two hours) or attendants who approach your car as you park and charge you according to how many hours you intend to stay. Hourly rates average 160 Ft. In most cases, overnight parking (generally after 6 PM and before 8 AM) in these areas is free. Budapest also has a number of parking lots and a few garages; two central-Pest garages are: V, Szervita tér and V, Aranykéz u. 4–6.

Smaller towns usually have free parking on the street, and some hourly-fee lots near main tourist zones. Throughout the country, no-parking zones are marked with the international "No Parking" sign: a white circle with a diagonal line through it.

ROAD CONDITIONS

There are four classes of roads: expressways (designated by the letter M and a single digit), main highways (a single digit), secondary roads (a two-digit number), and minor roads (a three-digit number). Highways, expressways, and secondary roads are generally in good condition. The conditions of minor roads vary considerably; keep in mind that tractors and horse-drawn carts may slow your route down in rural areas. In planning your driving route with a map, opt for the larger roadways whenever possible; you'll generally end up saving time even if there is a shorter but smaller road. It's not so much the condition of the smaller roads but the kind of traffic on them and the number of towns (where the speed limit is 50 kph [30 mph]) they pass through that will slow you down. If you're in no hurry, however, explore the smaller roads!

RULES OF THE ROAD

Hungarians drive on the right and observe the usual Continental rules of the road (but they revel in passing). Unless otherwise noted, the speed limit in developed areas is 50 kph (30 mph), on main roads 80–100 kph (50–62 mph), and on highways 120 kph (75 mph). Keep alert: Speed-limit signs are few and far between. Seat belts are compulsory (front-seat belts in lower speed zones, both front and back in higher speed zones), and drinking alcohol is totally prohibited—there is a zero-tolerance policy, and the penalties are very severe.

By Metro

Service on Budapest's subways is cheap, fast, frequent, and comfortable; stations are easily located on maps and streets by the big letter M (for metro). Tickets—95 Ft.; valid on all forms of mass transportation—can be bought at hotels, metro stations, newsstands, and kiosks. They are valid for one ride only; you can't change lines or direction. Tickets must be canceled in the time-clock machines in station entrances and should be kept until the end of the journey, as there are frequent checks by undercover inspectors; a fine for traveling without a validated ticket is about 1,300 Ft. A *napijegy* (day ticket) costs 740 Ft. (a three-day "tourist ticket," 1,500 Ft.) and allows unlimited travel on all services within the city limits.

Line 1 (marked FÖLDALATTI), which starts downtown at Vörösmarty tér and follows Andrássy út out past Gundel restaurant and City Park, is an antique tourist attraction in itself, built in the 1890s for the Magyar Millennium; its yellow trains with tank treads still work. Lines 2 and 3 were built 90 years later. Line 2 (red) runs from the eastern suburbs, past the Keleti (East) Station, through the city center, and under the Danube to the Déli (South) Station. (One of the stations, Moszkva tér, is where the *Várbusz* [Castle Bus] can be boarded.) Line 3 (blue) runs from the southeastern suburbs to Deák tér, through the city center, and northward to the Nyugati (West) Station and the northern suburbs. On all three lines, fare tickets are canceled in machines at the station entrance. All three metro lines meet at the Deák tér station and run from 4:30 AM to shortly after 11 PM.

By Taxi

Taxis are plentiful and a good value, but make sure they have a work-ing meter. The average initial charge is 125 Ft.–200 Ft. (toward the latter between 10 PM and 6 AM), plus about the same per km (½ mi) and 50 Ft.–70 Ft. (again, more at night) per minute of waiting time. Many drivers try to charge outrageous prices, especially if they sense that their passenger is a tourist. Avoid unmarked, "freelance" taxis; stick with those affiliated with an established company. Your safest and most reliable bet is to do what the locals do: Order a taxi by phone; it will arrive in about 5–10 minutes. The best rates are with **BudaTaxi** (☎ 1/233–3333)), **Citytaxi** (☎ 1/211–1111), **Fő taxi** (☎ 1/222–2222), **Tele 5 Taxi** (☎ 1/355–5555), and **6x6 Taxi** (☎ 1/266–6666).

Contacts and Resources

Apartment Rentals

Apartments, available for short- and long-term rental, can be the most economic lodging for families or groups. A short-term rental in Buda-pest may cost anywhere from $30 to $60 a day.

Amadeus Apartments (✉ IX, Üllői út 197, H-1091, ☎ 06/309–422–893, FAX 1/302–8268) oversees five well-kept apartments in downtown Budapest, each consisting of two rooms plus a fully equipped kitchen and bathroom. Free transportation from the train station or airport is included; guarded parking areas are provided for a fee for those with cars. The two-person, high-season rate is approximately $40 a night.

TRIBUS Hotel Service (✉ V, Apáczai Csere János u. 1, ☎ 1/318–5776, FAX 1/317–9099), open 24 hours a day, books private apartments, ar-ranges rooms in private homes, and reserves rooms in inns and hotels. **Cooptourist** (✉ XI, Bartók Béla út 4, ☎ 1/466–5349) arranges private apartments and rooms and makes reservations in its affiliated inns and hotels.

B&B Reservation Agencies

The rate per night for a double room in Budapest is around $20 (which usually includes the use of a bathroom but not breakfast). Two reli-able resources are: **TRIBUS Hotel Service** (☞ *above*) and **Cooptourist** (☞ *above*).

Car Rentals

Avis (main office, ✉ V, Szervita tér 8, ☎ 1/318–4240; Terminal 2A, ☎ 1/296–7265; Terminal 2B, ☎ 1/296–6421), **Budget** (main office, ✉ Hotel Mercure Buda, I, Krisztina krt. 41–43, ☎ 1/214–0420; Ter-minal 2A, ☎ 1/296–8481; Terminal 2B, ☎ 1/296–8197), and **Hertz** (also known in Hungary as Mercure Rent-a-Car; ✉ V, Marriott Hotel, Apáczai Csere János u. 4, ☎ 1/266–4361; Terminal 2A, ☎ 1/296–6988; Terminal 2B, ☎ 1/296–7171) are all here. Rates are high: Daily rates for automatics begin around $55–$60 plus 60¢ per km (½ mi); per-sonal, theft, and accident insurance (not required but recommended) runs an additional $25–$30 per day. Rates tend to be significantly lower if you arrange your rental *from home* through the American offices. Ask your travel agent for help.

Local companies offer lower rates. Inquire at **Americana Rent-a-Car** (✉ Ibis Hotel Volga, XIII, Dózsa György út 65, ☎ 1/350–2542 or 1/320–8287) about unlimited mileage weekend specials. Rates include free delivery and pickup of the car anywhere in the city. Also try **Fötaxi** (main office, ✉ VII, Kertész u. 24–28, ☎ 1/322–1471 or 1/351–0359.

Embassies and Consulates
Australian Embassy (⌧ XII, Királyhágó tér 8–9, ☎ 1/201–8899).
Canadian Embassy (⌧ XII, Zugligeti út 51–53, ☎ 1/275–1200). **British
Embassy** (⌧ V, Harmincad u. 6, ☎ 1/266–2888, FAX 1/266–0907). **U.S.
Embassy** (⌧ V, Szabadság tér 12, ☎ 1/475–4400).

Emergencies
Ambulance (☎ 104), or call **Falck–SOS** (⌧ II, Kapy u. 49/b, ☎ 1/200–
0100), a 24-hour private ambulance service with English-speaking
personnel. **Police** (☎ 107). **Doctor:** Ask your hotel or embassy for recommendations or visit the **R-Clinic** (⌧ II, Felsőzöldmáli út 13, ☎ 1/
325–9999), a private clinic staffed by English-speaking doctors offering 24-hour medical and ambulance service. The clinic accepts major
credit cards and prepares full reports for your insurance company. U.S.
and Canadian visitors are advised to take out full medical insurance.
U.K. visitors are covered for emergencies and essential treatment. **Dentist: Professional Dental Associates** (⌧ II, Sodrás u. 9, ☎ 1/200–4447
or 1/200–4448) is a private, English-speaking dental practice consisting of Western-trained dentists and hygienists; service is available 24
hours a day.

English-Language Bookstores
See Books *in* Shopping, *above.*

English-Language Periodicals
Several English-language weeklies have sprouted up to placate Budapest's large expatriate community. The *Budapest Sun* and the *Budapest Business Journal* are sold at major newsstands, hotels, and tourist
points. The mini-guidebook *Budapest in Your Pocket* appears fives times
a year and is also widely available. *Where Budapest,* a free monthly
magazine, is available only at major hotels.

Guided Tours
Orientation Tours: IBUSZ Travel (⌧ V, Ferenciek tere 10, ☎ 1/485–2762
or 1/317–7767) conducts three-hour bus tours of the city that operate
all year and cost about 5,500 Ft. Starting from Erzsébet tér, they take
in parts of both Buda and Pest. **Cityrama** (⌧ V, Báthori u. 22, ☎ 1/
302–4382) also offers a three-hour city bus tour (about 5,500 Ft. per
person). Both have commentary in English.

Special-Interest Tours: IBUSZ, Cityrama, and **Budapest Tourist** (☞ Visitor Information, *below*) organize a number of unusual tours, with trips
to the Buda Hills, goulash parties, and visits to such traditional sites
as the National Gallery and Parliament. These companies will provide
English-speaking personal guides on request. Also check at your hotel.

Boat Tours: From late March through October boats leave from the
dock at Vigadó tér on 1½-hour cruises between the railroad bridges
north and south of the Árpád and Petőfi bridges, respectively. The trip,
organized by **MAHART Tours** (☎ 1/318–1223), runs only on weekends
and holidays (once a day, at noon) in April and May, then twice daily
from May to October (at noon and 7); the cost is about 900 Ft. From
mid-June through August, the evening cruise leaves at 7:45 and has
live music and dancing for 100 Ft. more.

Hour-long evening sightseeing cruises on the *Danube Legend* depart
nightly at 8:15 in April and October, and three times nightly (at 8:15,
9, and 10) from May through September. Guests receive headphones
and listen to a recorded explanation of the sights in the language of
their choice. Drinks are also served. Boats depart from Pier 6–7 at Vigadó tér (☎ 1/317–2203 for reservations and information).

The *Duna-Bella* takes guests on two-hour tours on the Danube, including a one-hour walk on Margaret Island and shipboard cocktails. Recorded commentary is provided through earphones. The tour is offered July through August, six times a day; May through June and in September, three times a day; and April and October, once a day. Boats depart from Pier 6–7 at Vigadó tér (☎ 1/317–2203 for reservations and information).

Jewish-Heritage Tours: Chosen Tours (⊠ XII, Pagony u. 40, ☎ FAX 1/355–2202) offers a three-hour combination bus and walking tour ($17) called "Budapest Through Jewish Eyes," highlighting the sights and cultural life of the city's Jewish history. Tours run daily except Saturday and include free pickup and drop-off at central locations. Arrangements can also be made for off-season tours, as well as custom-designed tours.

Personal Guides: The major travel agencies—**IBUSZ Travel** and **Budapest Tourist** (☞ Visitor Information, *below*)—will arrange for guides.

Late-Night Pharmacies

Most pharmacies close between 6 PM and 8 PM, but several pharmacies stay open at night and on the weekend, offering 24-hour service, with a small surcharge for items that aren't officially stamped as urgent by a physician. You must ring the buzzer next to the night window and someone will respond over the intercom. Staff is unlikely to speak English; ask for help from someone who speaks Hungarian. Central ones in Pest include those at **Teréz körút 41** (☎ 1/311–4439) in the sixth district, near the Nyugati train station; and the one at **Rákóczi út 39** (☎ 1/314–3695) in the 8th district, near the Keleti train station. In Buda, there is one across the street from the Déli train station at **Alkotás utca 1/b** (☎ 1/355–4691), in the 12th district.

Language

Hungarian (*Magyar*) tends to look and sound intimidating at first because it is not an Indo-European language. Generally, older people speak some German, and many younger people speak at least rudimentary English, which has become the most popular language to learn. It's a safe bet that anyone in the tourist trade will speak at least one of the two languages. Also note that when giving names, Hungarians put the family name before the given name.

Mail

Airmail letters and postcards generally take seven days to travel between Hungary and the United States, sometimes more than twice as long, however, during the Christmas season.

In Hungary, go to Budapest's main **downtown post office** branch (⊠ Magyar Posta 4. sz., Városház u. 18, H-1052 Budapest). The post offices near Budapest's **Keleti** (East) (⊠ VIII, Baross tér) and **Nyugati** (West) (⊠ VI, Teréz krt. 51) train stations stay open until 9 PM on weekdays, the former just as long on weekends while the latter shuts its doors at 8 PM. The **American Express** office in Hungary is in Budapest (⊠ Deák Ferenc u. 10 H-1052 Budapest, ☎ 1/235–4330); there are poste restante services.

POSTAL RATES

Postage for an airmail letter to the United States costs about 160 Ft.; an airmail letter to the United Kingdom and elsewhere in Western Europe costs about 150 Ft. Airmail postcards to the United States cost about 110 Ft. and to the United Kingdom and the rest of Western Europe, about 100 Ft.

Money and Expenses

Eurocheque holders can cash personal checks in all banks and in most hotels. Many banks now also cash American Express and Visa traveler's checks. **American Express** has a full-service office in Budapest (✉ V, Deák Ferenc u. 10, ☎ 1/235–4330, FAX 1/267–2028), which also dispenses cash to its cardholders; a smaller branch on Castle Hill—at the Sisi Restaurant (☎ 1/264–0118)—has a currency exchange which operates daily from March to mid-January. Budapest also has a **Citibank** (✉ V, Vörösmarty tér 4) offering full services to account holders, including a 24-hour cash machine.

Plastic has recently entered Hungary's financial scene: Most major credit cards are accepted, though don't rely on them in smaller towns or less expensive accommodations and restaurants. Twenty-four-hour cash machines have sprung up throughout Budapest and in major towns around the country. Some accept Plus network bank cards and Visa credit cards, others Cirrus and MasterCard. You can withdraw forints only (automatically converted at the bank's official exchange rate) directly from your account. Most levy a 1% or $3 service charge. Instructions are in English. For those without plastic, many cash-exchange machines, into which you feed paper currency for forints, have also sprung up. Most bank automats and cash-exchange machines are clustered around their respective bank branches throughout downtown Pest.

COSTS

The forint was significantly devalued over the last few years and continues its decline, but at press time inflation had fallen under 10% from the 25% of five years ago. You'll receive more forints for your dollar but will find that prices have risen to keep up with inflation. More and more hotels now set their rates in hard currency to avoid the forint's instability. Still, even with inflation and the 25% value-added tax (VAT) in the service industry, enjoyable vacations with all the trimmings still remain less expensive than in nearby Western cities such as Vienna.

CURRENCY

Hungary's unit of currency is the forint (Ft.), no longer divided into fillérs as it was a few years ago. There are bills of 200, 500, 1,000, 2,000, 5,000, and 10,000 forints (at press time one of 20,000 forints was also planned); and coins of 1, 2, 5, 10, 20, 50, and 100 forints. The exchange rate was approximately 302 Ft. to the U.S. dollar, 204 Ft. to the Canadian dollar, and 427 Ft. to the pound sterling at press time. Although cash card and Eurocheque facilities are easy to find in big cities, it is probably still wise to bring traveler's checks, which can be cashed all over the country in banks and hotels. There is still a black market in hard currency, but changing money on the street is risky and illegal, and the bank rate almost always comes close. Stick with banks and official exchange offices.

SAMPLE PRICES

Cup of coffee, 120 Ft.–200 Ft.; bottle of beer, 350 Ft.–550 Ft.; soft drinks, 150 Ft.; ham sandwich, 200 Ft.; 2-km (1-mi) taxi ride, 300 Ft.; museum admission, 150 Ft.–300 Ft.

National Holidays

January 1; March 15 (Anniversary of 1848 Revolution); April 15–16, 2001 and March 31–April 1, 2002 (Easter and Easter Monday); May 1 (Labor Day); June 3–4, 2001 and May 19–20, 2002 (Pentecost); August 20 (St. Stephen's and Constitution Day); October 23 (1956 Revolution Day); December 24–26.

Opening and Closing Times

Banks are generally open weekdays until 3 or 4; most close by 2 on Friday. Museums are generally open Tuesday through Sunday from 10 to 6 and are closed on Monday; most stop admitting people 30 minutes before closing time. Some have a free-admission day; see individual listings in tours below, but double-check, as the days tend to change. Department stores are open weekdays 10–5 or 6, Saturday until 1. Grocery stores are generally open weekdays from 7 AM to 6 or 7 PM, Saturday until 1 PM; "nonstops," or *éjjel-nappali,* are (theoretically) open 24 hours.

Passports and Visas

Only a valid passport is required of U.S., British, and Canadian citizens; Australian citizens need a visa. For additional information contact the **Hungarian Embassy** in the United States (⊠ 3910 Shoemaker St. NW, Washington, DC 20008, ☎ 202/362–6730), in Canada (⊠ 299 Waverley St. Ottawa, Ontario K2P 0V9, ☎ 613/230–9614), in London (⊠ 35b Eaton Pl., London SW1X 8BY, ☎ 0171/235–5218), or in Australia (⊠ 17 Beale Crescent Deakin Act., Canberra 2600, ☎ 6126/282–3226).

Student and Youth Travel

In Hungary, as a general rule, only Hungarian citizens and students at Hungarian institutions qualify for student discounts on domestic travel fares and admission fees. Travelers under 25, however, qualify for excellent youth rates on international airfares; those under 26 are eligible for youth rates on international train fares. The International Student Identity Card (ISIC) is accepted in Budapest and other large Hungarian cities, but not as widely as it is in Western countries. If you buy your Student Identity Card in Budapest at the **Express Youth and Travel Office** (⊠ V, Zoltán u. 10, ☎ 1/311–6418; V, Szabadság tér 16, ☎ 1/331–6393; VIII, Keleti train station, ☎ 1/342–1772), which specializes in providing information on all aspects of student and youth travel throughout the country and abroad, it will cost about one-third the price of buying the card in the United States.

Telephones

Within Hungary, most towns can be dialed directly—dial 06 and wait for the buzzing tone; then dial the local number. Note that cellular phone numbers are treated like long-distance domestic calls: Dial 06 before the number (when giving their cellular phone numbers, most people include the 06 anyway).

Dial 198 for directory assistance for all of Hungary. Operators are unlikely to speak English. A safer bet is to consult *The Phone Book,* an English-language telephone directory full of important Budapest numbers as well as cultural and tourist information; it's provided in guest rooms of most major hotels, as well as at many restaurants and English-language bookstores. A similar, though much slimmer guide is *Budapest in Your Pocket,* which appears five times a year and can be found at newsstands and hotels.

Though continuously improving, the Hungarian telephone system is still antiquated, especially in the countryside. Be patient. With the slow improvements comes the problem of numbers changing—sometimes without forewarning. Tens of thousands of phone numbers in Budapest alone will be changed over the next few years; if you're having trouble getting through, ask your concierge to check the number for you.

The country code for Hungary is 36. When dialing from outside the country, drop the initial 06 prefix for area codes outside of Budapest.

INTERNATIONAL CALLS
Direct calls to foreign countries can be made from Budapest and all major provincial towns by dialing 00 and waiting for the international dialing tone; on pay phones the initial charge is 60 Ft. To reach an **AT&T** long-distance operator, dial ☎ 06–800–01111; for **MCI,** dial ☎ 06–800–01411; for **Sprint,** dial ☎ 06–800–01877.

LOCAL CALLS
Coin-operated pay phones accept 10-Ft., 20-Ft., 50-Ft., and 100-Ft. coins; the minimum initial amount is 20 Ft. Given that they often swallow up change without allowing a call in exchange, however, when possible use gray card-operated telephones, which outnumber coin-operated phones in Budapest and the Balaton region. The cards—available at post offices and most newsstands and kiosks—come in units of 60 (800 Ft.) and 90 (1,800 Ft.) calls. It is unnecessary to use the city code, 1, when dialing within Budapest. Don't be surprised if a flock of children gathers around your pay phone while you talk—collecting and trading used phone cards is a raging fad.

Tipping

Four decades of socialism have not restrained the extended palm in Hungary—so tip when in doubt. Hairdressers and taxi drivers expect 10%– 15% tips, while porters should get a dollar or two. Coatroom attendants receive 100 Ft.–200 Ft., as do gas-pump attendants if they wash your windows or check your tires; dressing-room attendants at thermal baths receive 50 Ft.–100 Ft. for opening and closing your locker. Gratuities are not included automatically on bills at most restaurants; when the waiter arrives with the bill, you should immediately add a 10%–15% tip to the amount, as it is not customary to leave the tip on the table. If a Gypsy band plays exclusively for your table, you should leave at least 200 Ft. in a plate discreetly provided for that purpose.

Travel Agencies

American Express (✉ V, Deák Ferenc u. 10, ☎ 1/235–4330, ℻ 1/267– 2028). **Getz International** (✉ V, Falk Miksa u. 5, ☎ 1/312–0645 or 1/ 312–0649, ℻ 1/312–1014). **Vista Travel Center** (✉ VI, Andrássy út 1, ☎ 1/269–6032 or 1/269–6033, ℻ 1/269–6031).

Visitor Information

Budapest Tourist (✉ I, Déli pályaudvar [South Railway Station]), ☎ 1/212–4625 or 1/355–7167; ✉ XIII, pedestrian underpass at Nyugati páaudvar [West Railway Station], ☎ 1/332–6565). **IBUSZ** (central branch: ✉ V, Ferenciek tere 10, ☎ 1/485–2700). **TRIBUS Hotel Service** (✉ V, Apáczai Csere János u. 1, ☎ 1/318–5776, ℻ 1/317–9099), open 24 hours. **Tourinform** (✉ V, Sütő u. 2, ☎ 1/317–9800). The **Tourism Office of Budapest** (✉ V, Március 15 tér 7, ☎ 1/266–0479; ✉ VI, Nyugati pályaudvar, ☎ 1/302–8580) has developed the **Budapest Card,** which entitles holders to unlimited travel on public transportation; free admission to many museums and sights; and discounts on various services from participating businesses. The cost (at press time) is 2,800 Ft. for two days, 3,400 Ft. for three days; one card is valid for an adult plus one child under 14.

4 PORTRAITS OF PRAGUE AND BUDAPEST

Further Reading

Vocabulary

FURTHER READING

Since the revolutions of 1989–90, a number of leading journalists have produced highly acclaimed books detailing the tumultuous changes experienced by Eastern and Central Europeans and the dramatic effects these changes have had on individual lives. Timothy Garten Ash's eyewitness account, *The Magic Lantern: The Revolution of '89 Witnessed in Warsaw, Budapest, Berlin, and Prague,* begins with Václav Havel's ringing words from his 1990 New Year's Address: "People, your government has returned to you!" Winner of both a National Book Award and a Pulitzer Prize, *The Haunted Land* is Tina Rosenberg's wide-ranging, incisive look at how Poland, the Czech Republic, and Slovakia (as well as Germany) are dealing with the memories of 40 years of communism.

In *Exit into History: A Journey Through the New Eastern Europe,* Eva Hoffman returns to her Polish homeland and five other countries—Hungary, Romania, Bulgaria, the Czech Republic, and Slovakia—and captures the texture of everyday life of a world in the midst of change. Isabel Fonseca's *Bury Me Standing: The Gypsies and Their Journey* is an unprecedented and revelatory look at the Gypsies—or Romany—of Eastern and Central Europe, the large and landless minority whose history and culture have long been obscure.

Travelogues worth reading, though less recent, include Claudio Magris's widely regarded *Danube,* which follows the river as it flows from its source in Germany to its mouth in the Black Sea; Brian Hall's *Stealing from a Deep Place,* a lively account of a solo bicycle trip through Romania and Bulgaria in 1982, followed by a stay in Budapest; Patrick Leigh Fermor's *Between the Woods and the Water,* which relates his 1934 walk through Hungary and Romania and captures life in these lands before their transformation during World War II and under the Soviets. Though its emphasis is on the countries on the eastern side of the Black Sea, Neal Ascherson's widely acclaimed *Black Sea* does touch on Bulgaria and Romania.

Forty-three writers from 16 nations of the former Soviet bloc are included in *Description of a Struggle: The Vintage Book of Contemporary Eastern European Writing,* edited by Michael March. Focusing on novels, poetry, and travel writing, the *Traveller's Literary Companion to Eastern and Central Europe* is a thorough guide to the vast array of literature from this region available in English translation. It includes country-by-country overviews, dozens of excerpts, reading lists, biographical discussions of key writers that highlight their most important works, and guides to literary landmarks.

Czech Republic

English readers have an excellent range of both fiction and nonfiction about the Czech Republic at their disposal. The most widely read Czech author of fiction in English is probably Milan Kundera, whose well-crafted tales illuminate both the foibles of human nature and the unique tribulations of life in Communist Czechoslovakia. *The Unbearable Lightness of Being* takes a look at the 1968 invasion and its aftermath through the eyes of a strained young couple. *The Book of Laughter and Forgetting* deals in part with the importance of memory and the cruel irony of how it fades over time; Kundera was no doubt coming to terms with his own forgetting as he wrote the book from his Paris exile. *The Joke,* Kundera's earliest work available in English, takes a serious look at the dire consequences of humorlessness among Communists.

Born and raised in the German-Jewish enclave of Prague, Franz Kafka scarcely left the city his entire life. *The Trial* and *The Castle* strongly convey the dread and mystery he detected beneath the 1,000 golden spires of Prague. Kafka worked as a bureaucrat for 14 years, in a job he detested; his books are, at least in part, an indictment of the bizarre bureaucracy of the Austro-Hungarian empire, though they now seem eerily prophetic of the even crueler and more arbitrary Communist system that was to come.

The most popular Czech authors at the close of the 20th century were those banned by the Communists after the Soviet invasion of 1968. Václav Havel and members of the Charter 77 illegally distributed self-published manuscripts, or *samizdat* as they were called, of these banned authors—among them, Bohumil Hrabel, Josef Škvorecký, and Ivan Klíma. Hrabel, perhaps the most beloved of all Czech writers, never left his homeland; many claim to have shared a table with him at his favorite pub in Prague, U Zlatéyho tygra. His books include *I Served the King of England* and the lyrical *Too Loud a Solitude,* narrated by a lonely man who spends his days in the basement compacting the world's greatest works of literature along with bloodied butcher paper into neat bundles before they get carted off for recycling and disposal. Škvorecký sought refuge and literary freedom in Toronto in the early 1970s. His book *The Engineer of Human Souls* reveals the double censorship of the writer in exile—censored in the country of his birth and unread in his adopted home. Still, Škvorecký did gain a following thanks to his translator, Paul Wilson—who lived in Prague in the 1960s and '70s until he was ousted for his assistance in dissident activities. Wilson also set up 68 Publishers, which is responsible for the bulk of Czech literature translated into English. Novelist, short story writer, and playwright Ivan Klíma is now one of the most widely read Czech writers in English; his books include the novels *Judge on Trial* and *Love and Garbage,* and *The Spirit of Prague,* a collection of essays about life in the post-Communist Czech Republic.

Václav Havel, one-time dissident playwright turned president of the Czech Republic, is essential nonfiction reading. The best place to start is probably *Living in Truth,* which provides an absorbing overview of his own political philosophy and of Czechoslovak politics and history over the last 30 years. Other recommended books by Havel include *Disturbing the Peace* (a collection of interviews with him) and *Letters to Olga.* Havel's plays explore the absurdities and pressures of life under the former Communist regime; the best example of his absurdist dramas is *The Memorandum,* which depicts a Communist bureaucracy more twisted than the streets of Prague's Old Town.

Among the most prominent of the younger Czech writers is Jáchym Topol, whose *A Visit to the Train Station* documents the creation of a new Prague with a sharp wit that cuts through the false pretenses of American youth occupying the city.

Hungary

Hungarians have played a central role in the intellectual life of the 20th century, although their literary masters are less well known to the west than those who have excelled in other arts, such as Béla Bartok in music and Andre Kertesz and Robert and Cornell Capa in photography.

Novelist and poet Daző Kosztolányi was prominent in European intellectual circles after World War I and was greatly admired by Thomas Mann. His novels, including *Anna Édes* and *Skylark,* are known for their keen psychological insight and social commentary. Also worth discovering is novelist and essayist György Konrád, one of Hungary's leading 20th-century dissidents, whose *The Loser* is a disturbing reflection on intellectual life in a totalitarian state. The English writer Tibor Fischer's novels *Under the Frog* and *The Thought Gang* deal with life in contemporary Hungary. John Lukacs's *Budapest 1900: A Historical Portrait of a City and Its Culture* is an oversize, illustrated study of Hungary's premier city at a particularly important moment in its history. For a more in-depth look at the city, András Török's *Budapest: A Critical Guide* offers detailed historical and architectural information, and is illustrated with excellent drawings.

VOCABULARY

Czech/Slovak

English	Czech/Slovak	Pronunciation
Basics		
Yes/no	Ano/ne	**ah**-no/neh
Please	Prosím	**pro**-seem
Thank you	Děkuji	**dyek**-oo-yee
Pardon me	Pardon	**par**-don
Hello.	Dobrý den	**dob**-ree den
Do you (m/f) speak English?	Mluvíte anglicky?	**mloo**-vit-eh ahng-**glit**-ski?
I don't speak Czech	Nemluvím česky	nem-**luv**-eem ches-ky
I don't understand	Nerozumím	neh-rohz-**oom**-eem
Please speak slowly	Prosím, mluvte pomalu	**pro**-seem, **mloov**-teh poh-**mah**-lo
Please write it down.	Prosím napište	**pro**-seem nah-**peesh**
Show me	Ukažte mně	oo-**kazh**-te mnye
I am American (m/f)	Jsem američan/ američanka	sem ah-**mer**-i-chan/ ah-mer-i--**chan**-ka
English (m/f)	Angličan/ angličanka	**ahn**-gli-chan/ ahn-gli-**chan**-ka
My name is . . .	Jmenuji se	**ymen** weh-seh
On the right/left	Napravo/nalevo	na-**pra**-vo/na-**leh**-vo
Arrivals	Přílety	**pshee**-leh-tee
Where is . . . ?	Kde je	g'deh yeh
the station?	Nádraží	nah-**drah**-zee
the train?	Vlak	vlahk
the bus/tram?	Autobus/tramvaj	**out**-oh-boos/**tram**-vie
the airport?	Letiště	**leh**-tish-tyeh
the post office?	Pošta	**po**-shta
the bank?	Banka	**bahn**-ka
Stop here	Zastavte tady	**zah**-stahv-teh **tah**-dee
I would like (m/f) . . .	Chtěl (chtěla) bych	kh'tyel (**kh'tyel**-ah) bihk
How much does it cost?	Kolik to stoji?	ko-**lik** toh **stoy**-ee?
Letter/postcard	Dopis/pohlednice	doh-**pis**-ee/poh-**hled**-nit-seh
By airmail	Letecky	**leh**-tet-skee
Help!	Pomoc!	**po**-motz!

Numbers

One	Jeden	ye-**den**
Two	Dva	dvah
Three	Tři	tshree
Four	Čtyři	ch'**ti**-zhee
Five	Pět	pyet
Six	Šest	shest
Seven	Sedm	**sed-oom**
Eight	Osm	**oh**-soom
Nine	Devět	**deh**-vyet
Ten	Deset	**deh**-set
One hundred	Sto	sto
Thousand	Tisíc	**tee**-seets

Days of the Week

Sunday	Neděle	**neh**-dyeh-leh
Monday	Pondělí	**pon**-dye-lee
Tuesday	žterý	**oo**-teh-ree
Wednesday	Středa	**stshreh**-da
Thursday	Čtvrtek	ch't'v'**r**-tek
Friday	Pátek	**pah**-tek
Saturday	Sobota	**so**-boh-ta

Where to Sleep

A room	Pokoj	**poh**-koy
The key	Klíč	kleech
With bath/shower	S koupelnou/sprcha	s'**ko**-pel-noh/**sp'r**-kho

Food

The menu	Jídelnílístek	**yee**-dell-nee lis-tek
The check, please.	Učet, prosím	**oo**-chet pro-seem
Breakfast	Snídaně	**snyee**-dan-ye
Lunch	Oběd	**ob**-yed
Dinner	Večeře	**ve**-cher-zhe
Bread	Chléb	khleb
Butter	Máslo	**mah**-slo
Salt/pepper	Sůl/pepř	sool-pepsh
Bottle	Láhev	**lah**-hev
Red/white wine	Červené/bílé víno	**cher**-ven-eh/**bee**-leh **vee**-no
Beer	Pivo	**piv**-oh
Mineral water	Minerálka voda	min-eh-**rahl**-ka **vo**-da
Milk	Mléko	**mleh**-koh
Coffee	Káva	**kah**-va
Tea (with lemon)	Čaj (s citrónem)	tchai (se tsi-**tro**-nem)

Hungarian

English	Hungarian	Pronunciation

Basics

English	Hungarian	Pronunciation
Yes/no	Igen/nem	**ee**-gen/nem
Please	Kérem	**kay**-rem
Thank you (very much)	Köszönöm (szépen)	**kuh**-suh-num (seh-pen)
Excuse me	Bocsánat	**noh**-chah-not
I'm sorry	Sajnálom	**shahee**-nah-lome
Hello/how do you do	Szervusz	**sair**-voose
Do you speak English?	Beszél angolul?	**bess**-el **on**-goal-ool?
I don't speak Hungarian	Nem tudok magyarul	nem **too**-dock **muh**-jor-ool.
I don't understand	Nem értem	nem **air**-tem
Please speak slowly	Kérem, beszéljen lassan	**kay**-rem, **bess**-el-yen **lush**-shun
Please write it down	Kérem, írja fel	**kay**-rem, **eer**-yuh fell
Please show me	Megmutatná nekem	meg-**moo**-taht-nah neh-kem
I am American	Amerikai vagyok	uh-**meh**-rick-ka-ee **vud**-yoke
I am English	Angol vagyok	**un**-goal **vud**-yoke
My name is . . .	vagyok	**vud**-yoke
Right/left	Bal/jobb	buhl/yobe
Open/closed	nyitva/zárva	**nit**-va/**zahr-voh**
Arrival/departures	Érkezés/indulás	**er**-keh-zesh/**In**-dool-ahsh
Where is . . . ?	Hol van	hole vun
the train station?	a pályaudvar	uh **pah**-yo-**oot**-var
the bus station?	a buszállomás	uh **boose**-ahlo-mahsh
the bus stop?	a megálló	uh **meg**-all-oh
the airport?	a repúl//oo//tér	uh rep-ewluh-**tair**
the post office?	a pósta	uh **pohsh**-tuh
the bank?	a bank	uh bonhk
Stop here	alljon meg itt	**all**-yon meg it
I would like . . .	Szeretnék	**sair**-et-neck
How much does it cost?	Mennyibe kerúl	**men**-yibe **kair**-ule
Letter/postcard	Levél/képeslap	**lev**-ehl/**kay**-pesh-lup
By airmail	Légi póstaval	**lay**-gee **pohsh**-tuh-vol
Help!	Segitség	**shay**-geet-shaig

Numbers

English	Hungarian	Pronunciation
One	Egy	edge
Two	Kettő	**ket**-tuh

Three	Három	**hah**-rome
Four	Négy	**nay**-ge
Five	Öt	ut
Six	Hat	huht
Seven	Hét	hate
Eight	Nyolc	nyolts
Nine	Kilenc	**kee**-lents
Ten	Tíz	teez
One hundred	Száz	sahz
One thousand	Ezer	**eh**-zer

Days of the Week

Sunday	Vasárnap	**vuh**-shar-nup
Monday	Hétfő	**hate**-fuh
Tuesday	Kedd	ked
Wednesday	Szerda	**ser**-duh
Thursday	Csütörtök	**chew**-tur-nuk
Friday	Péntek	**pain**-tek
Saturday	Szombat	**som**-but

Where to Sleep

A room	Egy szobá	edge **soh**-bah
The key	A kulcsot	uh **koolch**-oat
With a bath/a shower	fúrdőszo-bával/ egy zuhany	**fure**-duh-soh-bah-vul/ edge **zoo**-hon

Food

A restaurant	A vendéglő/ az étterem	uh **ven**-deh-gluh/ uz **eht**-teh-rem
The menu	A étlap	uh **ate**-lop
The check, please	A számlát kérem	uh **sahm**-lot **kay**-rem
I'd like to order this	Kéem ezt	**kay**-rem etz
Breakfast	Reggeli	**reg**-gell-ee
Lunch	Ebéd	**eb**-ehd
Dinner	Vacsora	**votch**-oh-rah
Bread	Kenyér	**ken**-yair
Butter	Vaj	voy
Salt/pepper	Só/bors	show/borsh
Bottle	Üveg	**ew**-veg
Red/white wine	Vörös/fehér bor	**vuh**-ruhsh/ **feh**-hehr bore
Beer	Sör	shur
Water/mineral water	Víz/kristályvíz	veez/**krish**-tah-**ee**-veez
Milk	Tej	tay
Coffee (with milk)	Káve/tejeskávé	**kah**-vay/ **tey**-esh-kah-tay
Tea (with lemon)	Tea (citrommal)	**tay**-oh **tsit**-rome-mol
Chocolate	Csokoládé	chaw-kaw-**law**-day

INDEX

Index 171

NOTES

NOTES

NOTES

NOTES